WEIGHT WATCHERS®
QUICK START PLUS PROGRAM®
MAKES THE IMPOSSIBLE POSSIBLE

More than two decades of experience have taught the Weight Watchers organization that the most successful diet is one that fits easily into people's life-styles. That's why they've created the Quick Start Plus Program—a program that is even easier and more flexible than ever before. Now you can delight in tantalizing temptations that everyone in the family will enjoy. Here's a sampling from the new Personal Choice® Food Selections section:

* ★ Belgian Waffles with ice cream
* ★ Crêpes Suzette with orange liqueur
* ★ Chocolate-Nut Squares
* ★ Puffy Brandied Apple Omelet with apple brandy
* ★ Pesto-Parmesan Sauce with pignolias
* ★ Soft-Shell Crab Sauté with sliced almonds
* ★ Peanut-Popcorn Balls
* ★ Banana-Pineapple Cocktail with rum
* ★ Frozen Strawberry Soufflé with raspberry liqueur
* ★ *And much more!*

A heavenly diet of guilt-free delights.

JEAN NIDETCH is the founder of the world's largest weight control organization, Weight Watchers International. In 1963, she created a landmark recipe for weight control by taking the basic ingredients of a nutritious diet and blending in healthy helpings of group support. Nidetch has proved that weight control can be achieved while dining in delicious and varied style not only with the popular Weight Watchers program, but in the best-selling *Weight Watchers Program Cookbook* and *Food Plan Diet Cookbook*, as well as the successful *Weight Watchers International Cookbook*, *Party & Holiday Cookbook*, *365-Day Menu Cookbook*, *Fast & Fabulous Cookbook*, and the recently published *Weight Watchers New International Cookbook*.

WEIGHT WATCHERS®
QUICK START PLUS PROGRAM® COOKBOOK

Including Personal Choice® Food Selections

by

Jean Nidetch

**Revised Edition of
WEIGHT WATCHERS®
QUICK START®
PROGRAM COOKBOOK**

A PLUME BOOK

NEW AMERICAN LIBRARY

A DIVISION OF PENGUIN BOOKS USA INC., NEW YORK

PUBLISHED IN CANADA BY
PENGUIN BOOKS CANADA LIMITED, MARKHAM, ONTARIO

Published simultaneously in Canada by
Penguin Books Canada Limited.

Design by Julian Hamer
Cover photography and photo insert by Gus Francisco
Drawings by Marcy Gold

For kindly lending us serving pieces for photography we thank:
Arzberg China, Hutschenreuther Corp., Portmeiron, Rorstrand,
Tirschenreuth, Villeroy & Boch Tableware Ltd., and Yamazaki
Tableware, Inc., all of New York City, New York.

Library of Congress Cataloging-in-Publication Data

Nidetch, Jean.
  Weight Watchers Quick Start Plus Program cookbook.

  1. Low-calorie diet—Recipes.   2. Weight Watchers
International.   I. Title.
RM222.2.N5224   1986   613.2'5   86-60524
ISBN 0-452-25831-6

SIGNET, SIGNET CLASSIC, MENTOR, ONYX, PLUME, MERIDIAN
and NAL BOOKS are published *in the United States* by
New American Library, a division of Penguin Books USA Inc.,
1633 Broadway, New York, New York 10019, *in Canada* by
Penguin Books Canada Limited, 2801 John Street, Markham,
Ontario L3R 1B4

First Plume Printing, July, 1986

25   26   27   28

Acknowledgments

What does it take to put together a really terrific cookbook? Not only does it take a combination of wonderful ingredients, a pinch of this and a touch of that, it also takes the input of some really dedicated people whose knowledge and expertise create the magic that makes a cookbook something to be treasured and used for years and years.

We want to thank the following members of the Weight Watchers staff for their indispensable assistance in making the magic that is now yours in the *Quick Start Plus Program Cookbook*. To Nina Procaccini, Christy Foley-McHale, Judi Rettmer, and Bianca Brown is due the credit for the development of the wonderful recipes that can now be enjoyed by everyone. To Eileen Pregosin, Patricia Barnett, Harriet Pollock, Elizabeth Resnick-Healy, and April Rozea are due the thanks for the research, writing, and editing that were necessary to complete this fine cookbook.

And, last, but certainly not least, we are grateful to Isabel Fleisher, Lucille Corsello, Carole Langroth, and Lola Sher for contributing their fine secretarial skills to the typing and revision of the manuscript.

Finally, a special note of thanks to Barbara Ecker-Gordon and Judy Marshel who, under the direction of Lawrence Appell, spent many hours developing the new Food Plan, and to Dr. Lelio Parducci and Steve Heyl, without whose guidance this Food Plan would not have been possible.

Weight Watchers International, Inc.

Contents

Dear Friends,

Welcome to the world of Weight Watchers!

For more than two decades, our Organization has been dedicated to listening as you share your successes, your difficulties, and your feelings. Through this sharing process, you have helped Weight Watchers Service and Product Development staff continue to bring you one of the best and most effective weight-control programs in the world.

We have always considered your wants and needs and, because of our desire to offer you the best possible help available, we have kept abreast of the latest findings in all weight-related fields in order to keep our Food Plan current. We have kept pace with an ever-changing world, listening and learning as science teaches us more about obesity and how to help the overweight. We have used this knowledge, along with recommended dietary guidelines, to periodically update the Food Plan.

Some time ago, we discovered that people need guidance to help them maintain their desired weight while still enjoying the foods they love, which is why we added a Maintenance Plan to the Program. We also discovered that food guidelines alone were not sufficient to help people lose weight or maintain their ideal weight, so we added a Self-Management Plan. We offer our members this Plan to help them acquire the invaluable skills needed to control the urge to overeat. In 1979, we added a moderate exercise plan to the Weight Watchers program to help members experience the sense of well-being, zest, and vitality that exercise can bring to their lives.

More recently you asked for a plan that was simple to understand and follow, a more flexible plan that could fit easily into any life-style, and, most important of all, a plan that would give you a faster start, and we gave you the Quick Start Program.

After many months of research and development, we were able to combine everything you've asked for with the most up-to-date scientific knowledge, and now we offer you the Quick Start Plus Program —all the advantages of the Quick Start Program, and . . .

- additional food selections such as sour cream and cream cheese
- expanded use of Optional calories from the very first week

1

- Personal Choice food selections so you can customize the Food Plan to fit your life-style (for example, enjoy chocolate and cookies without feeling guilty)

As our Program was changed, the Weight Watchers staff combined their culinary abilities and nutritional knowledge to incorporate these changes into our newest cookbook. It offers over 500 easy-to-follow, satisfying, delectable ways to fit our new Food Plan into every life-style.

We hope that you'll cherish this book and consider it your gift to yourself. It has been compiled by people who believe that together we care, we share, and we're there to help you as you help yourself. So use this volume to help you embark on a more rewarding, fulfilling life, and continue to use it as you progress toward a more slender world.

In the future, as our knowledge about the control of obesity expands, the Weight Watchers program will continue to be updated with an eye to meeting your needs as well as your wants. We will always strive to maintain the warmth and understanding that has sustained our growth from our beginnings over two decades ago to our current place as a world leader in the field of weight control.

Jean Nidetch
Founder, Weight Watchers International, Inc.

The Food Plan

THE purpose of this chapter is to introduce you to our phased Food Plan and to give you some help in building menus based on the recipes in this book. Menu planners have been included for Weeks 1 through 4. Subsequent chapters discuss each of the categories (called Exchanges) in our Food Plan, in addition to giving tested recipes for each category. You will find that our Food Plan is simpler and more flexible than ever before, and offers the added advantage of providing a faster start at weight loss.

Exchange Lists appear within each chapter. Each list indicates food servings with similar nutrient contents. You may substitute any item on an Exchange List for any other item on that list; however, you may only make these substitutions within the same Exchange List. For example, you may not exchange an item on the Bread List for one on the Fruit List.

Week 1—This is the Plan with which you should begin. It offers a balanced diet that allows for a faster start at weight loss.

Week 2—The number of daily Protein Exchanges that you may consume and weekly Optional Exchange calories have been increased. In addition, the Exchange Lists are slightly less restricted than those on Week 1.

Week 3—Your Total Daily Exchanges as well as weekly Optional calories have been further increased and the Exchange Lists incorporate additional variety allowing for more flexibility.

Week 4—This is the Plan that you will follow as you travel toward goal. It has been scientifically designed to provide a wide variety of nutritious foods. Choices have been built into this flexible Plan so that it can fit your individual needs and life-style.

Week 5—Personal Choice food selections are introduced this week. These additions help you to customize the Food Plan to fit your life-style.

◆ Pointers on Menu Planners

◆ The weights indicated on the menu planners for poultry, meats, and fish are net cooked (or drained canned) weights (without skin and bones). Refer to Pointers in each of the following chapters for explanations of food items and cooking procedures.

◆ The Total Daily Exchanges for each of the plans follows:

TOTAL DAILY EXCHANGES

	Fruit	Vegetables	Milk	Bread	Fat	Protein
Week 1						
Women	3	2 (at least)	2	2	3	6
Men	4	2 (at least)	2	4	3	8
Youths	4	2 (at least)	3	4	3	8
Week 2						
Women	3	2 (at least)	2	2	3	6 to 7
Men	4	2 (at least)	2	4	3	8 to 9
Youths	4	2 (at least)	3	4	3	8 to 9
Weeks 3 and 4						
Women	3	2 (at least)	2	2 to 3	3	6 to 8
Men	4 to 6	2 (at least)	2	4 to 5	3	8 to 10
Youths	4 to 6	2 (at least)	3 to 4	4 to 5	3	8 to 10

We suggest that you keep a food record each day; this will help you to keep track of your daily Exchanges and to plan ahead.

Note: To add interest to your menus and help you individualize the Food Plan, see The Optional Exchange section (page 405).

◆ It is recommended that you eat three meals a day; snacks are optional, but if you choose to have any, they should be planned. Exchanges eaten as snacks should be counted toward your daily total (see Total Daily Exchanges, above).

Breakfast is required. The morning meal provides essential nutrients as well as the energy that you need to perform your daily tasks. Breakfast-skippers tend to experience a mid-morning slump with a decrease in alertness. If you do not select at least 1 Protein Exchange at breakfast, you should eat 1 Bread Exchange with at least ½ Milk Exchange. If you select ¾ ounce cold cereal or ½ cup cooked hot cereal with at least ½ Milk Exchange, the cereal may be counted as 1 Protein Exchange *or* 1 Bread Exchange; count the milk toward the Milk Exchange. Although fruit is not required at breakfast, it is recommended.

You must have a minimum of 2 Protein Exchanges at both lunch and dinner.

◗ Bold type on the menu planners indicates that recipes are included in this book; menus are based on 1 serving of each recipe.

◗ Fruits that are high in vitamin C have been marked with an asterisk (*).

◗ You may consume additional vegetables daily, provided you follow the guidelines outlined in the Vegetable Exchange section (page 63).

◗ To increase the protein quality of dry beans, lentils, or peas, plan to supplement them with grains, poultry, meat, fish, egg, cheese, or milk (e.g., rice and beans, franks and lentils, etc.).

◗ We recommend that you eat the following per week:

no more than 4 eggs

no more than 4 ounces hard or semisoft cheese

no more than 4 ounces of asterisked (*) meats (Weeks 1 and 2); no more than 8 ounces of asterisked (*) meats (Week 3); no more than 12 ounces of asterisked (*) meats (Week 4 and beyond)

a minimum of 3 fish meals (about 12 Exchanges)

3 to 4 ounces liver (Weeks 1, 2, and 3); 4 to 6 ounces liver (Week 4)

no more than 150 Optional Exchange calories (Week 1); no more than 200 Optional Exchange calories (Week 2); no more than 250 Optional Exchange calories (Week 3); no more than 550 Optional Exchange calories (Week 4 and beyond)

◗ The menu planners on the following pages are designed for women. Additions for men and youths are noted on the menu planners.

MENU PLANNER I FOR WEEK 1

Men and Youths: Daily add 2 Protein Exchanges, 2 Bread Exchanges, and 1 Fruit Exchange

Youths only: Daily add 1 Milk Exchange

Day 1

BREAKFAST

* ½ cup Grapefruit Juice
¾ ounce Cold Cereal
1 cup Skim Milk
Coffee or Tea

LUNCH

Cottage-Cheddar Puff (see page 212)
Tossed Salad with Lemon Juice and Herbs
4 Melba Toast Slices
½ cup Peaches
Club Soda

DINNER

Broiled Veal Chops (see page 292)
½ cup Steamed Sliced Carrots
Mixed Green Salad with 2 teaspoons Vegetable Oil plus Wine Vinegar and Seasonings
Coffee or Tea

SNACKS, AT PLANNED TIMES

* 1 cup Melon; 1 cup Skim Milk

Day 2

BREAKFAST

½ cup Fruit Salad
⅓ cup Cottage Cheese
1 slice Bread
1 teaspoon Margarine
½ cup Skim Milk
Coffee or Tea

LUNCH

2 ounces Cooked Chicken
Marinated Pepper Salad (see page 96)
1 slice Bread
* 1 small Orange
1 cup Skim Milk

DINNER

3 ounces Cooked Fish
Quick Spinach Sauté (see page 97)
Tossed Salad with Lemon Juice and Herbs
Coffee or Tea

SNACKS, AT PLANNED TIMES

Black Cow (see page 116)

Day 3

BREAKFAST

* ½ medium Grapefruit
½ cup Cooked Cereal
1 cup Skim Milk
Coffee or Tea

LUNCH

Garden Cottage Cheese Salad (see page 207)
½ cup each Celery Sticks and Red Bell Pepper Strips
4 Melba Toast Slices
Coffee or Tea

DINNER

Easy Beef Liver Sauté (see page 373)
½ cup Steamed Cauliflower Florets
Lettuce Wedge with 2 teaspoons Vegetable Oil plus Wine Vinegar and Seasonings
* 1 small Orange
Coffee or Tea

SNACKS, AT PLANNED TIMES

½ cup Pineapple; ½ cup Plain Low-Fat Yogurt

6

Day 4

BREAKFAST
* ½ cup Orange Juice
⅓ cup Cottage Cheese
6 Sesame Melba Rounds
1 cup Skim Milk
Coffee or Tea

LUNCH
Tuna Salad with Lemon-French Dressing (see page 388)
½ cup each Carrot Sticks and Cucumber Slices
1 slice Bread
1 teaspoon Margarine
Sparkling Mineral Water with Lemon Slice

DINNER
3 ounces Cooked Chicken
6 Steamed Broccoli Spears
Tossed Salad with 1 teaspoon Vegetable Oil plus Wine Vinegar and Seasonings
Blender Applesauce (see page 37)
Coffee or Tea

SNACKS, AT PLANNED TIMES
½ cup Peaches; 1 cup Skim Milk

7

Day 5

BREAKFAST
* 1 cup Melon
¾ ounce Cold Cereal
1 cup Skim Milk
Coffee or Tea

LUNCH
2 ounces Swiss Cheese
Spinach-Mushroom Salad (see page 97)
4 Melba Toast Slices
1 teaspoon Margarine
½ cup Fruit Salad
Coffee or Tea

DINNER
Shrimp Scampi (see page 398)
½ cup each Steamed Whole Green Beans and Sliced Mushrooms
Tomato Slices on Lettuce Leaves with Lemon Juice and Herbs
Coffee or Tea

SNACKS, AT PLANNED TIMES
½ cup Pineapple; ½ cup Plain Low-Fat Yogurt

Day 6

BREAKFAST
* ½ medium Grapefruit
Puffy Cheese Omelet (see page 189)
1 slice Bread
¾ cup Skim Milk
Coffee or Tea

LUNCH
2 ounces Salmon with 1 teaspoon Mayonnaise
1-ounce Pita
1 small Apple
Coffee or Tea

DINNER
Chicken Curry (see page 272)
½ cup Steamed Sliced Zucchini
Tossed Salad with 1 teaspoon Vegetable Oil plus Wine Vinegar and Seasonings
Coffee or Tea

SNACKS, AT PLANNED TIMES
½ cup Peaches; 1 cup Skim Milk

Day 7

BREAKFAST
* ½ cup Orange Juice
¾ ounce Cold Cereal
1 cup Skim Milk
Coffee or Tea

LUNCH
2 ounces Cooked Chicken with 1½ teaspoons Mayonnaise
Cucumber-Orange Salad (see page 85)
1 slice Bread
Coffee or Tea

DINNER
Apple, Onion, and Chops (see page 338)
½ cup each Steamed Cauliflower and Broccoli Florets
Mixed Green Salad with Lemon Juice and Herbs
Coffee or Tea

SNACKS, AT PLANNED TIMES
* 1 cup Melon; ½ cup Plain Low-Fat Yogurt

MENU PLANNER II FOR WEEK 1

Men and Youths: Daily add 2 Protein Exchanges, 2 Bread Exchanges, and 1 Fruit Exchange

Youths only: Daily add 1 Milk Exchange

Day 1

BREAKFAST

* 1/2 cup Grapefruit Juice
1/3 cup Cottage Cheese
1 slice Bread
3/4 cup Skim Milk
Coffee or Tea

LUNCH

Zucchini-Mushroom Bake (see page 194)
1/2 cup each Cucumber Slices and Tomato Wedges
* 1 small Orange
Coffee or Tea

DINNER

Turkey-Stuffing Loaf (see page 286)
1/2 cup Steamed Broccoli Florets
Mixed Green Salad with 1 teaspoon Vegetable Oil plus Wine Vinegar and Herbs
Coffee or Tea

SNACKS, AT PLANNED TIMES

1/2 cup Plain Low-Fat Yogurt with 1/4 cup Fruit Salad

Day 2

BREAKFAST

* 1/2 cup Orange Juice
3/4 ounce Cold Cereal
1/2 cup Skim Milk
Coffee or Tea

LUNCH

Vegetable Soup (see page 102)
2 ounces Tuna with 2 teaspoons Mayonnaise
1/2 cup each Carrot Sticks and Green Bell Pepper Strips on Lettuce Leaves
1 cup Skim Milk

DINNER

Sautéed Livers 'n' Vegetables (see page 368)
1/2 cup Steamed Sliced Carrots
Tossed Salad with Lemon Juice and Herbs
1 slice Bread
* 1 cup Melon
Coffee or Tea

SNACKS, AT PLANNED TIMES

Amaretto Float (see page 117)

Day 3

BREAKFAST

1/2 cup Fruit Salad
1 Egg (prepared without fat)
1 slice Bread
1 cup Skim Milk
Coffee or Tea

LUNCH

2/3 cup Cottage Cheese
Marinated Green Bean Salad (see page 90)
1 slice Bread
1/2 teaspoon Margarine
* 1/2 medium Grapefruit
Coffee or Tea

DINNER

2 1/2 ounces Cooked Chicken
1/2 cup Steamed Spinach Leaves
Tomato Slices on Romaine Lettuce Leaves with **Lemon-Mustard Vinaigrette** (see page 163)
Coffee or Tea

SNACKS, AT PLANNED TIMES

1/2 cup Peaches; 1/2 cup Plain Low-Fat Yogurt

Day 4

BREAKFAST

*1 small Orange
1/2 cup Cooked Cereal
1 cup Skim Milk
Coffee or Tea

LUNCH

Salmon-Cheese Ball (see page 382)
1 cup Assorted Vegetable Sticks
6 Sesame Melba Rounds
*1 cup Melon
Sparkling Mineral Water with Lemon Slice

DINNER

Mushroom-Stuffed Flounder Roll-Ups (see page 379)
1/2 cup Steamed Whole Green Beans
1 teaspoon Margarine
Mixed Green Salad with Wine Vinegar and Herbs
Coffee or Tea

SNACKS, AT PLANNED TIMES
1/2 cup Pineapple; 1 cup Skim Milk

Day 5

BREAKFAST

*1/2 medium Grapefruit
1/3 cup Cottage Cheese
4 Melba Toast Slices
Coffee or Tea

LUNCH

1 1/2 ounces Tuna with 1 teaspoon Mayonnaise
Garden Salad (see page 183)
1-ounce Pita
1 cup Skim Milk
Coffee or Tea

DINNER

3 ounces Cooked Chicken
6 medium Steamed Broccoli Spears
Lettuce Wedge with 2 teaspoons Vegetable Oil plus Wine Vinegar and Seasonings
1 small Apple
Coffee or Tea

SNACKS, AT PLANNED TIMES
1/2 cup Fruit Salad; 1/2 cup Plain Low-Fat Yogurt

Day 6

BREAKFAST

*1 cup Melon
3/4 ounce Cold Cereal
1 cup Skim Milk
Coffee or Tea

LUNCH

2/3 cup Cottage Cheese
Mixed Green Salad with 2 teaspoons Vegetable Oil plus Wine Vinegar and Seasonings
1 slice Bread
1 teaspoon Margarine
*Citrus Cooler (see page 46)

DINNER

Teriyaki Lamb Burger (see page 334)
1/2 cup each Steamed Sliced Zucchini and Tomato Wedges
Tossed Salad with Lemon Juice and Herbs
Coffee or Tea

SNACKS, AT PLANNED TIMES
1/2 cup Peaches; 1 cup Skim Milk

Day 7

BREAKFAST

1/2 cup Pineapple
1/4 cup Part-Skim Ricotta Cheese
1 slice Bread
1/2 cup Skim Milk
Coffee or Tea

LUNCH

2 ounces Cooked Chicken with 1 1/2 teaspoons Mayonnaise
Cucumber in Yogurt Dressing (see page 84)
1 slice Bread
1/2 cup Fruit Salad
Coffee or Tea

DINNER

3 ounces Cooked Fish
Spiced Spinach Sauté (see page 98)
1/2 cup each Carrot Slices and Cauliflower Florets on Lettuce Leaves with 1 teaspoon Vegetable Oil plus Wine Vinegar and Seasonings
Coffee or Tea

SNACKS, AT PLANNED TIMES
*1 small Orange; 1/2 cup Plain Low-Fat Yogurt

9

MENU PLANNER I FOR WEEK 2

Men and Youths: Daily add 2 Protein Exchanges, 2 Bread Exchanges, and 1 Fruit Exchange

Youths only: Daily add 1 Milk Exchange

Day 1

BREAKFAST
* 1 small Orange
⅓ cup Cottage Cheese
½ cup Skim Milk
Coffee or Tea

LUNCH
2 ounces Cooked Chicken with 1 teaspoon Mayonnaise
½ small Bagel
½ cup each Cucumber Slices and Tomato Wedges on Lettuce Leaves
½ cup Pineapple
Sparkling Mineral Water with Lemon Slice

DINNER
Crab and Potato-Stuffed Peppers (see page 395)
6 medium Steamed Asparagus Spears
Tossed Salad with 1½ teaspoons French Salad Dressing
Coffee or Tea

SNACKS, AT PLANNED TIMES
Frozen Berry-Banana Yogurt (see page 109)

Day 2

BREAKFAST
Apricot-Glazed Banana Muffin (see page 40)
1 cup Skim Milk
Coffee or Tea

LUNCH
Zucchini-Ham Frittata (see page 348)
Mixed Green Salad with Lemon Juice and Herbs
6 Sesame Melba Rounds
* 1 cup Melon
Coffee or Tea

DINNER
4 ounces Cooked Chicken
½ cup Steamed Sliced Carrots
Spinach-Mushroom Salad (see page 97)
Coffee or Tea

SNACKS, AT PLANNED TIMES
½ cup Applesauce; 1 cup Skim Milk

Day 3

BREAKFAST
½ cup Peaches
¾ ounce Cold Cereal
¾ cup Skim Milk
Coffee or Tea

LUNCH
Scallion Appetizers (see page 201)
⅔ cup Cottage Cheese
Tossed Salad with 1½ teaspoons Vegetable Oil plus Wine Vinegar and Seasonings
Coffee or Tea

DINNER
4 ounces Cooked Liver
Twice-Baked Creamy Potatoes (see page 129)
½ cup each Steamed Sliced Mushrooms and Green Bell Pepper Rings
* 1 cup Strawberries
Coffee or Tea

SNACKS, AT PLANNED TIMES
½ cup Fruit Salad; ½ cup Plain Low-Fat Yogurt

10

Day 4

BREAKFAST
½ medium Banana
⅓ cup Cottage Cheese
½ small Bagel
1 cup Skim Milk
Coffee or Tea

LUNCH
Asparagus-Chili Dip (see page 73) with Assorted Vegetable Sticks
2 ounces Cooked Chicken
4 Melba Toast Slices
*1 small Orange
Club Soda

DINNER
Tuna Provençale (see page 392)
½ cup Steamed Whole Green Beans
Tossed Salad with 1½ teaspoons Italian Salad Dressing
Coffee or Tea

SNACKS, AT PLANNED TIMES
½ cup Pineapple; 1 cup Skim Milk

11

Day 5

BREAKFAST
*1 cup Strawberries
½ cup Cooked Cereal
½ cup Skim Milk
Coffee or Tea

LUNCH
3 ounces Salmon with 1 teaspoon Mayonnaise
Marinated Green Bean Salad (see page 90)
½ cup Peaches
½ cup Skim Milk
Coffee or Tea

DINNER
Apple-Pork Chop Bake (see page 337)
½ cup Steamed Cauliflower Florets
Mixed Green Salad with Lemon Juice and Herbs
Coffee or Tea

SNACKS, AT PLANNED TIMES
½ cup Plain Low-Fat Yogurt with ¼ cup Fruit Salad

Day 6

BREAKFAST
*1 small Orange
⅓ cup Cottage Cheese
½ cup Skim Milk
Coffee or Tea

LUNCH
2 Hard-Cooked Eggs
1½ teaspoons Mayonnaise
1 cup Assorted Vegetable Sticks
½ small Bagel
½ cup Skim Milk
Coffee or Tea

DINNER
Calamari Salad (see page 403)
1 slice Bread
*1 cup Strawberries
Coffee or Tea

SNACKS, AT PLANNED TIMES
Chocolate Shake (see page 114)

Day 7

BREAKFAST
½ medium Banana
¾ ounce Cold Cereal
¾ cup Skim Milk
Coffee or Tea

LUNCH
Cheese-Stuffed Celery Appetizer (see page 199)
2 ounces Tuna
Tossed Salad with 1 teaspoon Vegetable Oil plus Wine Vinegar and Seasonings
*1 cup Melon
Club Soda

DINNER
4 ounces Cooked Chicken
3 ounces Baked Potato with 1 teaspoon Margarine
Cauliflower-Pimiento Salad (see page 82)

SNACKS, AT PLANNED TIMES
½ cup Applesauce; 1 cup Skim Milk

MENU PLANNER II FOR WEEK 2

Men and Youths: Daily add 2 Protein Exchanges, 2 Bread Exchanges, and 1 Fruit Exchange

Youths only: Daily add 1 Milk Exchange

Day 1

BREAKFAST
1/2 cup Berries
3/4 ounce Cold Cereal
1 cup Skim Milk
Coffee or Tea

LUNCH
Tomato Sauce-Poached Eggs (see page 186)
1/2 cup each Cucumber Slices and Tomato Wedges on Lettuce Leaves
*1 small Orange
Coffee or Tea

DINNER
Scrod Florentine (see page 382)
1/2 cup Steamed Green Beans with 1/4 cup Steamed Sliced Mushrooms
Tossed Salad with 1 1/2 teaspoons French Salad Dressing
1 slice Bread
1/2 teaspoon Margarine
Coffee or Tea

SNACKS, AT PLANNED TIMES
1 medium Peach; 1 cup Skim Milk

Day 2

BREAKFAST
*1/2 medium Grapefruit sprinkled with Cinnamon
1/3 cup Cottage Cheese
2 Melba Toast Slices
1/2 cup Skim Milk
Coffee or Tea

LUNCH
3 ounces Tuna with 1 1/2 teaspoons Mayonnaise
Noodle Salad (see page 133)
1/2 cup Skim Milk
Coffee or Tea

DINNER
Brunswick Stew (see page 269)
Mixed Green Salad with Wine Vinegar and Seasonings
*1 cup Melon
Coffee or Tea

SNACKS, AT PLANNED TIMES
1/2 cup Fruit Salad; 1/2 cup Plain Low-Fat Yogurt

Day 3

BREAKFAST
Strawberry-Topped Crispies (see page 126)
3/4 cup Skim Milk
Coffee or Tea

LUNCH
2/3 cup Cottage Cheese
Mixed Green Salad with 1 1/2 teaspoons Vegetable Oil plus Wine Vinegar and Seasonings
3/4 cup Applesauce
Coffee or Tea

DINNER
4 ounces Roast Turkey
Twice-Baked Yams (see page 131)
1/2 cup Cauliflower Florets
Tomato Wedges and Bibb Lettuce Leaves with 1 1/2 teaspoons French Salad Dressing
Coffee or Tea

SNACKS, AT PLANNED TIMES
*1 small Orange; 1 cup Skim Milk

12

Day 4

BREAKFAST

* 1 cup Melon
¼ cup Part-Skim Ricotta Cheese
6 Sesame Melba Rounds
Coffee or Tea

LUNCH

2 ounces Salmon
Tossed Salad with 1½ teaspoons Russian Salad Dressing
1 cup Skim Milk

DINNER

Easy Beef Liver Sauté (see page 373)
3 ounces Baked Potato with 1 teaspoon Margarine
Mixed Green Salad with Lemon Juice and Herbs
* **Mixed Fruit Cooler** (see page 47)

SNACKS, AT PLANNED TIMES

½ cup Pineapple; ½ cup Plain Low-Fat Yogurt

13

Day 5

BREAKFAST

* ½ cup Orange Juice
¾ ounce Cold Cereal
½ cup Skim Milk
Coffee or Tea

LUNCH

2 ounces Broiled Chicken
Zesty Tomato-Cheese Salad (see page 209)
1 small Apple
½ cup Skim Milk
Coffee or Tea

DINNER

4 ounces Baked Veal Cutlet with **Quick Tomato Sauce** (see page 168)
½ cup Cooked Pasta
Ratatouille (see page 86)
Coffee or Tea

SNACKS, AT PLANNED TIMES

½ cup Peaches; 1 cup Skim Milk

Day 6

BREAKFAST

½ cup Fruit Salad
⅓ cup Cottage Cheese
2 Melba Toast Slices
½ cup Skim Milk

LUNCH

Cheddar, Potato, and Egg Pancake (see page 193)
Tossed Salad with 1½ teaspoons Thousand Island Salad Dressing
½ cup Skim Milk
Coffee or Tea

DINNER

Lamb and Eggplant Stew (see page 331)
Mixed Green Salad with Lemon Juice and Herbs
1 slice Bread
* 1 cup Melon
Coffee or Tea

SNACKS, AT PLANNED TIMES

½ medium Banana; ½ cup Plain Low-Fat Yogurt

Day 7

BREAKFAST

* ½ cup Grapefruit Juice
½ cup Cooked Cereal
1 cup Skim Milk
Coffee or Tea

LUNCH

2 ounces Cooked Chicken with 1½ teaspoons Mayonnaise
Vegetable-Swiss Broil (see page 100)
Sparkling Mineral Water with Lime Twist

DINNER

Baked Fish with Mushroom-Wine Sauce (see page 376)
½ cup Cooked Rice
½ cup Steamed Spinach Leaves
½ cup Berries
Coffee or Tea

SNACKS, AT PLANNED TIMES

1 small Apple; 1 cup Skim Milk

MENU PLANNER I FOR WEEK 3

Men and Youths: Daily add 2 Protein Exchanges, 2 Bread Exchanges, and 1 Fruit Exchange

Youths only: Daily add 1 Milk Exchange

Day 1

BREAKFAST

2 large Prunes
¾ ounce Cold Cereal
1 cup Skim Milk
Coffee or Tea

LUNCH

Three-Bean Soup (see page 242)
Mixed Green Salad with 1½ teaspoons French Salad Dressing
¾ ounce Breadsticks
*½ medium Grapefruit
Coffee or Tea

DINNER

4 ounces Cooked Chicken
½ cup Cooked Macaroni
½ cup Steamed Sliced Zucchini
Tossed Salad with 1½ teaspoons Vegetable Oil plus Wine Vinegar and Seasonings
Coffee or Tea

SNACKS, AT PLANNED TIMES

Baked Maple Apple (see page 37); 1 cup Skim Milk

Day 2

BREAKFAST

*1 cup Strawberries
⅓ cup Cottage Cheese
½ English Muffin
1 cup Skim Milk
Coffee or Tea

LUNCH

Salmon-Garbanzo Salad (see page 246)
½ cup each Carrot Sticks and Green Bell Pepper Strips
1 large Tangerine
Sparkling Mineral Water with Lime Twist

DINNER

Potted Lamb Chops in Apricot Sauce (see page 334)
3 ounces Baked Potato with 1 teaspoon Margarine
½ cup Steamed Sliced Green Beans
Mixed Green Salad with Lemon Juice and Herbs
Coffee or Tea

SNACKS, AT PLANNED TIMES

½ medium Banana; ½ cup Plain Low-Fat Yogurt

Day 3

BREAKFAST

*½ cup Orange Juice
½ cup Cooked Cereal
½ cup Skim Milk
Coffee or Tea

LUNCH

Asparagus-Cheese Casserole (see page 220)
Tossed Salad with 1½ teaspoons Italian Salad Dressing
¾ ounce Breadsticks
1 small Apple
Coffee or Tea

DINNER

3 ounces Cooked Chicken
6 medium Steamed Broccoli Spears
Chick-Pea Salad with Mustard Vinaigrette (see page 244)
Coffee or Tea

SNACKS, AT PLANNED TIMES

1 small Nectarine; 1 cup Skim Milk

14

Day 4

BREAKFAST

½ medium Banana
¼ cup Part-Skim Ricotta Cheese
½ English Muffin
1 cup Skim Milk
Coffee or Tea

LUNCH

Roast Beef Sandwich (3 ounces roast beef with mustard and lettuce leaves on 2 slices rye bread)
½ cup each Celery Sticks and Cauliflower Florets
*1 cup Strawberries
Coffee or Tea

DINNER

Flounder Florentine (see page 378)
½ cup Steamed Brussels Sprouts
Tossed Salad with 2 teaspoons Vegetable Oil plus Wine Vinegar and Seasonings
Coffee or Tea

SNACKS, AT PLANNED TIMES

2 large Prunes; ½ cup Plain Low-Fat Yogurt

Day 5

BREAKFAST

1 small Nectarine
¾ ounce Cold Cereal
1 cup Skim Milk
Coffee or Tea

LUNCH

Asparagus-Swiss Roll Appetizers (see page 200)
3 ounces Cooked Chicken with 1½ teaspoons Mayonnaise
2 Melba Toast Slices
Coffee or Tea

DINNER

*½ medium Grapefruit sprinkled with Cinnamon
4 ounces Cooked Liver
½ cup Cooked Rice with 1 teaspoon Margarine
Herb-Marinated Mushrooms (see page 94)
Coffee or Tea

SNACKS, AT PLANNED TIMES

1 small Apple; 1 cup Skim Milk

Day 6

BREAKFAST

*½ cup Orange Juice
1 Egg (prepared without fat)
½ English Muffin
½ teaspoon Margarine
1 cup Skim Milk
Coffee or Tea

LUNCH

Lemon Ring Mold with Tuna-Cheddar Salad (see page 386)
½ cup each Cucumber Slices and Tomato Wedges
¾ ounce Breadsticks
½ medium Banana
Coffee or Tea

DINNER

4 ounces Cooked Chicken
Sautéed Sweet 'n' Sour Beets (see page 76)
Tossed Salad with Lemon Juice and Herbs
*1 cup Strawberries
Coffee or Tea

SNACKS, AT PLANNED TIMES

2 cups Prepared Plain Popcorn; 1 cup Skim Milk

Day 7

BREAKFAST

*½ medium Grapefruit
¾ ounce Cold Cereal
½ cup Skim Milk
Coffee or Tea

LUNCH

2 Hard-Cooked Eggs with 1 teaspoon Mayonnaise
Mixed Green Salad with Lemon Juice and Herbs
1 slice Bread
1 small Nectarine
½ cup Skim Milk
Coffee or Tea

DINNER

4 ounces Cooked Fish
Oven "Fried" Potatoes (see page 131)
½ cup Steamed Spinach Leaves
Mixed Green Salad with 1½ teaspoons Thousand Island Salad Dressing
Coffee or Tea

SNACKS, AT PLANNED TIMES

2 large Prunes; ½ cup Plain Low-Fat Yogurt

15

MENU PLANNER II FOR WEEK 3

Men and Youths: Daily add 2 Protein Exchanges, 2 Bread Exchanges, and 1 Fruit Exchange

Youths only: Daily add 1 Milk Exchange

Day 1

BREAKFAST

*½ cup Grapefruit Juice
⅓ cup Cottage Cheese
2 Graham Crackers (2½-inch squares)
1 cup Skim Milk
Coffee or Tea

LUNCH

Pasta e Fagioli (Pasta and Bean Soup) (see page 238)
Tossed Salad with 1½ teaspoons Italian Salad Dressing
½ cup Applesauce
Club Soda

DINNER

4 ounces Roast Turkey
"Fried" Yam Sticks (see page 132)
½ cup Steamed Sliced Zucchini
Mixed Green Salad with Wine Vinegar and Seasonings
½ cup Fruit Salad
Coffee or Tea

SNACKS, AT PLANNED TIMES

1 cup Prepared Plain Popcorn; 1 cup Skim Milk

Day 2

BREAKFAST

½ cup Berries
¾ ounce Cold Cereal
1 cup Skim Milk
Coffee or Tea

LUNCH

Turkey-Cheddar Muffins (see page 289)
½ cup each Tomato Wedges and Cucumber Slices on Lettuce Leaves
*1 small Orange
Coffee or Tea

DINNER

4 ounces Cooked Fish with **Lemon Marinade** (see page 165)
½ cup Cooked Noodles
½ cup Cooked Sliced Beets
Tossed Salad with 1½ teaspoons Vegetable Oil plus Wine Vinegar and Seasonings
Coffee or Tea

SNACKS, AT PLANNED TIMES

20 small or 12 large Grapes; ½ cup Plain Low-Fat Yogurt

Day 3

BREAKFAST

*1 cup Melon
⅓ cup Cottage Cheese
1 slice Bread
1 teaspoon Margarine
½ cup Skim Milk
Coffee or Tea

LUNCH

Vegetarian Casserole (see page 248)
Tossed Salad with 1½ teaspoons French Salad Dressing
6 Sesame Melba Rounds
1 large Tangerine
½ cup Skim Milk
Coffee or Tea

DINNER

4 ounces Cooked Chicken
½ cup Cooked Rice
½ cup Cooked Spinach
Tomato Slices on Bibb Lettuce Leaves with Lemon Juice and Herbs
Coffee or Tea

SNACKS, AT PLANNED TIMES

Orange-Pineapple Delight (see page 50)

Day 4

BREAKFAST

* 1/2 cup Grapefruit Juice
3/4 ounce Cold Cereal
1 cup Skim Milk
Coffee or Tea

LUNCH

3 ounces Tuna with 1
teaspoon Mayonnaise
Mixed Green Salad with
Lemon Juice and Herbs
2 cups Prepared Plain
Popcorn
Coffee or Tea

DINNER

Beef and Pasta Casserole
(see page 317)
6 medium Steamed Broccoli
Spears
Mixed Green Salad with 1
teaspoon Vegetable Oil
plus Wine Vinegar and
Seasonings
1/2 cup Applesauce
Coffee or Tea

SNACKS, AT PLANNED TIMES

1/2 cup Fruit Salad; 1 cup Skim
Milk

17

Day 5

BREAKFAST

1/2 cup Berries
1/3 cup Cottage Cheese
1 cup Skim Milk
Coffee or Tea

LUNCH

Bean Dip Mexicali (see page
244) with 1 cup Assorted
Vegetable Sticks
6 Sesame Melba Rounds
Sparkling Mineral Water with
Lime Twist

DINNER

4 ounces Broiled Liver
1/2 cup Cooked Noodles with
1 1/2 teaspoons Margarine
1 cup Steamed Cauliflower
Florets with 1 teaspoon
Margarine
* 1 small Orange
Coffee or Tea

SNACKS, AT PLANNED TIMES

20 small or 12 large Grapes;
1/2 cup Plain Low-Fat Yogurt

Day 6

BREAKFAST

1 large Tangerine
1 Egg (prepared without fat)
1 slice Bread
1 teaspoon Margarine
1/2 cup Skim Milk
Coffee or Tea

LUNCH

2/3 cup Cottage Cheese
Tossed Salad with Wine
Vinegar and Seasonings
1/2 cup Fruit Salad
1/2 cup Skim Milk
Coffee or Tea

DINNER

Quick Jambalaya (see page
399)
Mixed Green Salad with
Lemon Juice and Herbs
* 1 cup Melon
Coffee or Tea

SNACKS, AT PLANNED TIMES

2 Graham Crackers (2 1/2-inch
squares); 1 cup Skim Milk

Day 7

BREAKFAST

* 1/2 cup Grapefruit Juice
1/2 cup Cooked Cereal
1 cup Skim Milk
Coffee or Tea

LUNCH

Ham Sandwich (3 ounces ham
with mustard and lettuce
leaves on 2 slices rye toast)
Mixed Green Salad with 1
tablespoon Russian Salad
Dressing
1/2 cup Applesauce
Coffee or Tea

DINNER

3 ounces Cooked Chicken
1/2 cup Steamed Sliced Carrots
with 1/2 teaspoon Margarine
Marinated Garbanzo Salad
(see page 245)
Coffee or Tea

SNACKS, AT PLANNED TIMES

1/2 cup Berries; 1/2 cup Plain
Low-Fat Yogurt

MENU PLANNER I FOR WEEK 4

Men and Youths: Daily
add 2 Protein Exchanges,
2 Bread Exchanges, and
1 Fruit Exchange

Youths only: Daily add
1 Milk Exchange

Day 1

BREAKFAST

Glazed Cinnamon Grapefruit
(see page 48)
3/4 ounce Cold Cereal
1/2 cup Skim Milk
Coffee or Tea

LUNCH

Vegetable-Cottage Cheese
(see page 209)
1/2 small Bagel
2 teaspoons Margarine
1/2 cup Skim Milk
*1 cup Strawberries
Coffee or Tea

DINNER

4 ounces Cooked Fish
1/2 cup Cooked Whole-Kernel
Corn
Tossed Salad with 1 1/2
teaspoons Thousand Island
Salad Dressing
Coffee or Tea

SNACKS, AT PLANNED TIMES

1 small Pear; 1 cup Skim Milk

Day 2

BREAKFAST

*1/2 cup Orange Sections
1/3 cup Cottage Cheese
1 cup Skim Milk
Coffee or Tea

LUNCH

2-ounce Frankfurter on 2-ounce
Roll with Mustard and 1
teaspoon Pickle Relish
**Coleslaw with Sour Cream
Dressing** (see page 79)
1/2 cup Fruit Salad
Coffee or Tea

DINNER

Creamed Parsley Chicken (see
page 274)
1 cup Steamed Sliced Carrots
Mixed Green Salad with 1 1/2
teaspoons Vegetable Oil
plus Wine Vinegar and
Seasonings
Coffee or Tea

SNACKS, AT PLANNED TIMES

1/2 medium Banana; 1/2 cup
Plain Low-Fat Yogurt

Day 3

BREAKFAST

Fruit 'n' Farina (see page 126)
Coffee or Tea

LUNCH

*1 cup Mixed Vegetable Juice
3 ounces Cooked Chicken
1 1/2 teaspoons Mayonnaise
3 Sesame Melba Rounds
Coffee or Tea

DINNER

**Artichoke-Stuffed Red
Snapper** (see page 383)
1/2 cup Cooked Wax Beans
Tossed Salad with Lemon
Juice and Herbs
Coffee or Tea

SNACKS, AT PLANNED TIMES

10 large Cherries; 1 cup Skim
Milk

18

Day 4

BREAKFAST
1/2 medium banana
1/4 cup Part-Skim Ricotta
  Cheese
Corn Muffins (see page 147)
1/2 cup Skim Milk
Coffee or Tea

LUNCH

3 ounces Tuna with 1 teaspoon
  Mayonnaise
Tossed Salad with Lemon
  Juice and Herbs
2 Melba Toast Slices
1/2 cup Skim Milk
Coffee or Tea

DINNER

4 ounces Cooked Liver
Vegetable Risotto (see page
  138)
Mixed Green Salad with Wine
  Vinegar and Seasonings
*1/2 medium Grapefruit
Coffee or Tea

SNACKS, AT PLANNED TIMES

1 small Pear; 1/2 cup Plain
  Low-Fat Yogurt

19

Day 5

BREAKFAST
*1/2 cup Orange Sections
3/4 ounce Cold Cereal
1 cup Skim Milk
Coffee or Tea

LUNCH

Tangy Egg Salad (see page
  186)
1/2 small Bagel
1/2 cup each Carrot Sticks and
  Zucchini Slices on Lettuce
  Leaves
*1 cup Mixed Vegetable Juice

DINNER

Carrot Soup (see page 79)
4 ounces Cooked Chicken
1/2 cup Cooked Green Peas
Tossed Salad with Lemon
  Juice and Herbs
Coffee or Tea

SNACKS, AT PLANNED TIMES

10 large Cherries; 1 cup Skim
  Milk

Day 6

BREAKFAST
*1/2 medium Grapefruit
  sprinkled with Cinnamon
1/3 cup Cottage Cheese
2 Graham Crackers (21/2-inch
  squares)
1 cup Skim Milk
Coffee or Tea

LUNCH

Cheddar Melt (2 ounces
  Cheddar cheese with
  tomato slices on 1 slice rye
  bread)
Mixed Green Salad with 1/2
  teaspoon Vegetable Oil plus
  Wine Vinegar and
  Seasonings
5 large Cherries
Coffee or Tea

DINNER

Creamed Shepherd's Pie (see
  page 321)
6 medium Steamed Asparagus
  Spears
Lettuce Wedge with 11/2
  teaspoons Italian Salad
  Dressing
1/2 cup Orange Sections with 2
  tablespoons Plain Low-Fat
  Yogurt
Coffee or Tea

SNACKS, AT PLANNED TIMES

Dutch Apple Yogurt (see page 111)

Day 7

BREAKFAST
1/2 medium Banana
3/4 ounce Cold Cereal
1 cup Skim Milk
Coffee or Tea

LUNCH

Greek Salad (see page 208)
6 Sesame Melba Rounds
*1/2 cup Orange Sections
Club Soda

DINNER

Fillet Diable (see page 384)
1/2 cup Cooked Rice
1/2 cup Steamed Sliced
  Zucchini
Tossed Salad with 11/2
  teaspoons French Salad
  Dressing
Coffee or Tea

SNACKS, AT PLANNED TIMES

1 small Pear; 1 cup Skim Milk

MENU PLANNER II FOR WEEK 4

Men and Youths: Daily add 2 Protein Exchanges, 2 Bread Exchanges, and 1 Fruit Exchange

Youths only: Daily add 1 Milk Exchange

Day 1

BREAKFAST

*½ cup Grapefruit Sections
¼ cup Part-Skim Ricotta Cheese
¾ cup Skim Milk
Coffee or Tea

LUNCH

*1 cup Tomato Juice
Open-Face Salmon Salad Sandwich (3 ounces salmon mixed with chopped celery and 1 teaspoon mayonnaise on 1 slice whole wheat toast)
Pickle Spears
½ cup each Carrot Slices and Red Bell Pepper Rings on Lettuce Leaves
Coffee or Tea

DINNER

Baked Stuffed Chicken Breasts (see page 266)
1 cup Spinach Leaves
Tossed Salad with 1½ teaspoons French Salad Dressing
Frozen Cantaloupe "Ice Cream" (see page 44)

SNACKS, AT PLANNED TIMES

½ cup Strawberries; 1 cup Skim Milk

Day 2

BREAKFAST

*½ cup Orange Juice
¾ ounce Cold Cereal
1 cup Skim Milk
Coffee or Tea

LUNCH

Hearty Lentil Soup (see page 239)
Tossed Salad with 1½ teaspoons Italian Salad Dressing
3 Melba Rounds
½ cup Pineapple
Coffee or Tea

DINNER

4 ounces Cooked Fish
3 ounces Baked Potato with ½ teaspoon Margarine
"Fried" Cauliflower (see page 82)
½ cup Steamed Wax Beans
Coffee or Tea

SNACKS, AT PLANNED TIMES

*¼ small Cantaloupe; ½ cup Plain Low-Fat Yogurt

Day 3

BREAKFAST

Crunchy Raisin Bars (see page 57)
⅓ cup Cottage Cheese
1 cup Skim Milk
Coffee or Tea

LUNCH

*½ cup Tomato Juice
Tuna Tacos (see page 388)
Mixed Green Salad with 1½ teaspoons French Salad Dressing
Coffee or Tea

DINNER

4 ounces Cooked Chicken
½ cup Cooked Noodles with 1 teaspoon Margarine
1 cup Steamed Sliced Yellow Squash
Coffee or Tea

SNACKS, AT PLANNED TIMES

*½ cup Grapefruit Sections; 1 cup Skim Milk

Day 4

BREAKFAST

*1 cup Honeydew Balls
Pancakes (see page 125)
Coffee or Tea

LUNCH

2/3 cup Cottage Cheese
Tossed Salad with Lemon
Juice and Herbs
2 Melba Toast Slices
1 small Apple
3/4 cup Skim Milk

DINNER

Steak Provençale (see page
310)
1/2 cup Cooked Pasta
1/2 cup Steamed Whole Green
Beans
Mixed Green Salad with 1 1/2
teaspoons Italian Salad
Dressing
Coffee or Tea

SNACKS, AT PLANNED TIMES

1/2 cup Pineapple; 1/2 cup Plain
Low-Fat Yogurt

Day 5

BREAKFAST

*1/2 cup Orange Juice
1 Egg (prepared without fat)
3 Melba Rounds
1/4 cup Skim Milk
Coffee or Tea

LUNCH

Baked Macaroni and Cheese
(see page 134)
Tossed Salad with 1/2 teaspoon
Imitation Bacon Bits and
1 1/2 teaspoons Vegetable
Oil plus Wine Vinegar and
Herbs
Sparkling Mineral Water with
Lime Slice

DINNER

4 ounces Cooked Fish
6 medium Steamed Asparagus
Spears
Green Salad with **Tomato-
Chive Dressing** (see page
164)

*1 cup Honeydew Balls
Coffee or Tea

SNACKS, AT PLANNED TIMES

*1/4 small Cantaloupe; 1/2 cup
Plain Low-Fat Yogurt

Day 6

BREAKFAST

2 tablespoons Raisins
1/2 cup Cooked Cereal
1 cup Skim Milk
Coffee or Tea

LUNCH

"Calzones" (see page 215)
1/2 cup Tomato Slices with 1
teaspoon Vegetable Oil plus
Basil Leaves on Lettuce
Leaves
1/2 cup Pineapple
Coffee or Tea

DINNER

*1 cup Tomato Juice
Deviled Calf Liver (see page
372)
1/2 cup Cooked Rice with 1
teaspoon Margarine
1/2 cup Steamed Brussels
Sprouts
Coffee or Tea

SNACKS, AT PLANNED TIMES

2 cups Prepared Plain Popcorn;
1 cup Skim Milk

Day 7

BREAKFAST

*1 cup Strawberries
1/4 cup Part-Skim Ricotta
Cheese
1/2 cup Skim Milk
Coffee or Tea

LUNCH

**BLT Sandwich with Spicy
Russian Dressing** (see page
352)
Mixed Green Salad with 1
teaspoon Vegetable Oil plus
Wine Vinegar and
Seasonings
1 small Apple
1/2 cup Skim Milk
Coffee or Tea

DINNER

4 ounces Cooked Chicken
6 medium Steamed Broccoli
Spears
Tossed Salad with **Sweet 'n'
Sour Salad Dressing** (see
page 413)
Coffee or Tea

SNACKS, AT PLANNED TIMES

*1 cup Honeydew Balls; 1/2 cup
Plain Low-Fat Yogurt

A NOTE ON THE RECIPE SYMBOLS

 The clock face on recipes indicates that they can be prepared in 30 minutes or less.

 The penny appears on budget recipes.

Recipe Information

◗ Pointers for Using Recipes with the Food Plan

◗ The recipes in this book were developed to fit the various stages of the Food Plan and are so noted. As you progress from Week 1 to Week 4, you may, of course, continue to use the recipes developed for the previous weeks. Starting on Week 5, you may choose recipes from the Personal Choice Selections chapter (see page 421 for further explanation).

◗ Always take time to measure and weigh ingredients carefully; this is vital to both recipe results and weight control. Don't try to judge portions by eye.

To weigh foods, use a scale.

To measure liquids, use a standard glass or clear plastic measuring cup. Place it on a level surface and read markings at eye level. Fill the cup just to the appropriate marking. To measure less than ¼ cup, use standard measuring spoons.

To measure dry ingredients, use metal or plastic measuring cups that come in sets of four: ¼ cup; ⅓ cup; ½ cup; and 1 cup. Spoon the ingredients into the cup, then level with the straight edge of a knife or metal spatula. To measure less than ¼ cup, use standard measuring spoons and, unless otherwise directed, level as for measuring cup.

To measure a dash, as a guide consider a dash to be about 1⁄16 of a teaspoon (½ of a ⅛-teaspoon measure or ¼ of a ¼-teaspoon measure).

◗ In any recipe for more than one serving it is important to mix ingredients well and to divide evenly so that each portion will be the same size. '

◗ Pointers on Our Ingredients

◗ Reading product labels is the best way to determine if the item you are using is what the recipe calls for. This may sound very simple, but the label contains a great deal of important information that will help you succeed on your Food Plan. Some recipes call for items of specific caloric content; some products are permissible on the Food Plan only if they meet certain nutritional guidelines. These facts, as well as other points of interest, can be found on items whose labels contain nutrition information. Get into the habit of reading labels and you'll find that your time, as well as your money, is being well spent.

In addition, the following pointers will help guide you through our ingredient lists.

◗ The herbs used in these recipes are dried unless otherwise indicated. If you are substituting fresh herbs, use approximately four times the amount of dried (e.g., 1 teaspoon chopped fresh basil instead of 1/4 teaspoon dried basil leaves). If you are substituting ground (powdered) herbs for dried leaves, use approximately half the amount of dried (e.g., 1/4 teaspoon ground thyme instead of 1/2 teaspoon dried thyme leaves).

◗ If you are substituting fresh spices for ground, generally use approximately eight times the amount of ground (e.g., 1 teaspoon minced ginger root instead of 1/8 teaspoon ground ginger).

◗ Generally, dried herbs and spices should not be kept for more than a year. Date the container at the time of purchase and check periodically for potency. Usually, if the herb (or spice) is aromatic, it is still potent; if the aroma has diminished, the recipe may require a larger amount of the seasoning.

◗ Unless otherwise specified, the raisins used in our recipes are dark seedless raisins.

◗ We've used fresh vegetables unless otherwise indicated. If you substitute frozen or canned vegetables, it may be necessary to adjust cooking times accordingly.

◗ When vegetable oil is called for, oils such as safflower, sunflower, soybean, corn, cottonseed, peanut, or any of these combined may be used. Since olive oil and Chinese sesame oil have distinctive flavors, they have been specifically indicated. There are two types of sesame oil: light and dark. The light oil is relatively flavorless and may be used as a substitute for any other vegetable oil. When sesame oil is specified, use the dark variety. This product, made from toasted sesame seeds, has a rich amber color and a characteristic sesame flavor.

◗ Pointers for Successful Results

◗ Read through a recipe completely before you begin. Make sure you understand the method and have all ingredients and utensils on hand. Gather all ingredients and any special utensils needed in one place and make sure that all items are at proper temperature (e.g., if you're beating evaporated skimmed milk, you'll want to chill the milk, bowl, and beaters; if you're beating egg whites, you'll want them at room temperature).

◗ Measure and/or weigh all ingredients carefully.

◗ When it is suggested that an ingredient be at room temperature, we are referring to a temperature of 68° to 72°F.

◗ It is recommended that foods not be marinated in aluminum containers. Certain foods react with aluminum and this can have an adverse effect. Using a plastic bag is an effective way of marinating foods. Place marinade and items to be marinated in a leakproof plastic bag; close bag securely and let marinate according to recipe directions. Using this method makes turning of foods easy, since all you have to do is turn the entire bag. After food has been marinated, the bag can be discarded and there's one pan less to clean.

◗ When pounding meat, if a meat mallet is unavailable a saucepan can be substituted. Pound with bottom of the saucepan and, unless otherwise specified, pound until meat is about ¼ inch thick.

◗ When using eggs, it's a good idea to break each one into a cup or bowl before combining with other ingredients or additional eggs. This will avoid wasting other items should one egg happen to be spoiled.

◗ When dissolving arrowroot, flour, or cornstarch in liquid, to avoid lumping add the dry ingredient to the liquid, not vice versa.

◗ When dissolving unflavored gelatin over direct heat, be sure to use a low heat and stir constantly. This is important since gelatin burns very easily.

◗ When a recipe calls for the use of custard cups, use items made of heatproof glass or heavy ceramic.

◗ The cooking times on most recipes are approximate and should be used as guides. There are many variables that can affect timing, such as temperature of food before it is cooked, type of heat being used, shape of food, type of cookware being used, etc. In addition, the flow of both gas and electricity to your appliances may be affected by the total amount being used within your area at the time you are cooking. If you are cooking at peak-load times, chances are a recipe may take a little longer than the suggested time; conversely, if a minimum amount of power is being utilized, the recipe may be done in a shorter period of time. Therefore, to ensure optimum results, be sure to always check for doneness as directed.

◗ Some recipes include instructions to preheat the oven. When preparing these recipes, if you do not preheat, generally allow an additional 5 to 10 minutes' cooking time.

◗ When baking, be sure that pans are placed on oven rack so that air can circulate freely. It's best to use one oven rack at a time. If you're using two racks, place them so that the oven is divided into thirds, then stagger the pans so that one is not directly above the other.

◗ When baking in a muffin pan and using only some of the cups, it's a good idea to partially fill the empty cups with water. This will prevent the pan from warping and/or burning. When ready to remove items from pan, drain off the water very carefully; remember, it will be boiling hot.

◗ When broiling, 4 inches is the standard distance from the heat source and should be used with any recipes that do not specify otherwise. If it is necessary to broil closer to or farther away from the heat, the appropriate distance will be indicated.

◗ If a dish is to be chilled or frozen after cooking, always allow it to cool slightly before refrigerating or freezing. Placing a very hot item into the refrigerator or freezer can adversely affect the functioning of the appliance. Cover all items that are to be refrigerated, and cover or properly wrap all items that are to be placed in the freezer. If a dish is not covered, odors from other foods may permeate it, or vice versa; drying may occur, particularly in frost-free refrigerators; the flavor may be spoiled by the accidental dripping of other foods; freezer-burn may occur.

◗ It is recommended that chilled foods be served on chilled plates and hot foods on warmed plates. Plates and glassware should be chilled in the refrigerator for approximately 5 minutes before serving. Plates and platters can be heated by placing them in a warm oven (no more than 200°F.) for 5 to 10 minutes before serving, in a warmer, or on a warming tray.

Oven Temperatures

Oven thermostats should be checked at least once a year. If your oven does not have a thermostat or regulator, the following chart will give you an idea of the equivalent amount of heat required for each temperature range:

250° to 275°F.	Very slow oven
300° to 325°F.	Slow oven
350° to 375°F.	Moderate oven
400° to 425°F.	Hot oven
450° to 475°F.	Very hot oven
500° to 525°F.	Extremely hot oven

An oven thermometer can be purchased and placed in the oven to help determine the degree of heat.

Microwave Ovens

Many of our recipes can be cooked in a microwave oven. Since there is no one standard that applies to all ovens, you will have to experiment with your unit and follow the manufacturer's advice for timing. Generally, you should allow about ¼ of the suggested cooking time. This means that if our recipe suggests 20 minutes, allow 5 minutes in your microwave oven (or slightly less, since it's wiser to undercook than overcook). Please note that our roasting procedures for beef, ham, lamb, and pork require the use of a rack so that fat can drain off into the pan. Racks designed for use in microwave ovens are available.

Slow Cookers

If you enjoy cooking with a slow cooker, there's no reason why you can't adapt many of our recipes to its use. For a headstart on Chicken Broth (see page 412), combine all ingredients; cook covered on low for 8 hours. Strain and proceed as in the basic recipe.

Metric Conversions

If you are converting the recipes in this book to metrics, use the following table as a guide:

Temperature

To change degrees Fahrenheit to degrees Celsius, subtract 32° and multiply by five-ninths.

Weight

To change	To	Multiply by
Ounces	Grams	30.0
Pounds	Kilograms	.48

Volume

To Change	To	Multiply by
Teaspoons	Milliliters	5.0
Tablespoons	Milliliters	15.0
Cups	Milliliters	250.0
Cups	Liters	.25
Pints	Liters	.5
Quarts	Liters	1.0
Gallons	Liters	4.0

Length

To Change	To	Multiply by
Inches	Millimeters	25.0
Inches	Centimeters	2.5
Feet	Centimeters	30.0
Yards	Meters	.9

Oven Temperatures

Degrees Fahrenheit =	Degrees Celsius
250	120
275	140
300	150
325	160
350	180
375	190
400	200
425	220
450	230
475	250
500	260
525	270

Symbol =	Metric Unit
g	gram
kg	kilogram
ml	milliliter
l	liter
°C	degrees Celsius
mm	millimeter
cm	centimeter
m	meter

Pan Substitutions

It's best to use the pan size that's recommended in a recipe; however, if your kitchen isn't equipped with that particular pan, chances are a substitution will work just as well. The pan size is determined by the volume of food. When substituting, use a pan as close to the recommended size as possible. Food cooked in too small a pan may boil over; food cooked in too large a pan may dry out or burn. To determine the dimensions of a baking pan, measure across the top, between the inside edges. To determine the volume, measure the amount of water the pan holds when completely filled.

When you use a pan that is a different size from the one recommended, it may be necessary to adjust the suggested cooking time. Depending on the size of the pan and the depth of the food in it, you may need to add or subtract 5 to 10 minutes. If you substitute glass or glass-ceramic for metal, it is recommended that the oven temperature be reduced by 25°F.

The following chart provides some common pan substitutions:

Recommended Size	Approximate Volume	Possible Substitutions
8 x 1½-inch round baking pan	1½ quarts	10 x 6 x 2-inch baking dish 9 x 1½-inch round baking pan 8 x 4 x 2-inch loaf pan 9-inch pie plate
8 x 8 x 2-inch baking pan	2 quarts	11 x 7 x 1½-inch baking pan 12 x 7½ x 2-inch baking pan 9 x 5 x 3-inch loaf pan two 8 x 1½-inch round baking pans
13 x 9 x 2-inch baking pan	3 quarts	14 x 11 x 2-inch baking dish two 9 x 1½-inch round baking pans three 8 x 1½-inch round baking pans

Sugar Substitutes

The use of sugar substitutes on the Weight Watchers food plan has always been optional. Natural sweetness is available in the form of fruits and honey. You may also use white and brown sugar, fructose, molasses, syrup, jams, jellies, and preserves. The use of sugar substitutes is completely optional, and we believe that the decision about using them should be made by you and your physician.

▶ Pointers on Nutrition

▶ Nutrition is defined as the process by which we utilize foods in order to maintain healthy bodily functions. Foods provide the nutrients necessary for energy, growth, and repair of body tissues, as well as for regulation and control of body processes. You need about forty different nutrients to stay healthy. These include proteins, fats, carbohydrates, vitamins, minerals, and water. It is the amount of proteins, carbohydrates, and fats in foods that determines their energy value (caloric content). The objective of daily menu planning is to provide yourself with basic nutrients while staying within your caloric limit.

▶ Proteins are necessary for building and maintaining body tissues. Poultry, meat, fish, eggs, milk, and cheese are the best sources of protein. Fats and carbohydrates provide energy in addition to assisting other body functions. Fruits, vegetables, cereals, and grains are rich in carbohydrates. Margarine, vegetable oils, poultry, meat, and fish supply the fats we need.

▶ Vitamins and minerals are also essential for the body's proper functioning. Sodium is especially important for maintaining body water balance and therefore has a significant effect on weight control. Sodium occurs naturally in some foods, and additional amounts are often added in processing prepared foods.

▶ *Variety* is the key to success. No single food supplies all the essential nutrients in the amounts needed. The greater the variety of food the less likely you are to develop either a deficiency or an excess of any single nutrient, and the more interesting and attractive your diet will be.

▶ Pointers for Using Exchange and Nutrition Information on the Recipes

▶ Each recipe in this book is followed by an Exchange Information statement. This statement provides information as to how one serving of the item prepared from that recipe fits into the Food Plan. You will find this statement useful when preparing your menus as it will help you keep track of your Exchanges. If you make any changes in the recipes, be sure to adjust the Exchange Information accordingly.

▶ Since many people are concerned about nutrition, on each recipe we have also included the per-serving nutrition analysis for calories, protein, fat, carbohydrate, calcium, sodium, and cholesterol. These figures were calculated using the most up-to-date data available; they will change if the recipe is altered, even if the substitution in ingredients does not affect the Exchange Information.

The Fruit Exchange

WHEN creating menus, be innovative and plan fruit selections that can appear in both starring and supporting roles. Set the stage for a successful solo by introducing our Glazed Cinnamon Grapefruit, or feature fruits in harmony with other "players," such as our Coconut-Topped Mixed Fruit.

The naturally pleasing shapes, the vivid variety of colors, and the full-flavored sweetness of fruit will delight the most exacting audience. You'll be sure to receive a standing ovation when you present any of the recipes in this section.

◗ Pointers on the Fruit Exchange

Daily Exchanges

	WEEKS 1 AND 2	WEEKS 3 AND 4
Women	3 Exchanges	3 Exchanges
Men and Youths	4 Exchanges	4 to 6 Exchanges

◗ Fruits supply fiber, vitamin A, and vitamin C. Since individual fruits vary widely in the amount of nutrients they supply, it is important that you take advantage of the wide variety supplied by the Exchange Lists.

◗ The fruits on the Exchange Lists that are marked with an asterisk (*) are excellent sources of vitamin C; you should select *at least* one of them every day. Because heating destroys vitamin C, if an asterisked fruit is cooked, you should select another asterisked fruit for one of your remaining Exchanges.

◗ Except for pineapple slices and spears, when using canned fruit, 1 Exchange is ½ cup *or* the fresh equivalent with up to 2 tablespoons juice (e.g., ½ cup canned sliced peaches *or* 2 canned peach halves). Two slices or 4 spears of canned pineapple is 1 Fruit Exchange.

◗ Measure frozen fruit in its frozen state, never thawed or partially thawed. Exchanges are the same as for fresh fruit.

◗ When using undiluted frozen concentrated fruit juice, 1 Fruit Exchange is:

2 tablespoons orange, grapefruit, or orange-grapefruit juice
4 teaspoons apple, grape, pineapple, or pineapple-orange juice

◗ One 3-ounce serving of approved commercially prepared vanilla or chocolate dietary frozen dessert provides 1 Fruit Exchange and ½ Milk Exchange.

FRUIT EXCHANGE LISTS

Week 1

Selections	One Exchange
Apple	1 small (about 4 ounces) or ¾ cup
Banana	½ medium (about 3 ounces with peel)
*Cantaloupe	¼ small (about 9 ounces with rind) or 1 cup
Fruit Salad	½ cup
*Grapefruit	½ medium (about 8 ounces with rind)
*Grapefruit Juice	½ cup
*Grapefruit Sections	½ cup
*Honeydew or similar melon	2 inch wedge (about 7 Inches long) or 1 cup
*Orange	1 small (about 6 ounces with rind)
*Orange-Grapefruit Juice	½ cup
*Orange Juice	½ cup
*Orange Sections	½ cup
Peach	1 medium (about 4 ounces with pit) or ½ cup
Pineapple	⅛ medium (about 4½ ounces with rind) or ½ cup
*Strawberries	1 cup whole or ¾ cup sliced
Watermelon	2 x 3-inch wedge or 1 cup

Week 2

You may use all of the items listed under Week 1 and may add the following to your Exchange List.

Selections	One Exchange
Applesauce, canned or homemade (no sugar added)	½ cup
Berries	
Blackberries	½ cup
Blueberries	½ cup
Boysenberries	½ cup
Elderberries	½ cup
Huckleberries	½ cup
Loganberries	½ cup
Mulberries	½ cup
Raspberries	½ cup

Week 3

You may use all of the items listed under Weeks 1 and 2 and may add the following to your Exchange List.

Selections	One Exchange
Grapes	20 small or 12 large
Nectarine	1 small (about 5 ounces with pit)
Prunes	2 large or 3 medium
Tangerine	1 large (about 4 ounces with rind)

Week 4

You may use all of the items listed under Weeks 1, 2, and 3 and may add the following to your Exchange List.

Selections	One Exchange
Apple Cider, unfermented (carbonated or noncarbonated)	1/3 cup
Apple Juice	1/3 cup
Apricots	2 medium (about 1 1/4 ounces each, with pit)
dried	4 halves
Berries	
Cranberries	1 cup
*Gooseberries	3/4 cup
Carambola (Star Fruit)	1 medium (about 4 1/2 ounces with rind)
Cherries	10 large
Crab Apples	2
Cranberry Juice, low-calorie	1 cup
*Currants, fresh	3/4 cup
dried	2 tablespoons
Dates, fresh or dried	2
Dried Fruit, mixed or individual varieties	3/4 ounce
Fig, fresh or dried	1 large
Genips	2
Grape Juice, carbonated or noncarbonated	1/3 cup
*Kiwi Fruit	1 medium (about 3 ounces with rind)
Kumquats	3 medium
Lichees, fresh	8
Loquats	10 pitted

Selections	One Exchange
Mandarin Orange	1 large (about 4¾ ounces with rind)
Mango	½ small (about 6½ ounces with rind, without pit)
*Mixed Vegetable Juice, canned or homemade (no sugar added)	1 cup
Murcot (Honey Tangerine)	1 medium (about 4¾ ounces with rind)
*Papaya	½ medium (about 8 ounces with rind) or ½ cup
Pear	1 small (about 5 ounces)
Persimmon, native	1 medium (about 2 ounces)
Pineapple Juice	⅓ cup
Pineapple-Orange Juice	⅓ cup
Plums	2 medium (about 2½ ounces each, with pit)
Prickly Pear (Cactus Pear)	1 medium
Prune Juice	⅓ cup
Quince	1 medium
Raisins	2 tablespoons
Soursop (Guanabana)	¼ cup
Sweetsop (Sugar Apple)	⅓ cup
Tamarinds	2
Tangelo	1 large
Tangerine Juice	½ cup
*Tomato Juice, canned or homemade (no sugar added)	1 cup
*Ugli Fruit	1 medium

Apple Clafouti ❶

WEEK 4 ∼ MAKES 4 SERVINGS

A clafouti is French fruit pudding, traditionally made with cherries; pancake batter is poured over the fruit, then baked. Our delicious version uses apples and may be served warm or at room temperature.

4 eggs
½ cup skim milk
¼ cup thawed frozen dairy
   whipped topping
2 teaspoons vanilla extract
¼ teaspoon each ground cinnamon
   and ground nutmeg
¾ cup self-rising flour

2 tablespoons granulated sugar
1 teaspoon margarine
4 small apples, cored, pared, and
   thinly sliced
1 tablespoon lemon juice
Brown sugar substitute to equal 2
   teaspoons brown sugar (optional)

Preheat oven to 375°F. In mixing bowl combine eggs, milk, whipped topping, vanilla, cinnamon, and nutmeg; using an electric mixer, beat until smooth. Gradually beat in flour and sugar and continue beating until mixture is thick and smooth.

Grease 10-inch pie plate or quiche dish with margarine; arrange apple slices in plate (or dish) in a single layer and sprinkle with lemon juice. Pour batter over fruit and, if desired, sprinkle with brown sugar substitute. Bake until browned, 35 to 40 minutes.

Each serving provides: 1 Protein Exchange; 1 Bread Exchange; 1 Fruit Exchange;
   65 calories Optional Exchange
Per serving: 285 calories; 10 g protein; 8 g fat; 42 g carbohydrate; 137 mg calcium;
   356 mg sodium; 275 mg cholesterol
With sugar substitute: 286 calories; 10 g protein; 9 g fat; 42 g carbohydrate;
   137 mg calcium; 356 mg sodium; 275 mg cholesterol

Baked Maple Apple ❶

WEEK 1 ⌇ MAKES 2 SERVINGS, 1 APPLE EACH

2 small apples
2 teaspoons reduced-calorie apricot
 spread (16 calories per 2
 teaspoons)

1 teaspoon reduced-calorie maple-
 flavored syrup (60 calories per
 fluid ounce)

Remove core from each apple to ½ inch from bottom. Remove a thin strip of peel from around center of each apple (this helps keep peel from bursting). Fill each apple with 1 teaspoon apricot spread and ½ teaspoon maple syrup. Place each apple upright in individual baking dish; cover dishes with foil and bake at 400°F. until apples are tender, 25 to 30 minutes.

Each serving provides: 1 Fruit Exchange; 13 calories Optional Exchange
Per serving: 75 calories; 0.2 g protein; 0.4 g fat; 19 g carbohydrate; 7 mg calcium;
 0 mg sodium; 0 mg cholesterol

Blender Applesauce ◑❶

WEEK 1 ⌇ MAKES 1 SERVING

1 small apple, cored and pared
1 tablespoon lemon juice

Granulated sugar substitute to
 equal 1 teaspoon sugar
Dash ground cinnamon (optional)

Chop apple into small pieces. In blender container combine apple and lemon juice and process until smooth (when necessary, stop machine and, using a rubber scraper, scrape apple from sides into bottom of container). Stir in sugar substitute and, if desired, cinnamon. Serve immediately or cover and refrigerate until chilled.

Each serving provides: 1 Fruit Exchange
Per serving: 62 calories; 0.2 g protein; 0.4 g fat; 20 g carbohydrate; 6 mg calcium;
 11 mg sodium; 0 mg cholesterol

Apple Pastry ❶

WEEK 4 ⬿ MAKES 1 SERVING

3 tablespoons all-purpose flour
Dash salt
2 teaspoons margarine
1 tablespoon plain low-fat yogurt
1 small apple

Dash each ground nutmeg and
  ground cinnamon
2 teaspoons reduced-calorie apricot
  spread (16 calories per 2
  teaspoons)

1. In small mixing bowl combine flour and salt; with pastry blender, or 2 knives used scissors-fashion, cut in margarine until mixture resembles coarse meal. Add yogurt and mix thoroughly. Form dough into a ball; wrap in plastic wrap and refrigerate for at least 1 hour (may be kept in refrigerator for up to 3 days).

2. Between 2 sheets of wax paper roll dough, forming a 4½-inch circle about ⅛ inch thick. Carefully remove wax paper and place dough on foil or small cookie sheet. Preheat oven to 350°F.

3. Core, pare, and thinly slice apple; arrange slices decoratively over dough and sprinkle with nutmeg and cinnamon. Bake until crust is golden, 20 to 30 minutes.

4. During last few minutes that pastry is baking, in small metal measuring cup or other small flameproof container heat apricot spread; as soon as pastry is done, brush with warm spread.

Each serving provides: 1 Bread Exchange; 2 Fat Exchanges; 1 Fruit Exchange;
  25 calories Optional Exchange
Per serving: 238 calories; 4 g protein; 8 g fat; 38 g carbohydrate; 39 mg calcium;
  228 mg sodium; 1 mg cholesterol

Baked Stuffed Apples with Custard Sauce

WEEK 4 ～ MAKES 4 SERVINGS, 1 STUFFED APPLE EACH

Serve at room temperature or chilled.

Stuffed Apples

15 large frozen pitted cherries,
   partially thawed, then chopped
1 tablespoon dried currants
2 teaspoons granulated sugar

1 tablespoon lemon juice, divided
1/8 teaspoon ground cinnamon
4 small Golden Delicious apples,
   cored

Sauce

1/2 cup evaporated skimmed milk
1 egg

2 teaspoons granulated sugar
1/4 teaspoon vanilla extract

To Prepare Apples: In small saucepan combine cherries, currants, sugar, 1 teaspoon lemon juice, and the cinnamon and bring to a boil; cook, stirring occasionally, until cherries are coated and mixture is slightly thickened, about 3 minutes. Let cool.

Preheat oven to 375°F. Starting at stem end of each apple, pare about 1/3 of the way down; brush pared section of each with 1/2 teaspoon lemon juice (this will prevent discoloring). Stuff each apple with 1/4 of the cherry mixture and set apples in baking pan that is just large enough to hold them upright; cover pan with foil and bake until apples are tender, 45 to 50 minutes. Let cool to room temperature or cool slightly, cover, and refrigerate until chilled.

To Prepare Sauce: In small saucepan heat milk until tiny bubbles form around edge. In bowl beat egg with sugar until thoroughly combined; gradually beat in milk. Pour mixture into top half of double boiler and stir in vanilla; cook over hot (*not boiling*) water, stirring constantly, until sauce is thick enough to thinly coat the back of a spoon. Pour sauce into a bowl, cover with plastic wrap, and refrigerate until cooled or chilled. Serve 1/4 of the sauce over each stuffed apple.

Each serving provides: 1 1/2 Fruit Exchanges; 1/4 Milk Exchange;
   40 calories Optional Exchange
Per serving: 144 calories; 4 g protein; 2 g fat; 29 g carbohydrate; 113 mg calcium;
   55 mg sodium; 70 mg cholesterol

Honey-Poached Apples ◖❸

WEEK 1 ∽ MAKES 2 SERVINGS

May be served warm or chilled.

2 small apples
2 teaspoons lemon juice, divided
¾ cup water

2-inch strip lemon peel
2 teaspoons honey
1 teaspoon vanilla extract

Core and pare apples; cut into thin wedges and place in bowl with water to cover. Add 1 teaspoon lemon juice and set aside.

In small saucepan combine the water and lemon peel; bring to a boil and cook for 5 minutes. Drain apples and add to saucepan along with honey, vanilla, and remaining teaspoon lemon juice. Cook until apples are tender, 8 to 10 minutes; remove and discard lemon peel. Serve apple wedges in poaching liquid.

Each serving provides: 1 Fruit Exchange; 20 calories Optional Exchange
Per serving: 87 calories; 0.2 g protein; 0.3 g fat; 21 g carbohydrate; 5 mg calcium;
 1 mg sodium; 0 mg cholesterol

Apricot-Glazed Banana Muffin ◖❸

WEEK 2 ∽ MAKES 2 SERVINGS, ½ MUFFIN EACH

Serve warm.

1 medium banana
1 raisin English muffin, split in half
 and toasted

2 teaspoons each margarine, melted,
 and reduced-calorie apricot
 spread (16 calories per 2
 teaspoons), heated
Ground cinnamon

Peel banana and cut in half crosswise, then cut each half in half lengthwise. Place muffin halves on broiling pan or on a sheet of foil; top each half with 2 banana quarters and drizzle with half of the melted margarine. Brush each banana quarter with ½ teaspoon apricot spread and sprinkle with dash cinnamon; broil until well heated.

Each serving provides: 1 Bread Exchange; 1 Fat Exchange; 1 Fruit Exchange;
 8 calories Optional Exchange
Per serving: 170 calories; 3 g protein; 5 g fat; 29 g carbohydrate; 6 mg calcium;
 190 mg sodium; 0 mg cholesterol

Cinnamon-Apricot Bananas ◑ ❸

WEEK 4 ⬦ MAKES 2 SERVINGS, 1 BANANA HALF EACH

4 graham crackers (2½-inch
  squares), made into crumbs
2 teaspoons shredded coconut
¼ teaspoon ground cinnamon
1 tablespoon plus 1 teaspoon
  reduced-calorie apricot spread
  (16 calories per 2 teaspoons)

1 medium banana, peeled and cut in
  half lengthwise

In small skillet combine crumbs, coconut, and cinnamon and toast lightly, being careful not to burn; transfer to sheet of wax paper or a paper plate and set aside.

In same skillet heat apricot spread until melted; remove from heat. Roll each banana half in spread, then quickly roll in crumb mixture, pressing crumbs so that they adhere to banana; place coated halves on plate, cover lightly, and refrigerate until chilled.

Each serving provides: 1 Bread Exchange; 1 Fruit Exchange;
  25 calories Optional Exchange
Per serving: 130 calories; 2 g protein; 2 g fat; 29 g carbohydrate; 13 mg calcium;
  95 mg sodium; 0 mg cholesterol

Variation: Coconut–Strawberry Bananas—Omit cinnamon and substitute reduced-calorie strawberry spread (16 calories per 2 teaspoons) for the apricot spread.

Banana-Chocolate Pudding Cake ❶

WEEK 4 ∽ MAKES 8 SERVINGS

¾ cup cake flour
⅓ cup instant nonfat dry milk powder
1 envelope (four ½-cup servings) reduced-calorie chocolate pudding mix
1 teaspoon double-acting baking powder
4 eggs, separated

2 tablespoons granulated sugar
½ cup evaporated skimmed milk
½ teaspoon vanilla extract
Dash salt
½ cup thawed frozen dairy whipped topping
2 medium bananas
1 tablespoon lemon juice

1. Preheat oven to 350°F. Line bottom of 8 x 8 x 2-inch baking pan with wax paper; spray bottom and sides with nonstick cooking spray and set aside.

2. Onto sheet of wax paper or a paper plate sift together flour, dry milk powder, chocolate pudding mix, and baking powder; set aside.

3. In large mixing bowl combine egg yolks and sugar; using electric mixer, beat for 2 minutes. Alternating ingredients, gradually beat in chocolate pudding mixture and milk; add vanilla extract. Beat at medium-high speed until mixture is thoroughly combined.

4. In separate bowl, using clean beaters, beat egg whites with salt until stiff peaks form. Gently stir ¼ of beaten egg whites into batter; carefully fold in remaining egg whites.

5. Pour batter into sprayed baking pan and set pan in middle of center oven rack; bake for 25 to 30 minutes (until a cake tester, inserted in center, comes out clean).

6. Let cake cool in pan for 5 minutes. Remove cake from pan and set on wire rack to cool.

7. Remove wax paper from cooled cake; transfer cake to serving platter and spread top with whipped topping. Peel and slice bananas; transfer slices to small bowl, add lemon juice, and toss gently. Decoratively arrange banana slices over whipped topping; to serve, cut cake into 8 equal pieces.

Each serving provides: ½ Protein Exchange; ½ Bread Exchange; ½ Fruit Exchange; ¼ Milk Exchange; 30 calories Optional Exchange
Per serving: 176 calories; 7 g protein; 4 g fat; 29 g carbohydrate; 127 mg calcium; 139 mg sodium; 138 mg cholesterol

Meringue Crêpes with Blueberry Custard Filling ◑

WEEK 4 ⬿ MAKES 4 SERVINGS, 2 CRÊPES EACH

---

1 cup evaporated skimmed milk
2 large eggs, separated
1 tablespoon plus 1 teaspoon
  granulated sugar, divided
2 teaspoons each cornstarch and
  lemon juice

2 cups blueberries (reserve 8
  berries for garnish)
8 crêpes (see Crêpes Suzette,
  page 433)

In 1-quart saucepan combine milk, egg yolks, and 1 tablespoon sugar; cook over low heat, stirring constantly, until slightly thickened and bubbles form around sides of mixture. In cup or small bowl dissolve cornstarch in lemon juice; gradually stir into milk mixture and cook, stirring constantly, until thick. Remove from heat and fold in blueberries; let cool.

Spoon ⅛ of custard onto center of each crêpe and fold sides over filling to enclose; arrange crêpes, seam-side down, in an 8 x 8 x 2-inch baking pan. In small bowl, using electric mixer on high speed, beat egg whites until soft peaks form; add remaining teaspoon sugar and continue beating until stiff peaks form. Fill pastry bag with egg whites and pipe an equal amount over each crêpe (if pastry bag is not available, spoon egg whites over crêpes); top each with a reserved blueberry and broil until meringue is lightly browned, 10 to 15 seconds. Serve immediately.

Each serving provides (includes crêpes): 1 Protein Exchange; 1 Bread Exchange;
  1 Fruit Exchange; ¾ Milk Exchange; 25 calories Optional Exchange
Per serving: 300 calories; 16 g protein; 6 g fat; 45 g carbohydrate; 298 mg calcium;
  180 mg sodium; 278 mg cholesterol

Frozen Cantaloupe "Ice Cream" ◑❸

WEEK 1 ⬦ MAKES 4 SERVINGS, ABOUT ½ CUP EACH

Soften **6 ounces vanilla dietary frozen dessert.** In work bowl of food processor puree **1 cup very ripe cantaloupe chunks or balls.** Add softened frozen dessert and process until smooth. Transfer mixture to freezer-safe bowl, cover with plastic wrap, and freeze until solid.

Break mixture into pieces and place in work bowl of food processor; process until smooth. Spoon into 4 freezer-safe dessert dishes, cover with plastic wrap, and freeze until firm. Remove from freezer 5 minutes before serving.

Each serving provides: ½ Fruit Exchange; ¼ Milk Exchange;
15 calories Optional Exchange
Per serving: 64 calories; 2 g protein; 1 g fat; 13 g carbohydrate; 78 mg calcium;
38 mg sodium; 0.1 mg cholesterol

Cherry-Apple Cobbler

WEEK 4 ⬦ MAKES 4 SERVINGS

2 slices raisin bread, made into
  crumbs
2 teaspoons each granulated sugar,
  divided, and margarine
⅛ teaspoon ground cinnamon
20 large frozen pitted cherries
  (no sugar added)

2 small apples, cored, pared, and
  sliced
¼ cup water, divided
1-inch piece cinnamon stick
1 teaspoon cornstarch

In small bowl combine crumbs, 1 teaspoon sugar, and the margarine and ground cinnamon; set aside.

In small saucepan combine fruit, 3 tablespoons water, and the cinnamon stick; cook over low heat for about 3 minutes. Combine remaining tablespoon water with cornstarch, stirring to dissolve; add to pan and cook, stirring constantly, until mixture is thickened. Remove from heat and remove and discard cinnamon stick; add remaining teaspoon sugar and stir to combine. Into each of four 6-ounce custard cups spoon ¼ of fruit mixture; top each with ¼ of crumb mixture and bake at 400°F. until topping is browned, about 15 minutes. Serve warm.

Each serving provides: ½ Bread Exchange; ½ Fat Exchange; 1 Fruit Exchange;
  15 calories Optional Exchange
Per serving: 114 calories; 1 g protein; 3 g fat; 23 g carbohydrate; 21 mg calcium;
  68 mg sodium; 0.4 mg cholesterol

Chilled Cherry Soup

WEEK 4 ～ MAKES 2 SERVINGS, ABOUT ½ CUP EACH

20 large frozen pitted cherries (no sugar added)
½ cup water
1½ teaspoons granulated sugar
2-inch cinnamon stick

1 strip lemon peel
2 tablespoons rosé wine
1 teaspoon cornstarch
¼ cup plain low-fat yogurt

In small saucepan combine cherries, water, sugar, cinnamon stick, and lemon peel; bring to a boil. Reduce heat, cover, and let simmer for 20 minutes.

Remove and discard cinnamon stick and lemon peel from cherry mixture. In measuring cup or small bowl combine wine and cornstarch, stirring to dissolve cornstarch; add to cherry mixture and, stirring constantly, bring to a boil. Reduce heat and let simmer until mixture thickens.

In heatproof bowl stir yogurt until smooth; add cherry mixture and stir to combine. Cover with plastic wrap and refrigerate until well chilled.

Each serving provides: 1 Fruit Exchange; ¼ Milk Exchange;
  35 calories Optional Exchange
Per serving: 98 calories; 2 g protein; 1 g fat; 19 g carbohydrate; 70 mg calcium;
  21 mg sodium; 2 mg cholesterol

Cherry-Vanilla "Ice Cream" ◐

WEEK 4 ∽ MAKES 2 SERVINGS

In work bowl of food processor or blender container process **6 ounces vanilla dietary frozen dessert** until smooth. Transfer to a 1-quart freezer-safe bowl and add **6 large fresh or frozen pitted cherries (no sugar added), cut into halves,** and **1 teaspoon vanilla extract**; stir to combine. Cover with plastic wrap and freeze until hardened; when ready to serve, scoop into serving dish and garnish with **4 large fresh or frozen pitted cherries (no sugar added).**

Each serving provides: 1½ Fruit Exchanges; ½ Milk Exchange
Per serving: 129 calories; 4 g protein; 1 g fat; 25 g carbohydrate; 154 mg calcium;
 70 mg sodium; 2 mg cholesterol

Citrus Cooler ◐❸

WEEK 1 ∽ MAKES 2 SERVINGS, 1¼ CUPS EACH

**1½ cups chilled lemon- or lemon-
lime-flavored diet soda (4 calories
per 12 fluid ounces)**
**1 cup chilled orange juice (no sugar
added)**

Garnish
2 cinnamon sticks (2 inches each)

Chill two 10-ounce glasses. In a 4-cup measure or pitcher combine soda and juice; pour half of mixture into each chilled glass and garnish each with a cinnamon stick.

Each serving provides: 1 Fruit Exchange; 2 calories Optional Exchange
Per serving: 58 calories; 1 g protein; 0.1 g fat; 14 g carbohydrate; 11 mg calcium;
 51 mg sodium; 0 mg cholesterol

Variation: Week 4—Substitute ⅔ cup apple juice (no sugar added) or unfermented apple cider (no sugar added) for the orange juice.

Per serving: 41 calories; 0.1 g protein; 0.1 g fat; 10 g carbohydrate; 6 mg calcium;
 53 mg sodium; 0 mg cholesterol

Iced Orange Punch ❸

WEEK 1 ⌁ MAKES 8 SERVINGS, ABOUT 1½ CUPS EACH

Ice Mold	Punch
Club soda	**1 quart each chilled orange juice**
1 lemon, sliced	**(no sugar added), club soda, and**
1 lime, sliced	**diet ginger ale (0 calories)**

To Prepare Ice Mold: Pour enough club soda into a 10- or 12-cup ring mold to fill mold; add lemon and lime slices, arranging them in an alternating pattern. Cover mold and carefully transfer to freezer; freeze until solid.

To Prepare Punch: In large punch bowl combine juice and sodas. Remove ice mold from ring mold and float ice mold in punch.

Each serving provides: 1 Fruit Exchange
Per serving: 56 calories; 1 g protein; 0.1 g fat; 14 g carbohydrate; 11 mg calcium;
    35 mg sodium; 0 mg cholesterol

Mixed Fruit Cooler ◐❸

WEEK 1 ⌁ MAKES 2 SERVINGS, ABOUT 1 CUP EACH

1 cup diet ginger ale (0 calories)	**8 ice cubes**
½ cup each grapefruit juice and	
orange juice (no sugar added)	**Garnish**
1 to 2 teaspoons lime juice (no	**2 lime or lemon wedges**
sugar added)	

Chill two 10-ounce glasses. In 2-cup glass measure combine all ingredients except ice cubes and garnish. Place 4 ice cubes in each chilled glass; pour half of juice mixture into each glass and garnish with lime or lemon wedge.

Each serving provides: 1 Fruit Exchange
Per serving: 53 calories; 1 g protein; 0.1 g fat; 13 g carbohydrate; 10 mg calcium;
    35 mg sodium; 0 mg cholesterol

Variation: Week 4—Substitute ⅓ cup apple juice (no sugar added) or unfermented apple cider (no sugar added) for the orange juice.

Per serving: 44 calories; 0.4 g protein; 1 g fat; 11 g carbohydrate; 8 mg calcium;
    36 mg sodium; 0 mg cholesterol

Meringue Fruit Cups ◑

WEEK 4 ∽ MAKES 4 SERVINGS

2 small oranges, cut crosswise into
  halves
1 cup strawberries, sliced
20 small seedless green grapes (or
  12 large, cut into halves)

1 egg white (at room temperature)
½ teaspoon each granulated sugar
  and vanilla extract

Over small bowl to catch juice and using a curved serrated knife, remove orange sections from shell halves into bowl; cut away and discard all membrane, reserving shells. Add strawberries and grapes to orange sections and toss lightly to combine; spoon ¼ of fruit mixture into each shell half and set aside.

In small mixing bowl, using electric mixer on high speed, beat egg white, gradually adding sugar and vanilla, until stiff peaks form. Spoon ¼ of meringue onto each filled fruit cup; transfer to baking sheet and broil until meringue is golden, 10 to 15 seconds. Serve immediately.

Each serving provides: 1 Fruit Exchange; 10 calories Optional Exchange
Per serving: 66 calories; 2 g protein; 0.4 g fat; 15 g carbohydrate; 36 mg calcium;
  13 mg sodium; 0 mg cholesterol

Glazed Cinnamon Grapefruit ◑❸

WEEK 1 ∽ MAKES 1 SERVING

Using the point of a sharp knife, remove seeds from ½ **medium grapefruit;** then, using a grapefruit knife, cut around each section to loosen from membrane and skin. Place grapefruit half in small shallow baking dish and spoon ½ **teaspoon honey** onto center of fruit; sprinkle with **dash ground cinnamon.** Broil 3 inches from heat source until fruit is lightly browned and honey has melted, 8 to 10 minutes.*

Each serving provides: 1 Fruit Exchange; 10 calories Optional Exchange
Per serving: 49 calories; 1 g protein; 0.1 g fat; 13 g carbohydrate; 16 mg calcium;
  0.2 mg sodium; 0 mg cholesterol

Variation: Substitute 2 teaspoons reduced-calorie orange marmalade or apricot spread (16 calories per 2 teaspoons) for the honey and cinnamon; increase Optional Exchange to 16 calories.

Per serving: 54 calories; 1 g protein; 0.1 g fat; 14 g carbohydrate; 14 mg calcium;
 0 mg sodium; 0 mg cholesterol

* This can be broiled in a conventional broiler or a toaster-oven.

Orange Baked Alaska ❶

WEEK 4 ∽ MAKES 2 SERVINGS

An easy-to-prepare dessert that makes an impressive and beautiful presentation.

Orange Filling

1 small orange, cut in half crosswise
3 ounces vanilla dietary frozen
 dessert, softened

Meringue

1 tablespoon plus 1 teaspoon
 reduced-calorie orange marmalade
 (16 calories per 2 teaspoons)
1 egg white (at room temperature)
1 teaspoon superfine sugar*

To Prepare Filling: Over small bowl to catch juice and using a curved serrated knife, remove orange sections from shell halves into bowl; cut away and discard all membrane, reserving shells. Add frozen dessert to fruit and stir to combine. Divide orange mixture into shell halves; cover with plastic wrap and freeze until hard, about 1 hour.

To Prepare Meringue and Bake: Just before serving, in metal measuring cup or other small flameproof container heat marmalade. Preheat broiler. In small mixing bowl, using electric mixer on high speed, beat egg white, gradually adding sugar, until stiff peaks form; gently fold in marmalade.

Remove filled orange halves from freezer and top each with half of the meringue; transfer to baking sheet and broil until meringue is golden, 10 to 15 seconds. Serve immediately.

Each serving provides: 1 Fruit Exchange; ¼ Milk Exchange;
 35 calories Optional Exchange
Per serving: 110 calories; 4 g protein; 1 g fat; 23 g carbohydrate; 102 mg calcium;
 60 mg sodium; 1 mg cholesterol

* If superfine sugar is not available, process granulated sugar in blender container until superfine.

Orange-Pineapple Delight ☯

WEEK 1 ∾ MAKES 2 SERVINGS

1 envelope unflavored gelatin
½ cup each orange juice (no sugar added), canned crushed pineapple (no sugar added), and water
1 tablespoon plus 1 teaspoon reduced-calorie orange marmalade (16 calories per 2 teaspoons)

1 cup plain low-fat yogurt
Granulated sugar substitute to equal 2 teaspoons sugar

In small saucepan sprinkle gelatin over orange juice and let stand to soften; cook over low heat, stirring constantly, until gelatin is completely dissolved. Remove from heat and add crushed pineapple, water, and marmalade; stir to combine. Add yogurt and sugar substitute and stir vigorously; into each of two 8-ounce dessert dishes pour half of mixture. Cover and refrigerate until set, 3 to 4 hours.

Each serving provides: 1 Fruit Exchange; 1 Milk Exchange; 16 calories Optional Exchange
Per serving: 165 calories; 10 g protein; 2 g fat; 28 g carbohydrate; 220 mg calcium; 83 mg sodium; 7 mg cholesterol

Coconut-Topped Mixed Fruit ☽

WEEK 4 ∾ MAKES 4 SERVINGS, ABOUT ½ CUP EACH

1 small orange
1 cup honeydew balls
1 medium banana, peeled and sliced
1 tablespoon lemon juice

½ teaspoon almond extract
1 tablespoon plus 1 teaspoon shredded coconut, toasted

Over medium bowl to catch juice, remove skin and membrane from orange and section orange into bowl. Add melon balls, banana slices, lemon juice, and extract; toss gently to combine. Divide into 4 dessert dishes; sprinkle each portion with ¼ of toasted coconut.

Each serving provides: 1 Fruit Exchange; 10 calories Optional Exchange
Per serving: 65 calories; 1 g protein; 1 g fat; 15 g carbohydrate; 18 mg calcium; 6 mg sodium; 0 mg cholesterol

Pears with Blueberry Sauce

WEEK 4 ⌒ MAKES 4 SERVINGS, 1 PEAR EACH

4 small pears, pared (leave stems attached)
¼ cup water
1 tablespoon thawed frozen concentrated orange juice (no sugar added)
2 teaspoons unsalted margarine, melted

2-inch cinnamon stick, broken in half
1 cup blueberries
1 tablespoon water
1 teaspoon each granulated sugar, cornstarch, and lemon juice

Preheat oven to 350°F. In shallow 1-quart casserole arrange pears on their sides. In 1-cup glass measure combine water, orange juice, and margarine; pour over fruit. Add cinnamon stick and bake until pears are tender, 20 to 30 minutes, basting occasionally and turning pears over once after 15 minutes. Using slotted spoon, transfer each pear, stem up, to a dessert dish; reserve pan juices.

In small saucepan combine pan juices with blueberries and bring to a boil. In a small cup or bowl combine water, sugar, cornstarch, and lemon juice, stirring to dissolve cornstarch; add to saucepan and, stirring constantly, bring to a boil. Reduce heat and cook, stirring frequently, until slightly thickened. To serve, pour ¼ of blueberry sauce over each pear.

Each serving provides: ½ Fat Exchange; 1½ Fruit Exchanges;
    15 calories Optional Exchange
Per serving: 128 calories; 1 g protein; 3 g fat; 28 g carbohydrate; 22 mg calcium;
    3 mg sodium; 0 mg cholesterol

Chocolate-Topped Pears ◑❸

WEEK 4 ∽ MAKES 4 SERVINGS, 2 PEAR HALVES EACH

1 tablespoon plus 1 teaspoon each
  unsweetened cocoa and
  granulated sugar
2 teaspoons cornstarch
1 cup evaporated skimmed milk,
  divided

¼ teaspoon vanilla extract
8 canned pear halves (no sugar
  added)

In small saucepan combine cocoa, sugar, and cornstarch; gradually add ¼ cup milk and stir until sugar is completely dissolved. Add remaining milk and vanilla and cook over medium heat, stirring constantly, until mixture comes to a boil; continue to stir and cook until thickened, about 2 minutes longer. Remove from heat, pour into a small bowl, and let cool; cover with plastic wrap and refrigerate until chilled.

To serve, into each of 4 dessert dishes place 2 pear halves and top each portion with ¼ of the sauce.

Each serving provides: 1 Fruit Exchange; ½ Milk Exchange;
  30 calories Optional Exchange
Per serving: 122 calories; 5 g protein; 0.5 g fat; 26 g carbohydrate; 194 mg calcium;
  77 mg sodium; 3 mg cholesterol

Pear Crumble ◑❸

WEEK 4 ∽ MAKES 2 SERVINGS, 2 PEAR HALVES EACH

Serve warm or chilled.

4 canned pear halves with ¼ cup
  juice (no sugar added)
1 teaspoon cornstarch
Dash ground cloves

2 slices raisin bread, made into
  crumbs
1 teaspoon firmly packed brown
  sugar
2 teaspoons margarine

Preheat oven to 400°F. In casserole just large enough to hold fruit in single layer arrange pear halves, cut-side down. Dissolve cornstarch in the ¼ cup juice and pour over pears; sprinkle with cloves.

In small bowl combine crumbs and sugar; add margarine and combine thoroughly. Sprinkle mixture over pears and bake until crumbs are golden, about 15 minutes.

Each serving provides: 1 Bread Exchange; 1 Fat Exchange; 1 Fruit Exchange;
   15 calories Optional Exchange
Per serving: 158 calories; 2 g protein; 5 g fat; 29 g carbohydrate; 28 mg calcium;
   140 mg sodium; 1 mg cholesterol

Prune Pockets ❶

WEEK 4 ⌒ MAKES 5 SERVINGS, 1 TURNOVER EACH

15 medium prunes, pitted and cut
   into quarters
1/2 cup water
1 teaspoon brandy extract
1/2 teaspoon grated orange peel
1 tablespoon granulated sugar

3/4 teaspoon cornstarch, dissolved
   in 1 tablespoon water
5-ounce package refrigerated
   buttermilk flaky biscuits (5
   biscuits)
1 teaspoon confectioners' sugar

In small saucepan combine prunes, water, extract, and orange peel and bring to a boil. Reduce heat and let simmer until mixture is a pasty consistency, about 5 minutes. Combine granulated sugar and dissolved cornstarch; add to prune mixture and stir until thoroughly combined. Remove from heat and let cool.

Preheat oven to 400°F. Separate biscuits and roll each between 2 sheets of wax paper, forming five 4-inch circles. Spoon 1/5 of prune mixture onto center of each circle and fold each in half, turnover style; moisten outer edges of dough and, using the tines of a fork, press edges to seal. Transfer turnovers to nonstick baking sheet and bake until golden brown, 10 to 12 minutes. Remove turnovers to wire rack to cool.

To serve, using a small tea strainer, sift an equal amount of confectioners' sugar onto each turnover.

Each serving provides: 1 Bread Exchange; 1 Fruit Exchange;
   20 calories Optional Exchange
Per serving: 155 calories; 3 g protein; 2 g fat; 32 g carbohydrate; 28 mg calcium;
   247 mg sodium; 0 mg cholesterol

Wine-Baked Plums

WEEK 4 ∽ MAKES 4 SERVINGS

8 medium sweet red plums, cut
   into halves and pitted
1/4 cup dry red wine
1 tablespoon firmly packed brown
   sugar

2 cinnamon sticks, broken into
   halves
1/4 cup thawed frozen dairy whipped
   topping

Preheat oven to 350°F. In 1½-quart casserole arrange plums in a single layer, cut-side down. In 1-cup glass measure combine wine and sugar and stir until sugar is dissolved; pour over fruit and add cinnamon sticks to casserole. Cover casserole and bake until plums are soft, about 30 minutes.

Remove and discard cinnamon sticks; peel plums and discard skin. Into each of 4 dessert dishes place 4 plum halves; spoon 1/4 of the cooking liquid over each portion and top each with 1 tablespoon whipped topping.

Each serving provides: 1 Fruit Exchange; 45 calories Optional Exchange
Per serving: 113 calories; 1 g protein; 2 g fat; 23 g carbohydrate; 24 mg calcium;
   2 mg sodium; 0 mg cholesterol

Strawberries Marsala

WEEK 2 ∽ MAKES 1 SERVING

1 cup strawberries
1 teaspoon Marsala wine
1/2 teaspoon granulated sugar

Dash lemon juice
2 teaspoons thawed frozen dairy
   whipped topping

In small bowl combine all ingredients except whipped topping; toss to coat thoroughly. Cover and refrigerate overnight.

To serve, transfer fruit mixture to dessert dish and top with whipped topping.

Each serving provides: 1 Fruit Exchange; 25 calories Optional Exchange
Per serving: 68 calories; 1 g protein; 1 g fat; 14 g carbohydrate; 22 mg calcium;
   2 mg sodium; 0 mg cholesterol

Strawberry-Cream Log

WEEK 4 ⌣ MAKES 8 SERVINGS

¾ cup cake flour
1 teaspoon double-acting baking
 powder
½ teaspoon salt
4 large eggs
¼ cup granulated sugar
4 cups strawberries, finely chopped
 (reserve 4 whole berries for
 garnish)

2 tablespoons reduced-calorie
 strawberry spread (16 calories
 per 2 teaspoons), melted
½ cup plus 1 tablespoon thawed
 frozen dairy whipped topping

1. Preheat oven to 400°F. Line 15½ x 10 x 1-inch jelly-roll pan with parchment paper and set aside. Onto sheet of wax paper or a paper plate sift together flour, baking powder, and salt 2 times; set aside.

2. In mixing bowl, using electric mixer on high speed, beat eggs until thick and lemon colored, about 5 minutes; gradually beat in sugar, then fold in sifted ingredients.

3. Pour batter into paper-lined pan and bake until golden, 9 to 10 minutes (top should spring back when touched lightly with finger).

4. Remove from oven and turn cake onto a towel; remove and discard parchment paper. Starting at narrow end, roll cake with towel; set on wire rack and let cool.

5. In bowl combine chopped strawberries and melted spread. Unroll cooled cake, remove towel, and spread berry mixture over cake surface; reroll cake and place, seam-side down, on serving platter. Spread whipped topping over top and sides of log; slice reserved berries and arrange slices attractively on log. To serve, cut into 8 equal slices.

Each serving provides: ½ Protein Exchange; ½ Bread Exchange; ½ Fruit Exchange; 50 calories Optional Exchange
Per serving: 147 calories; 4 g protein; 4 g fat; 23 g carbohydrate; 53 mg calcium; 221 mg sodium; 137 mg cholesterol

Orange-Frosted Carrot-Raisin Cake

WEEK 4 ~ MAKES 12 SERVINGS

Cake

⅓ cup plus 2 teaspoons unsalted margarine, softened, divided
2¼ cups all-purpose flour, divided
½ cup granulated sugar
1 tablespoon double-acting baking powder
3 cups shredded carrots

1 cup raisins, soaked in warm water until plumped, then drained
1 teaspoon ground cinnamon
4 eggs
¼ cup thawed frozen concentrated orange juice (no sugar added)
1 teaspoon vanilla extract

Frosting

2 tablespoons granulated sugar
1 envelope unflavored gelatin

¼ cup thawed frozen concentrated orange juice (no sugar added)
2 cups part-skim ricotta cheese

To Prepare Cake: Grease two 8-inch round cake pans with ½ teaspoon margarine each; sprinkle each with 1 teaspoon flour and set aside. Preheat oven to 325°F.

In mixing bowl combine remaining flour with the sugar and baking powder; stir in carrots, raisins, and cinnamon. In another bowl, using electric mixer, beat together eggs, orange juice, vanilla, and remaining ⅓ cup plus 1 teaspoon margarine; pour into dry ingredients and beat at medium speed until batter is smooth, about 1 minute. Pour half of batter into each sprayed pan and bake 35 to 40 minutes (until a cake tester, inserted in center, comes out clean). Let cakes cool in pans for 5 minutes, then remove cakes to wire rack to cool.

To Prepare Frosting: In saucepan sprinkle sugar and gelatin over juice; let stand to soften. Cook over low heat, stirring, until dissolved.

In blender container process cheese until smooth; remove center of blender cover and, with motor running, gradually add gelatin mixture, processing just until combined. Transfer frosting to a bowl, cover, and refrigerate until mixture is thick but not firm, about 10 minutes. Immediately spread a thin layer of frosting over top of 1 cake; top with remaining cake and spread remaining frosting over top and sides of entire cake. Cover lightly and refrigerate until frosting is firm. To serve, cut into 12 equal slices.

Each serving provides: 1 Protein Exchange; 1 Bread Exchange; ½ Vegetable Exchange; 1½ Fat Exchanges; 1 Fruit Exchange; 50 calories Optional Exchange
Per serving: 333 calories; 11 g protein; 11 g fat; 48 g carbohydrate; 200 mg calcium; 193 mg sodium; 104 mg cholesterol

Crunchy Raisin Bars ❶

WEEK 4 〜 MAKES 4 SERVINGS, 1 BAR EACH

3 ounces ready-to-eat crunchy
  nutlike cereal nuggets
¼ cup raisins, chopped
2 teaspoons shredded coconut

⅓ cup thawed frozen concentrated
  apple juice (no sugar added)
1 teaspoon honey
1 envelope unflavored gelatin

1. In small bowl combine cereal, raisins, and coconut; set aside.

2. In small saucepan combine juice and honey; sprinkle with gelatin and let stand to soften. Cook over low heat, stirring constantly, until gelatin is completely dissolved.

3. Pour juice mixture over cereal mixture and stir until thoroughly combined. Spray a 7⅜ x 3⅝ x 2¼-inch loaf pan with nonstick cooking spray and pack cereal mixture firmly into pan; cover and refrigerate until firm.

4. Using the point of a sharp knife, loosen edges of fruited cereal from pan; invert onto a plate and cut into 4 equal bars. Wrap each bar in plastic wrap and store in refrigerator until ready to use.

Each serving provides: 1 Bread Exchange; 1½ Fruit Exchanges;
  10 calories Optional Exchange
Per serving: 156 calories; 4 g protein; 0.5 g fat; 36 g carbohydrate; 18 mg calcium;
  156 mg sodium; 0 mg cholesterol

Raisin "Danish" with Orange Icing ◐

WEEK 4 ∽ MAKES 10 SERVINGS, 1 "DANISH" EACH

1¼ cups raisins
Hot water
1 tablespoon granulated sugar
1 to 2 teaspoons ground cinnamon
10-ounce package refrigerated
   buttermilk flaky biscuits (10
   biscuits)

3 tablespoons confectioners' sugar,
   sifted
½ to 1 teaspoon grated orange peel

Preheat oven to 400°F. Place raisins in bowl and add hot water to cover; let soak for 10 minutes. In small cup combine granulated sugar and cinnamon and set aside.

While raisins are soaking, separate biscuits; place biscuits in 2 lines (5 biscuits in each line), with edges touching so that they form one rectangle. Using fingers, flatten dough so that rectangle is about 13 x 8 inches, pressing edges of biscuits together to seal; sprinkle sugar mixture over entire surface of dough. Drain raisins and sprinkle over sugar mixture. Starting from one of the wide sides, roll dough jelly-roll fashion to enclose filling and press seam to seal; cut cross-wise into 10 equal pieces and place pieces, cut-side down, on non-stick baking sheet. Bake until browned, about 15 minutes; transfer "Danish" to wire rack to cool.

In small bowl combine confectioners' sugar and orange peel; add 1 to 1½ teaspoons hot water, a little at a time, stirring constantly until mixture is smooth and thoroughly combined. Drizzle an equal amount of icing over each "Danish"; serve immediately or refrigerate or freeze for future use.

Each serving provides: 1 Bread Exchange; 1 Fruit Exchange;
   25 calories Optional Exchange
Per serving: 147 calories; 3 g protein; 2 g fat; 31 g carbohydrate; 28 mg calcium;
   248 mg sodium; 0 mg cholesterol

Grape and Berry-Wine Mold

WEEK 3 ∽ MAKES 4 SERVINGS

1 envelope unflavored gelatin
2 teaspoons superfine sugar
½ cup water
1 cup dry white wine
1 tablespoon lemon juice

2 cups strawberries, cut into bite-
  size pieces
40 small seedless green grapes

Garnish

Lemon and lime slices

In small bowl combine gelatin and sugar. Pour water into small saucepan; sprinkle gelatin mixture over water and let stand for about 5 minutes to soften. Cook over low heat, stirring constantly, until gelatin is completely dissolved. Pour into 1-quart heatproof bowl; stir in wine and lemon juice. Cover and refrigerate until syrupy.

Spray 3-cup mold with nonstick cooking spray. Fold berries and grapes into syrupy gelatin mixture and transfer to sprayed mold; cover and refrigerate until firm.

To serve, unmold berry mixture onto serving platter and surround with lemon and lime slices.

Each serving provides: 1 Fruit Exchange; 70 calories Optional Exchange
Per serving: 122 calories; 2 g protein; 1 g fat; 19 g carbohydrate; 22 mg calcium;
  7 mg sodium; 0 mg cholesterol

Cran-Apple Gel

WEEK 4 ~ MAKES 8 SERVINGS, ABOUT 2 TABLESPOONS EACH

1 cup fresh or frozen cranberries*
2 tablespoons plus 1 teaspoon reduced-calorie strawberry spread (16 calories per 2 teaspoons)

¼ cup thawed frozen concentrated apple juice (no sugar added)
1 tablespoon granulated sugar
1 envelope unflavored gelatin

In blender container combine cranberries and strawberry spread and process until pureed, scraping down sides of container as necessary; transfer mixture to small bowl and set aside.

In small metal measuring cup or other small flameproof container sprinkle apple juice with sugar and gelatin and let stand to soften; cook over low heat, stirring constantly, until gelatin is completely dissolved. Pour gelatin mixture into pureed fruit and stir to combine.

Rinse a 1-cup mold with cold water; using rubber scraper, turn fruit mixture into mold. Cover with plastic wrap and refrigerate overnight; to serve, unmold onto serving platter.

Each serving provides: ½ Fruit Exchange; 15 calories Optional Exchange
Per serving: 34 calories; 0.1 g protein; 0.1 g fat; 9 g carbohydrate; 3 mg calcium;
2 mg sodium; 0 mg cholesterol

* If frozen berries are used, thaw after measuring.

Variation: Cran-Apple Sauce—Omit unflavored gelatin. In blender container combine all ingredients and process until pureed; refrigerate, covered, overnight to allow flavors to blend.

Per serving: 34 calories; 0.1 g protein; 0.1 g fat; 9 g carbohydrate; 3 mg calcium;
2 mg sodium; 0 mg cholesterol

Miniature Fruit Crescents ❶

WEEK 4 ⬦ MAKES 4 SERVINGS, 3 CRESCENTS EACH

⅓ cup plus 2 teaspoons all-purpose flour
Dash salt
1 tablespoon plus 1 teaspoon margarine
2 tablespoons plain low-fat yogurt
2 large pitted prunes, finely chopped

2 tablespoons golden raisins, finely chopped
2 teaspoons each granulated sugar and reduced-calorie apricot spread (16 calories per 2 teaspoons)
1 teaspoon confectioners' sugar, sifted

In mixing bowl combine flour and salt; with pastry blender, or 2 knives used scissors-fashion, cut in margarine until mixture resembles coarse meal. Add yogurt and mix thoroughly. Form dough into a ball; wrap in plastic wrap and refrigerate for at least 1 hour (may be kept in refrigerator for up to 3 days).

Preheat oven to 400°F. Between 2 sheets of wax paper roll dough, forming a circle about ⅛ inch thick; cut into 12 equal wedges.

In small bowl combine remaining ingredients except confectioners' sugar. Spoon an equal amount of mixture (about ¼ teaspoon) onto each wedge near curved end; roll each from curved end toward point and place on nonstick baking sheet, point-side down. Bake until golden brown, 18 to 20 minutes. Remove crescents to wire rack to cool; just before serving, sprinkle each with an equal amount of confectioners' sugar.

Each serving provides: ½ Bread Exchange; 1 Fat Exchange; ½ Fruit Exchange; 25 calories Optional Exchange
Per serving: 123 calories; 2 g protein; 4 g fat; 20 g carbohydrate; 21 mg calcium; 83 mg sodium; 0.5 mg cholesterol

Spiced Fruit Compote ◑

WEEK 4 ～ MAKES 2 SERVINGS, 1 COMPOTE EACH

Serve warm or at room temperature.

Pastry Topping

3 tablespoons all-purpose flour
Dash salt
2 teaspoons margarine
1 tablespoon plain low-fat yogurt

Fruit Mixture

4 dried apricot halves, chopped
2 tablespoons raisins
1 large dried fig, chopped
1 teaspoon each granulated brown
   sugar and lemon juice
1/4 teaspoon apple pie spice
1 small apple, cored, pared, diced,
   and sprinkled with lemon juice

To Prepare Pastry Topping: In mixing bowl combine flour and salt; with a pastry blender, or 2 knives used scissors-fashion, cut in margarine until mixture resembles coarse meal. Add yogurt and mix until thoroughly combined. Form dough into a ball; wrap in plastic wrap and refrigerate for about 1 hour (may be kept in refrigerator for up to 3 days).

To Prepare Fruit Mixture: In small saucepan combine all ingredients for fruit mixture except apple; cook over low heat, stirring constantly, until sugar begins to melt and glaze fruit mixture slightly (if necessary, add about 1 tablespoon water to keep fruit from burning). Let simmer until fruit softens and raisins are plump, about 5 minutes. Add apple and stir to combine.

To Prepare Compote: Preheat oven to 400°F. Divide fruit mixture into two 1-cup ovenproof dishes. Between 2 sheets of wax paper roll dough to about 1/8-inch thickness; carefully remove paper and cut dough in half. Place one half on top of each fruit mixture, molding dough to inside edges of dish. Bake until topping is golden brown, about 20 minutes.

Each serving provides: 1/2 Bread Exchange; 1 Fat Exchange; 2 Fruit Exchanges;
   15 calories Optional Exchange
Per serving: 188 calories; 3 g protein; 4 g fat; 37 g carbohydrate; 46 mg calcium;
   118 mg sodium; 0.4 mg cholesterol

The Vegetable Exchange

FROM A to Z—or asparagus to zucchini, you can discover a volume of vegetable suggestions to accent your meal planning.

Whether it's appealing appetizers like Parmesan-Stuffed Artichokes or Endives au Gratin or myriad vegetables baked and braised, "fried" and fruited, minted and marinated, here are zesty accompaniments to any meal.

◗ Pointers on the Vegetable Exchange

Daily Exchanges

WEEKS 1, 2, 3, and 4

Women, Men, and Youths   2 Exchanges (at least)

◗ Vegetables supply calcium, fiber, folic acid, iron, and vitamin A. In addition, because of their high bulk and water content, vegetables offer an excellent way to satisfy hunger. Remember, variety is the key to both satisfaction and good nutrition.

◗ One Vegetable Exchange is ½ cup (raw or cooked) or ½ medium (e.g., tomato, cucumber, zucchini, etc.) unless otherwise specified (see chart on pages 67-70). Although 2 Exchanges (1 cup) daily is the minimum, more is preferable.

◗ Canned and frozen vegetables that contain butter, sugar, cornstarch, or sauces are not permitted.

◗ Mixed vegetables that contain a starchy vegetable (e.g., corn, parsnips, peas, water chestnuts, etc.) should be considered a Bread Exchange; ½ cup is 1 Exchange.

◗ The liquid that vegetables have been cooked in contains water-soluble nutrients; it's a good idea to save this to use in soups, sauces, etc.

VEGETABLE EXCHANGE LISTS

Week 1

Selections	One Exchange
Arugula	½ cup
Asparagus	½ cup or 6 spears
Bamboo Shoots	½ cup
Beans, Green and Wax	½ cup
Broccoli	½ cup or 2 spears
Cabbage (all varieties including Chinese)	½ cup

Selections	One Exchange
Carrots	½ cup or ½ medium or large
Cauliflower	½ cup
Celery	½ cup
Chicory (Curly Endive)	½ cup
Cucumbers	½ cup, ½ medium, or 1 small
Endive, Belgian (French)	½ cup or 1 medium head (about 3 ounces)
Escarole	½ cup
Gherkins, fresh	½ cup or ½ medium
Kirbies	½ cup or ½ medium
Leeks	½ cup
Lettuce	½ cup
Mushrooms	½ cup
Mushrooms, dried	½ cup reconstituted or 2 large or 8 small
Onions	½ cup or 1 medium (about 2 ounces)
Peppers, banana	½ cup
Peppers, bell	½ cup or ½ medium
Peppers, chili	½ cup or 1 medium
Pimientos	½ cup or 3 whole
Radishes	½ cup or 12 whole
Scallions (Green Onions)	½ cup or 8 medium (about 4 ounces)
Shallots	½ cup
Spinach	½ cup or 8 leaves
Squash Leaves	½ cup
Squash, summer	
Caserta	½ cup
Chayote	½ cup
Cocozelle	½ cup
Mirleton	½ cup
Scallop (Pattypan, Cymling)	½ cup or ½ of 5-ounce squash
Spaghetti	½ cup
Yellow (Straightneck and Crookneck)	½ cup or ½ medium
Vegetable Marrow	½ cup
Zucchini	½ cup or ½ medium
Tomatoes	
Canned, all varieties (packed in their own juice or tomato puree)	½ cup
Cherry	6 small, medium, or large
Plum	1 large (about 1¾ to 2½ ounces) or 2 small (about 1 ounce each)
Regular, fresh	½ cup or ½ medium
Stewed	½ cup
Truffles	½ cup
Watercress	½ cup

Week 2

You may use all of the vegetables listed under Week 1 and may add the following to your Exchange List.

Selections	One Exchange
Alfalfa Sprouts	½ cup
Bean Sprouts	½ cup
Cardoon	½ cup
Eggplant	½ cup

Week 3

You may use all of the vegetables listed under Weeks 1 and 2 and may add the following to your Exchange List.

Selections	One Exchange
Beets	½ cup
Brussels Sprouts	½ cup
Fennel (Anise, Sweet Anise, or Finocchio)	½ cup
Kohlrabi	½ cup or 1 medium
Pumpkin	½ cup

Week 4

You may use all of the vegetables listed under Weeks 1, 2, and 3 and may add the following to your Exchange List.

Selections	One Exchange
Artichokes, whole, small	8-ounce
Artichoke Hearts	3 (about 4 ounces) or ½ cup
Bottle Gourd	½ cup
Cactus Leaves	½ cup
Celeriac	½ cup
Chinese Chard (Bok Choy)	½ cup
Chinese Pea Pods (Snow Peas)	½ cup
Chinese Winter Melon	½ cup
Comfrey Leaves	½ cup
Fiddlefern (Fiddlehead Greens)	½ cup
Grape Leaves	½ cup or 12 leaves

Selections	One Exchange
Greens	
Collard	½ cup
Dandelion	½ cup
Rutabaga	½ cup
Turnip	½ cup
Hearts of Palm (Palmetto)	½ cup
Jerusalem Artichokes (Sunchokes)	½ cup
Jicama	½ cup
Lamb's-Quarters	½ cup
Lotus Root	½ cup
Nasturtium Leaves	½ cup
Okra	½ cup
Peppergrass	½ cup
Pickles, unsweetened	½ cup or ½ medium
Rhubarb	½ cup
Rutabagas	½ cup
Salsify (Oyster Plant)	½ cup
Sauerkraut	½ cup
Sourgrass (Sorrel)	½ cup
Tomato Paste, Puree, or Sauce (limit to ¼ cup per day)	¼ cup
Turnips	½ cup

Average Approximate Size/Dimensions and Weight for Vegetables (fresh, including seeds and skin, unless otherwise specified)

Vegetables	Number	Approx. Size/ Dimensions	Approx. Weight	Number of Exchanges
Asparagus Spears	6		3 to 5 ounces	1
Broccoli, bunch	1	medium	1 pound	8
Cabbage, head:				
Chinese (celery)	1		12 ounces	8
green	1	medium	1 pound	12
red	1	medium	1½ pounds	18
leaves:				
green	2	medium/large	3¾ ounces	1
	3	small	3 ounces	1
red	1	medium/large	2½ ounces	1
	2	small	3 ounces	1

Vegetables	Number	Approx. Size/ Dimensions	Approx. Weight	Number of Exchanges
Carrots, whole	1	medium (1⅛-inch diameter at top x 7½ inches long) or large	3 to 4 ounces	2
sticks	6	3½ inches x ½ inch each		1
Cauliflower, head	1	medium (6- to 7-inch diameter)	1½ pounds	12
	1	small	1 pound	8
Celery, ribs	1	large (8 x 1½ inches)		1
	2	medium (6 inches x 1 inch each)		1
	3	small (5 inches x ¾ inch each)		1
sticks	6	3½ inches x ½ inch each		½
Cucumbers, whole	1	large (6½-inch circumference at widest part x 8¼ inches long)	9½ ounces	2¼
	1	medium (6-inch circumference at widest part x 7 inches long)	8 ounces	2
	1	small (5¼-inch circumference at widest part x 6¼ inches long)	6 ounces	1
sticks	6	4 inches x ½ inch each		½
Eggplants, whole	1	large	1½ pounds	8
	1	medium	1 to 1¼ pounds	6
	1	small	12 ounces	4
	1	tiny	8 ounces	3
slices, round	6	thin (¼ inch thick each)		1½

Vegetables	Number	Approx. Size/ Dimensions	Approx. Weight	Number of Exchanges
Endives (Belgian or French)	1	medium	3 ounces	1
Grape Leaves	12			1
Leeks (white portion only)	2	medium		1
Lettuce, head:				
Boston and Bibb	1	16-inch circumference at widest part	8 ounces	2½
iceberg	1	medium to large	2½ pounds	8
	1	small	1¼ pounds	4
romaine (cos) and	1	medium	1¼ pounds	12
loose-leafed	1	small	10 ounces	8
Lettuce, leaves:				
Boston and Bibb	8			1
iceberg	4	small, medium, and large		1
romaine (cos) and loose-leafed	4	small, medium, and large		1
Mushrooms, whole	3	large (2-inch diameter)	3¼ ounces	2
	7	medium (1½-inch diameter)	3 ounces	2
	18	small (1-inch diameter)	3½ ounces	2
caps	4	large	3 ounces	2
	8	medium	3 ounces	2
	16	small	3¼ ounces	2
Peppers:				
green/red bell, whole	1	large (3-inch diameter x 3¾ inches high)	7 ounces	4
	1	medium (2½-inch diameter x 2¾ inches high)	3¼ ounces	2
sticks	7	2¾ inches x ½ inch each		½
rings	4			1

Vegetables	Number	Approx. Size/ Dimensions	Approx. Weight	Number of Exchanges
Pickles, whole	1	large (5½-inch circumference at widest part x 4 inches long)	4¾ ounces	4
	1	medium (4-inch circumference at widest part x 3¾ inches long)	2¼ ounces	2
slices	3	large	1½ ounces	1
	5	medium	1⅛ ounces	1
Radishes	12	medium to large (2- to 4-inch circumference each at widest part)	2 to 3½ ounces	1
Squash:				
scallop (pattypan, cymling)	1	4-inch diameter	5 ounces	2
spaghetti	1		2½ to 3 pounds	8
zucchini	1	medium	5 ounces	2
Tomatoes, whole	1	large (3-inch diameter x 2⅛ inches high)	7 ounces	3
	1	medium (2½-inch diameter x 2 inches high)	4¾ ounces	2
	1	small (2¼-inch diameter)	3½ ounces	1½
slices:				
regular	4 to 6			1
thin	10	⅛ inch thick each		1
wedges	6	large		1½
	6	medium		1
	6	small		¾
Turnips	1	medium	2 ounces	1

Antipasto

WEEK 4 ∽ MAKES 8 SERVINGS

Dressing

2 tablespoons plus 2 teaspoons
olive or vegetable oil
2 tablespoons diced onion
1 tablespoon each red wine vinegar,
lemon juice, and drained capers

1 garlic clove, minced
¼ teaspoon each salt, pepper,
oregano leaves, and basil leaves

Marinated Vegetable Mixture

2 cups cauliflower florets, blanched
and kept warm
24 asparagus spears, blanched and
kept warm
1 package (9 ounces) frozen
artichoke hearts, cooked
according to package directions
and kept warm
¼ cup drained bottled cocktail
onions
1 ounce drained canned anchovies
(about 6 fillets)

Salad

8 romaine lettuce leaves
6 ounces each sliced turkey salami
(all turkey), sliced provolone
cheese, and drained canned
chick-peas
2 medium tomatoes, each cut into
eighths, or 24 cherry tomatoes
16 small pimiento-stuffed green
olives
8 large pitted black olives, sliced

To Prepare Dressing: In a small bowl combine all ingredients for dressing; set aside.

To Prepare Marinated Vegetable Mixture: In glass or stainless-steel bowl combine cauliflower, asparagus, artichoke hearts, cocktail onions, and anchovies; pour dressing over vegetable mixture and toss to coat. Cover and refrigerate for at least 2 hours, tossing several times (may be refrigerated overnight).

To Serve: Line a large serving platter with lettuce; arrange turkey salami around edges of platter. Wrap cheese around asparagus spears and arrange on platter. Toss marinated vegetable mixture; roll up anchovies and arrange on platter with a caper in the center of each roll. Spoon vegetable mixture onto center of platter; sprinkle chick-peas over entire mixture. Arrange tomatoes and olives decoratively over salad, alternating colors. Pour any remaining dressing over salad and serve.

Each serving provides: 2 Protein Exchanges; 2¼ Vegetable Exchanges;
 1 Fat Exchange; 15 calories Optional Exchange
Per serving: 273 calories; 17 g protein; 17 g fat; 18 g carbohydrate; 254 mg calcium;
 753 mg sodium; 26 mg cholesterol

Parmesan-Stuffed Artichokes

WEEK 4 ∽ MAKES 2 SERVINGS, 1 ARTICHOKE EACH

2 small artichokes (about 8 ounces each), thoroughly washed in cold water
Lemon juice
3 tablespoons plain dried bread crumbs

1 tablespoon chopped fresh parsley
2 teaspoons each grated Parmesan cheese and olive oil
1 small garlic clove, minced
½ teaspoon salt
Freshly ground pepper

Using large stainless-steel knife, cut off stem of each artichoke flush with base so that artichoke will stand upright; snap off any small or discolored leaves at base. Cut off and discard about 1 inch of the top; rub cut edges of each artichoke with lemon juice. Using stainless-steel scissors, remove barbed tips of leaves by cutting about ½ inch off tip of each leaf; rub cut edges of leaves with lemon juice.

In small bowl combine bread crumbs, parsley, cheese, oil, and garlic. Sprinkle each artichoke with ¼ teaspoon salt and dash pepper; spread leaves open and stuff half of crumb mixture into each artichoke.

Stand stuffed artichokes upright in deep baking pan (not aluminum) that is just large enough to hold them snugly; pour about 1 inch water into pan and cover with foil. Bake at 375°F. until base of each artichoke is tender when pierced with a fork, about 45 minutes. Serve immediately.

Each serving provides: ½ Bread Exchange; 1 Vegetable Exchange; 1 Fat Exchange; 10 calories Optional Exchange
Per serving: 121 calories; 4 g protein; 6 g fat; 14 g carbohydrate; 60 mg calcium; 682 mg sodium; 2 mg cholesterol

Asparagus-Chili Dip

WEEK 1 ⌒ MAKES 2 SERVINGS, ABOUT ½ CUP EACH

This is delicious served as a dip with fresh vegetables. May be frozen for future use.

12 asparagus spears, cooked and
  chopped
2 tablespoons drained canned mild
  green chilies
1 tablespoon chopped red onion
2 teaspoons olive oil

2 teaspoons lemon juice
½ teaspoon salt
½ garlic clove, crushed
Dash each ground nutmeg and
  pepper

In blender container or work bowl of food processor combine all ingredients and process until smooth. Refrigerate, covered, until chilled.

Each serving provides: 1⅛ Vegetable Exchanges; 1 Fat Exchange
Per serving: 66 calories; 2 g protein; 5 g fat; 5 g carbohydrate; 26 mg calcium;
  542 mg sodium; 0 mg cholesterol

Variation: Add ½ cup plain low-fat yogurt to processed ingredients and stir to combine; add ½ Milk Exchange to Exchange Information.

Per serving: 102 calories; 5 g protein; 6 g fat; 9 g carbohydrate; 128 mg calcium;
  581 mg sodium; 3 mg cholesterol

Asparagus Crêpes "Hollandaise"

WEEK 4 ～ MAKES 2 SERVINGS, 2 CRÊPES EACH

Crêpes

½ cup skim milk
⅓ cup plus 2 teaspoons all-purpose flour
1 egg
24 frozen asparagus spears, cooked

"Hollandaise" Sauce

1 egg
1 tablespoon margarine, melted (warm)
1 tablespoon lemon juice
Dash each salt and ground red pepper

To Prepare Crêpes: In blender container combine first 3 ingredients and process until smooth, about 30 seconds; let batter rest for about 15 minutes so that bubbles will subside.

Spray 6-inch nonstick skillet or crêpe pan with nonstick cooking spray and heat; pour ¼ of batter (about ¼ cup) into hot pan, quickly tilting pan to coat entire bottom with batter. Cook until underside of crêpe is lightly browned and edges are dry; using pancake turner, carefully turn crêpe over and cook other side briefly (just to dry), about 30 seconds. Slide crêpe onto plate and repeat procedure 3 more times, using remaining batter and making 3 more crêpes.

Preheat oven to 350°F. Arrange 6 asparagus spears in center of each crêpe so that 3 tip ends face one direction and 3 tip ends face the opposite direction; fold crêpes over to enclose asparagus and place seam-side down in casserole that is just large enough to hold them in 1 layer. Bake for 10 minutes.

To Prepare Sauce: Just before serving, in blender container process egg at high speed until thick and lemon colored; with motor running, slowly add margarine and continue processing until mixture is thickened. Add lemon juice and seasonings, processing just to blend. Pour sauce over hot crêpes and serve immediately.

Each serving provides: 1 Protein Exchange; 1 Bread Exchange;
2 Vegetable Exchanges; 1½ Fat Exchanges; ¼ Milk Exchange
Per serving: 277 calories; 15 g protein; 12 g fat; 29 g carbohydrate; 149 mg calcium;
236 mg sodium; 275 mg cholesterol

Meatless Borscht ❶

Delicious hot or chilled.

1 teaspoon margarine	1 cup shredded green cabbage
1/4 cup chopped onion	1/4 cup sliced carrot
1 cup coarsely shredded pared beets	2 tablespoons tomato paste
2 cups water	1 tablespoon lemon juice
2 packets instant beef broth and seasoning mix	1/2 teaspoon granulated sugar
1/2 bay leaf	1/8 teaspoon pepper
	2 tablespoons sour cream

In 1 1/2-quart saucepan heat margarine until bubbly and hot; add onion and sauté until softened, 1 to 2 minutes. Add beets and toss to combine; add water, broth mix, and bay leaf and bring to a boil. Cover pan and cook over medium heat for 10 minutes; stir in remaining ingredients except sour cream, cover, and let simmer until vegetables are tender, about 25 minutes. Remove and discard bay leaf. Pour borscht into 2 soup bowls and top each portion with 1 tablespoon sour cream.

Each serving provides: 2 3/4 Vegetable Exchanges; 1/2 Fat Exchange;
    50 calories Optional Exchange
Per serving: 129 calories; 4 g protein; 5 g fat; 12 g carbohydrate; 63 mg calcium;
    968 mg sodium; 6 mg cholesterol

Variation: Substitute 1/4 cup plain low-fat yogurt for the sour cream; top each portion of borscht with 2 tablespoons yogurt. Add 1/4 Milk Exchange to Exchange Information and reduce Optional Exchange to 15 calories.

Per serving: 117 calories; 5 g protein; 3 g fat; 13 g carbohydrate; 100 mg calcium;
    980 mg sodium; 2 mg cholesterol

Sautéed Sweet 'n' Sour Beets ◐❸

WEEK 3 ~ MAKES 2 SERVINGS

Serve hot or chilled.

2 teaspoons margarine
1 tablespoon diced onion
1 cup drained canned small whole
   beets, cut into quarters

1 tablespoon each lemon juice and
   water
⅛ teaspoon each salt and pepper
Dash granulated sugar substitute

In small nonstick skillet heat margarine over medium-high heat until bubbly and hot; add onion and sauté until softened, 1 to 2 minutes. Reduce heat to low and add remaining ingredients; cover pan and cook, stirring once, for 5 minutes longer.

Each serving provides: 1 Vegetable Exchange; 1 Fat Exchange
Per serving: 70 calories; 1 g protein; 4 g fat; 9 g carbohydrate; 22 mg calcium;
   385 mg sodium; 0 mg cholesterol

Orange Beets ❸

WEEK 4 ~ MAKES 2 SERVINGS

Marinating brings out the full flavor of this dish.

1 cup peeled and sliced cooked
   beets
2 teaspoons margarine
1 teaspoon firmly packed brown
   sugar
¼ cup orange juice (no sugar
   added)

1½ teaspoons lemon juice
1 teaspoon cornstarch
Dash salt
1 teaspoon orange marmalade

In 1-quart saucepan (not aluminum or cast-iron) combine beets, margarine, and sugar; cook over low heat, stirring constantly, until margarine and sugar are melted.

In 1-cup measure or small bowl combine juices, cornstarch, and salt, stirring to dissolve cornstarch; pour over beet mixture and, stirring constantly, bring to a boil. Continue cooking and stirring until mixture thickens. Reduce heat, add marmalade, and stir until combined. Remove from heat and let cool slightly; cover and refrigerate for at least 1 hour. Reheat before serving.

Each serving provides: 1 Vegetable Exchange; 1 Fat Exchange;
   35 calories Optional Exchange
Per serving: 97 calories; 1 g protein; 4 g fat; 15 g carbohydrate; 18 mg calcium;
   154 mg sodium; 0 mg cholesterol

Cabbage 'n' Potato Soup ✪

WEEK 4 ◇ MAKES 4 SERVINGS

This soup freezes well; for easy portion control, freeze in pre-measured servings.

2 teaspoons vegetable oil
4 cups shredded green cabbage
1 cup sliced onions
1 garlic clove, minced
3 cups water
6 ounces peeled potato, sliced

½ cup each sliced carrot and
   tomato puree
4 packets instant beef broth and
   seasoning mix
1 each bay leaf and whole clove

In 2-quart saucepan heat oil; add cabbage, onions, and garlic and sauté over medium heat, stirring frequently, until cabbage is soft, about 10 minutes. Reduce heat to low and add remaining ingredients; cook until vegetables are tender, about 30 minutes. Remove and discard bay leaf and clove before serving.

Each serving provides: ½ Bread Exchange; 3¼ Vegetable Exchanges;
   ½ Fat Exchange; 10 calories Optional Exchange
Per serving: 119 calories; 4 g protein; 3 g fat; 22 g carbohydrate; 67 mg calcium;
   900 mg sodium; 0 mg cholesterol

Coleslaw with Buttermilk Dressing ❶

WEEK 1 ⌒ MAKES 2 SERVINGS

½ cup buttermilk
1 tablespoon lemon juice
1 teaspoon granulated sugar
½ teaspoon salt

¼ teaspoon each celery seed and
   pepper
Dash garlic powder
2 cups shredded green cabbage

In medium bowl combine all ingredients except cabbage and stir to combine; add cabbage and toss to coat. Cover and refrigerate for at least 8 hours. Toss again just before serving.

Each serving provides: 2 Vegetable Exchanges; ¼ Milk Exchange;
   20 calories Optional Exchange
Per serving: 58 calories; 3 g protein; 1 g fat; 11 g carbohydrate; 125 mg calcium;
   622 mg sodium; 2 mg cholesterol

Caraway-"Bacon" Coleslaw

WEEK 4 ⌒ MAKES 2 SERVINGS

2 cups finely shredded green
   cabbage
2 tablespoons thinly sliced scallion
   (green onion)
¼ teaspoon caraway seed

3 tablespoons white wine vinegar
2 tablespoons water
2 teaspoons imitation bacon bits,
   divided
1 teaspoon olive oil

In medium bowl toss cabbage with scallion and caraway seed; set aside.

In small saucepan combine vinegar, water, 1 teaspoon bacon bits, and the oil; bring mixture to a boil. Pour over cabbage mixture and toss to combine. Cover and refrigerate for at least 3 hours.

Just before serving, sprinkle coleslaw with remaining teaspoon bacon bits and toss to combine.

Each serving provides: 2⅛ Vegetable Exchanges; ½ Fat Exchange;
   15 calories Optional Exchange
Per serving: 57 calories; 2 g protein; 3 g fat; 7 g carbohydrate; 52 mg calcium;
   116 mg sodium; 0 mg cholesterol

Coleslaw with Sour Cream Dressing ◐❶

WEEK 3 ∽ MAKES 2 SERVINGS

2 cups shredded green cabbage
1 cup shredded carrots
1 tablespoon each diced green
  bell pepper and celery
1½ teaspoons minced onion
1 tablespoon sour cream

1 teaspoon mayonnaise
½ teaspoon granulated sugar
⅛ teaspoon salt
Dash each celery seed (optional)
  and white pepper

In medium bowl combine cabbage, carrots, green pepper, celery, and onion. In small bowl combine remaining ingredients; pour over vegetables and toss until well coated. Cover and refrigerate until chilled.

Each serving provides: 3⅛ Vegetable Exchanges; ½ Fat Exchange;
  20 calories Optional Exchange
Per serving: 79 calories; 2 g protein; 4 g fat; 11 g carbohydrate; 60 mg calcium;
  191 mg sodium; 5 mg cholesterol

Variation: Week 1—Substitute plain low-fat yogurt for the sour cream; reduce Optional Exchange to 10 calories.

Per serving: 68 calories; 2 g protein; 2 g fat; 11 g carbohydrate; 64 mg calcium;
  192 mg sodium; 2 mg cholesterol

Carrot Soup ❶

WEEK 2 ∽ MAKES 2 SERVINGS, ABOUT 1 CUP EACH

1 tablespoon unsalted margarine
¼ cup each chopped onion and
  celery
½ small garlic clove, mashed
2 cups water

1 cup chopped carrots
3 ounces pared potato, chopped
2 packets instant chicken broth and
  seasoning mix

In 1-quart saucepan heat margarine until bubbly and hot; add onion, celery, and garlic and sauté, stirring constantly, until onion is soft. Add remaining ingredients and bring to a boil. Reduce heat, cover, and let simmer until vegetables are soft, about 20 minutes; let cool slightly. Pour mixture into blender container and process at low speed until smooth; reheat if necessary.

Each serving provides: ½ Bread Exchange; 1½ Vegetable Exchanges;
  1½ Fat Exchanges; 10 calories Optional Exchange
Per serving: 127 calories; 3 g protein; 6 g fat; 17 g carbohydrate; 37 mg calcium;
  882 mg sodium; 0 mg cholesterol

Carrot-Sprout Slaw

WEEK 2 ◇ MAKES 2 SERVINGS

1½ cups alfalfa sprouts (half of 4-ounce container)
1 cup shredded carrots
¼ cup diced celery
2 tablespoons chopped scallion (green onion)
1 tablespoon thawed frozen concentrated orange juice (no sugar added)

1½ teaspoons each Chinese sesame oil and lemon juice or lime juice (no sugar added)
⅛ teaspoon garlic powder
Dash salt
2 iceberg, romaine, or loose-leafed lettuce leaves

In medium bowl combine first 4 ingredients and toss until mixed. In small bowl combine remaining ingredients except lettuce and stir until well mixed; pour over vegetables and toss until combined. Cover bowl and refrigerate until slaw is chilled, at least 30 minutes.

To serve, line serving bowl with lettuce; toss slaw again and spoon onto lettuce leaves.

Each serving provides: 3 Vegetable Exchanges; ½ Fat Exchange;
25 calories Optional Exchange
Per serving: 83 calories; 2 g protein; 4 g fat; 12 g carbohydrate; 44 mg calcium;
102 mg sodium; 0 mg cholesterol

Glazed Carrots ◗●

WEEK 1 ◇ MAKES 2 SERVINGS

1 teaspoon margarine
1 cup slivered carrots, blanched
1 teaspoon granulated brown sugar

⅛ teaspoon powdered mustard
Dash each salt and hot sauce

In small skillet heat margarine until bubbly and hot; add remaining ingredients and sauté, stirring occasionally, until carrots are tender-crisp, about 5 minutes.

Each serving provides: 1 Vegetable Exchange; ½ Fat Exchange;
10 calories Optional Exchange
Per serving: 50 calories; 1 g protein; 2 g fat; 8 g carbohydrate; 24 mg calcium;
115 mg sodium; 0 mg cholesterol

Minted Julienne Carrots ◖❸

WEEK 1 ～ MAKES 4 SERVINGS

8 ounces carrots, trimmed and
   scraped
1/2 cup water
1/2 packet (about 1/2 teaspoon)
   instant chicken broth and
   seasoning mix

2 teaspoons margarine
1/2 teaspoon granulated sugar
1/4 teaspoon mint flakes or 3/4
   teaspoon chopped fresh mint

Cut carrots into matchstick pieces (should yield about 2 cups); set
aside.

In 8-inch skillet bring water to a boil; add broth mix and stir to
dissolve. Add carrots, cover, and cook for 5 minutes; add margarine,
sugar, and mint and cook, uncovered, until most of liquid has
evaporated and carrots are glazed, about 5 minutes.

Each serving provides: 1 Vegetable Exchange; 1/2 Fat Exchange;
   5 calories Optional Exchange
Per serving: 44 calories; 1 g protein; 2 g fat; 6 g carbohydrate; 22 mg calcium;
   153 mg sodium; 0 mg cholesterol

Oven-Braised Whole Baby Carrots ❸

WEEK 1 ～ MAKES 4 SERVINGS

1 package (12 ounces) whole baby
   carrots, trimmed and scraped
1/4 cup water
1 tablespoon plus 1 teaspoon
   unsalted margarine, melted

1 packet instant chicken broth and
   seasoning mix
1/4 to 1/2 teaspoon dillweed
2 tablespoons chopped fresh parsley

Preheat oven to 350°F. In 1-quart casserole arrange carrots. In small
bowl combine remaining ingredients except parsley; pour over
carrots and toss well to coat. Cover casserole and bake until carrots
are tender, 20 to 30 minutes. Just before serving, toss again and
sprinkle with chopped parsley.

Each serving provides: 1 1/2 Vegetable Exchanges; 1 Fat Exchange;
   3 calories Optional Exchange
Per serving: 73 calories; 1 g protein; 4 g fat; 9 g carbohydrate; 34 mg calcium;
   253 mg sodium; 0 mg cholesterol

Cauliflower-Pimiento Salad ◑

WEEK 1 ⮂ MAKES 2 SERVINGS

1 cup cauliflower florets, blanched
¼ cup chopped drained canned
  pimientos
1 tablespoon lemon juice
2 teaspoons olive oil
⅛ teaspoon minced fresh garlic or
  dash garlic powder

⅛ teaspoon Dijon-style mustard
Dash each salt and white pepper

Garnish
1 teaspoon chopped fresh parsley

In small bowl combine all ingredients except parsley. Toss well;
cover and refrigerate until chilled. Sprinkle with parsley just before
serving.

Each serving provides: 1¼ Vegetable Exchanges; 1 Fat Exchange
Per serving: 73 calories; 2 g protein; 5 g fat; 7 g carbohydrate; 24 mg calcium;
  98 mg sodium; 0 mg cholesterol

"Fried" Cauliflower ◑

WEEK 4 ⮂ MAKES 2 SERVINGS

1 egg
3 tablespoons plain dried bread
  crumbs
2 cups small cauliflower florets,
  blanched and cooled
1 tablespoon vegetable oil

⅛ teaspoon salt (optional)
Dash pepper (optional)

Garnish
Parsley sprigs

In shallow medium bowl beat egg lightly. Place bread crumbs in a
plastic or paper bag. Dip cauliflower into egg to coat, then place
florets in bag with crumbs; seal or close bag and shake well.

In 10-inch nonstick skillet heat oil; add coated cauliflower and
sauté until browned on all sides. Season with salt and pepper, if
desired, and serve garnished with parsley sprigs.

Each serving provides: ½ Protein Exchange; ½ Bread Exchange;
  2 Vegetable Exchanges; 1½ Fat Exchanges
Per serving: 186 calories; 8 g protein; 11 g fat; 17 g carbohydrate; 67 mg calcium;
  140 mg sodium; 137 mg cholesterol
With salt: 186 calories; 8 g protein; 11 g fat; 17 g carbohydrate; 68 mg calcium;
  280 mg sodium; 137 mg cholesterol

Cauliflower Parmesan ◗

WEEK 4 ～ MAKES 2 SERVINGS

2 teaspoons reduced-calorie
  margarine
1 teaspoon all-purpose flour
2 tablespoons sour cream (at room
  temperature)
2 teaspoons grated Parmesan
  cheese

Dash each salt, pepper, and ground
  nutmeg
1 cup cauliflower florets, blanched

Garnish

1 teaspoon chopped fresh parsley

In small saucepan heat margarine until bubbly and hot; stir in flour. Remove from heat and, using a wire whisk, blend in sour cream, cheese, salt, pepper, and nutmeg. Return to low heat and cook, stirring constantly, until smooth (*do not boil*). Add cauliflower and cook, stirring occasionally, until hot.

Transfer mixture to flameproof 1½-cup casserole; broil 6 inches from heat source until browned, about 1 minute. Serve sprinkled with parsley.

Each serving provides: 1 Vegetable Exchange; ½ Fat Exchange;
  50 calories Optional Exchange
Per serving: 77 calories; 3 g protein; 6 g fat; 5 g carbohydrate; 57 mg calcium;
  163 mg sodium; 8 mg cholesterol

Variation: Substitute plain low-fat yogurt for the sour cream; reduce Optional Exchange to 25 calories.

Per serving: 55 calories; 3 g protein; 3 g fat; 6 g carbohydrate; 67 mg calcium;
  165 mg sodium; 2 mg cholesterol

Minted Cauliflower ◑

WEEK 1 ∽ MAKES 2 SERVINGS

1 teaspoon vegetable oil
2 cups cauliflower florets, blanched
1/4 teaspoon mint flakes, crushed

1/8 teaspoon each salt and pepper
2 teaspoons to 1 tablespoon lemon
   juice

In 8-inch skillet heat oil; add cauliflower, mint, salt, and pepper and sauté until cauliflower is tender-crisp, about 5 minutes. Sprinkle with lemon juice and sauté for 2 minutes longer.

Each serving provides: 2 Vegetable Exchanges; 1/2 Fat Exchange
Per serving: 68 calories; 4 g protein; 3 g fat; 10 g carbohydrate; 43 mg calcium;
   174 mg sodium; 0 mg cholesterol

Cucumber in Yogurt Dressing ●

WEEK 1 ∽ MAKES 2 SERVINGS

Dijon-style mustard is excellent in this dressing.

1/2 cup plain low-fat yogurt
2 tablespoons chopped scallion
   (green onion)

1/4 teaspoon each salt, pepper,
   and prepared mustard
1 medium cucumber, scored and
   thinly sliced

In small bowl combine yogurt, scallion, salt, pepper, and mustard; add cucumber and mix well to coat with dressing. Cover and refrigerate for at least 1 hour.

Each serving provides: 1 1/8 Vegetable Exchanges; 1/2 Milk Exchange
Per serving: 52 calories; 4 g protein; 1 g fat; 8 g carbohydrate; 129 mg calcium;
   332 mg sodium; 3 mg cholesterol

Cucumber-Orange Salad ❶

WEEK 1 ❧ MAKES 2 SERVINGS

1 medium cucumber, scored and
   thinly sliced
1 small orange, peeled and
   sectioned
2 tablespoons minced Spanish onion

1 tablespoon lemon juice
½ teaspoon salt
¼ teaspoon pepper
1 teaspoon olive or vegetable oil
Lettuce leaves

In medium bowl combine cucumber, orange sections, and onion. In small bowl combine remaining ingredients except lettuce; pour over salad and toss to coat. Cover and refrigerate for 1 hour. Serve on bed of lettuce leaves.

Each serving provides: 1⅛ Vegetable Exchanges; ½ Fat Exchange;
   ½ Fruit Exchange
Per serving: 71 calories; 2 g protein; 3 g fat; 12 g carbohydrate; 12 mg calcium;
   548 mg sodium; 0 mg cholesterol

Eggplant Pesto

WEEK 2 ❧ MAKES 2 SERVINGS

Serve hot or chilled.

1 medium eggplant (about 1
   pound), cut crosswise into ½-
   to ¾-inch-thick rounds
Dash salt

2 tablespoons each chopped fresh
   basil and grated Parmesan cheese
1 tablespoon olive oil
1 small garlic clove, mashed
Dash freshly ground pepper

On 10 x 15-inch nonstick baking sheet arrange eggplant slices in a single layer; sprinkle with salt and bake at 425°F. until easily pierced with a fork, about 30 minutes.

In small bowl combine remaining ingredients; spread an equal amount of mixture over each eggplant slice. Transfer slices to 1½-quart casserole, return to oven, and bake until heated, about 10 minutes longer.

Each serving provides: 3 Vegetable Exchanges; 1½ Fat Exchanges;
   30 calories Optional Exchange
Per serving: 144 calories; 5 g protein; 9 g fat; 14 g carbohydrate; 122 mg calcium;
   163 mg sodium; 4 mg cholesterol

Ratatouille

WEEK 2 〜 MAKES 4 SERVINGS

1 tablespoon plus 1 teaspoon olive
  oil
1 cup each sliced onions and red or
  green bell peppers
3 garlic cloves, chopped
4 cups cubed eggplant (1-inch
  cubes)

1½ cups canned Italian tomatoes,
  chopped
1 cup sliced zucchini
3 tablespoons chopped fresh basil
  or 2 teaspoons dried
1 teaspoon salt
Dash freshly ground pepper

In 12-inch skillet heat oil over medium heat; add onions, bell peppers, and garlic and sauté until vegetables are tender-crisp. Add remaining ingredients and stir to combine. Reduce heat, cover, and let simmer until vegetables are tender, 20 to 25 minutes.

Each serving provides: 4¼ Vegetable Exchanges; 1 Fat Exchange
Per serving: 123 calories; 4 g protein; 5 g fat; 18 g carbohydrate; 62 mg calcium; 666 mg sodium; 0 mg cholesterol

Variations:
  1. Use Ratatouille as an omelet filling.
  2. Place Ratatouille in 10 x 6 x 2-inch baking dish; top with 4 ounces shredded hard cheese and bake at 350°F. until cheese is melted. Add 1 Protein Exchange to Exchange Information.

Per serving: 237 calories; 11 g protein; 15 g fat; 18 g carbohydrate; 267 mg calcium; 842 mg sodium; 30 mg cholesterol

Endives au Gratin

WEEK 4 ～ MAKES 4 SERVINGS

4 medium Belgian endives (about
  3 ounces each)
¾ cup water
½ teaspoon salt, divided
2 tablespoons each margarine and
  minced onion
3 tablespoons all-purpose flour

2 cups skim milk, heated
Dash each white and ground red
  pepper
4 ounces Swiss cheese, shredded
  (reserve 2 tablespoons for
  topping)
4 slices boiled ham (1 ounce each)

In 9-inch skillet combine endives, water, and ¼ teaspoon salt; bring water to a boil. Reduce heat, cover pan, and let endives simmer, turning once, until tender, 20 to 25 minutes (if necessary, add more water to prevent burning). Using a slotted spoon, remove endives from liquid; let drain.

While endives are draining, in 1-quart saucepan heat margarine until bubbly and hot; add onion and sauté until softened. Add flour and cook, stirring constantly, for 3 minutes; remove from heat and, using a wire whisk, gradually stir in milk, stirring until mixture is smooth. Add white and red pepper and remaining ¼ teaspoon salt; cook over medium heat, stirring constantly, until sauce is thickened. Reduce heat to low and continue cooking and stirring for 10 minutes longer; add all but reserved 2 tablespoons cheese and cook, continuing to stir, until cheese is melted and sauce is smooth. Remove from heat.

Preheat oven to 350°F. Into a shallow baking dish that is just large enough to hold endives in 1 layer pour ¼ of the cheese sauce. Roll 1 slice ham around each endive and place endives in baking dish; top with remaining sauce, then sprinkle with reserved 2 tablespoons cheese. Bake in upper-third section of oven for 15 minutes.

Each serving provides: 2 Protein Exchanges; 1 Vegetable Exchange;
  1½ Fat Exchanges; ½ Milk Exchange; 25 calories Optional Exchange
Per serving: 291 calories; 21 g protein; 16 g fat; 15 g carbohydrate; 15 mg calcium;
  672 mg sodium; 54 mg cholesterol

Endive-Tomato Salad with Sesame Dressing

WEEK 4 ⌢ MAKES 2 SERVINGS

Salad

5 medium Belgian endives (about
  3 ounces each)
½ cup chopped watercress leaves
6 cherry tomatoes, cut into quarters

Dressing

1 teaspoon each sesame seed,
  toasted, lemon juice, rice vinegar,
  and water
½ garlic clove, mashed
Dash salt

To Prepare Salad: Separate each endive into individual leaves. Line a clear 1-quart salad bowl with endive leaves with tips facing rim of bowl like flower petals. Fill center of bowl with chopped watercress; top watercress with cherry tomato quarters, arranged in a circular pattern. Refrigerate for at least 30 minutes.

To Prepare Dressing: Using a mortar and pestle, mash sesame seed. In small bowl or cup combine mashed seed with lemon juice, vinegar, water, garlic, and salt; mix well. Refrigerate for at least 30 minutes.

To Serve: Stir dressing and pour over salad.

Each serving provides: 3½ Vegetable Exchanges; 10 calories Optional Exchange
Per serving: 50 calories; 3 g protein; 1 g fat; 9 g carbohydrate; 57 mg calcium;
  86 mg sodium; 0 mg cholesterol

Braised Fennel ❶❸

WEEK 3 〰 MAKES 2 SERVINGS

1 teaspoon vegetable oil
2 garlic cloves, minced
3 cups sliced fennel
½ cup water

1 packet instant chicken broth and
 seasoning mix
¼ teaspoon each basil leaves and
 pepper

In small nonstick skillet heat oil; add garlic and sauté until golden. Add fennel and sauté over medium heat, stirring occasionally, for 2 to 3 minutes; add water, broth mix, basil, and pepper and bring to a boil. Reduce heat and let simmer until fennel is tender, about 15 minutes.

Each serving provides: 3 Vegetable Exchanges; ½ Fat Exchange;
 5 calories Optional Exchange
Per serving: 35 calories; 1 g protein; 2 g fat; 3 g carbohydrate; 25 mg calcium;
 458 mg sodium; 0 mg cholesterol

Fennel Salad

WEEK 4 〰 MAKES 2 SERVINGS

2 cups thinly sliced fennel
½ cup diced red bell pepper
4 black olives, pitted and chopped
2 tablespoons thinly sliced scallion
 (green onion)

1 tablespoon plus 1½ teaspoons
 white wine vinegar
2 teaspoons olive oil
½ garlic clove, minced
⅛ teaspoon each salt and pepper

In medium bowl combine fennel, red pepper, olives, and scallion. In jar with tight-fitting cover or small bowl combine remaining ingredients; cover and shake well or stir to mix thoroughly. Pour dressing over fennel mixture and toss to coat; cover with plastic wrap and refrigerate for at least 4 hours. Toss again just before serving.

Each serving provides: 2½ Vegetable Exchanges; 1 Fat Exchange;
 10 calories Optional Exchange
Per serving: 77 calories; 1 g protein; 6 g fat; 5 g carbohydrate; 31 mg calcium;
 234 mg sodium; 0 mg cholesterol

Marinated Green Bean Salad

WEEK 1 ～ MAKES 2 SERVINGS

Fresh green beans and fresh lemon juice make a big difference in this dish.

4 cups whole green beans (about
 1 pound)
1 cup water
¼ cup diced onion
2 tablespoons each drained capers
 and fresh lemon juice

1 tablespoon each olive oil and
 red wine vinegar
1 teaspoon oregano leaves
¼ teaspoon each salt and powdered
 mustard
1 egg, hard-cooked and chilled

Snap off and discard ends of beans. In 2-quart saucepan bring water to a boil; add beans and onion and cook until beans are tender-crisp, 5 to 8 minutes. Drain well.

In 1½- or 2-quart bowl combine remaining ingredients except egg; add warm beans and toss to coat. Cover bowl and refrigerate overnight or for at least 2 hours.

Just before serving, chop hard-cooked egg; toss salad again and sprinkle with egg.

Each serving provides: ½ Protein Exchange; 4¼ Vegetable Exchanges;
 1½ Fat Exchanges
Per serving: 182 calories; 7 g protein; 10 g fat; 20 g carbohydrate; 116 mg calcium;
 540 mg sodium; 137 mg cholesterol

Mixed Green Salad with Mustard Vinaigrette ◑

WEEK 1 ∿ MAKES 2 SERVINGS

2 cups torn chilled romaine lettuce
(bite-size pieces)
1 cup chilled watercress leaves
(stems removed)
1 tablespoon plus 2 teaspoons red
wine vinegar

2 teaspoons olive oil
¼ teaspoon Dijon-style mustard
Dash each salt and pepper

In salad bowl combine romaine lettuce with watercress. In small bowl combine remaining ingredients; pour over greens, toss to coat, and serve immediately.

Each serving provides: 3 Vegetable Exchanges; 1 Fat Exchange
Per serving: 47 calories; 1 g protein; 4 g fat; 3 g carbohydrate; 63 mg calcium;
98 mg sodium; 0 mg cholesterol

Mixed Green Salad with Buttermilk Dressing ◑

WEEK 1 ∿ MAKES 4 SERVINGS

4 cups chilled Boston lettuce leaves,
torn into bite-size pieces
3 cups chilled spinach leaves,
washed well and torn into bite-
size pieces

Buttermilk Dressing (see page 164)
1 egg, hard-cooked and chopped

In large salad bowl combine lettuce and spinach; add dressing and toss to coat. Sprinkle with chopped egg and serve immediately.

Each serving provides (includes Buttermilk Dressing): ½ Protein Exchange;
3½ Vegetable Exchanges; 1 Fat Exchange; 15 calories Optional Exchange
Per serving: 109 calories; 6 g protein; 7 g fat; 6 g carbohydrate; 110 mg calcium;
210 mg sodium; 141 mg cholesterol

Braised Jerusalem Artichokes ◐❸

WEEK 4 ∽ MAKES 2 SERVINGS

2 teaspoons olive or vegetable oil
½ cup diced onion
2 garlic cloves, minced
2 cups sliced pared Jerusalem
   artichokes (cut crosswise into
   ⅛-inch-thick slices)

½ teaspoon salt
¼ teaspoon pepper
½ cup each dry white wine and
   water
1 teaspoon chopped fresh parsley
   (optional)

In 8- or 9-inch nonstick skillet heat oil over medium-high heat; add onion and garlic and sauté until onion is lightly browned. Add artichoke slices, salt, and pepper and sauté for 5 minutes; add wine and cook until almost all liquid has evaporated. Add water, cover, and let simmer, stirring occasionally, until artichokes are tender, about 15 minutes. Serve sprinkled with parsley if desired.

Each serving provides: 2½ Vegetable Exchanges; 1 Fat Exchange;
   60 calories Optional Exchange
Per serving: 164 calories; 4 g protein; 5 g fat; 29 g carbohydrate; 40 mg calcium;
   545 mg sodium; 0 mg cholesterol

Quick Caesar Salad ◐

WEEK 1 ∽ MAKES 2 SERVINGS

4 cups torn chilled romaine lettuce
   (bite-size pieces)
2 slices white bread, toasted and
   cut into cubes

1 tablespoon each grated Parmesan
cheese, lemon juice, and Caesar
salad dressing

In 1-quart bowl toss lettuce with bread cubes and cheese; add lemon juice and dressing and toss to coat thoroughly. Let stand for 5 to 10 minutes; toss again just before serving.

Each serving provides: 1 Bread Exchange; 4 Vegetable Exchanges; 1 Fat Exchange;
   15 calories Optional Exchange
Per serving: 129 calories; 5 g protein; 5 g fat; 17 g carbohydrate; 137 mg calcium;
   278 mg sodium; 3 mg cholesterol

Mushroom-Cheese Pâté ❶

WEEK 4 ∽ MAKES 2 SERVINGS

4 cups sliced mushrooms
2 tablespoons sliced scallion
 (green onion)
2 teaspoons dry red wine
1 packet instant onion broth and
 seasoning mix
⅔ cup cottage cheese

3 tablespoons plain dried bread
 crumbs
2 large lettuce leaves

Garnish

Watercress sprigs and 4 sliced
 radishes

In 8- or 9-inch nonstick skillet combine mushrooms, scallion, wine, and broth mix; cook over medium heat, stirring occasionally, until all liquid has evaporated.

Spoon mixture into blender container or work bowl of food processor and process until smooth. Turn motor off and add cheese and bread crumbs; process until combined. Spray two 6-ounce custard cups (or two ¾-cup nonstick molds) with nonstick cooking spray and spoon half of cheese mixture into each; tap cups (or molds) on hard surface to release air bubbles. Cover with plastic wrap and refrigerate for at least 2 hours.

To unmold and serve, run the point of a small knife around the edge of each cup (or mold); on each of 2 plates place a lettuce leaf and invert pâtés onto lettuce. Garnish with watercress and radish slices.

Each serving provides: 1 Protein Exchange; ½ Bread Exchange;
 4½ Vegetable Exchanges; 10 calories Optional Exchange
Per serving: 170 calories; 15 g protein; 4 g fat; 18 g carbohydrate; 71 mg calcium;
 782 mg sodium; 12 mg cholesterol

Herb-Marinated Mushrooms

WEEK 1 ✎ MAKES 4 SERVINGS

6 cups small mushroom caps*
2 tablespoons each lemon juice and
  cider vinegar
2 teaspoons olive oil

1 teaspoon salt
½ teaspoon each tarragon leaves
  and pepper
¼ teaspoon ground thyme

In small saucepan (not aluminum or cast-iron) combine all ingredients; bring to a boil. Reduce heat and let simmer for 5 minutes, stirring occasionally. Let cool, then cover and refrigerate for at least 8 hours.

Each serving provides: 3 Vegetable Exchanges; ½ Fat Exchange
Per serving: 50 calories; 3 g protein; 2 g fat; 7 g carbohydrate; 18 mg calcium;
  558 mg sodium; 0 mg cholesterol

* Save and freeze the mushroom stems for later use in soup or sauce.

Okra Caponata

WEEK 4 ✎ MAKES 4 SERVINGS, ABOUT ½ CUP EACH

2 teaspoons olive or vegetable oil
¼ cup each diced onion, celery,
  and red bell pepper
1 garlic clove, minced
½ cup each sliced okra, sliced
  mushrooms, and chopped zucchini

½ cup canned whole tomatoes,
  chopped
2 tablespoons dry red wine
1½ teaspoons drained capers
3 each pitted black and pimiento-
  stuffed green olives, sliced

In 9- or 10-inch nonstick skillet heat oil; add onion, celery, red pepper, and garlic and sauté, stirring constantly, until onion is translucent, about 3 minutes. Stir in okra, mushrooms, and zucchini and sauté, stirring occasionally, until vegetables are lightly browned; stir in tomatoes, wine, and capers and cook until liquid has evaporated. Stir in olives and transfer mixture to 2-cup glass or stainless-steel bowl; cover and refrigerate for at least 8 hours to allow flavors to blend.

Each serving provides: 1¼ Vegetable Exchanges; ½ Fat Exchange;
  15 calories Optional Exchange
Per serving: 61 calories; 2 g protein; 4 g fat; 6 g carbohydrate; 32 mg calcium;
  175 mg sodium; 0 mg cholesterol

Onion Soup

WEEK 1 ～ MAKES 4 SERVINGS

2 tablespoons reduced-calorie
  margarine, divided
2 cups thinly sliced onions
1 quart water
4 packets instant beef broth and
  seasoning mix
2 teaspoons Worcestershire sauce

½ bay leaf
Dash pepper
4 slices French bread (½ ounce
  each)
2 teaspoons grated Parmesan
  cheese

In 2-quart saucepan heat 1 tablespoon plus 1 teaspoon margarine until bubbly and hot; add onions and sauté until translucent, 2 to 3 minutes. Add water, broth mix, and seasonings and bring to a boil. Reduce heat, partially cover pan, and let simmer for 30 minutes. Remove and discard bay leaf.

While soup is simmering, spread each slice of bread with ½ teaspoon margarine and sprinkle each with ½ teaspoon Parmesan cheese; transfer to baking sheet and bake at 350°F. until browned and crisp, 25 to 30 minutes.

To serve, place 1 slice of baked bread in each of 4 soup bowls and pour ¼ of the soup into each bowl.

Each serving provides: ½ Bread Exchange; 1 Vegetable Exchange; ½ Fat Exchange; 25 calories Optional Exchange
Per serving: 110 calories; 4 g protein; 4 g fat; 16 g carbohydrate; 40 mg calcium; 941 mg sodium; 1 mg cholesterol

Pickle-Mustard Relish ◐ ⬤

WEEK 4 ～ MAKES 8 SERVINGS, ABOUT 2 TABLESPOONS EACH

Serve with Baked Smoked Ham with Pineapple Rings (see page 346).

3 medium dill pickles, minced
2 tablespoons minced drained
  canned pimientos

2 teaspoons Dijon-style mustard

In small bowl thoroughly combine all ingredients; cover and refrigerate until chilled.

Each serving provides: ¾ Vegetable Exchange
Per serving: 5 calories; 0.2 g protein; 0.2 g fat; 1 g carbohydrate; 6 mg calcium; 380 mg sodium; 0 mg cholesterol

Marinated Pepper Salad

WEEK 1 ∽ MAKES 2 SERVINGS

---

2 teaspoons olive oil
½ cup thinly sliced onion
1 garlic clove, minced
1½ cups each thinly sliced green
  and red bell peppers

2 teaspoons red wine vinegar
1½ teaspoons drained capers
½ teaspoon salt
Dash each oregano leaves, pepper,
  and granulated sugar substitute

In 9-inch nonstick skillet heat oil; add onion and garlic and sauté briefly (just until onion is tender-crisp). Add sliced peppers and toss lightly; cover and cook until peppers are tender-crisp, 3 to 5 minutes.

Transfer vegetable mixture to medium bowl; add remaining ingredients and toss. Cover and refrigerate for at least 2 hours before serving.

Each serving provides: 3½ Vegetable Exchanges; 1 Fat Exchange
Per serving: 127 calories; 4 g protein; 6 g fat; 18 g carbohydrate; 50 mg calcium;
  502 mg sodium; 0 mg cholesterol

Rutabaga-Carrot Whip ◖❶

WEEK 4 ∽ MAKES 2 SERVINGS

---

2 cups pared and cubed rutabaga
  (about ¾ pound)
1 cup sliced carrots
½ teaspoon salt

1 tablespoon reduced-calorie
  pancake syrup (30 calories per
  tablespoon)
2 teaspoons margarine
Dash ground cinnamon

In 1½-quart saucepan combine vegetables and salt; add water to cover and bring to a boil. Reduce heat to medium-low and cook until tender.

Drain vegetables and transfer to work bowl of food processor; add syrup and margarine and process until mixture is smooth. Transfer pureed mixture to serving bowl and sprinkle with cinnamon.

Each serving provides: 3 Vegetable Exchanges; 1 Fat Exchange;
  15 calories Optional Exchange
Per serving: 151 calories; 3 g protein; 4 g fat; 28 g carbohydrate; 139 mg calcium;
  616 mg sodium; 0 mg cholesterol

Spinach-Mushroom Salad ◐

WEEK 1 ∿ MAKES 2 SERVINGS

3 cups spinach leaves, washed well
  and drained
1 cup thinly sliced mushrooms
3 tablespoons lemon juice
2 teaspoons olive oil
½ teaspoon basil leaves

Granulated sugar substitute to
  equal ½ teaspoon sugar
½ garlic clove, minced
¼ teaspoon each pepper and
  Dijon-style mustard
⅛ teaspoon salt

In salad bowl combine spinach and mushrooms. In small bowl combine remaining ingredients; pour over spinach mixture and toss gently to combine.

Each serving provides: 4 Vegetable Exchanges; 1 Fat Exchange
Per serving: 82 calories; 4 g protein; 5 g fat; 7 g carbohydrate; 93 mg calcium;
  229 mg sodium; 0 mg cholesterol

Quick Spinach Sauté ◐

WEEK 1 ∿ MAKES 1 SERVING, ABOUT 1 CUP

1 teaspoon olive oil
⅛ teaspoon minced fresh garlic
12 ounces spinach leaves, washed
  well and drained

Dash each salt and pepper

In 10-inch skillet heat oil; add garlic and sauté just until garlic begins to turn golden. Add spinach, salt, and pepper and cook, stirring frequently, until spinach is cooked, about 5 minutes.

Each serving provides: 2 Vegetable Exchanges; 1 Fat Exchange
Per serving: 131 calories; 11 g protein; 6 g fat; 15 g carbohydrate; 318 mg calcium;
  371 mg sodium; 0 mg cholesterol

Variation: Sprinkle cooked spinach with 2 teaspoons grated Parmesan cheese; add 20 calories Optional Exchange to Exchange Information.

Per serving: 151 calories; 12 g protein; 7 g fat; 15 g carbohydrate; 364 mg calcium;
  433 mg sodium; 3 mg cholesterol

Spiced Spinach Sauté ◐

WEEK 1 ⌒ MAKES 4 SERVINGS, ABOUT ½ CUP EACH

1 pound spinach
2 teaspoons margarine
¼ cup diced onion
½ garlic clove, minced

⅛ teaspoon salt
Dash each pepper and ground
   nutmeg

Wash spinach thoroughly and drain; remove and discard stems and coarsely chop leaves. In 9- or 10-inch nonstick skillet, over high heat and using only the water that clings to spinach leaves after washing, cook spinach, covered, until wilted; remove from pan and set aside.

In same skillet heat margarine until bubbly and hot; add onion and garlic and sauté until onion is translucent. Add spinach and stir to combine; season and sauté until thoroughly heated.

Each serving provides: 1 Vegetable Exchange; ½ Fat Exchange
Per serving: 51 calories; 4 g protein; 2 g fat; 6 g carbohydrate; 6 mg calcium;
   174 mg sodium; 0 mg cholesterol

Olive-Stuffed Tomatoes

WEEK 4 ⌒ MAKES 2 SERVINGS, 1 TOMATO EACH

2 medium tomatoes
2 teaspoons margarine
2 tablespoons each diced onion
   and green bell pepper
4 large pimiento-stuffed green
   olives, chopped

1 tablespoon plus 1½ teaspoons
   seasoned dried bread crumbs
⅛ teaspoon salt
Dash pepper

Cut thin slice from stem end of each tomato and scoop out pulp, reserving shells; set shells upside-down on paper towels and let drain. Drain off excess liquid from pulp; chop pulp and set aside.

In small nonstick skillet heat margarine until bubbly and hot; add onion and green pepper and sauté until soft. Add reserved tomato pulp and cook until all moisture has evaporated; remove from heat.

Preheat oven to 375°F. Add olives, bread crumbs, salt, and pepper to tomato pulp mixture and stir to combine; spoon ¼ of mixture into each reserved tomato shell. Place stuffed tomatoes in shallow ovenproof dish that is just large enough to hold them upright; bake until tomatoes are soft, 25 to 30 minutes.

Each serving provides: 2¼ Vegetable Exchanges; 1 Fat Exchange;
  30 calories Optional Exchange
Per serving: 92 calories; 2 g protein; 5 g fat; 10 g carbohydrate; 24 mg calcium;
  530 mg sodium; 0.3 mg cholesterol

Broiled Crumb-Topped Tomatoes ◖◗ ❸

WEEK 4 ⬠ MAKES 2 SERVINGS, 1 TOMATO EACH

2 medium tomatoes, cut crosswise
  into halves
2 teaspoons margarine
1 tablespoon minced onion
3 tablespoons plain dried bread
  crumbs

2 teaspoons grated Parmesan
  cheese
1½ teaspoons chopped fresh basil
  or ½ teaspoon dried

Preheat broiler. Place tomatoes cut-side up on a nonstick baking sheet and broil 6 inches from heat source until lightly browned, about 5 minutes.

While tomatoes are broiling, in small skillet heat margarine until bubbly and hot; add onion and cook until translucent. Remove from heat, add remaining ingredients, and stir to combine.

Remove tomatoes from broiler and spoon half of crumb mixture over each; return tomatoes to broiler and broil until topping is browned, 1 to 2 minutes.

Each serving provides: ½ Bread Exchange; 2 Vegetable Exchanges; 1 Fat Exchange;
  10 calories Optional Exchange
Per serving: 113 calories; 4 g protein; 5 g fat; 14 g carbohydrate; 63 mg calcium;
  153 mg sodium; 2 mg cholesterol

Vegetable Relish ◐

WEEK 1 ∽ MAKES 2 SERVINGS

1 large cucumber (about 8 inches long), pared and seeded
1 tablespoon each diced drained canned pimiento and coarsely grated carrot
2 teaspoons finely chopped scallion (green onion)

1 tablespoon plus 1 teaspoon white wine vinegar
1 teaspoon olive oil
1/4 teaspoon salt
1/8 teaspoon each powdered mustard and pepper
Dash granulated sugar substitute (optional)

Coarsely grate cucumber into a small bowl and pour off any liquid; add pimiento, carrot, and scallion. In another small bowl combine remaining ingredients except pepper; pour over cucumber mixture and toss well. Serve sprinkled with pepper.

Each serving provides: 1¼ Vegetable Exchanges; ½ Fat Exchange
Per serving: 41 calories; 1 g protein; 3 g fat; 4 g carbohydrate; 21 mg calcium;
 279 mg sodium; 0 mg cholesterol

Vegetable-Swiss Broil

WEEK 2 ∽ MAKES 2 SERVINGS

1 cup cubed eggplant (1-inch cubes)
1/4 teaspoon salt, divided
1 teaspoon olive oil
1/2 cup diced onion
1/2 garlic clove, minced, or dash garlic powder
1 medium zucchini (about 5 ounces), cut into 1/4-inch-thick slices

1/2 medium green bell pepper, seeded and cut into 1-inch squares
1/8 teaspoon each basil leaves and pepper
1 cup canned whole tomatoes
Dash hot sauce
1½ teaspoons chopped fresh parsley
2 ounces Swiss cheese, shredded

Spread eggplant on double layer of paper towels and sprinkle with 1/8 teaspoon salt; let stand for 30 minutes, then pat dry.

In 1-quart saucepan heat oil; add onion and minced garlic and sauté until onion is softened (if garlic powder is used, do not add at this time). Add eggplant, zucchini, and green pepper and sauté for 3 minutes; sprinkle with basil, pepper, remaining ⅛ teaspoon salt, and, if used, garlic powder. Stir in tomatoes and hot sauce and bring to a boil. Reduce heat, cover, and let simmer for 15 minutes. Stir in parsley and simmer, uncovered, until liquid has evaporated slightly, about 5 minutes.

Transfer mixture to a 1-quart flameproof casserole;* sprinkle with cheese and broil until cheese is melted and lightly browned.

Each serving provides: 1 Protein Exchange; 4 Vegetable Exchanges;
⅟₂ Fat Exchange
Per serving: 200 calories; 12 g protein; 11 g fat; 17 g carbohydrate; 329 mg calcium;
445 mg sodium; 26 mg cholesterol

* Individual 1½-cup flameproof casseroles may be substituted; sprinkle each portion with 1 ounce cheese.

Vegetable Sauté ◑

WEEK 1 ❧ MAKES 2 SERVINGS

1½ teaspoons peanut or vegetable oil
½ teaspoon Chinese sesame oil
½ cup julienne-cut carrot

½ garlic clove, minced, or ⅛ teaspoon garlic powder
1 cup broccoli florets
½ cup sliced mushrooms

In small nonstick skillet combine oils and heat over medium-high heat; add carrot and garlic (or garlic powder) and sauté for about 2 minutes. Reduce heat, cover, and cook for 3 minutes (carrot sticks should still be crisp); add broccoli and mushrooms and sauté until vegetables are tender-crisp, about 5 minutes.

Each serving provides: 2 Vegetable Exchanges; 1 Fat Exchange
Per serving: 79 calories; 3 g protein; 5 g fat; 7 g carbohydrate; 40 mg calcium;
32 mg sodium; 0 mg cholesterol

Variation: Broccoli-Carrot Sauté—Omit mushrooms and proceed as directed; reduce Vegetable Exchange to 1½ Exchanges.

Per serving: 74 calories; 3 g protein; 5 g fat; 7 g carbohydrate; 39 mg calcium;
29 mg sodium; 0 mg cholesterol

Vegetable Soup ❶

WEEK 1 ∽ MAKES 2 SERVINGS

¼ cup diced onion
1 garlic clove, minced
1 cup each thinly sliced carrots and
 zucchini
2 teaspoons chopped fresh parsley

¼ teaspoon each thyme leaves and
 salt
⅛ teaspoon pepper
2 cups water

In 1½-quart nonstick saucepan combine onion and garlic and cook until onion is translucent; add carrots, zucchini, parsley, thyme, salt, and pepper. Cover and cook over low heat, stirring occasionally, until vegetables are tender, about 10 minutes; add water and bring to a boil. Reduce heat to medium and cook until vegetables are soft, about 20 minutes. Remove from heat and let cool slightly.

Remove ½ cup soup from pan and reserve. Pour remaining soup into blender container and process at low speed until smooth; return pureed and reserved mixture to saucepan and cook, stirring constantly, until thoroughly combined and heated.

Each serving provides: 2¼ Vegetable Exchanges
Per serving: 45 calories; 2 g protein; 0.2 g fat; 10 g carbohydrate; 53 mg calcium;
 299 mg sodium; 0 mg cholesterol

Wine-Braised Zucchini ❶

WEEK 2 ∽ MAKES 2 SERVINGS

2 teaspoons olive oil
2 medium zucchini (about 5 ounces
 each), thinly sliced
¼ cup minced shallots

½ teaspoon basil leaves
¼ teaspoon each salt and pepper
¼ cup dry white wine
1 teaspoon lemon juice

In 10-inch skillet heat oil; add zucchini, shallots, basil, salt, and pepper and sauté for 3 minutes. Add wine and lemon juice, cover, and let simmer, stirring occasionally, for 10 minutes.

Each serving provides: 2¼ Vegetable Exchanges; 1 Fat Exchange;
 30 calories Optional Exchange
Per serving: 107 calories; 2 g protein; 5 g fat; 10 g carbohydrate; 61 mg calcium;
 275 mg sodium; 0 mg cholesterol

The Milk Exchange

THIS "milky way" offers a galaxy of recipes guaranteed to brighten any day. With our Amaretto Float, Honey Shake, or Frozen Berry Yogurt there's no need to wish upon a falling star for recipes that fulfill your nutritional needs and still provide heavenly taste appeal.

◗ Pointers on the Milk Exchange

Daily Exchanges

	WEEKS 1 AND 2	WEEKS 3 AND 4
Women and Men	2 Exchanges	2 Exchanges
Youths	3 Exchanges	3 to 4 Exchanges

◗ Items from the Milk Exchange supply calcium, phosphorus, protein, riboflavin, and vitamins A and D.

◗ Use *skim milk* containing up to 90 calories per cup.

◗ You may select up to 2 Exchanges per day of *reduced-calorie flavored milk beverages or puddings* that contain at least 6 grams of protein and 200 milligrams of calcium; you may select up to 1 Exchange per day of products that contain 5 to 6 grams of protein and 150 to 200 milligrams of calcium.

◗ One 3-ounce serving of approved commercially prepared vanilla or chocolate *dietary frozen dessert* provides 1 Fruit Exchange and ½ Milk Exchange.

MILK EXCHANGE LISTS

Weeks 1, 2, and 3

Selections	*One Exchange*
Milk, skim	1 cup
Milk, nonfat, dry	⅓ cup powder
Buttermilk, made from whole milk	¾ cup
made from skim milk	1 cup
Flavored Milk Beverages, reduced-calorie	1 packet or serving
Flavored Milk Puddings, reduced-calorie	½ cup prepared
Yogurt, skim or low-fat (plain)	½ cup

Week 4

You may use all of the items listed under Weeks 1, 2, and 3 and may add the following to your Exchange List.

Selections	One Exchange
Milk, low-fat (1% milk fat)	1 cup (omit 20 Optional Exchange calories)
Milk, low-fat (2% milk fat)	1 cup (omit 40 Optional Exchange calories)
Milk, evaporated, skimmed	½ cup

Creamy Chicken-Mushroom Soup

WEEK 4 ⬲ MAKES 2 SERVINGS, ABOUT 1 CUP EACH

2 teaspoons margarine
2 tablespoons minced onion
2 cups sliced mushrooms
1 tablespoon all-purpose flour
1½ cups water
1 packet instant chicken broth and
   seasoning mix

Dash ground thyme
½ cup evaporated skimmed milk
2 teaspoons dry sherry
Dash each salt and white pepper
1 teaspoon chopped fresh parsley

In 1-quart saucepan heat margarine until bubbly and hot; add onion and sauté, stirring occasionally, until softened. Add mushrooms and sauté for 5 minutes longer; remove and reserve 2 tablespoons of mushroom mixture. Sprinkle flour over vegetables in saucepan and stir quickly to combine; cook, stirring constantly, for 2 minutes. Gradually stir in water; add broth mix and thyme and, stirring constantly, bring mixture to a boil. Reduce heat, cover, and let simmer for 15 minutes.

Pour 2 cups soup into blender container and process until smooth; transfer mixture to a 1-quart bowl and repeat procedure with remaining soup.

Pour soup back into saucepan. Stir in milk, sherry, and reserved mushroom mixture and let simmer for 5 minutes; season with salt and pepper and serve garnished with parsley.

Each serving provides: 2⅛ Vegetable Exchanges; 1 Fat Exchange;
   ½ Milk Exchange; 25 calories Optional Exchange
Per serving: 135 calories; 8 g protein; 4 g fat; 16 g carbohydrate; 198 mg calcium;
   611 mg sodium; 3 mg cholesterol

Cream of Broccoli Soup ◐❸

WEEK 4 ∿ MAKES 4 SERVINGS, ABOUT ¾ CUP EACH

2 teaspoons margarine
½ cup diced onion
1 package (10 ounces) thawed
   frozen chopped broccoli
½ teaspoon salt

1 bay leaf
1 teaspoon all-purpose flour
1 cup evaporated skimmed milk
½ cup canned chicken broth

In 10-inch nonstick skillet heat margarine until bubbly and hot; add onion and sauté until translucent. Add broccoli, salt, and bay leaf and stir to combine. Sprinkle vegetables with flour and stir quickly to combine; cook, stirring constantly, for 1 minute. Continuing to stir, gradually add milk; add broth and, stirring constantly, bring just to a boil. Reduce heat and simmer, stirring, until mixture thickens slightly. Remove and discard bay leaf. Transfer soup to blender container and process at low speed until smooth; if necessary, reheat (*do not boil*).

Each serving provides: 1¼ Vegetable Exchanges; ½ Fat Exchange;
   ½ Milk Exchange; 10 calories Optional Exchange
Per serving: 104 calories; 8 g protein; 2 g fat; 14 g carbohydrate; 238 mg calcium;
   480 mg sodium; 3 mg cholesterol

Cream of Celery Soup ◐❸

WEEK 4 ∿ MAKES 2 SERVINGS, ABOUT 1 CUP EACH

2 teaspoons margarine
½ cup diced onion
2 cups diced celery
1 teaspoon all-purpose flour
1 packet instant chicken broth and
   seasoning mix

1 cup skim milk
Dash each ground nutmeg and
   white pepper

In 8-inch nonstick skillet heat margarine until bubbly and hot; add onion and sauté until translucent. Add celery and stir to combine. Reduce heat, cover, and cook until celery is soft. Sprinkle flour and broth mix over vegetables and stir quickly to combine; cook, stirring constantly, for 1 minute. Continuing to stir, gradually add milk and bring just to a boil. Reduce heat, season with nutmeg and pepper and simmer, stirring, until mixture thickens. Transfer soup to blender container and process at low speed until smooth; reheat if necessary (*do not boil*).

Each serving provides: 2½ Vegetable Exchanges; 1 Fat Exchange;
  ½ Milk Exchange; 10 calories Optional Exchange
Per serving: 124 calories; 7 g protein; 4 g fat; 16 g carbohydrate; 213 mg calcium;
  681 mg sodium; 2 mg cholesterol

Cream of Spinach Soup ❶❸

WEEK 4 ⟋ MAKES 4 SERVINGS, ABOUT 1⅛ CUPS EACH

---

2 tablespoons margarine
1 cup diced onions
2 packets instant chicken broth
  and seasoning mix
1 tablespoon all-purpose flour
3 cups skim milk (at room
  temperature)

1 package (10 ounces) frozen
  chopped spinach, cooked
  according to package directions
  and thoroughly drained
Dash ground nutmeg (optional)

In 1½-quart saucepan heat margarine until bubbly and hot; add onions, sprinkle with broth mix, and sauté until onions are soft. Sprinkle onions with flour and stir quickly to combine; cook, stirring constantly, for 1 minute (*be careful not to burn*). Continuing to stir, gradually add milk and bring just to a boil. Reduce heat and simmer, stirring, until mixture thickens; stir in cooked spinach, remove from heat, and let cool slightly.

Pour 2 cups soup into blender container and process at low speed until thoroughly blended, about 30 seconds. Transfer mixture to 2-quart bowl and repeat procedure with remaining soup, 2 cups at a time, until all soup has been processed; pour soup back into saucepan and heat (*do not boil*).

Each serving provides: 1½ Vegetable Exchanges; 1½ Fat Exchanges;
  ¾ Milk Exchange; 15 calories Optional Exchange
Per serving: 161 calories; 10 g protein; 6 g fat; 18 g carbohydrate; 323 mg calcium;
  624 mg sodium; 4 mg cholesterol

Yogurt-Mint Dip ◖◗

WEEK 1 ◇ MAKES 2 SERVINGS, ABOUT ¼ CUP EACH

Serve with crudités.

½ cup plain low-fat yogurt
2 tablespoons finely chopped fresh
  mint leaves

1 teaspoon lemon juice
Dash each white pepper, ground
  red pepper, and salt

In small bowl combine all ingredients and mix well. Cover and refrigerate until chilled.

Each serving provides: ½ Milk Exchange
Per serving: 37 calories; 3 g protein; 1 g fat; 4 g carbohydrate; 106 mg calcium;
  104 mg sodium; 3 mg cholesterol

Frozen Berry Yogurt

WEEK 4 ◇ MAKES 4 SERVINGS, ABOUT ¾ CUP EACH

3 cups strawberries
2 cups plain low-fat yogurt
2 tablespoons thawed frozen
  concentrated orange juice (no
  sugar added)
Granulated sugar substitute to
  equal 4 teaspoons sugar

2 egg whites (from large eggs), at
  room temperature
1 tablespoon plus 1 teaspoon
  confectioners' sugar
1 teaspoon vanilla extract

1. Set aside 4 strawberries for garnish. In 2-quart mixing bowl, using fork, crush remaining berries; stir in yogurt, orange juice, and sugar substitute.

2. In another bowl, using electric mixer on high speed, beat egg whites until soft peaks form; add sugar and extract and continue beating until stiff but not dry.

3. Fold beaten whites into strawberry mixture; transfer mixture to 2 freezer trays or a shallow baking pan, cover, and freeze until almost firm, about 45 minutes. Chill mixing bowl.

4. Turn berry yogurt into chilled bowl and, using electric mixer on high speed, beat until thick and creamy. Cover with plastic wrap and freeze until just firm.

5. To serve, let yogurt mixture soften slightly, just until it can be easily spooned out; spoon into 4 ice cream or dessert dishes and garnish each with a reserved berry.

Each serving provides: 1 Fruit Exchange; 1 Milk Exchange;
  30 calories Optional Exchange
Per serving: 143 calories; 9 g protein; 2 g fat; 23 g carbohydrate; 228 mg calcium;
  106 mg sodium; 7 mg cholesterol

Frozen Berry-Banana Yogurt

WEEK 1 ⟿ MAKES 4 SERVINGS

½ envelope (about 1½ teaspoons)
  unflavored gelatin
2 tablespoons water
2 cups strawberries
1 medium banana, peeled and cut
  into chunks

2 cups plain low-fat yogurt
Granulated sugar substitute to
  equal 4 teaspoons sugar
¼ teaspoon vanilla extract

In small saucepan or metal measuring cup sprinkle gelatin over water and let stand to soften; cook over low heat, stirring constantly, until gelatin is completely dissolved.

In blender container combine strawberries, banana, and dissolved gelatin and process until smooth; add yogurt, sugar substitute, and vanilla and process until combined. Pour mixture into shallow metal 1½-quart pan; cover and freeze, stirring every 30 minutes, until mixture is the consistency of ice cream.

Each serving provides: 1 Fruit Exchange; 1 Milk Exchange
Per serving: 127 calories; 7 g protein; 2 g fat; 21 g carbohydrate; 217 mg calcium;
  88 mg sodium; 7 mg cholesterol

Strawberry-Pineapple Sherbet

WEEK 1 〜 MAKES 4 SERVINGS, ABOUT 1 CUP EACH

Acidic foods, such as pineapple, may react with aluminum. Therefore, be sure to use non-aluminum containers for freezing.

2 cups strawberries
1 cup canned crushed pineapple
  (no sugar added)
1½ cups buttermilk

1 tablespoon granulated sugar
2 teaspoons vanilla extract
Granulated sugar substitute to equal
  1 teaspoon sugar

Set aside 4 strawberries for garnish. In blender container combine remaining berries with the pineapple and process until smooth; add remaining ingredients except garnish and process to combine. Pour mixture into two 8-inch square nonstick baking pans (not aluminum) or any non-aluminum shallow freezer containers; cover and freeze until partially frozen, about 30 minutes. Chill 2-quart mixing bowl.

Spoon partially frozen sherbet into chilled bowl and, using electric mixer, beat until fluffy; cover bowl with plastic wrap and freeze until sherbet is almost firm. Spoon sherbet into 4 ice cream or dessert dishes, garnish each with a reserved berry, and serve immediately.

Each serving provides: 1 Fruit Exchange; ½ Milk Exchange;
  15 calories Optional Exchange
Per serving: 117 calories; 4 g protein; 1 g fat; 24 g carbohydrate; 126 mg calcium;
  98 mg sodium; 4 mg cholesterol

Mandarin Mold ❶

WEEK 4 ⌁ MAKES 2 SERVINGS

1 envelope unflavored gelatin
2 tablespoons thawed frozen
  concentrated orange juice (no
  sugar added)
½ cup boiling water

1 cup plain low-fat yogurt
½ cup canned mandarin orange
  sections (no sugar added)
2 teaspoons granulated sugar

In small heatproof bowl sprinkle gelatin over orange juice and let stand to soften; add boiling water and stir until gelatin is dissolved.

In separate bowl combine yogurt, orange sections, and sugar; gently fold in juice mixture. Rinse 2-cup mold with cold water and pour mixture into mold; cover and refrigerate until firm, about 4 hours. To serve, unmold onto serving plate.

Each serving provides: 1 Fruit Exchange; 1 Milk Exchange;
  20 calories Optional Exchange
Per serving: 150 calories; 10 g protein; 2 g fat; 25 g carbohydrate; 218 mg calcium;
  85 mg sodium; 7 mg cholesterol

Dutch Apple Yogurt ❶❶

WEEK 2 ⌁ MAKES 2 SERVINGS, ABOUT ½ CUP EACH

In small bowl combine ½ **cup plain low-fat yogurt,** ½ **cup applesauce (no sugar added), 1 tablespoon chunky Dutch apple jam,** and **dash ground cinnamon;** cover and refrigerate until chilled.

Each serving provides: ½ Fruit Exchange; ½ Milk Exchange;
  25 calories Optional Exchange
Per serving: 90 calories; 3 g protein; 1 g fat; 18 g carbohydrate; 107 mg calcium;
  42 mg sodium; 3 mg cholesterol

Buttermilk Custard Pie ❶

WEEK 4 ∽ MAKES 8 SERVINGS

Crust
¾ cup all-purpose flour
¼ teaspoon salt
2 tablespoons plus 2 teaspoons
  margarine
¼ cup plain low-fat yogurt
1 teaspoon white vinegar

Filling
¼ cup each margarine and
  granulated sugar
4 eggs, separated
3 tablespoons all-purpose flour
1 teaspoon each grated orange peel,
  lemon juice, and vanilla extract
1½ cups buttermilk

To Prepare Crust: In mixing bowl combine flour and salt; with pastry blender, or 2 knives used scissors-fashion, cut in margarine until mixture resembles coarse meal. Add yogurt and vinegar and mix thoroughly; form dough into a ball, wrap in plastic wrap, and refrigerate for at least 1 hour (may be kept in refrigerator for up to 3 days).

Between 2 sheets of wax paper roll dough, forming a 10-inch circle about ⅛ inch thick. Fit dough into a 9-inch pie plate and flute edges; wrap in plastic wrap and return to refrigerator.

To Prepare Filling and Bake: Preheat oven to 450°F. In large mixing bowl, using electric mixer, cream margarine with sugar until light and fluffy; beat in egg yolks. Add flour, orange peel, juice, and vanilla and beat until well blended; stir in buttermilk.

In small mixing bowl, using clean beaters, beat egg whites until stiff but not dry; fold into yolk mixture. Pour filling into prepared pie crust and bake for 15 minutes. Reduce oven temperature to 350°F. and continue baking for 45 to 50 minutes longer. Remove pie plate to wire rack and let cool; cover and refrigerate for at least 1 hour before serving.

Each serving provides: ½ Protein Exchange; ½ Bread Exchange;
  2½ Fat Exchanges; ¼ Milk Exchange; 45 calories Optional Exchange
Per serving: 228 calories; 7 g protein; 13 g fat; 21 g carbohydrate; 88 mg calcium;
  226 mg sodium; 139 mg cholesterol

Yogurt-Fruit Pie

WEEK 3 ～ MAKES 8 SERVINGS

Crust

16 graham crackers (2½-inch squares), made into crumbs

2 tablespoons plus 2 teaspoons margarine, softened

Filling

¼ cup thawed frozen concentrated orange juice (no sugar added)

2 tablespoons plus 2 teaspoons granulated sugar

1 envelope unflavored gelatin

2 cups plain low-fat yogurt

½ cup canned crushed pineapple (no sugar added)

1 teaspoon vanilla extract

Topping

40 small seedless green grapes

2 small nectarines, pitted and sliced

¾ cup sliced strawberries

To Prepare Crust: Preheat oven to 350°F. Spray 9-inch glass pie plate with nonstick cooking spray; set aside.

In small bowl combine crumbs and margarine, mixing thoroughly; using the back of a spoon, press crumb mixture over bottom and up sides of sprayed pie plate. Bake until crust is crisp and brown, about 10 minutes; remove to wire rack and let cool.

To Prepare Filling: Pour orange juice into small saucepan. Combine sugar and gelatin and sprinkle over juice; let stand for 1 minute to soften. Cook over medium-low heat, stirring constantly, until sugar and gelatin are completely dissolved; set aside.

In medium bowl, using a wire whisk, gently stir together yogurt and pineapple; add gelatin mixture and vanilla and stir until completely blended. Pour mixture into cooled pie crust; cover and refrigerate until firm, overnight or at least 4 hours.

To Serve: Arrange fruit decoratively over filling; serve immediately or cover and refrigerate until ready to use.

Each serving provides: 1 Bread Exchange; 1 Fat Exchange; 1 Fruit Exchange; ½ Milk Exchange; 20 calories Optional Exchange
Per serving: 202 calories; 6 g protein; 6 g fat; 33 g carbohydrate; 121 mg calcium; 179 mg sodium; 3 mg cholesterol

Honeyed Pear Parfait ◑❸

WEEK 4 ～ MAKES 2 SERVINGS, 1 PARFAIT EACH

2 very ripe small pears, cored,
  pared, and diced
1 teaspoon each lemon juice and
  honey
Dash ground cinnamon

1 cup plain low-fat yogurt
1 teaspoon vanilla extract
2 graham crackers (2½-inch
  squares), crushed

Chill 2 parfait glasses. In small bowl combine pears, lemon juice, honey, and cinnamon; cover and refrigerate until chilled. In another small bowl combine yogurt and vanilla; cover and refrigerate until chilled.

To serve, spoon ¼ of fruit mixture into each chilled glass and top with ¼ of yogurt mixture; repeat layers with remaining fruit and yogurt mixture. Sprinkle each parfait with half of the graham cracker crumbs.

Each serving provides: ½ Bread Exchange; 1 Fruit Exchange; 1 Milk Exchange;
  10 calories Optional Exchange
Per serving: 194 calories; 7 g protein; 3 g fat; 36 g carbohydrate; 223 mg calcium;
  126 mg sodium; 7 mg cholesterol

Chocolate Shake ◑❸

WEEK 1 ～ MAKES 1 SERVING, ABOUT 1 CUP

½ cup skim milk
3 ounces chocolate dietary frozen
  dessert

1 teaspoon reduced-calorie
  chocolate-flavored syrup (30
  calories per tablespoon)
¼ teaspoon vanilla extract

In blender container combine all ingredients and process until smooth, about 1 minute. Serve immediately or cover and chill in freezer for 1 to 2 minutes, then reprocess.

Each serving provides: 1 Fruit Exchange; 1 Milk Exchange;
  10 calories Optional Exchange
Per serving: 157 calories; 8 g protein; 1 g fat; 27 g carbohydrate; 301 mg calcium;
  134 mg sodium; 4 mg cholesterol

Honey "Eggnog" ◗❸

WEEK 2 ◡ MAKES 2 SERVINGS

1 cup skim milk
3 ounces vanilla dietary frozen
dessert
2 tablespoons thawed frozen dairy
whipped topping

1 teaspoon honey
¼ teaspoon each rum and brandy
extracts
Ground nutmeg

In blender container combine all ingredients except nutmeg; process until smooth. Pour into 2 champagne glasses and sprinkle each with dash nutmeg.

Each serving provides: ½ Fruit Exchange; ¾ Milk Exchange;
25 calories Optional Exchange
Per serving: 121 calories; 6 g protein; 2 g fat; 20 g carbohydrate; 226 mg calcium;
99 mg sodium; 3 mg cholesterol

Honey Shake ◗❸

WEEK 4 ◡ MAKES 1 SERVING, ABOUT 1 CUP

½ cup low-fat milk (2% milk fat)
3 ounces vanilla dietary frozen
dessert

½ teaspoon honey
¼ teaspoon vanilla extract

In blender container combine all ingredients and process until smooth, about 1 minute; serve immediately.

Each serving provides: 1 Fruit Exchange; 1 Milk Exchange;
30 calories Optional Exchange
Per serving: 176 calories; 8 g protein; 3 g fat; 29 g carbohydrate; 298 mg calcium;
131 mg sodium; 12 mg cholesterol

Mango Shake ◑

WEEK 4 ～ MAKES 2 SERVINGS, ABOUT 1 CUP EACH

½ very ripe small mango, pared
  and pitted
½ cup low-fat milk (2% milk fat)
1 tablespoon lemon juice
2 ice cubes

¼ cup thawed frozen dairy whipped
  topping

Garnish

Mint sprigs

Chill two 8-ounce glasses. In blender container combine mango, milk, and lemon juice and process until smooth; with motor running add ice cubes, 1 at a time, processing after each addition until all ice is dissolved. Add whipped topping and process just to combine. Pour half of mixture into each chilled glass, garnish, and serve immediately.

Each serving provides: ½ Fruit Exchange; ¼ Milk Exchange;
  35 calories Optional Exchange
Per serving: 90 calories; 2 g protein; 3 g fat; 14 g carbohydrate; 80 mg calcium;
  33 mg sodium; 5 mg cholesterol

Black Cow ◑◐

WEEK 1 ～ MAKES 1 SERVING

Chill a tall glass. Into chilled glass pour **1 cup diet root beer (0 calories)**; scoop **3 ounces vanilla dietary frozen dessert** into glass and top with **1 tablespoon prepared low-calorie whipped topping mix (6 calories per 2 tablespoons).** Serve with a straw and long-handled spoon.

Each serving provides: 1 Fruit Exchange; ½ Milk Exchange;
  3 calories Optional Exchange
Per serving: 103 calories; 4 g protein; 1 g fat; 20 g carbohydrate; 147 mg calcium;
  70 mg sodium; 2 mg cholesterol

Amaretto Float ◐❸

WEEK 1 ∿ MAKES 1 SERVING

In 8-ounce mug combine **½ cup hot black coffee** and **⅛ teaspoon almond extract;** add **3 ounces vanilla dietary frozen dessert,** stir, and serve immediately.

Each serving provides: 1 Fruit Exchange; ½ Milk Exchange
Per serving: 102 calories; 4 g protein; 1 g fat; 19 g carbohydrate; 149 mg calcium;
 70 mg sodium; 2 mg cholesterol

Sweet Carob Milk in a Mug ◐❸

WEEK 1 ∿ MAKES 1 SERVING

1½ teaspoons unsweetened carob   **¾ cup skim milk**
 powder   **⅛ teaspoon vanilla extract**
½ teaspoon granulated sugar   **Cinnamon stick**

In small saucepan combine carob powder and sugar; using a wire whisk, gradually stir in milk. Add vanilla and, over medium heat, bring mixture to a boil, beating with whisk until frothy; pour into a mug, add cinnamon stick stirrer, and serve immediately.

Each serving provides: ¾ Milk Exchange; 20 calories Optional Exchange
Per serving: 86 calories; 7 g protein; 1 g fat; 13 g carbohydrate; 247 mg calcium;
 97 mg sodium; 4 mg cholesterol

The Bread Exchange

WE'VE proved you can have bread without exchanging taste for "waist." However, for those who choose *not* to live by bread alone, we offer a variety of recipes using grains, crackers, and starchy vegetables, from lively breakfast beginnings like Strawberry-Topped Crispies or Oatmeal-Blueberry Muffins to Couscous Salad, Vegetable Risotto, and Baked Alaska.

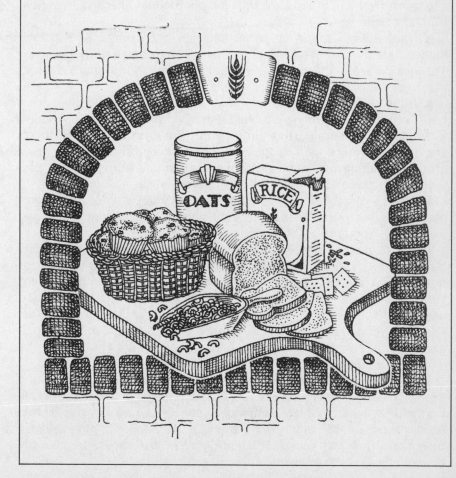

◗ Pointers on the Bread Exchange

Daily Exchanges

	WEEKS 1 AND 2	WEEKS 3 AND 4
Women	2 Exchanges	2 to 3 Exchanges
Men and Youths	4 Exchanges	4 to 5 Exchanges

◗ Items from the Bread Exchange supply B vitamins, carbohydrates, iron, and fiber.

◗ *Breads* may contain up to 80 calories per Exchange. You may select 2 slices of thin-sliced, high-fiber, diet, or low-calorie bread as 1 Bread Exchange if 2 slices are about 1 ounce and no more than 80 calories.

◗ *Bread and pasta* should be made with enriched or whole-grain flour; white *rice* should be enriched. Enriched products contain added vitamins and minerals (thiamin, niacin, riboflavin, and iron) to restore the nutrients lost during milling and processing. Whole-grain products contain the inner parts of the seed and kernel, which provide good sources of vitamins and minerals.

◗ Mixed vegetables that contain a *starchy vegetable* (e.g., corn, parsnips, peas, water chestnuts, etc.) should be considered a Bread Exchange; ½ cup is 1 Exchange.

◗ Use ¾ ounce uncooked weight as 1 Exchange for *Grain* selections (except barley, buckwheat groats, cracked wheat, and rice; for these use 1 ounce). Bear in mind that uncooked weight may not yield the indicated cooked amount; this is due to the cooking method used, length of cooking time, amount of water, and other variables. For most items the nutritional difference is negligible. For very small macaroni products (e.g., pastina, orzo, tubettini, etc.), use *only* the uncooked weight, then cook according to package directions.

◗ Three-fourths ounce cold *cereal* or ½ cup cooked hot cereal is 1 Bread Exchange. However, if you eat this amount of cereal at breakfast with at least ½ Milk Exchange, you may count it as 1 Protein Exchange; count the milk toward the Milk Exchange. If you eat more than this amount of cereal, the additional cereal should be counted toward the Bread Exchange.

▶ *Cereals* should not have descriptive names or titles indicating that they are sweetened; they may contain up to 110 calories per ounce and up to 8.5 grams of sucrose and other related sugars per ounce. However, some cereals with fruit contain 110 calories per ounce and may have a slightly higher sugar content due to the fruit (e.g., bran flakes with raisins cereal); this is permitted.

▶ You may prepare *popcorn* in a hot-air popper or by following package directions. Whichever you choose, 1 Exchange is 2 cups popped *or* 1 ounce unpopped.

BREAD EXCHANGE LISTS

Week 1

Selections	One Exchange
Biscuit, refrigerated	1 ounce
Bread, enriched or whole grain (any type)	1 slice (1 ounce)
Cereal, cold	¾ ounce
Cereal, hot	¾ ounce dry or ½ cup cooked
Cornflake Crumbs	¾ ounce (5 tablespoons)
Frankfurter Roll	½ (1 ounce)
Hamburger Roll	½ (1 ounce)
Melba Toast, all varieties	6 rounds or 4 slices
Pita Bread	1 ounce
Roll, fresh or refrigerated	1 ounce

Week 2

You may use all of the items listed under Week 1 and may add the following to your Exchange List.

Selections	One Exchange
Bagel, small	½ (1 ounce)
English Muffin	½ (1 ounce)
Pasta, enriched or whole grain (Macaroni, Noodles, Spaghetti, etc.)	½ cup cooked or ¾ ounce uncooked
Potato Flakes (Instant Mashed Potatoes)	⅓ cup flakes
Potato, sweet or white	3 ounces
Rice, enriched, brown, or wild	½ cup cooked or 1 ounce uncooked
Yam	3 ounces

Week 3

You may use all of the items listed under Weeks 1 and 2 and may add the following to your Exchange List.

Selections	One Exchange
Breadsticks	¾ ounce
Dry Beans, Lentils, Peas	2 ounces cooked or ¾ ounce uncooked
Graham Crackers (Cinnamon, Honey, Plain)	2 (2½-inch squares)
Popcorn, plain	2 cups popped or 1 ounce unpopped

Week 4

You may use all of the items listed under Weeks 1, 2, and 3 and may add the following to your Exchange List.

Selections	One Exchange
Breads	
Bread Crumbs, dried (plain or seasoned)	3 tablespoons
Taco Shell	1
Tortilla, Corn	1 (6-inch diameter)
Tostada Shell	1
Grains	
Barley	½ cup cooked or 1 ounce uncooked
Buckwheat Groats (Kasha)	½ cup cooked or 1 ounce uncooked
Cornmeal	½ cup cooked or ¾ ounce (2 tablespoons) uncooked
Couscous	½ cup cooked or ¾ ounce uncooked
Cracked Wheat (Bulgur)	½ cup cooked or 1 ounce uncooked
Flour, enriched or whole grain (sifted or unsifted)	3 tablespoons
Hominy, grits or whole	½ cup cooked or ¾ ounce uncooked
Millet	⅓ cup cooked or ¾ ounce uncooked

Selections	One Exchange
Crackers	
Crispbreads	¾ ounce
Matzo (Egg, Regular, Whole Wheat)	½ board
Matzo Cake Meal	3 tablespoons
Matzo Meal	3 tablespoons
Oyster Crackers	20
Saltines	6
Rice Cakes	2
Zwieback	2
Starchy Vegetables	
Chestnuts, small	6
Corn	
whole-kernel (fresh, frozen, or canned)	
cream-style (homemade without sugar and/or cream, or canned)	½ cup
ear	1 small (approximately 5 inches long)
Lima Beans, green	½ cup
Parsnips	½ cup
Peas, green	½ cup
Squash, winter	
(Acorn [Table Queen], Banana, Buttercup, Butternut, Calabaza, Cushaw, Des Moines, Gold Nugget, Hubbard, Peppercorn)	½ cup or 4 ounces
Succotash	½ cup
Water Chestnuts	3 ounces
Wonton Skins (Wrappers)	5 skins (3 x 3-inch squares)

Quick Corn Chowder ◑ ❸

WEEK 4 ～ MAKES 2 SERVINGS, ABOUT 1¼ CUPS EACH

For a thicker and sweeter soup, use canned cream-style corn instead of whole-kernel corn.

2 teaspoons margarine
½ cup each diced onion and celery
2 teaspoons all-purpose flour
1 cup each skim milk and drained
  canned whole-kernel corn
1 teaspoon imitation bacon bits,
  crushed

⅛ teaspoon each salt and powdered
  mustard
Dash white pepper

Garnish

Ground nutmeg

In 1-quart saucepan heat margarine until bubbly and hot; add onion and celery and sauté until onion is translucent. Add flour and cook, stirring constantly, for 1 minute; gradually stir in milk and, stirring constantly, bring to a boil. Reduce heat and cook, stirring, until mixture is smooth and thickened, 2 to 3 minutes; add remaining ingredients except nutmeg and, stirring constantly, cook until thoroughly combined and hot. Pour into 2 bowls and sprinkle each portion with dash nutmeg.

Each serving provides: 1 Bread Exchange; 1 Vegetable Exchange;
  1 Fat Exchange; ½ Milk Exchange; 15 calories Optional Exchange
Per serving: 219 calories; 9 g protein; 5 g fat; 39 g carbohydrate; 185 mg calcium;
  640 mg sodium; 2 mg cholesterol

Mixed Rice Soup ◑

WEEK 4 ～ MAKES 4 SERVINGS, ABOUT 1 CUP EACH

1 tablespoon plus 1 teaspoon
  margarine
¼ cup minced onion
1 tablespoon plus 1 teaspoon
  all-purpose flour
2¼ cups water
¼ cup dry sherry

3 packets instant chicken broth and
  seasoning mix
½ cup each cooked wild and
  long-grain white rice*
½ cup evaporated skimmed milk
1 tablespoon plus 1 teaspoon
  chopped fresh parsley

In 1½-quart saucepan heat margarine until bubbly and hot; add onion and sauté, stirring constantly, until translucent. Add flour and stir quickly to combine; gradually stir in water. Add sherry and broth mix and, stirring constantly, bring to a boil. Reduce heat to low and cook, stirring, until mixture thickens.

Remove pan from heat; add rice and milk and stir to combine. Return to low heat and cook until soup is heated through (*do not boil*); serve each portion garnished with 1 teaspoon chopped parsley.

Each serving provides: ½ Bread Exchange; 1 Fat Exchange; ¼ Milk Exchange;
  35 calories Optional Exchange
Per serving: 149 calories; 5 g protein; 4 g fat; 19 g carbohydrate; 107 mg calcium;
  709 mg sodium; 1 mg cholesterol

* This soup may be prepared with 1 cup cooked long-grain white rice instead of ½ cup white and ½ cup wild.
Per serving: 147 calories; 5 g protein; 4 g fat; 19 g carbohydrate; 110 mg calcium;
  708 mg sodium; 1 mg cholesterol

Pancakes ◖◗ ❸

WEEK 4 ◇ MAKES 2 SERVINGS, 3 PANCAKES EACH

½ cup plus 1 tablespoon all-purpose
  flour
½ cup skim milk
2 large eggs
2 teaspoons margarine
1 teaspoon superfine sugar

½ teaspoon double-acting baking
  powder
¼ teaspoon vanilla extract
Dash salt
2 tablespoons low-calorie pancake
  syrup (14 calories per tablespoon)

In blender container combine all ingredients except syrup; process at low speed until smooth, scraping down sides of container as necessary.

Spray 12-inch nonstick skillet with nonstick cooking spray and heat; pour ⅙ of batter (about 3 tablespoons) into hot skillet, forming a circle about 5 inches in diameter. Cook until bottom is browned and bubbles appear on surface; using a pancake turner, turn pancake over and cook until other side is browned. Remove pancake to serving platter and keep warm. Repeat procedure 5 more times, spraying pan each time and making 5 more pancakes. For each portion, serve 3 pancakes topped with 1 tablespoon syrup.

Each serving provides: 1 Protein Exchange; 1½ Bread Exchanges; 1 Fat Exchange;
  ¼ Milk Exchange; 25 calories Optional Exchange
Per serving: 292 calories; 12 g protein; 10 g fat; 38 g carbohydrate; 163 mg calcium;
  313 mg sodium; 275 mg cholesterol

Fruit 'n' Farina ◑

WEEK 4 〰 MAKES 1 SERVING

1 cup skim milk
2 dates, pitted and chopped
Dash salt
¾ ounce uncooked quick farina

½ teaspoon granulated sugar
¼ teaspoon vanilla extract
1 teaspoon margarine
Dash ground cinnamon

In small saucepan combine milk, dates, and salt and bring to a boil; gradually stir in farina. Add sugar and vanilla and cook, stirring constantly, until thickened, 2 to 3 minutes. Spoon into a bowl, stir in margarine, and sprinkle with cinnamon.

Each serving provides: 1 Bread Exchange;* 1 Fat Exchange; 1 Fruit Exchange; 1 Milk Exchange; 10 calories Optional Exchange
Per serving: 256 calories; 11 g protein; 5 g fat; 42 g carbohydrate; 421 mg calcium; 356 mg sodium; 5 mg cholesterol

* If this dish is eaten at breakfast, the farina may be counted as 1 Protein Exchange instead of 1 Bread Exchange.

Strawberry-Topped Crispies ◑

WEEK 1 〰 MAKES 2 SERVINGS

1 cup strawberries
Granulated sugar substitute to
   equal 2 teaspoons sugar
½ teaspoon grated orange peel

¼ cup plain low-fat yogurt
1½ ounces ready-to-eat oven-
   toasted rice cereal

In blender container combine berries, sugar substitute, and orange peel and process until pureed; stir in yogurt (do not process).* Pour ¾ ounce cereal into each of 2 bowls and top each portion with half of the strawberry puree.

Each serving provides: 1 Bread Exchange; ½ Fruit Exchange; ¼ Milk Exchange
Per serving: 128 calories; 3 g protein; 1 g fat; 27 g carbohydrate; 66 mg calcium; 284 mg sodium; 2 mg cholesterol

* Processing yogurt will thin it considerably; therefore, if thinner consistency is desired, process yogurt along with berries.

Hot Potato Salad with Vinegar Dressing ◐❸

WEEK 2 ⌒ MAKES 2 SERVINGS

---

2 teaspoons vegetable oil
¼ cup thinly sliced onion
2 teaspoons imitation bacon bits
2 tablespoons cider vinegar

1 teaspoon granulated sugar
Dash each salt and pepper
6 ounces peeled cooked potatoes,
 thinly sliced

In small skillet heat oil over medium heat; add onion slices and bacon bits and sauté until onion is translucent. Add vinegar, sugar, salt, and pepper and cook, stirring occasionally, until mixture starts to boil. Add potatoes and cook, stirring gently, until thoroughly heated. Serve hot.

Each serving provides: 1 Bread Exchange; ¼ Vegetable Exchange;
 1 Fat Exchange; 20 calories Optional Exchange
Per serving: 124 calories; 3 g protein; 5 g fat; 18 g carbohydrate; 17 mg calcium;
 163 mg sodium; 0 mg cholesterol

Potato and Pea Curry ❸

WEEK 4 ⌒ MAKES 2 SERVINGS

---

1 teaspoon margarine
4½ ounces pared potatoes, cut
 into ½-inch cubes
½ cup canned Italian tomatoes,
 crushed

¼ cup fresh or frozen peas
¾ teaspoon curry powder
⅛ teaspoon salt
½ cup water

In small skillet heat margarine until bubbly and hot; add potatoes and tomatoes and sauté for 5 minutes. Add peas, curry powder, and salt, then stir in water; cover and let simmer, stirring occasionally, until potatoes and peas are tender, about 25 minutes (if necessary, add more water to prevent sticking).

Each serving provides: 1 Bread Exchange; ½ Vegetable Exchange;
 ½ Fat Exchange
Per serving: 96 calories; 3 g protein; 2 g fat; 17 g carbohydrate; 18 mg calcium;
 243 mg sodium; 0 mg cholesterol
With frozen peas: 95 calories; 3 g protein; 2 g fat; 17 g carbohydrate;
 18 mg calcium; 268 mg sodium; 0 mg cholesterol

Potato Torte ❶

WEEK 4 ❦ MAKES 8 SERVINGS

May be served warm or at room temperature.

¾ cup all-purpose flour
3 tablespoons warm water
1 tablespoon plus 1 teaspoon
  vegetable oil
Salt
2 tablespoons plus 2 teaspoons
  margarine
1 cup chopped scallions (green
  onions)

12 ounces peeled cooked potatoes,
  mashed
1⅓ cups cottage cheese
4 eggs
¼ teaspoon freshly ground pepper
1 tablespoon plus 1 teaspoon grated
  Parmesan cheese

1. In small mixing bowl combine flour, water, oil, and dash salt; using hands, knead dough to form a smooth ball (dough should hold together but not be sticky; if necessary, add up to 1 more tablespoon warm water to adjust consistency). Wrap dough in plastic wrap and set aside while preparing filling (plastic wrap will prevent dough from cracking).

2. In small nonstick skillet heat margarine until bubbly and hot; add scallions and sauté over low heat until soft. Set aside.

3. In work bowl of food processor or in large mixing bowl combine mashed potatoes, cottage cheese, 3 eggs, 1 teaspoon salt, and the pepper; process, or beat with electric mixer, until smooth. Stir in sautéed scallions.

4. Preheat oven to 350°F. Between 2 sheets of wax paper roll dough, forming a rectangle about ⅛ inch thick; remove paper and fit dough into a 10 x 6 x 2-inch baking dish so that edges of dough extend slightly over sides of dish. Spoon potato mixture over dough and bring up sides of dough over edges of filling, leaving center uncovered.

5. In small bowl beat remaining egg with Parmesan cheese; pour over entire surface of torte. Bake until browned, 35 to 40 minutes. Remove from oven and let stand until set, about 15 minutes.

Each serving provides: 1 Protein Exchange; 1 Bread Exchange;
  ¼ Vegetable Exchange; 1½ Fat Exchanges; 5 calories Optional Exchange
Per serving: 213 calories; 10 g protein; 11 g fat; 18 g carbohydrate; 61 mg calcium;
  532 mg sodium; 143 mg cholesterol

Twice-Baked Creamy Potatoes ❸

WEEK 2 ⌇ MAKES 2 SERVINGS

2 potatoes (3 ounces each), well
   scrubbed and baked
1/4 cup plain low-fat yogurt

2 teaspoons margarine, melted
1 teaspoon chopped chives
Dash each salt and white pepper

Preheat oven to 350°F. Cut each baked potato in half lengthwise. Scoop pulp from 2 halves into bowl, leaving firm shells; reserve shells. Scoop pulp from remaining 2 halves, discarding skins; mash pulp until smooth. Add remaining ingredients and stir to combine. Spoon half of potato mixture into each reserved shell; transfer to baking sheet and bake until thoroughly heated, about 20 minutes.

Each serving provides: 1 Bread Exchange; 1 Fat Exchange; 1/4 Milk Exchange
Per serving: 117 calories; 3 g protein; 4 g fat; 17 g carbohydrate; 60 mg calcium;
   132 mg sodium; 2 mg cholesterol

Potato-Vegetable Sauté ❶❸

WEEK 2 ⌇ MAKES 2 SERVINGS

2 teaspoons vegetable oil
2 tablespoons diced onion
1/2 garlic clove, minced
6 ounces peeled cooked potatoes,
   cut into cubes

1/2 cup each cubed red and green
   bell peppers (1/2-inch cubes)
Dash each salt and pepper

In 8- or 9-inch skillet heat oil; add onion and garlic and sauté until onion is soft. Add potatoes and bell peppers and sauté, stirring, until potatoes are lightly browned and peppers are tender-crisp; stir in salt and pepper and sauté for 2 minutes longer.

Each serving provides: 1 Bread Exchange; 1 1/8 Vegetable Exchanges;
   1 Fat Exchange
Per serving: 122 calories; 3 g protein; 5 g fat; 18 g carbohydrate; 17 mg calcium;
   77 mg sodium; 0 mg cholesterol

Potato Rosettes ◐❸

WEEK 2 ∽ MAKES 4 SERVINGS, 2 ROSETTES EACH

8 ounces sliced pared potatoes,
  cooked and drained
2 tablespoons buttermilk
1 tablespoon plus 1 teaspoon each
  grated Parmesan cheese, divided,
  and margarine

1½ teaspoons each minced fresh
  parsley and frozen or chopped
  fresh chives
¼ teaspoon salt
Dash white pepper

Force potatoes through food mill or coarse sieve into a 1-quart mixing bowl; add milk, 1 tablespoon cheese, and the margarine and seasonings and combine thoroughly.

Spray baking sheet with nonstick cooking spray. Fit a pastry bag with a large rosette tube and fill bag with potato mixture; pipe out mixture onto sheet, forming 8 spiral cones, each about 2 inches in diameter (if pastry bag is not available, spoon potato mixture onto sprayed sheet, forming 8 mounds). Sprinkle each potato cone (or mound) with ⅛ teaspoon cheese and broil, about 6 inches from heat source, just until golden brown.

Each serving provides: ½ Bread Exchange; 1 Fat Exchange;
  25 calories Optional Exchange
Per serving: 88 calories; 2 g protein; 4 g fat; 10 g carbohydrate; 40 mg calcium;
  221 mg sodium; 2 mg cholesterol

Crispy Potato Slices ◐❸

WEEK 2 ∽ MAKES 2 SERVINGS

Using a vegetable brush, thoroughly scrub a **6-ounce potato.** Preheat oven to 450°F. Using a sharp knife, cut potato into ¼-inch-thick round slices, or slice in work bowl of food processor fitted with slicing disk. On nonstick baking sheet arrange potato slices in 1 layer and sprinkle with **dash each salt and white pepper.** Bake for 10 minutes; using a pancake turner, turn slices over, sprinkle with **dash each salt and white pepper,** and bake for 10 minutes longer.

Each serving provides: 1 Bread Exchange
Per serving: 65 calories; 2 g protein; 0.1 g fat; 15 g carbohydrate; 7 mg calcium;
  142 mg sodium; 0 mg cholesterol

Oven "Fried" Potatoes ❶

WEEK 2 ∾ MAKES 2 SERVINGS

Preheat oven to 350°F. Pare **6 ounces baking potatoes** and cut potatoes into thin strips. In medium bowl combine potato strips, **2 teaspoons vegetable oil,** and **dash each salt and pepper;** toss thoroughly so that all oil is used to coat potatoes.

On nonstick baking sheet arrange potatoes, leaving space between strips; bake for 20 minutes. Using a spatula, turn potatoes over; bake until browned and crisp, about 20 minutes longer.

Each serving provides: 1 Bread Exchange; 1 Fat Exchange
Per serving: 106 calories; 2 g protein; 5 g fat; 15 g carbohydrate; 7 mg calcium;
   67 mg sodium; 0 mg cholesterol

Twice-Baked Yams ❶

WEEK 2 ∾ MAKES 4 SERVINGS, ½ YAM EACH

2 yams (6 ounces each), well
   scrubbed and dried
2 teaspoons margarine, melted,
   divided

Dash each salt, white pepper, and
   ground nutmeg

1. Using tines of fork, pierce potatoes; transfer to oven rack and bake at 400°F. for 35 to 40 minutes.

2. Cut each potato in half lengthwise and scoop out pulp, being careful not to break skin; transfer pulp to work bowl of food processor and reserve skins.

3. Add 1 teaspoon melted margarine and the seasonings to processor and process until smooth. Spoon ¼ of mixture into each reserved potato skin and, using the tines of a fork, swirl a design in each. Sprinkle each portion with ¼ of the remaining melted margarine. Wrap and refrigerate until ready to bake or proceed immediately with Step 4.

4. Place unwrapped stuffed potatoes on nonstick baking sheet and bake at 350°F. until hot, 10 to 15 minutes; turn oven control to broil and broil potatoes until lightly browned, 2 to 3 minutes.

Each serving provides: 1 Bread Exchange; ½ Fat Exchange
Per serving: 103 calories; 2 g protein; 2 g fat; 20 g carbohydrate; 18 mg calcium;
   63 mg sodium; 0 mg cholesterol

"Fried" Yam Sticks ❶

WEEK 2 ∽ MAKES 2 SERVINGS

1 medium yam   ¼ teaspoon salt
1 teaspoon each margarine and
   vegetable oil

On baking sheet bake yam at 400°F. until just tender, 35 to 40 minutes (*do not overbake*); let yam cool, then peel and discard skin. Cut potato into 2 x ¼-inch sticks; weigh 6 ounces (any remaining yam can be frozen for use at another time).

In 9-inch skillet combine margarine and oil and heat until margarine is bubbly and hot; add yam sticks and cook over medium heat, turning frequently with pancake turner, until crispy outside and tender inside. Serve sprinkled with salt.

Each serving provides: 1 Bread Exchange; 1 Fat Exchange
Per serving: 136 calories; 1 g protein; 4 g fat; 23 g carbohydrate; 14 mg calcium;
   299 mg sodium; 0 mg cholesterol

Variation: Omit salt and sprinkle "fried" sticks with ½ teaspoon granulated brown sugar; add 5 calories Optional Exchange to Exchange Information.

Per serving: 140 calories; 1 g protein; 4 g fat; 25 g carbohydrate; 14 mg calcium;
   29 mg sodium; 0 mg cholesterol

Honey-Stuffed Sweet Potatoes ❶

WEEK 2 ∽ MAKES 2 SERVINGS, ½ POTATO EACH

Using a vegetable brush, scrub **one 6-ounce sweet potato** well; using tines of fork, pierce potato. Wrap potato in foil and place on baking sheet; bake at 400°F. until tender, 35 to 40 minutes. Remove foil and let potato stand until cool enough to handle.

Cut potato in half lengthwise; scoop out pulp into medium bowl and reserve shells. Add **1 teaspoon honey** and **dash each ground cinnamon and ground nutmeg** to bowl and, using electric mixer, beat until potato mixture is smooth and fluffy. Spoon half of mixture into each reserved shell. Bake on baking sheet at 350°F. until heated through, 15 to 20 minutes.

Each serving provides: 1 Bread Exchange; 10 calories Optional Exchange
Per serving: 108 calories; 1 g protein; 0.4 g fat; 25 g carbohydrate; 28 mg calcium;
   9 mg sodium; 0 mg cholesterol

Noodle Salad ❶

WEEK 2 ～ MAKES 2 SERVINGS

1 cup cooked egg bows (bow-tie
  noodles)
1 medium tomato, diced
¼ cup each diced celery and thinly
  sliced scallions (green onions)

1 tablespoon bottled red wine
  vinegar and oil salad dressing
Dash each salt and pepper

In salad bowl combine all ingredients; toss to coat with dressing. Cover and refrigerate for at least 1 hour. Toss again just before serving.

Each serving provides: 1 Bread Exchange; 1½ Vegetable Exchanges;
  1 Fat Exchange
Per serving: 158 calories; 4 g protein; 5 g fat; 24 g carbohydrate; 30 mg calcium;
  205 mg sodium; 25 mg cholesterol

Green and White Pasta Salad

WEEK 4 ～ MAKES 4 SERVINGS

1 garlic clove
Dash each salt and pepper
2 tablespoons plus 2 teaspoons
  olive oil
2 tablespoons chopped fresh basil
1 tablespoon chopped fresh parsley
1 teaspoon mashed drained canned
  anchovies (optional)

2 cups cooked small macaroni
  shells (1 cup regular macaroni
  and 1 cup spinach macaroni)
1 medium red bell pepper, seeded
  and chopped
¼ cup grated Parmesan cheese
8 pitted black olives, sliced

Using mortar and pestle or back of knife, crush garlic with salt and pepper. In small bowl combine garlic mixture with oil, basil, parsley, and if desired, anchovies; set aside.

    In salad bowl combine remaining ingredients; add garlic mixture and toss well to coat. Cover and refrigerate until chilled.

Each serving provides: 1 Bread Exchange; ½ Vegetable Exchange;
  2 Fat Exchanges; 45 calories Optional Exchange*
Per serving with anchovies: 224 calories; 7 g protein; 14 g fat; 18 g carbohydrate;
  133 mg calcium; 241 mg sodium; 16 mg cholesterol

* If anchovies are not used, decrease Optional Exchange to 40 calories.

Without anchovies: 219 calories; 6 g protein; 14 g fat; 18 g carbohydrate;
  130 mg calcium; 229 mg sodium; 16 mg cholesterol

Baked Macaroni and Cheese ❶

WEEK 4 ∽ MAKES 2 SERVINGS

2 teaspoons margarine, divided
1/2 cup chopped onion
1 1/2 cups cooked elbow macaroni
3 ounces Cheddar cheese, shredded
3/4 cup evaporated skimmed milk

1 large egg
1/4 teaspoon salt
Dash ground red pepper
1/4 teaspoon paprika

Preheat oven to 350°F. In small nonstick skillet heat 1 teaspoon margarine until bubbly and hot; add onion and sauté until translucent (*do not brown*).

In bottom of 1-quart casserole spread 3/4 cup macaroni; top with 1 1/2 ounces cheese, then half of the sautéed onion. Repeat layers. In small bowl combine milk, egg, salt, and pepper, mixing well; pour over macaroni mixture and sprinkle with paprika. Dot with remaining teaspoon margarine and bake until set, 20 to 25 minutes.

Each serving provides: 2 Protein Exchanges; 1 1/2 Bread Exchanges;
  1/2 Vegetable Exchange; 1 Fat Exchange; 3/4 Milk Exchange
Per serving: 451 calories; 25 g protein; 21 g fat; 39 g carbohydrate; 620 mg calcium;
  725 mg sodium; 185 mg cholesterol

Vegetables 'n' Pasta in Cheese Sauce

WEEK 4 ∽ MAKES 2 SERVINGS

1 tablespoon margarine
1 tablespoon plus 1 1/2 teaspoons
  all-purpose flour
1 cup skim milk
1/8 teaspoon each salt, paprika, and
  powdered mustard
Dash each ground nutmeg
  (optional) and white pepper

2 ounces Gruyère or Swiss cheese,
  shredded
2 cups cooked broccoli florets
1 cup each cooked pearl onions
  and small mushroom caps
3/4 cup cooked macaroni shells

In 2-quart saucepan heat margarine until bubbly and hot; add flour and cook over low heat, stirring constantly, for 3 minutes. Remove pan from heat and, using small wire whisk, gradually stir in milk and continue stirring until mixture is smooth; add seasonings and cook over medium heat, stirring constantly, until thickened. Reduce heat to low and cook for 10 minutes longer, stirring occasionally; add cheese and cook, stirring constantly, until cheese is melted. Add vegetables and macaroni and cook, stirring gently, until vegetables and shells are thoroughly coated and heated.

Each serving provides: 1 Protein Exchange; 1 Bread Exchange;
  4 Vegetable Exchanges; 1½ Fat Exchanges; ½ Milk Exchange
Per serving with Gruyère cheese: 374 calories; 21 g protein; 16 g fat;
  40 g carbohydrate; 537 mg calcium; 406 mg sodium; 34 mg cholesterol
With Swiss cheese: 363 calories; 21 g protein; 15 g fat; 41 g carbohydrate;
  523 mg calcium; 385 mg sodium; 29 mg cholesterol

Lasagna Rolls

WEEK 4 ⌒ MAKES 2 SERVINGS, 2 ROLLS EACH

½ cup part-skim ricotta cheese
1 egg, beaten
1 ounce shredded mozzarella
  cheese
2 tablespoons grated Parmesan
  cheese, divided
⅛ teaspoon each oregano leaves
  and basil leaves
Dash garlic powder

4 curly-edged lasagna noodles
  (12 x 3-inch pieces),* cooked
  according to package directions
  and drained
½ cup tomato sauce

Garnish
Italian (flat-leaf) parsley leaves

1. Preheat oven to 350°F. Spray 2 individual casseroles with non-stick cooking spray; set aside.

2. In small bowl combine ricotta cheese, egg, mozzarella cheese, 1 tablespoon Parmesan cheese, and the seasonings, mixing well.

3. Place cooked lasagna on a damp towel and spoon ¼ of the cheese mixture lengthwise along the center of each noodle; starting from narrow end, carefully roll each noodle to enclose filling.

4. Place 2 rolls in each sprayed casserole and spoon 2 tablespoons sauce over each roll; sprinkle each roll with ¾ teaspoon Parmesan cheese and bake until thoroughly heated, 35 to 40 minutes. Serve garnished with parsley.

Each serving provides: 2 Protein Exchanges; 1 Bread Exchange;
  1 Vegetable Exchange; 30 calories Optional Exchange
Per serving: 404 calories; 22 g protein; 15 g fat; 45 g carbohydrate; 343 mg calcium;
  556 mg sodium; 219 mg cholesterol

* Will yield about 1 cup cooked macaroni.

Spaghetti Pie

WEEK 4 ⌒ MAKES 4 SERVINGS

Crust

2 cups cooked thin spaghetti
1 ounce grated Parmesan cheese
1 egg, beaten

1 tablespoon plus 1 teaspoon
   margarine, softened

Filling

2/3 cup part-skim ricotta cheese
2 teaspoons margarine
1/2 cup each diced onion and red
   or green bell pepper
1 garlic clove, minced
6 ounces cooked ground beef,
   crumbled

1 cup canned whole tomatoes,
   drained and chopped (reserve
   liquid)
2 teaspoons tomato paste
2 ounces mozzarella cheese,
   shredded

To Prepare Crust: In medium bowl combine all ingredients for crust. Spray a 9-inch glass pie plate with nonstick cooking spray; spread spaghetti mixture over bottom and up sides of plate to form a crust.

To Prepare Filling and Pie: Preheat oven to 350°F. Carefully spread ricotta cheese over bottom of crust and set aside.

In 8-inch nonstick skillet heat margarine until bubbly and hot; add onion, bell pepper, and garlic and sauté until onion is translucent. Add beef, tomatoes, reserved liquid, and paste and cook, stirring constantly, until mixture is slightly thickened and thoroughly heated; spoon beef mixture over ricotta cheese and bake until pie is thoroughly heated, 20 to 25 minutes. Sprinkle pie with mozzarella cheese and bake until cheese is melted and just begins to brown, about 5 minutes; remove from oven and let stand for 5 minutes before cutting.

Each serving provides: 3 Protein Exchanges; 1 Bread Exchange;
   1 Vegetable Exchange; 1½ Fat Exchanges; 20 calories Optional Exchange
Per serving: 444 calories; 27 g protein; 26 g fat; 26 g carbohydrate; 316 mg calcium;
   454 mg sodium; 138 mg cholesterol

Spanish Rice ❶

Good!

WEEK 4 ⌇ MAKES 2 SERVINGS

2 teaspoons olive or vegetable oil
1 cup each diced green bell peppers
  and onions
1 small garlic clove, mashed
2 ounces uncooked regular long-
  grain rice
¾ cup water

½ cup tomato puree
2 packets instant chicken broth and
  seasoning mix

Garnish

Chopped fresh parsley

In 2½-quart saucepan heat oil until hot; add peppers, onions, and garlic and sauté until vegetables are soft, 3 to 4 minutes. Stir in remaining ingredients except parsley and bring to a boil. Reduce heat, cover, and let simmer, stirring occasionally, until rice is tender and liquid is absorbed, 20 to 25 minutes; serve sprinkled with parsley.

Each serving provides: 1 Bread Exchange; 3 Vegetable Exchanges;
  1 Fat Exchange; 10 calories Optional Exchange
Per serving: 229 calories; 6 g protein; 5 g fat; 41 g carbohydrate; 45 mg calcium;
  1,100 mg sodium; 0 mg cholesterol

Raisin-Rice Custard ❶

WEEK 4 ⌇ MAKES 2 SERVINGS, ABOUT ¾ CUP EACH

1 cup skim milk
1 envelope (two 4-ounce servings)
  reduced-calorie custard mix
½ cup cooked long-grain rice
¼ cup raisins

½ teaspoon vanilla extract

Garnish

Ground cinnamon or ground nutmeg

In small saucepan heat milk to a simmer; stirring constantly, add custard mix and cook until dissolved, at least 1 minute. Allow to cool for 3 to 5 minutes.

In bowl combine rice, raisins, and vanilla; stir into cooled custard. Into each of two 6-ounce custard cups or dessert dishes spoon half of mixture; garnish each portion with dash cinnamon or nutmeg. Cover and refrigerate until set.

Each serving provides: ½ Bread Exchange; 1 Fruit Exchange; 1 Milk Exchange
Per serving: 195 calories; 8 g protein; 0.1 g fat; 42 g carbohydrate; 16 mg calcium;
  107 mg sodium; 0 mg cholesterol

Vegetable Risotto ❶

WEEK 4 ∽ MAKES 2 SERVINGS

2 teaspoons peanut oil
¼ cup each diced onion and celery
2 tablespoons each diced carrot
 and green bell pepper
1 garlic clove, minced
1 cup water

1 ounce uncooked regular long-
 grain rice
1 packet instant chicken broth and
 seasoning mix
1½ teaspoons sesame seed,
 toasted

In small saucepan heat oil over medium heat; add onion, celery, carrot, green pepper, and garlic and sauté until vegetables are tender-crisp. Stir in water, rice, and broth mix and bring to a boil. Reduce heat, cover, and let simmer, stirring occasionally, until rice is tender and liquid is absorbed, 15 to 20 minutes. Stir in sesame seed and serve hot.

Each serving provides: ½ Bread Exchange; ¾ Vegetable Exchange;
 1 Fat Exchange; 20 calories Optional Exchange
Per serving: 126 calories; 3 g protein; 6 g fat; 16 g carbohydrate; 22 mg calcium;
 444 mg sodium; 0 mg cholesterol

Cheese Polenta

WEEK 4 ∽ MAKES 6 SERVINGS

4½ ounces (about ¾ cup) uncooked
 yellow cornmeal
½ cup cold water
3 cups boiling water

1 tablespoon margarine
1 ounce grated Parmesan cheese
2 ounces Swiss cheese, shredded

In 1½-quart saucepan combine cornmeal and cold water; add boiling water and cook over high heat, stirring constantly, until mixture comes to a boil and thickens. Reduce heat, cover, and cook, stirring occasionally, until mixture is smooth, 8 to 10 minutes.

 Preheat oven to 350°F. Spray shallow flameproof 2-quart casserole with nonstick cooking spray. Using a spatula, spread half of cooked cornmeal over bottom of casserole; dot with 1½ teaspoons margarine and sprinkle with ½ ounce Parmesan cheese. Repeat with remaining cornmeal, margarine, and Parmesan cheese; top with Swiss cheese and bake until cheese is hot and bubbly, 20 to 25 minutes. Turn oven control to broil and broil polenta until cheese is browned, about 1 minute.

Each serving provides: ½ Protein Exchange; 1 Bread Exchange; ½ Fat Exchange
Per serving: 151 calories; 6 g protein; 6 g fat; 17 g carbohydrate; 158 mg calcium;
   135 mg sodium; 12 mg cholesterol

Couscous Salad ❶

WEEK 4 ⌁ MAKES 4 SERVINGS

Serve with cheese or chilled cooked meat, poultry, or shrimp.

2 tablespoons olive or vegetable oil, divided
1 packet instant chicken broth and seasoning mix
¼ teaspoon each ground cinnamon and ground ginger
1½ cups water
3 ounces uncooked couscous (dry precooked semolina)
½ cup raisins
1 medium tomato, diced

½ cup each grated or shredded zucchini and carrot
¼ cup diced onion
1 tablespoon freshly squeezed lemon juice
¼ teaspoon salt
8 iceberg or romaine lettuce leaves

Garnish
Parsley sprigs

In 1-quart saucepan combine 1 tablespoon oil with the broth mix, cinnamon, and ginger; add water and bring to a boil. Stir in couscous and raisins; return mixture to a boil and cook until liquid is absorbed. Transfer to large bowl and let cool.

Add tomato, zucchini, carrot, onion, lemon juice, salt, and remaining tablespoon oil to cooled couscous mixture and toss to combine; cover and refrigerate for several hours to allow flavors to blend (may be refrigerated overnight).

Just before serving, toss salad again; serve on bed of lettuce leaves and garnish with parsley sprigs.

Each serving provides: 1 Bread Exchange; 1½ Vegetable Exchanges;
   1½ Fat Exchanges; 1 Fruit Exchange; 3 calories Optional Exchange
Per serving: 219 calories; 5 g protein; 7 g fat; 32 g carbohydrate; 32 mg calcium;
   355 mg sodium; 0 mg cholesterol

Roasted Chestnuts ❶

WEEK 4 ∽ MAKES 6 SERVINGS, 6 CHESTNUTS EACH

Can be used in desserts, stuffings, or for snacks.

Use: **36 small chestnuts**

To Roast: Using a sharp paring knife, cut an X through the flat side of each chestnut, partially penetrating top portion of nutmeat. Place in shallow baking pan and add just enough water to cover the bottom of pan. Roast at 350°F. until peel on cut side begins to separate, 30 to 40 minutes. Serve hot or peel and freeze for future use.

To Peel: Place roasted chestnuts in bowl of warm water. Peel off outer shell and brown inner skin, keeping chestnuts whole if possible.

To Freeze: Place peeled chestnuts in plastic freezer bags and seal securely, pressing out as much air as possible; freeze for future use.

Each serving provides: 1 Bread Exchange
Per serving: 105 calories; 2 g protein; 1 g fat; 23 g carbohydrate; 15 mg calcium;
    3 mg sodium; 0 mg cholesterol

Chestnut Stuffing ❶

WEEK 4 ∽ MAKES 6 SERVINGS

This stuffing may be prepared in advance and frozen for future use.

2 tablespoons vegetable oil
1 cup chopped onions
½ cup each chopped celery and red or green bell pepper
2 packets instant chicken broth and seasoning mix
2 garlic cloves, minced
2 cups sliced mushrooms

18 peeled Roasted Chestnuts (see above), chopped
1½ cups cooked long-grain rice
⅓ cup plus 2 teaspoons raisins
2 tablespoons chopped fresh parsley
¼ teaspoon ground allspice
Dash freshly ground pepper

In 12-inch skillet heat oil; add onions, celery, bell pepper, broth mix, and garlic and sauté over medium heat until vegetables are tender-crisp, about 5 minutes. Add mushrooms and continue sautéing for 5 minutes longer.

Transfer vegetable mixture to large mixing bowl; add remaining ingredients and toss well to combine. Transfer to shallow 2-quart casserole and bake at 325°F. for 20 minutes.

Each serving provides: 1 Bread Exchange; 1¼ Vegetable Exchanges;
 1 Fat Exchange; ½ Fruit Exchange; 5 calories Optional Exchange
Per serving: 195 calories; 4 g protein; 5 g fat; 35 g carbohydrate; 38 mg calcium;
 302 mg sodium; 0 mg cholesterol

Candied Acorn Squash Rings

WEEK 4 〜 MAKES 4 SERVINGS, 2 SQUASH RINGS EACH

2 small acorn squash (about 12 ounces each) *
¼ teaspoon each salt and pepper

1 tablespoon plus 1 teaspoon each firmly packed brown sugar and margarine
1 tablespoon water

Preheat oven to 350°F. Trim off ends of each squash. Cut each squash crosswise into 4 rings, each about ¾ inch wide; discard seeds and membranes from slices. On nonstick jelly-roll pan arrange rings in a single layer and sprinkle with salt and pepper; cover with foil and bake until squash is slightly tender, 35 to 40 minutes.

In small saucepan combine sugar, margarine, and water and cook over medium heat until bubbly. Remove squash from oven, uncover, and spoon an equal amount of sugar mixture over each squash ring; return to oven and bake, uncovered, until squash is tender, 10 to 15 minutes, basting occasionally with pan juices. Transfer rings to serving platter and top with any remaining pan juices.

Each serving provides: 1 Bread Exchange; 1 Fat Exchange;
 20 calories Optional Exchange
Per serving: 109 calories; 2 g protein; 4 g fat; 19 g carbohydrate; 47 mg calcium;
 181 mg sodium; 0 mg cholesterol

* A 12-ounce acorn squash will yield about 1 cup cooked squash.

Lima and Pepper Sauté ◑

WEEK 4 〜 MAKES 2 SERVINGS

1 teaspoon each olive oil and
 margarine
½ garlic clove, minced
½ cup each diced onion and red
 bell pepper
1 cup frozen green lima beans,
 thawed to room temperature

1½ teaspoons chopped fresh basil
 or ½ teaspoon dried
1 teaspoon dry white wine
⅛ teaspoon salt
Dash pepper, or to taste

In 12-inch nonstick skillet combine oil and margarine and heat until margarine is bubbly and hot; add garlic and sauté for 1 minute (*be careful not to burn*). Add onion and red pepper and sauté until onion is translucent; add remaining ingredients, stirring to combine. Reduce heat, cover, and cook, stirring occasionally, for about 15 minutes or until vegetables are done to taste.

Each serving provides: 1 Bread Exchange; 1 Vegetable Exchange; 1 Fat Exchange;
 3 calories Optional Exchange
Per serving: 163 calories; 8 g protein; 5 g fat; 24 g carbohydrate; 66 mg calcium;
 172 mg sodium; 0 mg cholesterol

Hot Cross Buns ❶

WEEK 4 ∽ MAKES 12 SERVINGS, 1 BUN EACH

1 cup plus 1 tablespoon skim milk, divided
1/3 cup plus 2 teaspoons margarine, divided
1/4 cup granulated sugar
2 packets (1/4 ounce each) active dry yeast or 2 cakes (0.6 ounce each) compressed yeast
2 1/4 cups all-purpose flour

1/3 cup plus 2 teaspoons raisins, soaked in warm water until plumped, then drained
1 teaspoon grated orange peel
2 tablespoons confectioners' sugar, sifted
1 teaspoon water
1/8 teaspoon grated lemon peel (optional)

1. In small saucepan combine 1 cup milk and 1/3 cup margarine and heat over low heat until slightly warmed, *not hot* (margarine need not be melted).

2. In work bowl of food processor or in medium mixing bowl combine sugar and yeast; add flour and gradually pour in warm milk mixture. Process, or beat lightly with electric mixer, until thoroughly combined (dough will be sticky); stir in raisins and orange peel.

3. Shape dough into 12 equal balls, about 2 1/4 ounces each, and arrange on nonstick baking sheet, leaving a space of about 2 inches between each; cover with a towel, place in a draft-free area, and allow to rise until buns are doubled in volume, about 1 hour.

4. Preheat oven to 350°F. In metal measuring cup, or other small flameproof container, melt remaining 2 teaspoons margarine; add remaining tablespoon milk and stir to combine. Brush mixture evenly over each bun, then using a sharp knife, cut a cross in the top of each; bake until buns are golden brown, about 25 minutes. Using a spatula, remove buns to a wire rack; let cool thoroughly.

5. In small bowl combine confectioners' sugar, water, and if desired, lemon peel; drizzle icing evenly over each bun in the shape of a cross.

Each serving provides: 1 Bread Exchange; 1 1/2 Fat Exchanges; 50 calories Optional Exchange
Per serving: 184 calories; 4 g protein; 6 g fat; 29 g carbohydrate; 36 mg calcium; 80 mg sodium; 0.4 mg cholesterol

Apple Crumb Muffins ❷

WEEK 4　～　MAKES 12 SERVINGS, 1 MUFFIN EACH

Muffins freeze well so they can be prepared in advance and kept for future use; thaw at room temperature.

Batter

2 cups all-purpose flour
¼ cup granulated sugar
1 tablespoon double-acting baking
　powder
1 teaspoon apple pie spice

1 cup skim milk
1 small Golden Delicious apple,
　cored, pared, and shredded
¼ cup margarine, melted
1 egg

Crumb Topping

¼ cup all-purpose flour
2 tablespoons plus 1 teaspoon
　granulated sugar

2 tablespoons margarine, melted
⅛ teaspoon ground cinnamon

To Prepare Batter: Line twelve 2½-inch-diameter muffin pan cups with paper baking cups and set aside. Preheat oven to 400°F.

In mixing bowl combine first 4 ingredients. In 2-cup measure or bowl combine milk, apple, margarine, and egg; pour into dry ingredients and stir until combined (*do not beat or overmix; batter should be lumpy*). Fill each baking cup with an equal amount of batter (each will be about ⅔ full).

To Prepare Topping and Bake: In small bowl combine all ingredients for topping, stirring until thoroughly combined; sprinkle an equal amount of topping over each muffin and bake for 15 to 20 minutes (until muffins are golden brown and a toothpick, inserted in center, comes out dry). Remove muffins to wire rack and let cool.

Each serving provides: 1 Bread Exchange; 1½ Fat Exchanges;
　50 calories Optional Exchange
Per serving: 183 calories; 4 g protein; 6 g fat; 28 g carbohydrate; 88 mg calcium;
　186 mg sodium; 23 mg cholesterol

Apple-Orange Spice Muffins

WEEK 4 ∽ MAKES 4 SERVINGS, 2 MUFFINS EACH

3/4 cup all-purpose flour
1 1/2 teaspoons double-acting baking
  powder
1/2 teaspoon ground cinnamon
1/4 teaspoon baking soda
Dash each salt, ground nutmeg,
  and ground cloves
1/3 cup instant nonfat dry milk
  powder
2 tablespoons plus 2 teaspoons
  margarine

1 tablespoon plus 1 teaspoon firmly
  packed brown sugar
1 large egg, separated
2 small apples, cored, pared, and
  grated
2 tablespoons raisins
1 tablespoon plus 1 teaspoon
  thawed frozen concentrated apple
  juice (no sugar added)
1 teaspoon grated orange peel
Dash cream of tartar

Preheat oven to 375°F. Into small bowl sift together flour, baking powder, cinnamon, baking soda, salt, nutmeg, and cloves; stir in milk powder and set aside.

In mixing bowl cream margarine with sugar; add egg yolk and, using electric mixer on medium speed, beat until thick and creamy. Add apples, raisins, juice, and orange peel and stir to combine; add flour mixture and beat until well blended.

In separate bowl, using clean beaters and mixer on high speed, beat egg white with cream of tartar until stiff but not dry; fold into batter. Spray eight 2 1/2-inch-diameter nonstick muffin pan cups with nonstick cooking spray; spoon 1/8 of batter into each sprayed cup (each will be about 2/3 full) and partially fill remaining cups with water (this will prevent pan from burning and/or warping). Bake 20 to 25 minutes (until cake tester, inserted in center, comes out clean). Remove pan from oven and carefully drain off water (remember, it will be boiling hot); remove muffins to wire rack and let cool.

Each serving provides: 1 Bread Exchange; 2 Fat Exchanges; 1 Fruit Exchange;
  1/4 Milk Exchange; 40 calories Optional Exchange
Per serving: 267 calories; 6 g protein; 9 g fat; 40 g carbohydrate; 177 mg calcium;
  343 mg sodium; 70 mg cholesterol

Bran Muffins ◖❸

WEEK 4 ∽ MAKES 12 SERVINGS, 1 MUFFIN EACH

Muffins freeze well so they can be prepared in advance and kept for future use; thaw at room temperature.

3 ounces ready-to-eat bran flakes with dates or bran flakes with raisins cereal
1½ cups whole wheat flour
¼ cup granulated sugar
1 tablespoon double-acting baking powder

1 cup skim milk
⅓ cup plus 2 teaspoons unsalted margarine, melted
1 egg, beaten

Preheat oven to 400°F. In medium bowl, using a fork, combine cereal, flour, sugar, and baking powder. In 2-cup measure thoroughly blend milk, margarine, and egg; add milk mixture to dry mixture and, using a fork, stir to combine (*do not overmix or beat*). Using a 12-cup non-stick muffin pan that has 2½-inch-diameter cups,* spoon an equal amount of batter into each cup; bake for 15 to 20 minutes (until muffins are browned and a toothpick, inserted in center of muffin, comes out dry). Remove muffins to wire rack to cool.

Each serving provides: 1 Bread Exchange; 1½ Fat Exchanges;
    35 calories Optional Exchange
Per serving with bran flakes with dates cereal: 156 calories; 4 g protein; 7 g fat;
    21 g carbohydrate; 86 mg calcium; 171 mg sodium; 23 mg cholesterol

With bran flakes with raisins cereal: 153 calories; 4 g protein; 7 g fat;
    21 g carbohydrate; 89 mg calcium; 171 mg sodium; 23 mg cholesterol

* If nonstick pan is not available, spray pan with nonstick cooking spray.

Corn Muffins ◑

WEEK 4 ⌒ MAKES 12 SERVINGS, 1 MUFFIN EACH

1 cup less 1 tablespoon all-purpose
  flour
5¼ ounces (1 cup less 2
  tablespoons) uncooked yellow
  cornmeal
2 tablespoons granulated sugar
1 tablespoon plus 1 teaspoon
  double-acting baking powder

1 teaspoon salt
1 cup skim milk
¼ cup margarine, melted, or
  vegetable oil
1 egg, beaten

Preheat oven to 425°F. Spray a 12-cup muffin pan that has 2½-inch diameter cups with nonstick cooking spray; set aside.

In bowl combine flour, cornmeal, sugar, baking powder, and salt. In separate bowl combine milk, margarine (or oil), and egg; pour milk mixture into dry mixture, stirring to combine. Fill each muffin pan cup with an equal amount of batter (each cup will be about ⅔ full); bake for 15 to 20 minutes (until muffins are golden brown and a toothpick, inserted in center, comes out dry). Remove muffins to wire rack to cool.

Each serving provides: 1 Bread Exchange; 1 Fat Exchange;
  25 calories Optional Exchange
Per serving with margarine: 138 calories; 3 g protein; 5 g fat; 21 g carbohydrate;
  101 mg calcium; 377 mg sodium; 23 mg cholesterol
With oil: 146 calories; 3 g protein; 5 g fat; 21 g carbohydrate; 99 mg calcium;
  333 mg sodium; 23 mg cholesterol

Oatmeal-Blueberry Muffins

WEEK 4 〜 MAKES 12 SERVINGS, 1 MUFFIN EACH

Muffins freeze well so they can be prepared in advance and kept for future use; thaw at room temperature.

1 cup plus 2 tablespoons all-purpose
  flour
6 ounces uncooked quick or
  old-fashioned oats
1/3 cup plus 1 tablespoon
  granulated sugar, divided
1 tablespoon double-acting baking
  powder

1/2 teaspoon salt
1 cup skim milk
1 egg
1/4 cup vegetable oil
1 cup blueberries*
1 teaspoon ground cinnamon

1. Preheat oven to 425°F. Line twelve 2½-inch-diameter muffin pan cups with paper baking cups; set aside.

2. In medium mixing bowl combine flour, oats, 1/3 cup sugar, and the baking powder and salt.

3. In small bowl, using a fork, combine milk, egg, and oil; add to flour mixture and beat until all ingredients are blended. Fold in blueberries. Pour an equal amount of batter into each baking cup (each will be about 2/3 full).

4. Combine remaining tablespoon of sugar with the cinnamon and sprinkle evenly over muffins; bake for 20 to 25 minutes (until lightly browned and a toothpick, inserted in center, comes out dry).

Each serving provides: 1 Bread Exchange; 1 Fat Exchange;
  65 calories Optional Exchange
Per serving: 188 calories; 5 g protein; 6 g fat; 29 g carbohydrate; 92 mg calcium;
  210 mg sodium; 23 mg cholesterol

* If fresh berries are not available, 1 cup frozen (no sugar added) may be substituted; thaw before using.
Per serving: 187 calories; 5 g protein; 6 g fat; 28 g carbohydrate; 92 mg calcium;
  210 mg sodium; 23 mg cholesterol

Sugar Muffins ◐❸

WEEK 4 ⌒ MAKES 4 SERVINGS, 2 MUFFINS EACH

¾ cup cake flour
3 tablespoons granulated sugar,
  divided
1½ teaspoons double-acting baking
  powder
2 tablespoons plus 2 teaspoons
  unsalted margarine, softened,
  divided

2 eggs, beaten
¼ cup evaporated skimmed milk
1 teaspoon vanilla extract

Preheat oven to 425°F. In bowl combine flour, 2 tablespoons sugar, and the baking powder; with a pastry blender, or 2 knives used scissors-fashion, cut in 2 tablespoons plus 1 teaspoon margarine until mixture resembles coarse meal. In small bowl combine eggs, milk, and vanilla; add to flour mixture and stir to blend, forming a thin batter.

Spray eight 2½-inch-diameter muffin pan cups with nonstick cooking spray; divide batter into sprayed cups (each will be about half full). Partially fill empty cups with water (this will prevent pan from burning and/or warping). Bake until muffins are golden brown, about 10 minutes.

While muffins are baking, in small metal measuring cup or other small flameproof container melt remaining teaspoon margarine. Remove baked muffins from oven and immediately brush each with ⅛ of the melted margarine; sprinkle each with ⅛ of the remaining tablespoon sugar and return to oven for 2 minutes longer. Remove pan from oven and carefully drain off water (remember, it will be boiling hot); remove muffins to wire rack and let cool.

Each serving provides: ½ Protein Exchange; 1 Bread Exchange; 2 Fat Exchanges;
  55 calories Optional Exchange
Per serving: 226 calories; 6 g protein; 11 g fat; 26 g carbohydrate; 142 mg calcium;
  207 mg sodium; 138 mg cholesterol

Lemon Cookies ◑❸

WEEK 4 ◇ MAKES 4 SERVINGS, 2 COOKIES EACH

1 tablespoon plus 2 teaspoons
  margarine
2½ teaspoons granulated sugar
1½ teaspoons freshly squeezed
  lemon juice

¼ teaspoon grated lemon peel
⅓ cup plus 2 teaspoons cake flour

Preheat oven to 300°F. In small mixing bowl, using electric mixer, combine all ingredients except flour, beating until light and smooth; add flour and beat until flour has been incorporated and mixture forms sticky batter.

Using wet hands, roll batter into 8 small balls (about 1 tablespoon batter for each ball); arrange balls on nonstick baking sheet, leaving about 2 inches between each. Using tines of fork, lightly press each ball down to flatten, then press down lightly in opposite direction to create a checkerboard pattern. Transfer baking sheet to lowest oven rack and bake until edges of cookies are lightly browned, about 15 minutes; using a spatula, remove cookies to wire rack to cool.

Each serving provides: ½ Bread Exchange; 1 Fat Exchange;
  25 calories Optional Exchange
Per serving: 93 calories; 1 g protein; 5 g fat; 12 g carbohydrate; 4 mg calcium;
  56 mg sodium; 0 mg cholesterol

Coconut Dreams ❸

WEEK 4 ∾ MAKES 16 SERVINGS, 2 COOKIES EACH

These cookies may be frozen for future use; thaw at room temperature.

⅔ cup margarine
¼ cup granulated sugar
1½ teaspoons grated lemon peel
1½ cups all-purpose flour
3 ounces (about ½ cup) uncooked
   instant farina

Cold water
1 teaspoon lemon juice
1 egg white
½ cup shredded coconut

1. Preheat oven to 325°F. In medium mixing bowl cream margarine with sugar and lemon peel; add flour, cereal, 1 tablespoon water, and the lemon juice and mix until thoroughly combined (dough should just hold together but not be too sticky; if necessary, add up to 1 more tablespoon water to adjust consistency).

2. In small bowl combine egg white with 1 teaspoon water; set aside.

3. Form dough into a narrow loaf and cut into 32 equal pieces; roll each piece into a round, then flatten with palm of hand.

4. Dip one side of each flattened round into egg white mixture, then press same side into shredded coconut; arrange rounds coconut-side up on nonstick baking sheet and bake until golden brown, 20 to 25 minutes. Using a spatula, remove cookies to wire rack to cool.

Each serving provides: ½ Bread Exchange; 2 Fat Exchanges;
  50 calories Optional Exchange
Per serving: 155 calories; 2 g protein; 9 g fat; 17 g carbohydrate; 32 mg calcium;
  106 mg sodium; 0 mg cholesterol

Rice-Crisp Cookies ❶❸

WEEK 4 ❧ MAKES 4 SERVINGS, 3 COOKIES EACH

1 tablespoon granulated sugar	1 egg, beaten
2 teaspoons unsalted margarine, softened	3 tablespoons self-rising flour, sifted
½ teaspoon vanilla extract	¾ ounce ready-to-eat oven-toasted rice cereal

Preheat oven to 350°F. In mixing bowl combine sugar, margarine, and vanilla and mix until creamy; add egg and beat well. Blend in sifted flour, then fold in cereal until just combined (*do not overmix or beat*). Onto nonstick cookie sheet drop batter by heaping teaspoonsful, forming 12 cookies and leaving a space of about 2 inches between each; using moistened tines of a fork, flatten each cookie slightly. Bake until cookies are golden brown, 8 to 10 minutes. Using a spatula, remove cookies to wire rack to cool.

Each serving provides: ½ Bread Exchange; ½ Fat Exchange;
35 calories Optional Exchange
Per serving: 93 calories; 2 g protein; 3 g fat; 12 g carbohydrate; 24 mg calcium;
146 mg sodium; 69 mg cholesterol

Variations:

1. *Lemon-Crisp Cookies*—Add 2 teaspoons each grated lemon peel and lemon juice to batter before adding cereal.
Per serving: 94 calories; 2 g protein; 3 g fat; 13 g carbohydrate; 26 mg calcium;
147 mg sodium; 69 mg cholesterol

2. *Raisin Cookies*—Add ¼ cup raisins to batter before adding cereal; add ½ Fruit Exchange to Exchange Information.
Per serving: 120 calories; 3 g protein; 3 g fat; 20 g carbohydrate; 29 mg calcium;
147 mg sodium; 69 mg cholesterol

3. *Spiced Raisin Cookies*—When preparing Raisin Cookies, add ½ teaspoon ground cinnamon and dash ground ginger to sifted flour.
Per serving: 121 calories; 3 g protein; 3 g fat; 20 g carbohydrate; 32 mg calcium;
148 mg sodium; 69 mg cholesterol

4. *Chocolate Cookies*—Decrease sugar to 2 teaspoons. Add 1 teaspoon chocolate syrup to batter before adding cereal.
Per serving: 93 calories; 2 g protein; 3 g fat; 12 g carbohydrate; 24 mg calcium;
147 mg sodium; 69 mg cholesterol

Vanilla-Strawberry Cookies ❶

WEEK 4 ～ MAKES 4 SERVINGS, 3 COOKIES EACH

⅓ cup plus 2 teaspoons all-purpose
flour
¼ teaspoon double-acting baking
powder
1 tablespoon plus 1 teaspoon
margarine
1 tablespoon granulated sugar

½ teaspoon vanilla extract
¼ teaspoon grated lemon peel
1 tablespoon ice water
2 teaspoons reduced-calorie
strawberry spread (16 calories
per 2 teaspoons)

Onto sheet of wax paper or a paper plate sift together flour and
baking powder; set aside. In small bowl cream margarine with sugar;
add vanilla and lemon peel and stir to combine. Add sifted flour and
ice water and mix to form dough.

Preheat oven to 375°F. Between 2 sheets of wax paper roll dough
to about ⅛-inch thickness; remove top sheet of paper and, using a
2½-inch round cookie cutter, cut out cookies, placing cookies on
nonstick baking sheet. Form scraps of dough into ball and repeat
rolling and cutting procedures until all dough has been used (should
yield 12 cookies). Bake for 10 to 12 minutes; using a spatula, remove
cookies to wire rack to cool. Top center of each cooled cookie with
an equal amount of spread.

Each serving provides: ½ Bread Exchange; 1 Fat Exchange;
20 calories Optional Exchange
Per serving: 96 calories; 1 g protein; 4 g fat; 13 g carbohydrate; 16 mg calcium;
70 mg sodium; 0 mg cholesterol

Orange Sponge Cake ❶

WEEK 4 ～ MAKES 12 SERVINGS

Make this ahead and keep in the freezer for that special meal when you'd like to serve a delicious dessert but don't have time to fuss; freeze whole or sliced. Thaw at room temperature.

1 cup plus 2 tablespoons cake flour
½ teaspoon salt
⅓ cup plus 2 teaspoons thawed
  frozen concentrated orange juice
  (no sugar added)

2 teaspoons grated orange peel
6 large eggs, separated (at room
  temperature)
¼ teaspoon cream of tartar
¼ cup granulated sugar

1. Onto sheet of wax paper or a paper plate sift together flour and salt; set aside.

2. In 1-cup measure combine juice with enough water to make ½ cup liquid; add orange peel and set aside.

3. Preheat oven to 350°F. In medium mixing bowl, using electric mixer on high speed, beat egg yolks until thick and lemon colored; using mixer on low speed, alternately beat in sifted flour and juice mixture.

4. In large mixing bowl combine egg whites and cream of tartar and, using clean beaters, beat at high speed until soft peaks form. Gradually beat in sugar, beating until sugar is dissolved and stiff peaks form.

5. Using a wire whisk, fold ¼ of beaten whites into yolk mixture; pour yolk mixture into remaining beaten whites and fold gently just until evenly blended. Turn batter into a 10-inch tube pan that has a removable bottom;* run a knife through batter to release air bubbles.

6. Bake 35 to 40 minutes (until cake is golden brown and springs back when touched with tip of finger). To cool, invert cake pan and place on neck of a bottle; let stand for about 1 hour.

7. Remove sides of pan;* to serve, cut into 12 equal slices.

Each serving provides: ½ Protein Exchange; ½ Bread Exchange;
  35 calories Optional Exchange
Per serving: 110 calories; 4 g protein; 3 g fat; 17 g carbohydrate; 20 mg calcium;
  126 mg sodium; 137 mg cholesterol

* If tube pan with removable bottom is not available, a solid tube pan may be used. To remove cake from pan, run a spatula around sides of pan and around tube to loosen cake.

Pound Cake ❶

WEEK 4 ~ MAKES 8 SERVINGS

¾ cup all-purpose flour
1½ teaspoons double-acting baking
  powder
¼ cup each unsalted margarine
  and granulated sugar

2 eggs
2 teaspoons vanilla extract

Spray a 7⅜ x 3⅝ x 2¼-inch loaf pan with nonstick cooking spray; set aside. Onto sheet of wax paper or a paper plate sift together flour and baking powder; set aside.

Preheat oven to 350°F. In mixing bowl, using electric mixer, cream margarine; gradually add sugar and beat until light and fluffy. Beat in eggs, 1 at a time, beating after each addition until thoroughly combined; beat in vanilla, then gradually beat in sifted ingredients, beating just until blended. Pour batter into sprayed loaf pan and bake 20 to 30 minutes (until cake is golden brown and a cake tester, inserted in center of loaf, comes out clean). Transfer pan to wire rack and let cake cool in pan. To serve, cut into 8 equal slices.

Each serving provides: ½ Bread Exchange; 1½ Fat Exchanges;
  50 calories Optional Exchange
Per serving: 142 calories; 3 g protein; 7 g fat; 16 g carbohydrate; 48 mg calcium;
  95 mg sodium; 69 mg cholesterol

Serving Suggestion: Toast 1 slice cake and place on serving plate; top with a 3-ounce scoop of vanilla dietary frozen dessert and ½ teaspoon chocolate syrup. Add 1 Fruit Exchange and ½ Milk Exchange to Exchange Information and increase Optional Exchange to 60 calories.

Per serving: 249 calories; 7 g protein; 8 g fat; 37 g carbohydrate; 196 mg calcium;
  165 mg sodium; 70 mg cholesterol

Coconut Custard Pie ●

WEEK 4 ～ MAKES 8 SERVINGS

Crust

¾ cup all-purpose flour
¼ teaspoon salt
2 tablespoons plus 2 teaspoons
 margarine
¼ cup plain low-fat yogurt

Filling

2 cups skim milk
2 envelopes (two 4-ounce servings
 each) reduced-calorie custard
 mix
2 tablespoons plus 2 teaspoons
 shredded coconut, toasted

To Prepare Crust: In mixing bowl combine flour and salt; with pastry blender, or 2 knives used scissors-fashion, cut in margarine until mixture resembles coarse meal. Add yogurt and mix thoroughly to form dough. Form dough into a ball; wrap in plastic wrap and refrigerate for at least 1 hour (may be kept in refrigerator for up to 3 days).

Preheat oven to 400°F. Between 2 sheets of wax paper roll dough, forming a 10-inch circle about ⅛ inch thick. Carefully remove paper and fit dough into a 9-inch pie plate; fold under any dough that extends beyond edge of plate and flute or crimp edge. Using a fork, prick bottom and sides of pie shell; bake until lightly browned, 15 to 20 minutes. Remove pie plate to wire rack and let cool; while crust is cooling, prepare filling.

To Prepare Filling: In 1-quart saucepan heat milk just to a simmer (*do not boil*); add custard mix and cook over low heat, stirring constantly, until powder is completely dissolved, about 1 minute. Stir in coconut and remove from heat; let cool slightly, then pour into cooled crust. Cover and refrigerate until firm, about 1 hour.

Each serving provides: ½ Bread Exchange; 1 Fat Exchange; ½ Milk Exchange;
 15 calories Optional Exchange
Per serving: 130 calories; 4 g protein; 5 g fat; 17 g carbohydrate; 92 mg calcium;
 169 mg sodium; 2 mg cholesterol

Baked Alaska ❶

WEEK 4 ⌁ MAKES 4 SERVINGS

12 ounces chocolate dietary frozen
  dessert, softened
2 egg whites (at room temperature)
Dash cream of tartar, sifted

3 tablespoons confectioners' sugar,
  sifted
8 graham crackers (2½-inch
  squares)

Spray a 7⅜ x 3⅝ x 2¼-inch loaf pan with nonstick cooking spray and line bottom and sides of pan with wax paper. Pack frozen dessert into prepared pan, cover with plastic wrap, and freeze until firm.

In small bowl, using electric mixer, beat egg whites with cream of tartar until soft peaks form; gradually add sugar and continue beating until egg whites are stiff but not dry.

Preheat broiler. Remove frozen dessert from pan onto a flameproof serving plate; remove wax paper. Arrange graham crackers along sides and over top of loaf; spread beaten egg whites over entire surface of loaf and broil until egg whites are browned, 1 to 2 minutes. Serve immediately.

Each serving provides: 1 Bread Exchange; 1 Fruit Exchange; ½ Milk Exchange;
  55 calories Optional Exchange
Per serving: 183 calories; 7 g protein; 2 g fat; 35 g carbohydrate; 154 mg calcium;
  188 mg sodium; 2 mg cholesterol

Cinnamon Sweet Popcorn ◐❶

WEEK 3 ∾ MAKES 8 SERVINGS, 1 CUP EACH

4 ounces unpopped popping corn
(about ½ cup)
¼ cup water

3 tablespoons vegetable oil
⅓ cup granulated sugar
Dash ground cinnamon

In small bowl combine popping corn and water; let soak for about 10 minutes. In 4-quart saucepan heat oil; add sugar, stirring to combine. Add popping corn and water and partially cover pan, leaving just enough space for steam to escape; cook, shaking pan over burner, until all corn has popped. Remove from heat, sprinkle with cinnamon, and toss to coat.

Each serving provides: ½ Bread Exchange; 1 Fat Exchange;
45 calories Optional Exchange
Per serving: 130 calories; 2 g protein; 6 g fat; 18 g carbohydrate; 2 mg calcium;
1 mg sodium; 0 mg cholesterol

The Fat Exchange

THERE'S no mystery about fat. Once you investigate, you'll find that the truth of the matter is you can "exchange" boring meals for interesting ones and still uncover a weight loss. Whether it's a little bit of mayonnaise, margarine, oil, or salad dressing, a touch of fat can go a long way to enhance the flavor of classic favorites. The proof is in our Tartar Sauce, "Hollandaise" Sauce, Stove-Top Chicken Gravy, Buttermilk Dressing, and a raft of other recipes.

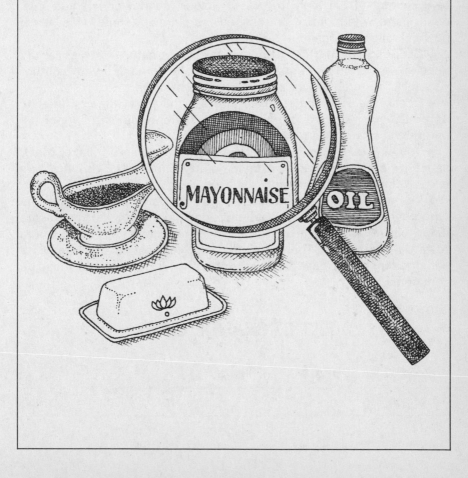

◗ Pointers on the Fat Exchange

Daily Exchanges

WEEKS 1, 2, 3, AND 4	
Women, Men, and Youths	3 Exchanges

◗ Fats supply polyunsaturated fatty acids and vitamin E.

◗ When measuring fats, be sure your measurements are level.

◗ You may use any of the following *vegetable oils,* alone or in combination; they are listed in order of their polyunsaturated fatty acid content—from high to low: safflower; sunflower; walnut; soybean; corn; wheat germ; cottonseed; sorghum; sesame; rice; bran; peanut; rapeseed (canola); olive.

◗ Chili oil is permitted; however, due to its nature, it is generally used in very small amounts. Chili oil may be combined with another vegetable oil to obtain a measurable amount of oil.

◗ Check the label on regular and reduced-calorie margarines to determine if they are permitted; use margarines with a polyunsaturated to saturated fat ratio (P/S ratio) of 2 to 1.

◗ You may use your Fat Exchanges to broil, pan-broil, bake, roast, sauté, or stir-fry all foods except poultry and game with the skin and raw beef, ham, lamb, pork, and tongue.

◗ You may use Fat Exchanges as part of a marinade (do not use with poultry and game that have not been skinned or the raw meats listed above); all of the marinade must be consumed and counted toward the Food Plan. Therefore, all pan juices that accumulate while cooking foods that have been marinated in Fat Exchanges must be consumed.

FAT EXCHANGE LISTS

Weeks 1, 2, 3, and 4

Selections	*One Exchange*
Margarine	1 teaspoon
Margarine, reduced-calorie	2 teaspoons

Selections	One Exchange
Mayonnaise, commercial and homemade	1 teaspoon
Mayonnaise, reduced-calorie	2 teaspoons
Salad Dressing, any type	1½ teaspoons
Vegetable Oil	1 teaspoon

Anchovy Vinaigrette ◑

WEEK 4 ⬥ MAKES 2 SERVINGS, ABOUT 2½ TABLESPOONS EACH

**2 tablespoons plus 1½ teaspoons
red wine vinegar
2 teaspoons mashed drained
canned anchovies**

**1 tablespoon plus 1 teaspoon
olive oil
⅛ teaspoon each basil leaves and
mashed fresh garlic**

In small bowl gradually stir vinegar into anchovies, mixing well to combine. Add oil in a thin stream, beating constantly. Add basil and garlic and stir to combine.

Each serving provides: 2 Fat Exchanges; 10 calories Optional Exchange
Per serving: 94 calories; 1 g protein; 10 g fat; 1 g carbohydrate; 12 mg calcium;
53 mg sodium; 3 mg cholesterol

Apple Vinaigrette ◑❸

WEEK 4 ⬥ MAKES 2 SERVINGS, ABOUT 3 TABLESPOONS EACH

Delicious when combined with fruit for a piquant fruit salad.

**⅓ cup apple juice (no sugar added)
2 teaspoons vegetable oil
1 teaspoon each cider vinegar and
lemon juice**

**¼ teaspoon powdered mustard
Dash each salt, pepper, and ground
ginger**

In small bowl or jar with tight-fitting cover combine all ingredients; stir or cover and shake to mix.

Each serving provides: 1 Fat Exchange; ½ Fruit Exchange
Per serving: 63 calories; 0.1 g protein; 5 g fat; 5 g carbohydrate; 5 mg calcium;
66 mg sodium; 0 mg cholesterol

Herb Vinaigrette ◑

WEEK 1 ⌒ MAKES 1 SERVING, ABOUT 2 TABLESPOONS

1 teaspoon each olive oil, vegetable oil, red wine vinegar, and water
1 teaspoon chopped fresh parsley

½ teaspoon Worcestershire sauce
Dash each salt, pepper, and granulated sugar substitute

In small bowl combine all ingredients; using a whisk or fork, beat until well mixed.

Each serving provides: 2 Fat Exchanges
Per serving: 88 calories; 0.3 g protein; 9 g fat; 1 g carbohydrate; 4 mg calcium;
    158 mg sodium; 0 mg cholesterol

Variations:
  1. Substitute chopped fresh basil for the parsley.
  2. Substitute lemon juice for the vinegar.
  3. Substitute ¼ teaspoon granulated sugar for the sugar substitute; add 5 calories Optional Exchange to Exchange Information.

Per serving: 93 calories; 0.2 g protein; 9 g fat; 2 g carbohydrate; 4 mg calcium;
    158 mg sodium; 0 mg cholesterol

Honey-Citrus Dressing ◑

WEEK 3 ⌒ MAKES 1 SERVING, ABOUT 2 TABLESPOONS

Delicious with fruit salad.

2 tablespoons sour cream
1 tablespoon thawed frozen concentrated orange juice (no sugar added)

1 teaspoon each chopped chives and Chinese sesame oil
½ teaspoon honey
Dash each salt and pepper

In small bowl or jar with tight-fitting cover combine all ingredients; stir or cover and shake to mix.

Each serving provides: 1 Fat Exchange; ½ Fruit Exchange;
    75 calories Optional Exchange
Per serving: 141 calories; 1 g protein; 11 g fat; 11 g carbohydrate; 41 mg calcium;
    148 mg sodium; 13 mg cholesterol

Lemon-Mustard Vinaigrette ●❶

WEEK 1 ～ MAKES 4 SERVINGS, ABOUT 1 TABLESPOON EACH

1 tablespoon plus 1 teaspoon olive
  or vegetable oil
1 tablespoon each white wine
  vinegar and fresh lemon juice

2 teaspoons Dijon-style mustard
Dash white pepper

In small jar that has a tight-fitting cover combine all ingredients; cover tightly and shake well. Refrigerate until chilled. Shake again just before serving.

Each serving provides: 1 Fat Exchange
Per serving: 45 calories; trace protein; 5 g fat; 1 g carbohydrate; 0.5 mg calcium;
  75 mg sodium; 0 mg cholesterol

Sesame Vinaigrette ●

WEEK 4 ～ MAKES 2 SERVINGS, ABOUT 2½ TABLESPOONS EACH

1 tablespoon plus 1 teaspoon
  vegetable oil
1 teaspoon sesame seed
½ garlic clove, minced

¼ cup rice vinegar
1 teaspoon granulated sugar
¼ teaspoon salt
Dash pepper

In small skillet combine oil and sesame seed and cook over low heat, stirring constantly, until seeds are lightly browned. Stir in garlic and remove from heat.

  In small bowl combine vinegar, sugar, salt, and pepper; add sesame seed mixture and mix well.

Each serving provides: 2 Fat Exchanges; 20 calories Optional Exchange
Per serving: 104 calories; 1 g protein; 10 g fat; 4 g carbohydrate; 4 mg calcium;
  270 mg sodium; 0 mg cholesterol

Buttermilk Dressing ◐❶

WEEK 1 ～ MAKES 4 SERVINGS, ABOUT 3 TABLESPOONS EACH

---

1 egg, well beaten
1 tablespoon plus 1 teaspoon
  mayonnaise
1 tablespoon white vinegar, heated

2 teaspoons Dijon-style mustard
½ cup buttermilk
½ teaspoon Worcestershire sauce
Dash white pepper

In small bowl combine egg, mayonnaise, vinegar, and mustard, mixing well; gradually beat in milk and seasonings.

Each serving provides: 1 Fat Exchange; 35 calories Optional Exchange
Per serving: 70 calories; 3 g protein; 6 g fat; 2 g carbohydrate; 44 mg calcium;
  158 mg sodium; 73 mg cholesterol

Tomato-Chive Dressing ◐

WEEK 4 ～ MAKES 4 SERVINGS, ABOUT ¼ CUP EACH

---

1 cup tomato juice
1 tablespoon each chopped chives
  and rice vinegar
2 teaspoons olive oil

1 garlic clove, chopped
¼ teaspoon salt
⅛ teaspoon pepper

In blender container combine all ingredients and process at high speed until blended.

Each serving provides: ½ Fat Exchange; 15 calories Optional Exchange
Per serving: 35 calories; 1 g protein; 2 g fat; 3 g carbohydrate; 7 mg calcium;
  255 mg sodium; 0 mg cholesterol

Barbecue Marinade ◐ ❸

WEEK 1 ∽ MAKES 2 SERVINGS, ABOUT ¼ CUP EACH, *OR* 4 SERVINGS, ABOUT 2 TABLESPOONS EACH

Use as a marinade with poultry.

2 teaspoons vegetable oil
¼ cup diced onion
2 tablespoons plus 2 teaspoons
  low-calorie ketchup (6 calories
  per tablespoon)

2 tablespoons water
1 teaspoon each Worcestershire
  sauce and red wine vinegar
½ teaspoon powdered mustard
¼ to ½ teaspoon hot sauce

In small saucepan heat oil; add onion and sauté until softened. Stir in remaining ingredients and simmer, stirring constantly, for 3 minutes; let cool.

Each ¼-cup serving provides: ¼ Vegetable Exchange; 1 Fat Exchange; 8 calories Optional Exchange
Per serving: 60 calories: 1 g protein; 5 g fat; 3 g carbohydrate; 6 mg calcium; 56 mg sodium; 0 mg cholesterol
Each 2-tablespoon serving provides: ⅛ Vegetable Exchange; ½ Fat Exchange; 4 calories Optional Exchange
Per serving: 30 calories; 0.5 g protein; 2.5 g fat; 1.5 g carbohydrate; 3 mg calcium; 28 mg sodium; 0 mg cholesterol

Lemon Marinade

WEEK 1 ∽ MAKES 2 SERVINGS, ABOUT 2 TABLESPOONS EACH

Use as a marinade with fish.

3 tablespoons lemon juice
2 teaspoons olive oil
2 garlic cloves, minced

½ teaspoon oregano leaves
¼ teaspoon salt
⅛ teaspoon pepper

In small bowl combine all ingredients, mixing well.

Each serving provides: 1 Fat Exchange
Per serving: 52 calories; 0.3 g protein; 5 g fat; 3 g carbohydrate; 12 mg calcium; 274 mg sodium; 0 mg cholesterol

Chinese-Style Marinade ◖❸

WEEK 1 ⌇ MAKES 2 SERVINGS, ABOUT 2 TABLESPOONS EACH

Use as a marinade with poultry or fish.

2 tablespoons teriyaki sauce
1 tablespoon lemon juice
2 teaspoons peanut oil

1 teaspoon each minced pared
   ginger root and honey
1 medium garlic clove, minced

In small bowl combine all ingredients, mixing well.

Each serving provides: 1 Fat Exchange; 10 calories Optional Exchange
Per serving: 73 calories; 1 g protein; 5 g fat; 8 g carbohydrate; 2 mg calcium;
   606 mg sodium; 0 mg cholesterol

Variation: Week 2—Substitute 2 tablespoons dry sherry for the lemon juice and proceed as directed; increase Optional Exchange to 25 calories.

Per serving: 88 calories; 1 g protein; 5 g fat; 8 g carbohydrate; 2 mg calcium;
   605 mg sodium; 0 mg cholesterol

Brown Gravy ❸

WEEK 4 ⌇ MAKES 4 SERVINGS, ABOUT 3 TABLESPOONS EACH

---

1 tablespoon each margarine and
   all-purpose flour
2 tablespoons each diced carrot,
   celery, and onion
1 cup water
2 tablespoons tomato puree

1 packet instant beef broth and
   seasoning mix
1 bay leaf
½ garlic clove
Dash each pepper and thyme leaves

In small saucepan heat margarine over medium heat until bubbly and hot; add flour and cook, stirring constantly, for 3 minutes. Add carrot, celery, and onion and continue to stir and cook until vegetables are lightly browned, about 5 minutes; remove from heat and gradually stir in water. Add remaining ingredients, stirring to combine; return pan to heat and, stirring constantly, bring mixture to a boil. Reduce heat and let simmer, stirring occasionally, for 45 minutes.

Let mixture cool slightly, then remove and discard bay leaf; transfer gravy to blender container and process until smooth.

Each serving provides: ¼ Vegetable Exchange; ½ Fat Exchange;
  20 calories Optional Exchange
Per serving: 43 calories; 1 g protein; 3 g fat; 4 g carbohydrate; 7 mg calcium;
  258 mg sodium; 0 mg cholesterol

Stove-Top Chicken Gravy ◐❸

WEEK 4 ⌒ MAKES 4 SERVINGS, ABOUT ¼ CUP EACH

2 teaspoons margarine
½ cup each diced carrot and
  chopped celery leaves
1½ cups water, divided

2 teaspoons cornstarch
2 packets instant chicken broth and
  seasoning mix

In small nonstick skillet heat margarine until bubbly and hot; add vegetables and sauté until softened. In small cup combine 1 tablespoon water with the cornstarch, stirring to dissolve cornstarch; add to vegetable mixture along with remaining water and broth mix. Stirring constantly, bring to a boil. Reduce heat and let simmer for 5 minutes; let cool slightly.

Pour vegetable mixture into blender container and process at low speed until smooth; return to skillet and heat.

Each serving provides: ½ Vegetable Exchange; ½ Fat Exchange;
  10 calories Optional Exchange
Per serving: 35 calories; 1 g protein; 2 g fat; 4 g carbohydrate; 12 mg calcium;
  464 mg sodium; 0 mg cholesterol

Gruyère Sauce

WEEK 4 ∽ MAKES 4 SERVINGS

Delicious over cooked cauliflower, broccoli, asparagus, or potato; top cooked vegetable with sauce, then broil until lightly browned.

2 tablespoons each margarine and
 all-purpose flour
1 cup skim milk
2 ounces Gruyère cheese, shredded

¼ teaspoon salt
Dash each white pepper and ground
 red pepper

In small saucepan heat margarine over medium heat until bubbly and hot; add flour and cook, stirring constantly, for 2 minutes. Set aside.

In another small saucepan heat milk just to the boiling point; remove from heat. Add flour mixture, a little at a time, beating well with wire whisk after each addition. Cook over medium heat, stirring constantly, until thickened; add cheese, salt, and peppers and continue cooking and stirring until cheese is melted. Reduce heat as low as possible and cook, stirring occasionally, for 30 minutes.

Each serving provides: ½ Protein Exchange; 1½ Fat Exchanges; ¼ Milk Exchange;
 15 calories Optional Exchange
Per serving: 146 calories; 7 g protein; 10 g fat; 6 g carbohydrate; 223 mg calcium;
 281 mg sodium; 17 mg cholesterol

Quick Tomato Sauce ◐

WEEK 1 ∽ MAKES 4 SERVINGS, ABOUT ½ CUP EACH

---

2 cups canned whole tomatoes
8 fresh basil leaves or ½ teaspoon
 dried
6 parsley sprigs, stems removed,
 or 1 teaspoon parsley flakes
1 tablespoon plus 1 teaspoon olive oil

1 tablespoon chopped onion
½ teaspoon salt
1 small garlic clove
Dash each oregano leaves and
 freshly ground pepper

In blender container combine all ingredients and process until smooth; pour into 1-quart saucepan and bring to a boil. Reduce heat, cover, and let simmer for 10 minutes.

Each serving provides: 1 Vegetable Exchange; 1 Fat Exchange
Per serving: 70 calories; 1 g protein; 5 g fat; 6 g carbohydrate; 17 mg calcium;
 426 mg sodium; 0 mg cholesterol

Variation: If blender is not available, this sauce can be totally prepared in a saucepan. Use canned crushed tomatoes and mince the basil, parsley, and garlic. In saucepan heat oil; add onion and garlic and sauté briefly (*do not brown*). Add tomatoes and bring to a boil. Reduce heat and stir in remaining ingredients; let simmer for 10 to 15 minutes.

Red Clam Sauce ◑

WEEK 4 〜 MAKES 4 SERVINGS, ABOUT ¾ CUP EACH

Serve over cooked linguini or spaghetti.

2 teaspoons olive oil
½ cup chopped onion
2 garlic cloves, minced
3 cups canned Italian tomatoes,
   crushed
1 cup bottled clam juice
2 teaspoons basil leaves

½ teaspoon salt
Dash each oregano leaves and
   pepper
8 ounces drained canned minced
   clams
2 tablespoons chopped fresh parsley

In 1½-quart saucepan heat oil; add onion and garlic and sauté for about 2 minutes. Add remaining ingredients except clams and parsley and bring to a boil. Reduce heat and let simmer, stirring occasionally, for about 15 minutes. Add clams and parsley and cook until thoroughly heated, about 3 minutes longer.

Each serving provides: 2 Protein Exchanges; 1¾ Vegetable Exchanges;
   ½ Fat Exchange; 10 calories Optional Exchange
Per serving: 138 calories; 13 g protein; 4 g fat; 13 g carbohydrate; 70 mg calcium;
   814 mg sodium; 41 mg cholesterol

White Clam Sauce ◑

WEEK 4 ⌒ MAKES 4 SERVINGS, ABOUT ½ CUP EACH

Serve over cooked linguini or spaghetti.

2 teaspoons olive oil
1 garlic clove, minced
2 cups bottled clam juice
½ teaspoon each oregano leaves
  and salt

⅛ teaspoon white pepper
8 ounces drained canned minced
  clams
2 tablespoons chopped fresh parsley

In 1-quart saucepan heat oil; add garlic and sauté just until golden. Add remaining ingredients except clams and parsley and bring to a boil. Reduce heat and let simmer for 5 minutes. Add clams and parsley and cook until thoroughly heated, about 3 minutes longer.

Each serving provides: 2 Protein Exchanges; ½ Fat Exchange;
  20 calories Optional Exchange
Per serving: 101 calories; 12 g protein; 4 g fat; 4 g carbohydrate; 40 mg calcium;
  818 mg sodium; 47 mg cholesterol

Curry Sauce ◑❶

WEEK 4 ⌒ MAKES 4 SERVINGS

2 teaspoons margarine
1 tablespoon each minced onion
  and all-purpose flour

1 teaspoon curry powder
1 cup skim milk, heated
Dash each salt and white pepper

In small saucepan heat margarine until bubbly and hot; add onion and sauté until softened. Add flour and cook over low heat, stirring constantly, for 3 minutes. Add curry powder and continue to stir and cook for 1 minute longer; remove from heat. Using a small wire whisk, gradually stir in heated milk, stirring until mixture is smooth; add salt and pepper and cook over low heat, stirring frequently, for 10 minutes.

Each serving provides: ½ Fat Exchange; ¼ Milk Exchange;
  10 calories Optional Exchange
Per serving: 49 calories; 2 g protein; 2 g fat; 5 g carbohydrate; 81 mg calcium;
  87 mg sodium; 1 mg cholesterol

Creole Sauce ❸

WEEK 1 ∽ MAKES 4 SERVINGS, ABOUT ½ CUP EACH

2 teaspoons vegetable oil
½ cup diced onion
1 garlic clove, minced
1 cup each diced green bell pepper
   and sliced mushrooms
½ cup chopped celery
1 cup canned Italian tomatoes,
   drained and chopped (reserve
   liquid)

¾ cup canned beef broth
1 bay leaf
1 tablespoon chopped fresh parsley
¼ teaspoon salt
Dash pepper

In 1½-quart saucepan heat oil; add onion and garlic and sauté until onion is softened. Add green pepper, mushrooms, and celery and sauté for 5 minutes. Add tomatoes, reserved liquid, broth, and bay leaf; cover and let simmer for 20 minutes, stirring occasionally. Stir in parsley, salt, and pepper; remove bay leaf before serving.

Each serving provides: 2 Vegetable Exchanges; ½ Fat Exchange;
   10 calories Optional Exchange
Per serving: 63 calories; 3 g protein; 3 g fat; 8 g carbohydrate; 28 mg calcium;
   388 mg sodium; 0 mg cholesterol

Tartar Sauce ◖❸

WEEK 4 ∽ MAKES 4 SERVINGS, ABOUT 2 TABLESPOONS EACH

Delicious with fish.

¼ cup reduced-calorie mayonnaise
1 teaspoon Dijon-style mustard
⅛ teaspoon each Worcestershire
   sauce and lemon juice

1 tablespoon pickle relish
1 teaspoon chopped drained capers
½ teaspoon chopped fresh parsley

In small bowl mix mayonnaise with mustard, Worcestershire sauce, and lemon juice; stir in pickle relish, capers, and parsley. Serve immediately or cover and refrigerate until ready to use.

Each serving provides: 1½ Fat Exchanges; 10 calories Optional Exchange
Per serving: 47 calories; 0.1 g protein; 4 g fat; 3 g carbohydrate; 1 mg calcium;
   196 mg sodium; 5 mg cholesterol

Apple-Sour Cream Sauce ◑❸

WEEK 3 ⬠ MAKES 1 SERVING

Serve with baked or broiled chicken.

2 teaspoons reduced-calorie
  margarine
1 small Red Delicious apple, cored
  and diced

1 teaspoon chopped chives
3 tablespoons sour cream
Dash ground nutmeg

In small skillet heat margarine over medium heat until bubbly and hot; add apple and chives and sauté, stirring occasionally, until apple pieces are soft. Remove from heat* and stir in sour cream and nutmeg; serve hot.

Each serving provides: 1 Fat Exchange; 1 Fruit Exchange;
  100 calories Optional Exchange
Per serving: 188 calories; 2 g protein; 13 g fat; 18 g carbohydrate; 60 mg calcium;
  114 mg sodium; 19 mg cholesterol

* To prevent curdling, be sure to remove skillet from heat before stirring in sour cream.

Variation: Week 1—Substitute ¼ cup plain low-fat yogurt for the sour cream. Add ½ Milk Exchange to Exchange Information and omit Optional Exchange.

Per serving: 131 calories; 3 g protein; 5 g fat; 20 g carbohydrate; 114 mg calcium;
  131 mg sodium; 3 mg cholesterol

White Sauce ◑❸

WEEK 4 ⬠ MAKES 4 SERVINGS, ABOUT ½ CUP EACH

May be frozen for future use.

2 tablespoons margarine
3 tablespoons all-purpose flour
2 cups skim milk, heated

⅛ teaspoon salt
Dash each ground nutmeg
  (optional) and white pepper

In 1-quart saucepan heat margarine until bubbly and hot; add flour and cook over low heat, stirring constantly, for 3 minutes.

Remove pan from heat; using small wire whisk, gradually stir in milk and continue stirring until mixture is smooth. Add remaining ingredients and cook over medium heat, stirring constantly, until sauce is thickened. Reduce heat to low and cook for 10 minutes longer, stirring occasionally.

Each serving provides: 1½ Fat Exchanges; ½ Milk Exchange;
  25 calories Optional Exchange
Per serving: 116 calories; 5 g protein; 6 g fat; 11 g carbohydrate; 156 mg calcium;
  201 mg sodium; 2 mg cholesterol

"Hollandaise" Sauce ◑❸

WEEK 4 ⬿ MAKES 4 SERVINGS, ABOUT 2 TABLESPOONS EACH

½ cup canned chicken broth
1 tablespoon cornstarch
2 tablespoons each margarine and
  mayonnaise

1½ teaspoons lemon juice
Dash each salt, white pepper, and
  ground red pepper

In small saucepan combine broth and cornstarch, stirring to dissolve cornstarch; cook over medium heat, stirring constantly, until mixture comes to a boil. Continue cooking and stirring until thickened, about 1 minute longer.

Remove sauce from heat and add margarine, stirring until margarine is melted; add remaining ingredients and stir to combine.

Each serving provides: 3 Fat Exchanges; 15 calories Optional Exchange
Per serving: 114 calories; 1 g protein; 11 g fat; 2 g carbohydrate; 5 mg calcium;
  241 mg sodium; 4 mg cholesterol

Velouté Sauce ◐❶

WEEK 4 ～ MAKES 4 SERVINGS, ABOUT 3 TABLESPOONS EACH

1 tablespoon plus 1 teaspoon each margarine and all-purpose flour
1 cup canned chicken broth

⅛ teaspoon salt
Dash white pepper

In small saucepan heat margarine until bubbly and hot; add flour and cook over low heat, stirring constantly, for 2 minutes. Set aside.

In another saucepan bring broth to a boil; remove from heat. Add margarine mixture, a little at a time, beating well with wire whisk after each addition. Cook over medium heat, stirring constantly, until thickened; season with salt and pepper. Reduce heat as low as possible and continue cooking for 15 minutes longer, stirring occasionally.

Each serving provides: 1 Fat Exchange; 20 calories Optional Exchange
Per serving: 54 calories; 2 g protein; 4 g fat; 2 g carbohydrate; 5 mg calcium;
318 mg sodium; 0 mg cholesterol

Variation: Tomato-Herb Velouté—Before serving, stir 1½ teaspoons chopped fresh parsley and ½ teaspoon tomato paste into sauce.

Per serving: 55 calories; 2 g protein; 4 g fat; 3 g carbohydrate; 6 mg calcium;
323 mg sodium; 0 mg cholesterol

The Protein Exchange

THE wide variety of Protein Exchanges offers endless ways to help you reduce and at the same time add variety and interest to meal planning. Choose from this cornucopia of recipes featuring eggs, cheese, peanut butter, tofu, legumes, poultry, fish, liver, veal, and meats.

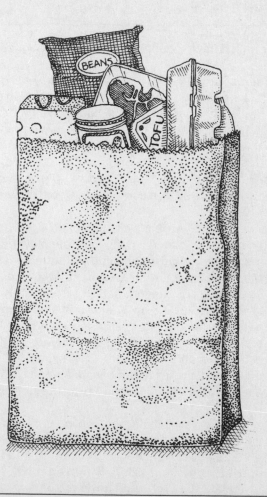

◗ Pointers on the Protein Exchange

Daily Exchanges

	WEEK 1	WEEK 2	WEEKS 3 AND 4
Women	6	6 to 7	6 to 8
Men and Youths	8	8 to 9	8 to 10

◗ The Protein Exchange supplies B vitamins, calcium, iron, and protein.

◗ You may select up to 4 *eggs* a week; they may be small, medium, large, or extra-large in size, white or brown in color. If you are going to consume raw eggs, inspect shells carefully for cracks; cracked eggs may contain salmonella, a bacteria that causes intestinal upset.

◗ You may select up to 4 ounces of hard or semisoft *cheese* a week.

◗ Since *peanut butter* and *tahini* have a high fat content, 1 Fat Exchange must be omitted for each tablespoon of peanut butter or tahini that you use.

◗ As a rule of thumb, ¾ ounce of uncooked *dry beans, lentils, or peas* will yield about 2 ounces cooked. You may use canned and frozen products; they should be packed without sugar.

◗ To determine the amount of *boneless raw meat and fish or skinned and boned poultry* needed, as a rule of thumb, take the total cooked weight desired, divide by 4, and add this number to the desired cooked weight; for raw meat and fish with bone, take the total skinned and boned cooked weight desired, divide by 2, and add this number to the desired cooked weight (for examples and for whole poultry and poultry parts refer to the charts on page 177). If a fraction results from these calculations, round up to the nearest whole number.

As a rule of thumb, raw whole chicken or cut-up parts will yield about 33 percent skinned cooked meat; raw chicken breasts (bone in) will yield about 50 percent skinned cooked meat and raw Cornish hen will yield about 40 percent skinned cooked meat. Use the charts on page 177 as a guide to purchasing birds of the appropriate size.

Meat, Fish, and Poultry	Desired Skinned & Boned Cooked Weight	Divided by	Equals (ounces)	Start with (raw weight)
Boneless Meat or Fish or Skinned & Boned Poultry	1 pound	4	4	1¼ pounds
	12 ounces	4	3	15 ounces
	9 ounces	4	2¼	12 ounces
Meat or Fish with Bone	1 pound	2	8	1½ pounds
	12 ounces	2	6	1 pound 2 ounces
	9 ounces	2	4½	14 ounces

Whole or Cut-Up Poultry (raw with skin and bone)	Approx. Yield (skinned and boned cooked meat)
Chicken	
6 pounds	2 pounds
5 pounds	1 pound 11 ounces
4½ pounds	1½ pounds
4 pounds	1 pound 5 ounces
3½ pounds	1 pound 3 ounces
3 pounds	1 pound
Cornish Hen	
1½ pounds	10 ounces
1¼ pounds	8 ounces

Chicken Breasts (raw with skin and bone)	Approx. Yield (skinned and boned cooked meat)
2 pounds	1 pound
1½ pounds	12 ounces
8 ounces	4 ounces
6 ounces	3 ounces

▶ *Clams, lobsters, mussels, oysters, and shrimp* are exceptions to the rule of thumb.

—Count 3 small clams, mussels, oysters, or shrimp as 1 Protein Exchange.

—A 1½-pound lobster will yield about 6 ounces cooked lobster meat; a 6-ounce lobster tail will yield about 3 ounces cooked lobster meat.

▶ *Poultry, veal, game, fish, organ meats, and liver* may be boiled, poached, stewed, broiled, pan-broiled, baked, roasted, sautéed, or stir-fried. Since skin is a concentrated source of fat, you should remove skin of poultry and game before pan-broiling, sautéing, stir-frying, or stewing. If you bake, broil, roast, boil, or poach poultry or game with the skin on, remove and discard skin and any additional ingredients (e.g., vegetables, liquid, etc.) after cooking.

▶ Use lean *meat* and remove all visible fat. Raw beef, ham, lamb, pork, and tongue should be cooked on a rack (baked, roasted, or broiled) or boiled; discard fat that cooks out of meat.

▶ Uncooked whole poultry and game and raw meats marked with an asterisk (*) may not be stuffed prior to cooking.

▶ *Frankfurters, knockwurst, sausages, bologna, and luncheon meat* may be made from beef, chicken, turkey, veal, or a combination of these items; pork may be used in combination with these items, but all-pork products are not permitted. If made from chicken, turkey, veal, or a combination of these items, count as a poultry/veal selection; if made in combination with beef or pork, count as a beef/pork selection.

▶ We recommend that you have a minimum of 3 *fish* meals (about 12 Exchanges) each week. Canned fish should be well drained; do not consume the liquid. If you are following Weeks 1, 2, or 3, you may use canned fish that is packed in water or oil; on Week 4, you may also use fish packed in tomato sauce, gelatin, broth, or mustard sauce.

▶ *Liver* is an important source of iron; beef, calf, chicken, lamb, pork, and turkey livers may be selected.

PROTEIN EXCHANGE LISTS

The weights indicated for dry beans (etc.), poultry, meats, and fish are net cooked (or drained canned) weights (without skin and bones).

Week 1

You may select up to 4 Exchanges weekly from the meats marked with an asterisk (*).

Since liver is an important source of iron, we recommend that you consume 3 to 4 ounces per week.

Selections	One Exchange
*Beef	1 ounce
Cheese	
Cottage	⅓ cup
Hard	1 ounce
Pot	⅓ cup
Ricotta, part-skim	¼ cup
Semisoft	1 ounce
Chicken	1 ounce
Cornish Hen	1 ounce
Egg	1
Fish	1 ounce
Frankfurter and Knockwurst, chicken,	
turkcy, or veal	1 ounce
Lamb	1 ounce
Liver	1 ounce
Luncheon Meats, chicken, turkey,	
or veal	1 ounce
*Pork	1 ounce
Sausage, chicken, turkey, or veal	1 ounce
Turkey	1 ounce

Week 2

You may use all of the items listed under Week 1 and may add *Ham, 1 ounce, to your Exchange List.

Week 3

You may use all of the items listed under Weeks 1 and 2 and may add Dry Beans, Lentils, and Peas, 2 ounces cooked, to your Exchange List; you may now select up to 8 Exchanges per week from the meats marked with an asterisk (*).

Week 4

You may use all of the items listed under Weeks 1, 2, and 3 and may add the following selections to your Exchange List; you may now select up to 12 Exchanges per week from the meats marked with an asterisk (*).

We recommend that you consume 4 to 6 ounces of liver per week.

Selections	One Exchange
*Bacon, Canadian-style	1 ounce
*Beefalo	1 ounce
*Bologna	1 ounce
Capon	1 ounce
*Frankfurter and Knockwurst, beef or beef and pork combined	1 ounce
Game	1 ounce
*Liverwurst	1 ounce
*Luncheon Meat, beef or beef and pork combined	1 ounce
*Organ Meats	1 ounce
Peanut Butter	1 tablespoon (omit 1 Fat Exchange)
*Sausage, beef or beef and pork combined	1 ounce
Tahini	1 tablespoon (omit 1 Fat Exchange)
Tempeh (Fermented Soybean Cake)	1 ounce
Tofu (Soybean Curd)	3 ounces
*Tongue	1 ounce

Eggs

Egg-stra, Egg-stra, read all about some egg-cellent ways to serve eggs. Our collection includes hors d'oeuvres, salads, custards, and quiches, all scrambling to make headlines. And here's a bit of news—there's no nutritional difference between white- and brown-shelled eggs, so you can use either in these recipes and expect sensational results.

Chicken Egg-Drop Soup ◐ ❸

WEEK 1 〰 MAKES 1 SERVING, ABOUT 1 CUP

1 packet instant chicken broth and
  seasoning mix
¾ cup water
2 teaspoons thinly sliced scallion
  (green onion), green portion only

1 large egg, beaten
¼ teaspoon soy sauce (optional)

Empty packet of broth mix into small saucepan; add water and stir
to combine. Add scallion and bring to a boil. Remove from heat and
gradually stir in egg and, if desired, soy sauce; serve immediately.

Each serving provides: 1 Protein Exchange; 10 calories Optional Exchange
Per serving with soy sauce: 92 calories; 7 g protein; 6 g fat; 3 g carbohydrate;
  34 mg calcium; 1,015 mg sodium; 274 mg cholesterol
Without soy sauce: 91 calories; 7 g protein; 6 g fat; 2 g carbohydrate;
  33 mg calcium; 904 mg sodium; 274 mg cholesterol

"Caviar"-Topped Eggs Hors d'Oeuvres

WEEK 4 〰 MAKES 4 SERVINGS, 1 EGG EACH

8 large black olives, pitted and
  minced
1 tablespoon mashed drained capers
1 teaspoon each lemon juice and
  olive oil
½ teaspoon mashed drained canned
  anchovies
⅛ teaspoon garlic powder

4 eggs, hard-cooked and chilled
8 iceberg, romaine, or loose-leafed
  lettuce leaves
1 tablespoon plus 1 teaspoon minced
  onion

Garnish

Parsley sprigs

In small bowl combine olives, capers, lemon juice, oil, anchovies,
and garlic powder, mixing well; cover and refrigerate overnight to
allow flavors to blend.

To serve, cut eggs lengthwise into halves. Arrange lettuce leaves
on serving platter and top with egg halves; spoon ⅛ of "caviar"
mixture onto each half, mounding mixture. Sprinkle each half with
½ teaspoon minced onion and garnish platter with parsley.

Each serving provides: 1 Protein Exchange; ½ Vegetable Exchange;
  20 calories Optional Exchange
Per serving: 109 calories; 7 g protein; 8 g fat; 2 g carbohydrate; 42 mg calcium;
  192 mg sodium; 274 mg cholesterol

Deviled Eggs

WEEK 4 ～ MAKES 4 SERVINGS, 1 EGG EACH

4 eggs, hard-cooked and cut
 lengthwise into halves
1 tablespoon plus 1 teaspoon each
 mayonnaise and pickle relish
½ teaspoon spicy brown mustard
Dash each salt, onion powder, and
 garlic powder

Garnish

¼ teaspoon paprika, 8 pimiento
 strips (1 inch long each), and
 8 small parsley sprigs

Carefully remove yolks from egg halves to a small bowl and set
whites aside; mash yolks. Add remaining ingredients except garnish
and whites and stir well to combine.

Using a spoon or pastry bag, fill each reserved white half with ⅛
of the yolk mixture; sprinkle each with an equal amount of paprika
and top with a pimiento strip and parsley sprig. Arrange eggs on
serving platter, cover loosely, and refrigerate for at least 30 minutes.

Each serving provides: 1 Protein Exchange; 1 Fat Exchange;
 10 calories Optional Exchange
Per serving: 121 calories; 6 g protein; 9 g fat; 3 g carbohydrate; 30 mg calcium;
 171 mg sodium; 277 mg cholesterol

Garden Salad ◑

WEEK 1 ～ MAKES 4 SERVINGS

4 cups torn mixed salad greens
1 medium tomato, cut into wedges
½ cup each sliced radishes and
 chopped scallions (green onions)
2 eggs, hard-cooked and cut into
 wedges

¼ cup low-calorie blue cheese salad
 dressing (10 calories per
 tablespoon)

In salad bowl combine salad greens, tomato wedges, radishes, and
scallions; toss lightly to combine. Arrange egg wedges on top of
salad and serve with dressing.

Each serving provides: ½ Protein Exchange; 3 Vegetable Exchanges;
 10 calories Optional Exchange
Per serving: 74 calories; 5 g protein; 4 g fat; 6 g carbohydrate; 61 mg calcium;
 192 mg sodium; 137 mg cholesterol

Vegetable-Cheese Appetizer Puffs ❶

WEEK 4 ᕽ MAKES 4 SERVINGS, 6 PUFFS EACH

Puff Shells

¼ cup margarine
½ cup each water and all-purpose
  flour

3 medium eggs

Filling

⅔ cup cottage cheese
3 tablespoons each minced celery
  and carrot
2 tablespoons minced scallion
  (green onion)

2 teaspoons Dijon-style mustard
1 teaspoon prepared horseradish
⅛ teaspoon paprika
Dash salt

To Prepare Puff Shells: Preheat oven to 400°F. Place margarine in 1-quart saucepan; add water and bring to a boil. Add flour all at once and, using a wooden spoon, stir vigorously until mixture leaves sides of pan and forms a ball; remove from heat. Add eggs, 1 at a time, beating well after each addition until mixture is smooth (dough should be smooth and shiny).

Spray a heavy aluminum baking sheet with nonstick cooking spray; drop dough by rounded ½ teaspoonsful onto sprayed baking sheet, making 24 mounds and leaving a space of about 1½ inches between each. Bake for 15 minutes. Reduce oven temperature to 350°F. and bake for 15 minutes longer.

Turn oven off and remove baking sheet. Using the point of a sharp knife, pierce side of each shell; return to turned-off oven and let stand for 10 minutes, leaving oven door ajar. Carefully transfer shells to wire rack away from drafts and let cool.

To Prepare Filling: In small bowl combine all ingredients for filling; mix until well blended.

To Prepare Puffs: Shortly before serving, using a sharp knife, slice off top of each puff shell. Spoon an equal amount of vegetable-cheese filling (about 1½ teaspoons) into each shell; replace tops and serve.

Each serving provides: 1 Protein Exchange; ½ Bread Exchange;
  ¼ Vegetable Exchange; 3 Fat Exchanges; 35 calories Optional Exchange
Per serving: 258 calories; 11 g protein; 17 g fat; 15 g carbohydrate; 54 mg calcium;
  448 mg sodium; 186 mg cholesterol

Antipasto (page 71)

Green and White Pasta Salad (page 133)

Top: Lasagna Rolls (page 135)
Middle: Spaghetti Pie (page 136)
Bottom: Fettuccine and Asparagus in
          Parmesan Sauce (page 224)

Cherry-Vanilla "Ice Cream" (page 46)

Top: Hoisin Beef and Vegetables (page 315)
Middle: Butterfly Shrimp with Honey Sauce (page 398)
Bottom: Sweet and Sour Pineapple Pork (page 342)

Kiwi-Lemon Chiffon Pie (page 418)

Top: Gazpacho Shrimp Cocktail (page 401)
Middle: Hot Deviled Crab (page 396)
Bottom: Scallops en Brochette (page 402)

Sausage and Onion Parmigiana Hero (page 302)

Egg 'n' Endive Salad with Lemon-Mustard Vinaigrette

WEEK 1 ∾ MAKES 4 SERVINGS

2 Belgian endives (about 4 ounces each), each cut lengthwise into eighths
12 cherry tomatoes, cut into halves
4 eggs, hard-cooked and cut into quarters
Lemon-Mustard Vinaigrette (see page 163)

On each of 4 salad plates arrange 4 endive pieces; top each portion with 6 cherry tomato halves, cut-side down, and 4 egg quarters. Cover and refrigerate until chilled. To serve, pour ¼ of vinaigrette over each portion of salad.

Each serving provides (includes Lemon-Mustard Vinaigrette): 1 Protein Exchange; 1¼ Vegetable Exchanges; 1 Fat Exchange
Per serving: 143 calories; 7 g protein; 11 g fat; 5 g carbohydrate; 78 mg calcium; 153 mg sodium; 274 mg cholesterol

Pimiento-Egg Salad ❶

WEEK 4 ∾ MAKES 4 SERVINGS

½ cup each minced celery and dill pickle
¼ cup chopped drained canned pimientos
2 tablespoons plus 2 teaspoons mayonnaise
1 tablespoon plus 1 teaspoon minced onion
2 teaspoons Dijon-style mustard
8 eggs, hard-cooked and chopped
¼ teaspoon each salt and pepper
8 iceberg or romaine lettuce leaves

In medium bowl combine celery, pickle, pimientos, mayonnaise, onion, and mustard, mixing well; add eggs, salt, and pepper and combine thoroughly. Cover and refrigerate until chilled. To serve, line serving platter with lettuce leaves and top with egg salad.

Each serving provides: 2 Protein Exchanges; 1⅛ Vegetable Exchanges; 2 Fat Exchanges
Per serving: 240 calories; 13 g protein; 19 g fat; 4 g carbohydrate; 75 mg calcium; 696 mg sodium; 554 mg cholesterol

Tangy Egg Salad 🌗

WEEK 4 〜 MAKES 2 SERVINGS

½ cup diced celery
2 tablespoons each chopped scallion
  (green onion), sour cream, and
  reduced-calorie mayonnaise
1 tablespoon chili sauce
2 teaspoons each pickle relish and
  chopped drained capers

¼ teaspoon pepper
Dash salt
4 eggs, hard-cooked and coarsely
  chopped
8 iceberg or romaine lettuce leaves

In medium bowl combine all ingredients except eggs and lettuce; add eggs and mix well. Cover and refrigerate until chilled. To serve, line serving plate with lettuce leaves and top with egg salad.

Each serving provides: 2 Protein Exchanges; 1½ Vegetable Exchanges;
  1½ Fat Exchanges; 50 calories Optional Exchange
Per serving: 259 calories; 14 g protein; 18 g fat; 10 g carbohydrate; 119 mg calcium;
  578 mg sodium; 559 mg cholesterol

Variation: Substitute plain low-fat yogurt for the sour cream; reduce Optional Exchange to 30 calories.

Per serving: 238 calories; 14 g protein; 16 g fat; 10 g carbohydrate; 128 mg calcium;
  581 mg sodium; 554 mg cholesterol

Tomato Sauce-Poached Eggs 🌓

WEEK 2 〜 MAKES 1 SERVING

1 teaspoon olive oil
¼ cup diced onion
¼ garlic clove, mashed with ⅛
  teaspoon salt
1 cup canned crushed tomatoes

¼ teaspoon oregano leaves,
  crumbled
Dash pepper
2 large eggs
½ cup cooked long-grain rice (hot)

In small nonstick skillet heat oil over medium-high heat; add onion and sauté until tender. Add mashed garlic and sauté for about 30 seconds. Stir in tomatoes and seasonings, reduce heat to low, and let simmer until mixture thickens slightly.

Make 2 indentations in tomato mixture. Break 1 egg into small cup, being careful not to break yolk; carefully slide egg into one of the indentations. Repeat with remaining egg. Cover skillet and let simmer until eggs are set, 3 to 4 minutes; slide eggs and sauce over hot rice.

Each serving provides: 2 Protein Exchanges; 1 Bread Exchange;
 2½ Vegetable Exchanges; 1 Fat Exchange
Per serving: 374 calories; 17 g protein; 16 g fat; 40 g carbohydrate; 148 mg calcium;
 807 mg sodium; 548 mg cholesterol

Pipérade ◑

WEEK 1 ∽ MAKES 4 SERVINGS

A simple baked omelet dressed up with onions, peppers, and tomatoes—easy to prepare and attractive to serve. Vegetables can be cooked ahead and refrigerated, then combined with eggs and baked just before serving.

**1 tablespoon plus 1 teaspoon
 olive oil**
1 cup thinly sliced onions
**1 cup each sliced red and green
 bell peppers (2 x ¼-inch strips)**
**½ garlic clove, mashed with ¼
 teaspoon salt**

1 cup canned crushed tomatoes
½ teaspoon salt
⅛ teaspoon pepper
8 large eggs, lightly beaten
**1 tablespoon plus 1 teaspoon grated
 Parmesan cheese**

In 10-inch nonstick skillet heat oil over medium heat; add onions and sauté until translucent, about 2 minutes. Add red and green peppers and mashed garlic and cook, stirring occasionally, until peppers are tender, 2 to 3 minutes longer. Reduce heat, stir in tomatoes and seasonings, and let simmer until liquid has evaporated; remove from heat.

Preheat oven to 350°F. Spray shallow 2-quart casserole with nonstick cooking spray; add vegetable mixture and stir in eggs. Sprinkle egg mixture with Parmesan cheese and bake until set, 10 to 12 minutes.

Each serving provides: 2 Protein Exchanges; 2 Vegetable Exchanges;
 1 Fat Exchange; 10 calories Optional Exchange
Per serving: 244 calories; 14 g protein; 17 g fat; 9 g carbohydrate; 111 mg calcium;
 678 mg sodium; 549 mg cholesterol

Egg Foo Yung (Chinese Omelet)

WEEK 4 ~ MAKES 2 SERVINGS, 3 TO 4 OMELET PATTIES EACH

Egg Mixture

4 ounces shelled and deveined cooked shrimp, skinned and boned cooked chicken, or boned cooked pork, chopped

2 large eggs, beaten with 2 teaspoons water

1 cup bean sprouts

¼ cup chopped scallions (green onions)

⅛ teaspoon salt

Dash each garlic powder and white pepper

2 teaspoons peanut or vegetable oil

Sauce

1½ teaspoons soy sauce

1 teaspoon each cornstarch and rice vinegar

Dash ground ginger

½ cup water

To Prepare Egg Mixture: In bowl combine shrimp (or chicken or pork), beaten eggs, bean sprouts, scallions, and seasonings, mixing well. In 9-inch nonstick skillet heat oil; drop a scant ¼ cup of egg mixture into hot oil and cook until set and lightly browned on bottom. Turn patty over and brown other side; remove to a warmed platter and keep warm. Repeat procedure with remaining egg mixture, using scant ¼ cup mixture for each patty.

To Prepare Sauce: In small saucepan combine soy sauce, cornstarch, vinegar, and ginger, stirring to dissolve cornstarch; gradually stir in water. Stirring constantly, bring mixture to a boil and cook until sauce thickens.

To Serve: Transfer patties to 2 warmed plates and top each portion with half of the sauce.

Each serving provides: 3 Protein Exchanges; 1¼ Vegetable Exchanges;
  1 Fat Exchange; 5 calories Optional Exchange
Per serving with shrimp: 212 calories; 22 g protein; 11 g fat; 7 g carbohydrate;
  112 mg calcium; 622 mg sodium; 359 mg cholesterol
With chicken: 254 calories; 25 g protein; 14 g fat; 6 g carbohydrate; 56 mg calcium;
  592 mg sodium; 324 mg cholesterol
With pork: 283 calories; 23 g protein; 18 g fat; 6 g carbohydrate; 52 mg calcium;
  582 mg sodium; 325 mg cholesterol

Puffy Cheese Omelet ◐

WEEK 1 〜 MAKES 2 SERVINGS

¼ cup part-skim ricotta cheese
1 ounce provolone cheese, shredded
2 eggs, separated
½ teaspoon Worcestershire sauce

⅛ teaspoon pepper
Dash salt
1 teaspoon margarine

1. In medium bowl mix ricotta cheese with provolone cheese, egg yolks, Worcestershire sauce, and pepper until well combined.

2. In small mixing bowl, using electric mixer on high speed, beat whites with salt until stiff but not dry. Beat ⅓ of the beaten whites into cheese mixture, then fold in remaining whites.

3. Preheat broiler. In small omelet pan or skillet that has a metal or removable handle heat margarine until bubbly and hot; tilt pan to coat entire bottom with melted margarine. Pour omelet mixture into pan and cook over medium heat until partially set, about 2 minutes.

4. Transfer pan to broiler and broil until top of omelet is golden brown; using a spatula, loosen edges of omelet and carefully slide onto warmed plate.

Each serving provides: 2 Protein Exchanges; ½ Fat Exchange
Per serving: 190 calories; 13 g protein; 14 g fat; 3 g carbohydrate; 221 mg calcium;
  333 mg sodium; 293 mg cholesterol

Crustless Asparagus Quiche

WEEK 4 ∽ MAKES 2 SERVINGS

2 teaspoons margarine, divided
¼ cup chopped scallions (green onions)
1 cup cooked chopped asparagus (½-inch pieces)
½ cup evaporated skimmed milk

2 eggs, beaten
2 ounces shredded Swiss cheese, divided
¼ teaspoon pepper
Dash each salt and ground red pepper

Preheat oven to 375°F. In small skillet heat 1 teaspoon margarine until bubbly and hot; add scallions and sauté until softened. In medium bowl combine sautéed scallions with asparagus, milk, eggs, 1 ounce cheese, and the seasonings.

Grease 7-inch pie plate with remaining teaspoon margarine and pour in egg mixture; sprinkle with remaining 1 ounce cheese and bake for 35 minutes (until a knife, inserted in center, comes out clean).

Each serving provides: 2 Protein Exchanges; 1¼ Vegetable Exchanges;
1 Fat Exchange; ½ Milk Exchange
Per serving: 296 calories; 22 g protein; 18 g fat; 14 g carbohydrate; 515 mg calcium;
327 mg sodium; 303 mg cholesterol

Matzo "Quiche" ❶

WEEK 4 ∽ MAKES 4 SERVINGS

2 tablespoons margarine
1 cup diced onions
1 garlic clove, minced
4 eggs
¼ teaspoon each paprika and salt
⅛ teaspoon pepper

4 ounces sharp Cheddar cheese, shredded
2 egg matzo boards, broken into halves
2 medium tomatoes, sliced

1. Preheat oven to 375°F. In small skillet heat margarine until bubbly and hot; add onions and garlic and sauté until onions are softened.

2. In medium bowl beat eggs; add sautéed onions, paprika, salt, and pepper; add cheese and stir until well combined.

3. In 8 x 8 x 2-inch nonstick baking pan place 2 matzo halves; top with half of the tomato slices, then half of the egg mixture. Repeat layers with remaining matzo halves, tomato slices, and egg mixture.

4. Bake "quiche" for 30 minutes (until a knife, inserted in center, comes out clean). Remove from oven and, keeping warm, let stand for 5 minutes before cutting.

Each serving provides: 2 Protein Exchanges; 1 Bread Exchange;
  1½ Vegetable Exchanges; 1½ Fat Exchanges
Per serving: 346 calories; 17 g protein; 21 g fat; 22 g carbohydrate; 260 mg calcium;
  452 mg sodium; 304 mg cholesterol

Quick "Quiche Lorraine" ❸

WEEK 4 ∽ MAKES 1 SERVING

A mixed green salad is the perfect accompaniment to this delicious dish.

½ cup evaporated skimmed milk   1 teaspoon imitation bacon bits
1 large egg, beaten   Dash pepper
1 ounce Swiss cheese, shredded   1 teaspoon grated Parmesan cheese

Preheat oven to 350°F. Spray 10-ounce custard cup or 1½-cup casserole with nonstick cooking spray and set aside. In small bowl beat together milk and egg; stir in Swiss cheese, bacon bits, and pepper. Pour into sprayed cup (or casserole) and sprinkle with Parmesan cheese; place cup (or casserole) in 8 x 8 x 2-inch baking pan and fill pan with boiling water to a depth of about 1 inch. Bake for 25 to 30 minutes (until a knife, inserted in center, comes out clean). Remove from water and, keeping warm, let stand for about 5 minutes before serving.

Each serving provides: 2 Protein Exchanges; 1 Milk Exchange;
  20 calories Optional Exchange
Per serving: 302 calories; 25 g protein; 15 g fat; 17 g carbohydrate; 698 mg calcium;
  415 mg sodium; 307 mg cholesterol

Broccoli-Cheddar Soufflé 🌓

WEEK 4 〜 MAKES 4 SERVINGS

4 large eggs, separated
1 tablespoon plus 1 teaspoon each
 margarine and minced onion
2 tablespoons all-purpose flour
1 cup skim milk, heated
1/4 teaspoon salt
Dash each white pepper, ground red
 pepper, and ground nutmeg

4 ounces extra-sharp Cheddar
 cheese, shredded
1 cup each cooked long-grain rice
 and cooked broccoli florets
Dash cream of tartar

1. In small bowl beat egg yolks and set aside.

2. In small saucepan heat margarine over medium heat until bubbly and hot; add onion and sauté until softened. Reduce heat to low; add flour and cook, stirring constantly, for 3 minutes. Remove from heat and, using small wire whisk, gradually stir in hot milk, stirring until mixture is smooth; add salt, white and red pepper, and nutmeg.

3. Return saucepan to medium heat and cook, stirring constantly, until mixture is thickened. Reduce heat to low and cook, stirring frequently, for 10 minutes longer. Add cheese and cook, stirring constantly, until cheese is melted; gradually stir beaten egg yolks into cheese sauce, stirring until well blended. Remove sauce from heat. Preheat oven to 350°F.

4. Gently stir rice into cheese sauce and transfer mixture to a large mixing bowl; gently fold in broccoli.

5. In another large bowl beat egg whites with cream of tartar until stiff but not dry. Lightly stir 1/4 of the whites into broccoli mixture, then fold in remaining whites.

6. Spray 1 1/2-quart soufflé or ovenproof glass dish with nonstick cooking spray; turn broccoli mixture into dish. To form a crown, using the back of a spoon, make a shallow indentation about 1 inch from edge of dish all the way around soufflé. Bake for 40 minutes; serve immediately.

Each serving provides: 2 Protein Exchanges; 1/2 Bread Exchange;
 1/2 Vegetable Exchange; 1 Fat Exchange; 1/4 Milk Exchange;
 15 calories Optional Exchange
Per serving: 322 calories; 18 g protein; 19 g fat; 20 g carbohydrate; 335 mg calcium;
 464 mg sodium; 305 mg cholesterol

Cheddar, Potato, and Egg Pancake ◐❸

WEEK 2 ∽ MAKES 4 SERVINGS

1 tablespoon plus 1 teaspoon
  vegetable oil
6 ounces thinly sliced pared
  potatoes, thoroughly dried with
  paper towels
4 ounces sharp Cheddar cheese,
  coarsely shredded

1 tablespoon chopped chives
1/8 teaspoon powdered mustard
Dash ground red pepper
4 eggs
1/8 teaspoon salt

In 12-inch nonstick skillet that has an oven-safe or removable handle heat oil; brush pan with oil to coat entire bottom. Spread potato slices over bottom of pan, overlapping slices slightly; using a pancake turner, press slices down. Cook over medium heat, occasionally pressing down with turner but not stirring, until potatoes are tender and underside forms a crisp, brown crust; remove from heat.

Preheat oven to 350°F. In small bowl combine cheese, chives, mustard, and red pepper; sprinkle over potato crust, leaving a 1/2-inch border all around. Break 1 egg into small cup and carefully slide egg onto cheese mixture; repeat with remaining 3 eggs, 1 at a time, spacing eggs evenly. Sprinkle eggs with salt and bake for 5 to 7 minutes or until done to taste. Using spatula, loosen edges of pancake from skillet; slide pancake onto serving plate and cut into wedges.

Each serving provides: 2 Protein Exchanges; 1/2 Bread Exchange; 1 Fat Exchange
Per serving: 268 calories; 14 g protein; 20 g fat; 8 g carbohydrate; 238 mg calcium;
  317 mg sodium; 304 mg cholesterol

Baked Eggs in Spinach Cups ❶

WEEK 4 ⟋ MAKES 2 SERVINGS

2 teaspoons margarine
1 garlic clove, chopped
1 cup well-drained cooked chopped
  spinach
2 teaspoons all-purpose flour
1 cup skim milk

¼ teaspoon salt
⅛ teaspoon each ground nutmeg
  and pepper
2 ounces Swiss cheese, shredded
2 eggs

Preheat oven to 350°F. In 8-inch skillet heat margarine until bubbly and hot; add garlic and sauté for 1 minute. Add spinach and cook over medium heat, stirring constantly, for 3 minutes. Sprinkle flour over spinach and stir quickly to combine; gradually stir in milk and cook, stirring constantly, until slightly thickened. Remove from heat and stir in salt, nutmeg, and pepper; add cheese and stir to combine.

Spray two 10-ounce custard cups with nonstick cooking spray; fill each with half of the spinach mixture. Using the back of a spoon, make a depression in the center of each portion. Being careful not to break yolk, break 1 egg into a small dish, then slide into depression in 1 portion of spinach mixture; repeat with remaining egg and spinach mixture. Bake until eggs are firm, 12 to 15 minutes.

Each serving provides: 2 Protein Exchanges; 1 Vegetable Exchange;
  1 Fat Exchange; ½ Milk Exchange; 10 calories Optional Exchange
Per serving: 297 calories; 22 g protein; 18 g fat; 14 g carbohydrate; 543 mg calcium;
  567 mg sodium; 303 mg cholesterol

Zucchini-Mushroom Bake

WEEK 1 ⟋ MAKES 4 SERVINGS

1 tablespoon plus 1 teaspoon olive
  oil, divided
½ cup chopped onion
2 garlic cloves, minced
2 cups thinly sliced zucchini
1 cup sliced mushrooms

½ cup diced red bell pepper
½ teaspoon basil leaves
¼ teaspoon each salt and pepper
4 eggs
4 ounces shredded Monterey Jack
  cheese, divided

Preheat oven to 400°F. In 12-inch skillet heat 1 tablespoon oil; add onion and garlic and sauté until onion is translucent. Add zucchini, mushrooms, red pepper, and seasonings and, stirring constantly, sauté until vegetables are tender-crisp, about 5 minutes; remove from heat.

In medium bowl beat eggs; add 2 ounces cheese and the sautéed vegetables and stir to combine.

Grease an 8 x 8 x 2-inch baking dish with remaining teaspoon oil; transfer vegetable mixture to dish and sprinkle with remaining 2 ounces cheese. Bake for 25 to 30 minutes (until puffy and browned and a knife, inserted in center, comes out clean).

Each serving provides: 2 Protein Exchanges; 2 Vegetable Exchanges; 1 Fat Exchange
Per serving: 259 calories; 15 g protein; 19 g fat; 8 g carbohydrate; 273 mg calcium; 364 mg sodium; 274 mg cholesterol

Apple Custard 🌀

WEEK 1 〜 MAKES 2 SERVINGS

May be served warm or chilled.

2 teaspoons margarine
2 small Golden Delicious apples, cored, pared, and sliced
2 whole cloves
1/8 teaspoon ground cinnamon

1 cup skim milk
2 large eggs
1 tablespoon granulated sugar
1/2 teaspoon vanilla extract

Preheat oven to 350°F. In small saucepan heat margarine; add apples, cloves, and cinnamon. Cover and cook, stirring occasionally, until apples just begin to soften, about 2 minutes; remove and discard cloves. Divide mixture into two 10-ounce custard cups.

In small bowl combine remaining ingredients and beat until well mixed; pour half of mixture into each custard cup and bake until custard is set, 35 to 40 minutes.

Each serving provides: 1 Protein Exchange; 1 Fat Exchange; 1 Fruit Exchange; 1/2 Milk Exchange; 30 calories Optional Exchange
Per serving: 241 calories; 10 g protein; 10 g fat; 28 g carbohydrate; 188 mg calcium; 178 mg sodium; 276 mg cholesterol

Caramel Egg Custard

WEEK 1 ∽ MAKES 2 SERVINGS

May be served warm or chilled.

Caramel
1 tablespoon granulated sugar
2 teaspoons water

Custard
½ cup skim milk
2 eggs, beaten
2 teaspoons vanilla extract
1 teaspoon granulated sugar

To Prepare Caramel: Spray two 6-ounce custard cups with nonstick cooking spray. Place cups in 8 x 8 x 2-inch baking pan and pour boiling water into pan to a depth of about 1 inch; set aside.

Fill a second baking pan with ice water; set aside. In small nonstick saucepan combine sugar and water and cook over medium heat, stirring constantly, until sugar dissolves and browns (*be very careful not to burn*); immediately pour half of mixture into each sprayed cup, tilting each cup to coat sides. Transfer custard cups from pan of boiling water to pan of ice water to harden caramel.

To Prepare Custard: Preheat oven to 325°F. In bowl thoroughly combine all ingredients for custard; pour half of mixture into each caramel-coated cup. Set cups in 8 x 8 x 2-inch baking pan and pour boiling water into pan to a depth of about 1 inch; bake for 20 to 30 minutes (until a knife, inserted in center of custard, comes out clean). Remove baking pan from oven and cups from water bath; let custard stand at room temperature for 10 to 15 minutes.

Unmold custard by loosening edges with point of sharp knife; invert onto serving plate.

Each serving provides: 1 Protein Exchange; ¼ Milk Exchange;
  40 calories Optional Exchange
Per serving: 150 calories; 8 g protein; 6 g fat; 12 g carbohydrate; 104 mg calcium;
  101 mg sodium; 275 mg cholesterol

Cheese

Picture yourself smiling and saying cheese. To help you, we've developed a colorful collage of culinary delights using Cheddar, ricotta, feta, Monterey Jack, Swiss, and Parmesan, among others. From Quick and Easy Cheddar Sauce that can be prepared in a flash to Fettuccine Supreme, these are recipes that capture the spotlight and help you set the scene for smiles.

Cheddar Soup ◐❶

WEEK 4 ∿ MAKES 2 SERVINGS, ABOUT 1 CUP EACH

1 tablespoon margarine
¼ cup diced onion
2 tablespoons each diced celery
  and carrot
2 teaspoons all-purpose flour
1 packet instant chicken broth and
  seasoning mix, dissolved in ¾
  cup hot water

1 cup skim milk (at room
  temperature)
4 ounces sharp Cheddar cheese,
  shredded
Dash pepper

In small saucepan heat margarine until bubbly and hot; add vegetables and sauté, stirring frequently, until tender. Sprinkle flour over vegetables and stir quickly to combine; gradually stir in dissolved broth mix and cook, stirring constantly, until mixture is smooth and thickened. Stir in milk and cook, stirring occasionally, until thoroughly heated (*do not boil*). Add cheese and cook over low heat, stirring constantly, until cheese is melted; season with pepper and serve immediately.

Each serving provides: 2 Protein Exchanges; ½ Vegetable Exchange;
  1½ Fat Exchanges; ½ Milk Exchange; 15 calories Optional Exchange
Per serving: 350 calories; 20 g protein; 25 g fat; 12 g carbohydrate; 575 mg calcium;
  914 mg sodium; 62 mg cholesterol

Broccoli au Gratin Soup

WEEK 1 ∿ MAKES 4 SERVINGS, ABOUT 1 CUP EACH

2 teaspoons margarine
½ cup diced onion
1 package (10 ounces) frozen
  chopped broccoli, thawed
1 cup skim milk

½ cup canned chicken broth
1 cup part-skim ricotta cheese
1 tablespoon plus 1 teaspoon grated
  Parmesan cheese, divided

In 2-quart saucepan heat margarine until bubbly and hot; add onion and sauté until translucent. Add broccoli and cook until heated, 2 to 3 minutes. Add milk and broth and stir to combine; stirring occasionally, bring just to a boil. Transfer mixture to blender container and process at low speed until smooth; add ricotta cheese and process until combined. Reheat if necessary (*do not boil*); serve each portion sprinkled with 1 teaspoon Parmesan cheese.

Each serving provides: 1 Protein Exchange; 1¼ Vegetable Exchanges;
½ Fat Exchange; ¼ Milk Exchange; 15 calories Optional Exchange
Per serving: 165 calories; 13 g protein; 8 g fat; 12 g carbohydrate; 317 mg calcium;
279 mg sodium; 22 mg cholesterol

Cheese-Stuffed Celery Appetizer ❸

WEEK 1 ◇ MAKES 4 SERVINGS, 2 CELERY RIBS EACH

**¼ cup each minced celery and
scallions (green onions)
4 ounces extra-sharp Cheddar
cheese, shredded
1 teaspoon Dijon-style mustard**

**Dash each garlic powder and
Worcestershire sauce
½ cup plain low-fat yogurt
8 medium celery ribs**

Spray top half of double boiler with nonstick cooking spray; add celery and scallions, cover, and cook directly over low heat until celery is tender, stirring occasionally to prevent sticking or burning. Place over hot water and add cheese, mustard, garlic powder, and Worcestershire sauce to vegetable mixture; cook, stirring constantly, until cheese is melted.

Spoon yogurt into a bowl and, using a wire whisk, gradually stir in cheese mixture, stirring until thoroughly blended; cover and refrigerate until firm.

To serve, fill each celery rib with ⅛ of the cheese mixture.

Each serving provides: 1 Protein Exchange; 1¼ Vegetable Exchanges;
¼ Milk Exchange
Per serving: 151 calories; 9 g protein; 10 g fat; 7 g carbohydrate; 292 mg calcium;
344 mg sodium; 31 mg cholesterol

Asparagus-Swiss Roll Appetizers ◑

WEEK 1 ⌖ MAKES 4 SERVINGS, 3 ROLLS EACH

Also delicious as a quick and easy hors d'oeuvre.

2 ready-to-bake refrigerated buttermilk flaky biscuits (1 ounce each)	12 frozen asparagus spears, thawed 2 ounces sliced Swiss cheese, cut into 12 equal strips

Preheat oven to 400°F. Roll each biscuit between 2 sheets of wax paper, forming two 5-inch squares; remove top sheet of paper and cut each square into 6 equal strips. Wrap 1 strip in a spiral pattern around each asparagus spear; place on nonstick baking sheet and bake until dough is golden brown, 8 to 10 minutes. Remove baking sheet from oven and turn oven off.

Place 1 strip of cheese over each wrapped spear and return to turned-off oven just long enough for cheese to melt slightly, about 1 minute.

Each serving provides: ½ Protein Exchange; ½ Bread Exchange; ½ Vegetable Exchange
Per serving: 103 calories; 7 g protein; 5 g fat; 9 g carbohydrate; 154 mg calcium; 161 mg sodium; 13 mg cholesterol

"Bacon" Cheddar Pinwheel Appetizers ❸

WEEK 4 ⌖ MAKES 4 SERVINGS

¾ cup all-purpose flour 2 ounces Cheddar cheese, shredded 2 teaspoons each imitation bacon bits, crushed, and onion flakes, reconstituted ⅛ teaspoon each salt and ground red pepper 2 tablespoons plus 2 teaspoons margarine	¼ cup plain low-fat yogurt 2 tablespoons each Dijon-style mustard and chopped fresh parsley or chives 1 tablespoon plus 1 teaspoon grated Parmesan cheese

In small mixing bowl combine flour, Cheddar cheese, bacon bits, onion flakes, salt, and pepper. With pastry blender, or 2 knives used scissors-fashion, cut in margarine until mixture resembles coarse meal; add yogurt and mix thoroughly. Form dough into a ball, wrap in plastic wrap, and refrigerate for at least 1 hour.

Between two sheets of wax paper roll dough, forming a rectangle about ⅛-inch thick. Spread mustard over dough and sprinkle with parsley (or chives), then roll up jelly-roll fashion; wrap in plastic wrap and freeze until dough slices easily, about 30 minutes.

Preheat oven to 400°F. Cut rolled dough into ¼-inch-thick pinwheels; place on parchment-lined or nonstick baking sheet. Sprinkle each pinwheel with an equal amount of Parmesan cheese and bake until lightly browned, about 15 minutes.

Each serving provides: ½ Protein Exchange; 1 Bread Exchange; 2 Fat Exchanges; 25 calories Optional Exchange
Per serving: 245 calories; 8 g protein; 14 g fat; 22 g carbohydrate; 165 mg calcium; 562 mg sodium; 17 mg cholesterol

Scallion Appetizers ❶❸

WEEK 1 ◦ MAKES 4 SERVINGS, 2 SCALLIONS EACH

2 teaspoons margarine
½ teaspoon Dijon-style mustard
8 large scallions (green onions),
   about 5 inches long (white
   portion and some green)

2 ounces sharp Cheddar cheese,
   shredded

In small bowl combine margarine and mustard and stir to form a paste; spread white and part of green portion of each scallion with ⅛ of mixture. Roll each scallion in cheese, then place in palm of hand and squeeze to tightly secure cheese. Arrange on serving plate, cover, and refrigerate until chilled.

Each serving provides: ½ Protein Exchange; ¼ Vegetable Exchange; ½ Fat Exchange
Per serving: 93 calories; 4 g protein; 7 g fat; 5 g carbohydrate; 119 mg calcium; 131 mg sodium; 15 mg cholesterol

Swiss and "Bacon" Pinwheel Appetizers ❶

WEEK 2 ∽ MAKES 4 SERVINGS, 5 PINWHEELS EACH

These can be prepared ahead and refrigerated until ready to bake.

4 slices white bread, lightly toasted
1 tablespoon plus 1 teaspoon
  reduced-calorie margarine

2 ounces Swiss cheese, shredded
1 tablespoon plus 1 teaspoon
  imitation bacon bits, crushed

1. Using a rolling pin, lightly roll each slice of toast as flat as possible without breaking the bread. Spread 1 teaspoon margarine on each slice.

2. In small bowl combine cheese and bacon bits; sprinkle ¼ of mixture over each slice of toast, covering entire surface.

3. Roll each slice jelly-roll fashion and wrap tightly in wax paper or plastic wrap; freeze for 30 minutes.

4. Preheat oven to 350°F. Unwrap bread rolls and cut each into 5 equal pinwheels, securing each pinwheel with a toothpick; transfer pinwheels, cut-side down, to nonstick baking sheet and bake for 10 minutes.

Each serving provides: ½ Protein Exchange; 1 Bread Exchange; ½ Fat Exchange;
  10 calories Optional Exchange
Per serving: 142 calories; 7 g protein; 7 g fat; 13 g carbohydrate; 161 mg calcium;
  296 mg sodium; 14 mg cholesterol

Broccoli-Cheese Canapés ◑

WEEK 4 ∽ MAKES 4 SERVINGS, 4 CANAPES EACH

1 cup cooked broccoli florets,
  pureed
¼ cup evaporated skimmed milk
1 tablespoon plus 1 teaspoon
  mayonnaise
½ teaspoon salt
⅛ teaspoon each garlic powder and
  freshly ground pepper

4 slices white bread, toasted
4 ounces Gruyère or Swiss cheese,
  thinly sliced
1 tablespoon plus 1 teaspoon grated
  Parmesan cheese

Garnish

8 small pimiento squares

In small bowl combine broccoli, milk, mayonnaise, and seasonings. On nonstick baking sheet arrange toast slices; top each slice with 1 ounce Gruyère (or Swiss) cheese and ¼ of the broccoli mixture.

Sprinkle each with 1 teaspoon Parmesan cheese and bake at 400°F. until cheese is melted, about 10 minutes. Cut each slice into 4 triangles and garnish each with a pimiento square.

Each serving provides: 1 Protein Exchange; 1 Bread Exchange;
½ Vegetable Exchange; 1 Fat Exchange; 20 calories Optional Exchange
Per serving with Gruyère cheese: 244 calories; 14 g protein; 14 g fat;
16 g carbohydrate; 197 mg calcium; 566 mg sodium; 37 mg cholesterol
With Swiss cheese: 234 calories; 13 g protein; 13 g fat; 17 g carbohydrate;
190 mg calcium; 544 mg sodium; 32 mg cholesterol

Spinach-Cheese Bundles

WEEK 4 ～ MAKES 2 SERVINGS

A delicious appetizer or hors d'oeuvre.

Pastry

⅓ cup plus 2 teaspoons all-purpose flour
1 tablespoon plus 1 teaspoon margarine
Dash salt
2 tablespoons plain low-fat yogurt

Filling

¼ cup well-drained cooked chopped spinach
1 ounce shredded Fontina or grated Parmesan cheese
Dash each onion powder, salt, and freshly ground pepper

To Prepare Pastry: In small bowl combine flour, margarine, and salt; with pastry blender, or 2 knives used scissors-fashion, cut in margarine until mixture resembles coarse meal. Add yogurt and mix thoroughly. Form dough into a ball; wrap in plastic wrap and chill for about 1 hour (may be kept in the refrigerator for up to 3 days).

To Prepare Filling and Bake: In small bowl combine spinach, cheese, and seasonings. Preheat oven to 400°F. Between two sheets of wax paper roll dough to about ⅛-inch thickness; remove paper and, using 2½-inch round cookie cutter, cut dough into rounds; roll scraps of dough and continue cutting until all dough has been used. Spoon an equal amount of spinach mixture onto each round and fold in half to enclose filling; using the tines of a fork, press edges to seal. Transfer bundles to parchment-lined or nonstick baking sheet and bake until lightly browned, 15 to 20 minutes.

Each serving provides: ½ Protein Exchange; 1 Bread Exchange;
¼ Vegetable Exchange; 2 Fat Exchanges; 10 calories Optional Exchange
Per serving with Fontina cheese: 225 calories; 8 g protein; 13 g fat;
21 g carbohydrate; 133 mg calcium; 239 mg sodium; 17 mg cholesterol
With Parmesan cheese: 235 calories; 10 g protein; 12 g fat; 21 g carbohydrate;
250 mg calcium; 503 mg sodium; 12 mg cholesterol

Ricotta-Parmesan Torte

WEEK 4 〜 MAKES 8 SERVINGS

Serve warm or at room temperature.

Dough

¾ cup all-purpose flour
3 tablespoons warm water
1 tablespoon plus 1 teaspoon
   vegetable oil

Dash salt

Filling

1 tablespoon plus 1 teaspoon
   margarine
1 cup each chopped scallions
   (green onions) and grated
   zucchini
½ cup grated carrot
2 garlic cloves, minced

2 cups cooked long-grain rice
1 cup part-skim ricotta cheese
4 eggs
3 tablespoons grated Parmesan
   cheese, divided
Dash each salt and freshly ground
   pepper

To Prepare Dough: In small mixing bowl combine flour, water, oil, and salt; using your hands, knead dough into a smooth ball (dough should hold together but not be sticky; if necessary, add up to 1 more tablespoon warm water to adjust consistency). Wrap dough in plastic wrap and set aside while preparing filling (plastic wrap will prevent dough from cracking).

To Prepare Filling: In 10-inch nonstick skillet heat margarine until bubbly and hot; add vegetables and garlic and sauté over medium-low heat, stirring occasionally, until vegetables are soft, about 3 minutes. Set aside and let cool.

  In large mixing bowl combine rice, ricotta cheese, 3 eggs, 2 tablespoons Parmesan cheese, and the salt and pepper; beat until smooth. Add cooled vegetables and stir to combine.

To Prepare Torte: Preheat oven to 350°F. Between 2 sheets of wax paper roll dough, forming a rectangle about ⅛ inch thick; remove paper and fit dough into a 10 x 6 x 2-inch baking dish so that edges of dough extend slightly over sides of dish. Spoon cheese mixture over dough and bring up sides of dough over edges of filling, leaving center uncovered.

In small bowl beat remaining egg with remaining tablespoon Parmesan cheese; pour over entire surface of torte. Bake until browned, about 1 hour; remove from oven and let stand until set, about 15 minutes.

Each serving provides: 1 Protein Exchange; 1 Bread Exchange;
½ Vegetable Exchange; 1 Fat Exchange; 10 calories Optional Exchange
Per serving: 231 calories; 10 g protein; 10 g fat; 24 g carbohydrate; 148 mg calcium;
167 mg sodium; 148 mg cholesterol

Baked Stuffed Eggplant Appetizers

WEEK 4 ◇ MAKES 4 SERVINGS, 2 STUFFED EGGPLANT HALVES EACH

4 baby eggplants (about 4 ounces each)
2 teaspoons olive oil
2 tablespoons each diced onion and red bell pepper
1 garlic clove, minced
½ cup part-skim ricotta cheese
1 egg, beaten

3 tablespoons seasoned dried bread crumbs
¼ teaspoon each basil leaves, oregano leaves, and salt
Dash pepper
3 ounces shredded mozzarella cheese, divided

1. Cut each eggplant in half lengthwise; scoop out pulp, leaving ¼-inch-thick shells. Reserve shells; chop pulp and reserve.

2. Preheat oven to 350°F. In small skillet heat oil; add onion, pepper, eggplant pulp, and garlic and sauté until vegetables are tender. Remove from heat and stir in ricotta cheese, then egg, bread crumbs, and seasonings.

3. Spray 10 x 6 x 2-inch flameproof baking dish with nonstick cooking spray. Spoon ⅛ of eggplant mixture into each reserved shell and transfer shells to sprayed dish. Bake until mixture is hot and shells are tender, about 25 minutes.

4. Remove shells from oven and sprinkle each with an equal amount of mozzarella cheese; broil until cheese is melted.

Each serving provides: 1½ Protein Exchanges; 1½ Vegetable Exchanges;
½ Fat Exchange; 25 calories Optional Exchange
Per serving: 196 calories; 11 g protein; 11 g fat; 13 g carbohydrate; 228 mg calcium;
342 mg sodium; 95 mg cholesterol

Parmesan Puff Hors d'Oeuvres ◐❶

WEEK 1 ～ MAKES 10 SERVINGS, 2 PUFFS EACH

Preheat oven to 400°F. Using a **10-ounce package of refrigerated buttermilk flaky biscuits (10 biscuits),** separate biscuits and cut each in half. In small skillet melt **3 tablespoons plus 1 teaspoon margarine.** Spoon ⅓ **cup grated Parmesan cheese** onto sheet of wax paper. Dip each biscuit half into melted margarine, then dredge in cheese to coat; arrange coated biscuits on nonstick baking sheet, leaving a space of about 1 inch between each. Bake until biscuits are puffed and golden brown, 8 to 10 minutes.

Each serving provides: 1 Bread Exchange; 1 Fat Exchange;
   15 calories Optional Exchange
Per serving: 124 calories; 3 g protein; 6 g fat; 13 g carbohydrate; 53 mg calcium;
   340 mg sodium; 2 mg cholesterol

Molded Cheese Salad

WEEK 1 ～ MAKES 4 SERVINGS

Mold

1 envelope (four ½-cup servings) low-calorie lime-flavored gelatin (8 calories per serving)
1 cup boiling water
½ cup cold water
2 ounces Swiss cheese, shredded

½ cup each shredded carrot and zucchini
½ cup canned crushed pineapple (no sugar added)
1 tablespoon lemon juice
Dash each salt and pepper

Dressing

⅔ cup cottage cheese
2 tablespoons mayonnaise
Dash each salt, pepper, and powdered mustard

2 tablespoons chopped scallion (green onion)

Garnish

Lettuce leaves and 1 medium tomato, cut into 8 wedges

To Prepare Mold: In large heatproof bowl dissolve gelatin in boiling water; stir in cold water. Add remaining ingredients for mold and combine thoroughly. Spray 1-quart mold with nonstick cooking spray and pour in gelatin mixture; cover with plastic wrap and refrigerate until firm, about 3 hours.

To Prepare Dressing: In blender container combine cottage cheese, mayonnaise, and seasonings; process until smooth, about 1 minute. Transfer mixture to small serving dish and stir in scallion; cover and refrigerate until ready to serve.

To Serve: Line platter with bed of lettuce leaves. Using point of small knife, loosen edges of mold; dip mold into warm (*not hot*) water for a few seconds. Invert mold onto lettuce and surround with tomato wedges; serve with dressing.

Each serving provides: 1 Protein Exchange; 1 Vegetable Exchange;
   1½ Fat Exchanges; 20 calories Optional Exchange
Per serving: 180 calories; 11 g protein; 11 g fat; 9 g carbohydrate; 177 mg calcium;
   306 mg sodium; 23 mg cholesterol

Garden Cottage Cheese Salad ◑❸

WEEK 1 ～ MAKES 2 SERVINGS

1⅓ cups cottage cheese
½ cup seeded and diced pared
   cucumber
¼ cup each chopped watercress
   and coarsely grated carrot
2 tablespoons each sliced drained
   canned pimiento and minced
   onion

½ teaspoon Dijon-style mustard
⅛ teaspoon each white pepper
   and Worcestershire sauce
4 iceberg lettuce leaves

Garnish

2 pimiento strips

In bowl combine all ingredients except lettuce and garnish; mix well. Line each of 2 salad plates with 2 lettuce leaves and spoon half of cheese mixture onto each portion of lettuce; garnish each serving with a pimiento strip.

Each serving provides: 2 Protein Exchanges; 1¾ Vegetable Exchanges
Per serving: 177 calories; 20 g protein; 7 g fat; 9 g carbohydrate; 114 mg calcium;
   661 mg sodium; 22 mg cholesterol

Greek Salad

WEEK 4 ～ MAKES 4 SERVINGS

Salad

1 garlic clove, cut in half

8 cups torn salad greens (romaine, escarole, and chicory leaves)

2 medium tomatoes, each cut into 8 wedges

1 cup each sliced green bell pepper and pared cucumber

½ cup sliced radishes

¼ cup each sliced red onion and scallions (green onions)

4 each pitted black olives and pimiento-stuffed green olives, sliced

6 ounces feta cheese, cubed or crumbled

2 ounces drained canned anchovies, chopped

Dressing

1 to 2 tablespoons lemon juice

1 tablespoon plus 1 teaspoon olive oil

1 tablespoon red wine vinegar

½ teaspoon oregano leaves

Dash each salt and pepper

1. Rub inside of a large wooden salad bowl with cut garlic; mash garlic and reserve.

2. Add all salad ingredients except garlic, cheese, and anchovies to bowl; cover and refrigerate for 1 hour.

3. In small bowl combine all ingredients for dressing; add mashed garlic and stir to combine. Cover and refrigerate until chilled.

4. To serve, pour dressing over chilled salad and toss thoroughly to combine; add cheese and anchovies and toss gently.

Each serving provides: 2 Protein Exchanges; 6½ Vegetable Exchanges; 1 Fat Exchange; 10 calories Optional Exchange
Per serving: 257 calories; 13 g protein; 17 g fat; 16 g carbohydrate; 374 mg calcium; 778 mg sodium; 46 mg cholesterol

Vegetable-Cottage Cheese ◐❸

WEEK 4 ◇ MAKES 1 SERVING

6 cherry tomatoes
⅔ cup cottage cheese
2 tablespoons chopped scallion
  (green onion)
2 pimiento-stuffed green olives,
  sliced

1 tablespoon chopped fresh parsley
  (optional)
Lettuce leaves

Cut 5 tomatoes into quarters; reserve remaining tomato for garnish. In small bowl combine all ingredients except lettuce and garnish; mix well. Line a salad plate with lettuce leaves, top with cheese mixture, and garnish with reserved cherry tomato.

Each serving provides: 2 Protein Exchanges; 1¼ Vegetable Exchanges;
  10 calories Optional Exchange
Per serving: 187 calories; 20 g protein; 8 g fat; 9 g carbohydrate; 114 mg calcium;
  805 mg sodium; 23 mg cholesterol

Zesty Tomato-Cheese Salad ◐

WEEK 1 ◇ MAKES 4 SERVINGS

8 large romaine or loose-leafed
  lettuce leaves, torn into bite-size
  pieces
4 medium tomatoes, sliced
4 ounces provolone cheese, sliced

2 tablespoons chilled Italian salad
  dressing

Garnish

Chopped fresh parsley

Line salad bowl with lettuce; arrange tomato and cheese slices over lettuce, alternating and overlapping slices. Cover and refrigerate until chilled. Just before serving, drizzle dressing over salad and sprinkle with parsley.

Each serving provides: 1 Protein Exchange; 2½ Vegetable Exchanges;
  1 Fat Exchange
Per serving: 168 calories; 9 g protein; 11 g fat; 9 g carbohydrate; 249 mg calcium;
  312 mg sodium; 20 mg cholesterol

Spicy Cheese 'n' Caper Dip ◑

WEEK 3 ◇ MAKES 8 SERVINGS, ABOUT ¼ CUP EACH

Serve with crudités.

1⅓ cups cottage cheese
½ cup sour cream
2 tablespoons plus 2 teaspoons
 ketchup
2 tablespoons each chopped scallion
 (green onion) and chopped
 drained capers

2 teaspoons prepared mustard
⅛ teaspoon Worcestershire sauce

In blender container combine all ingredients and process at low speed, scraping down sides of container as necessary, until mixture is smooth, about 30 seconds. Pour into a serving bowl, cover, and refrigerate for at least 30 minutes.

Each serving provides: ½ Protein Exchange; 40 calories Optional Exchange
Per serving: 74 calories; 5 g protein; 5 g fat; 3 g carbohydrate; 41 mg calcium;
 281 mg sodium; 12 mg cholesterol

Variation: Week 1—Substitute buttermilk for the sour cream; reduce Optional Exchange to 15 calories.

Per serving: 50 calories; 5 g protein; 2 g fat; 3 g carbohydrate; 42 mg calcium;
 289 mg sodium; 6 mg cholesterol

Blue Cheese Dressing ◑

WEEK 1 ◇ MAKES 4 SERVINGS, ABOUT 3 TABLESPOONS EACH

---

2 ounces blue cheese, crumbled
2 tablespoons rice vinegar
2 teaspoons olive oil

½ teaspoon Dijon-style mustard
Dash pepper
½ cup buttermilk

In small bowl, using a fork, mix blue cheese with vinegar, oil, mustard, and pepper; gradually stir in buttermilk.

Each serving provides: ½ Protein Exchange; ½ Fat Exchange;
 15 calories Optional Exchange
Per serving: 85 calories; 4 g protein; 7 g fat; 2 g carbohydrate; 111 mg calcium;
 249 mg sodium; 12 mg cholesterol

Easy Cheese Sauce ◐❸

WEEK 4 ～ MAKES 2 SERVINGS

2 teaspoons each margarine and
   all-purpose flour
½ cup skim milk

2 ounces Cheddar cheese, shredded
½ teaspoon Worcestershire sauce
¼ teaspoon powdered mustard

In small nonstick saucepan heat margarine until bubbly and hot; add flour and stir quickly to combine. Remove from heat and gradually stir in milk, stirring until thoroughly combined. Set over low heat and add remaining ingredients; cook, stirring constantly, until cheese is melted and sauce thickens, about 2 minutes.

Each serving provides: 1 Protein Exchange; 1 Fat Exchange; ¼ Milk Exchange;
   10 calories Optional Exchange
Per serving: 182 calories; 10 g protein; 13 g fat; 6 g carbohydrate; 283 mg calcium;
   266 mg sodium; 31 mg cholesterol

Quick and Easy Cheddar Sauce ◐❸

WEEK 1 ～ MAKES 2 SERVINGS, ABOUT 6 TABLESPOONS EACH

½ cup skim milk
⅓ cup instant nonfat dry
   milk powder
2 ounces sharp Cheddar cheese,
   shredded

Dash each Worcestershire sauce,
   hot sauce, salt, and pepper

In small saucepan combine skim milk and milk powder and heat to just below the boiling point; remove pan from heat and stir in remaining ingredients. Cook over low heat, stirring constantly, until cheese is melted.

Each serving provides: 1 Protein Exchange; ¾ Milk Exchange
Per serving: 176 calories; 13 g protein; 10 g fat; 9 g carbohydrate; 419 mg calcium;
   341 mg sodium; 33 mg cholesterol

Cottage-Cheddar Puff ❶

WEEK 1 〜 MAKES 2 SERVINGS

⅓ cup cottage cheese
1 ounce Cheddar cheese, shredded
2 eggs, separated
1 teaspoon instant minced onion,
  reconstituted in 2 teaspoons
  warm water

1 teaspoon Dijon-style mustard
Dash Worcestershire sauce

Preheat oven to 375°F. Spray two 10-ounce custard cups with non-stick cooking spray; set aside.

In blender container combine cheeses, egg yolks, reconstituted onion, mustard, and Worcestershire sauce and process until smooth, scraping down sides of container as necessary; set aside.

In small mixing bowl beat egg whites until stiff but not dry; fold ⅓ of cheese mixture into beaten whites, then fold in remaining cheese mixture. Spoon half of mixture into each sprayed cup; place cups on baking sheet and bake until puffs are golden brown, about 25 minutes.

Each serving provides: 2 Protein Exchanges
Per serving: 178 calories; 14 g protein; 12 g fat; 2 g carbohydrate; 153 mg calcium;
  383 mg sodium; 294 mg cholesterol

Cheddar Muffins ❶

WEEK 4 〜 MAKES 6 SERVINGS, 1 MUFFIN EACH

1 cup plus 2 tablespoons all-purpose
  flour
1 tablespoon granulated sugar
2 teaspoons double-acting baking
  powder

5 ounces Cheddar cheese, shredded
½ cup skim milk
1 egg
2 tablespoons unsalted margarine,
  melted

1. Preheat oven to 400°F. Line a 6-cup muffin pan (2½-inch-diameter cups) with paper baking cups and set aside.

2. In bowl combine flour, sugar, and baking powder; stir in cheese until coated with flour mixture.

3. In 1-cup measure combine milk, egg, and margarine; pour into dry ingredients and, using a fork, stir until all ingredients are moist (mixture will be thick and lumpy).

4. Divide batter into paper baking cups (each will be about ⅔ full); bake for 15 minutes (until muffins are golden brown). Transfer muffins to wire rack to cool.

Each serving provides: 1 Protein Exchange; 1 Bread Exchange; 1 Fat Exchange; 20 calories Optional Exchange
Per serving: 246 calories; 10 g protein; 13 g fat; 22 g carbohydrate; 273 mg calcium; 306 mg sodium; 71 mg cholesterol

Cheese Pancakes ◑❸

WEEK 4 ⌣ MAKES 2 SERVINGS, 4 PANCAKES EACH

⅓ cup plus 2 teaspoons all-purpose flour
½ teaspoon double-acting baking powder
¼ teaspoon salt
⅛ teaspoon paprika

2 eggs
2 ounces Monterey Jack cheese, shredded
2 tablespoons finely chopped scallion (green onion)
2 teaspoons margarine, divided

Onto sheet of wax paper or a paper plate sift together flour, baking powder, salt, and paprika. In medium bowl beat eggs slightly; gradually stir in flour mixture, stirring until smooth. Stir in cheese and scallion.

In 9-inch skillet heat 1 teaspoon margarine until bubbly and hot; drop 4 heaping tablespoonsful batter into hot skillet, making 4 pancakes. Cook until bubbles appear on surface and edges are browned; turn pancakes over and brown other side. Set aside and keep warm. Repeat procedure, using remaining margarine and batter and making 4 more pancakes.

Each serving provides: 2 Protein Exchanges; 1 Bread Exchange; ⅛ Vegetable Exchange; 1 Fat Exchange
Per serving: 307 calories; 16 g protein; 18 g fat; 19 g carbohydrate; 303 mg calcium; 643 mg sodium; 299 mg cholesterol

Serving Suggestion: Serve each portion of pancakes with ½ cup applesauce (no sugar added) and 2 tablespoons sour cream. Add 1 Fruit Exchange and 65 calories Optional Exchange to Exchange Information.

Per serving: 421 calories; 17 g protein; 24 g fat; 34 g carbohydrate; 340 mg calcium; 660 mg sodium; 311 mg cholesterol

Pita Pizza ◗❸

WEEK 4 ∿ MAKES 1 SERVING

---

1 mini pita pocket (1 ounce), cut in half horizontally and toasted	1 tablespoon diced onion
2 tablespoons tomato sauce	2 ounces mozzarella cheese, shredded
3 tablespoons sliced mushrooms	Oregano leaves and garlic powder

Preheat broiler. On baking sheet place toasted pita halves and spread 1 tablespoon tomato sauce over each; top each with half of the mushrooms and 1½ teaspoons onion, then sprinkle each with 1 ounce cheese and dash each oregano leaves and garlic powder. Broil until cheese melts, 1 to 2 minutes.

Each serving provides: 2 Protein Exchanges; 1 Bread Exchange;
   1 Vegetable Exchange
Per serving: 255 calories; 15 g protein; 13 g fat; 19 g carbohydrate; 300 mg calcium; 363 mg sodium; 44 mg cholesterol

Blueberry-Cheese Blintzes with Blueberry Sauce

WEEK 4 ∿ MAKES 4 SERVINGS, 2 BLINTZES EACH

Blintze Wraps

1 cup skim milk	1 teaspoon unsalted margarine, melted
¾ cup all-purpose flour	
2 eggs	

Filling

1⅔ cups pot or cottage cheese	½ cup blueberries
1 egg, beaten	⅛ teaspoon ground cinnamon
2 tablespoons granulated sugar	1 tablespoon unsalted margarine

Sauce

½ cup sour cream	½ cup blueberries
1 teaspoon vanilla extract	

To Prepare Blintze Wraps: In blender container combine milk, flour, and eggs and process until smooth, scraping down sides of container as necessary. Refrigerate, covered, for 1 hour.

Heat an 8-inch nonstick crêpe pan or skillet; brush ⅛ of the melted margarine over bottom of pan and pour in ⅛ of batter (about ¼ cup), quickly swirling batter so that it covers entire bottom of pan. Cook until bottom of blintze wrap is lightly browned; using pancake turner, carefully turn wrap over and brown other side. Slide blintze wrap onto a plate and repeat procedure 7 more times, using remaining batter and melted margarine and making 7 more blintze wraps.

To Prepare Blintzes: Force pot (or cottage) cheese through a sieve Into a small bowl; add egg and sugar and stir until thoroughly blended. Fold in blueberries and cinnamon. Spoon ⅛ of filling onto center of each blintze wrap; fold sides of wrap in and roll to enclose filling. In 12-inch skillet melt margarine; place blintzes seam-side down in skillet and cook until golden on all sides.

To Prepare Sauce: In small bowl combine sour cream and vanilla and stir until smooth; fold in blueberries and spoon sauce over blintzes.

Each serving provides: 2 Protein Exchanges; 1 Bread Exchange; 1 Fat Exchange;
  ½ Fruit Exchange; ¼ Milk Exchange; 95 calories Optional Exchange
Per serving with pot cheese: 378 calories; 22 g protein; 15 g fat; 37 g carbohydrate;
  195 mg calcium; 485 mg sodium; 223 mg cholesterol
With cottage cheese: 400 calories; 21 g protein; 18 g fat; 37 g carbohydrate;
  190 mg calcium; 457 mg sodium; 233 mg cholesterol

"Calzones"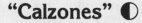

WEEK 2　～　MAKES 4 SERVINGS, 1 "CALZONE" EACH

1 cup part-skim ricotta cheese
4 ounces mozzarella cheese,
  shredded
4 ounces finely chopped (or ground)
  cooked ham

2 teaspoons oregano leaves
4 ready-to-bake refrigerated
  buttermilk flaky biscuits (1 ounce
  each)

Preheat oven to 400°F. In bowl combine first 4 ingredients; set aside.

Roll each biscuit between 2 sheets of wax paper, forming four 6-inch circles; spoon ¼ of cheese mixture onto center of each. Moisten edges of dough slightly, then fold each circle over, turnover style, forming 4 "calzones"; using tines of fork, press edges to seal.

Spray baking sheet with nonstick cooking spray and place turnovers on sheet; bake until golden brown, 10 to 12 minutes. Serve immediately.

Each serving provides: 3 Protein Exchanges; 1 Bread Exchange
Per serving: 299 calories; 22 g protein; 15 g fat; 17 g carbohydrate; 345 mg calcium;
  686 mg sodium; 66 mg cholesterol

Broccoli Crêpes Gratinées ❶

WEEK 4 ～ MAKES 4 SERVINGS, 2 CRÊPES EACH

Crêpes

4 eggs
¾ cup all-purpose flour

½ cup water
⅛ teaspoon salt

Cheese Sauce

2 tablespoons plus 2 teaspoons
  margarine
¼ cup minced shallots or onion
2 tablespoons plus 2 teaspoons
  all-purpose flour

2 cups skim milk
8 ounces Cheddar cheese, shredded
2 teaspoons Worcestershire sauce
½ teaspoon prepared mustard

Filling

4 cups cooked chopped broccoli

⅛ teaspoon each salt and pepper

To Prepare Crêpes: In blender container combine first 4 ingredients and process until smooth. Let stand about 15 minutes so that bubbles will subside.

Lightly spray 9-inch nonstick skillet or omelet pan with nonstick cooking spray and heat (to test, sprinkle pan with drop of water; if water sizzles, pan is hot enough). Pour ⅛ of batter (about ¼ cup) into pan and quickly swirl batter so that it covers entire bottom of pan; cook over medium-high heat until edges and underside of crêpe are dry. Using pancake turner, carefully turn crêpe over; cook other side briefly just to dry, about 30 seconds. Slide crêpe onto a plate and repeat procedure 7 more times, using remaining batter and making 7 more crêpes; set aside.

To Prepare Sauce: In 1½-quart nonstick saucepan heat margarine until bubbly and hot; add shallots (or onion) and sauté briefly (*do not brown*). Add flour and stir quickly to combine; remove from heat and gradually stir in milk, stirring until mixture is smooth. Set over low heat and add cheese, Worcestershire sauce, and mustard; cook, stirring briskly, until cheese is melted and sauce thickens, about 2 minutes.

To Prepare Crêpes Gratinées: Preheat oven to 400°F. In small bowl combine broccoli, seasonings, and half of the cheese sauce. Spoon ⅛ of filling onto center of each crêpe and roll crêpes to enclose filling; place seam-side down in shallow 4-quart flameproof casserole. Top with remaining cheese sauce and bake until sauce begins to bubble; turn oven control to broil and broil until lightly browned.

Each serving provides: 3 Protein Exchanges; 1 Bread Exchange;
  $2\frac{1}{8}$ Vegetable Exchanges; 2 Fat Exchanges; $\frac{1}{2}$ Milk Exchange;
  20 calories Optional Exchange
Per serving with shallots: 584 calories; 33 g protein; 33 g fat; 41 g carbohydrate;
  702 mg calcium; 779 mg sodium; 336 mg cholesterol
With onion: 581 calories; 33 g protein; 33 g fat; 40 g carbohydrate; 701 mg calcium;
  779 mg sodium; 336 mg cholesterol

Welsh Rarebit ❶❸

WEEK 4 ❧ MAKES 2 SERVINGS

4 ounces Cheddar cheese, shredded
1 tablespoon plus 1 teaspoon
  all-purpose flour
$\frac{1}{4}$ cup beer
2 teaspoons margarine

$\frac{1}{2}$ teaspoon Worcestershire sauce
$\frac{1}{4}$ teaspoon powdered mustard
Dash ground red pepper
1 English muffin, split and toasted
1 medium tomato, sliced

In 1-quart nonstick saucepan combine cheese with flour; gradually stir in beer. Add margarine and seasonings and cook over low heat, stirring constantly, until cheese is melted and mixture is smooth and thick.

Place each muffin half in a shallow individual flameproof casserole; top each half with half of the tomato slices, then half of the cheese mixture. Broil 3 inches from heat source until cheese is browned, about 1 minute.

Each serving provides: 2 Protein Exchanges; 1 Bread Exchange;
  1 Vegetable Exchange; 1 Fat Exchange; 35 calories Optional Exchange
Per serving: 377 calories; 18 g protein; 23 g fat; 22 g carbohydrate; 422 mg calcium;
  559 mg sodium; 60 mg cholesterol

Zucchini-Cheese Casserole ◖◑

WEEK 1 ∾ MAKES 2 SERVINGS

4 medium zucchini (about 5 ounces
 each), cut lengthwise into
 ½-inch-thick strips
½ teaspoon salt
4 ounces Muenster cheese,
 shredded*

½ cup plain low-fat yogurt
1 teaspoon each minced onion and
 Dijon-style mustard

Into 12-inch skillet pour water to a depth of about 1 inch and bring
to a boil; add zucchini and salt, cover, and cook until tender-crisp,
about 3 minutes.

Spray 2-quart flameproof casserole with nonstick cooking spray;
drain zucchini and transfer to casserole. In small bowl combine remaining ingredients, mixing well; spread over zucchini and broil
until cheese melts and begins to brown, 4 to 5 minutes.

Each serving provides: 2 Protein Exchanges; 4 Vegetable Exchanges;
 ½ Milk Exchange
Per serving: 296 calories; 20 g protein; 18 g fat; 15 g carbohydrate; 591 mg calcium;
 742 mg sodium; 58 mg cholesterol

* Swiss or provolone cheese may be substituted for the Muenster cheese.
Per serving with Swiss cheese: 300 calories; 22 g protein; 17 g fat;
 17 g carbohydrate; 729 mg calcium; 533 mg sodium; 56 mg cholesterol
With provolone cheese: 286 calories; 21 g protein; 16 g fat; 16 g carbohydrate;
 613 mg calcium; 882 mg sodium; 42 mg cholesterol

Cheese 'n' Eggplant Pie ◑

WEEK 2 ∾ MAKES 2 SERVINGS

1 large eggplant (about 1½
 pounds), pared and cut lengthwise
 into ¼-inch-thick slices
2 ounces each mozzarella cheese
 and sharp Cheddar cheese,
 shredded
1 medium tomato, diced

½ cup each diced green bell
 pepper, diced onion, and sliced
 mushrooms
Dash each oregano leaves and garlic
 powder
2 teaspoons grated Parmesan
 cheese

On baking sheet arrange eggplant slices in a single layer; broil,
turning once, for 3 to 5 minutes on each side (slices should be crisp

and brown). Remove eggplant from broiler and set oven temperature at 350°F.

In small bowl combine mozzarella and Cheddar cheeses. In 9-inch nonstick pie pan arrange eggplant in a circular pattern, overlapping slices; press edges of eggplant together to resemble a pie crust. Spread vegetables evenly over eggplant and sprinkle with oregano and garlic powder; top evenly with combined cheeses, then sprinkle with Parmesan cheese. Bake until cheese is melted and browned, 20 to 25 minutes. Cut into 4 equal wedges and serve 2 wedges per portion.

Each serving provides: 2 Protein Exchanges; 6½ Vegetable Exchanges;
   10 calories Optional Exchange
Per serving: 331 calories; 20 g protein; 17 g fat; 30 g carbohydrate; 440 mg calcium;
   334 mg sodium; 53 mg cholesterol

Mixed Vegetable-Cheese Bake

WEEK 4 ∾ MAKES 4 SERVINGS
---

1 small eggplant (about 12 ounces),
   cut into cubes
1 package (9 ounces) frozen
   artichoke hearts
2 medium tomatoes, each cut into
   8 wedges
1 cup chopped onions
2 garlic cloves, minced

½ teaspoon each oregano leaves,
   basil leaves, and salt
¼ teaspoon pepper
1 tablespoon plus 1 teaspoon olive
   oil
4 ounces provolone cheese,
   shredded

Preheat oven to 425°F. In shallow 2-quart casserole combine all vegetables; sprinkle with seasonings, then drizzle oil over entire mixture. Cover casserole and bake until vegetables are tender, about 45 minutes.

Remove cover and sprinkle vegetables with provolone cheese; return to oven and bake, uncovered, until cheese is melted, 8 to 10 minutes.*

Each serving provides: 1 Protein Exchange; 3½ Vegetable Exchanges;
   1 Fat Exchange
Per serving: 213 calories; 11 g protein; 13 g fat; 16 g carbohydrate; 254 mg calcium;
   555 mg sodium; 20 mg cholesterol

* If crisper topping is desired, broil for about 1 minute; if mixture is to be broiled, be sure to use a flameproof casserole.

Asparagus-Cheese Casserole

WEEK 1 ∽ MAKES 4 SERVINGS

1 tablespoon plus 1 teaspoon
  margarine, melted, divided
24 asparagus spears, cooked
6 ounces sharp Cheddar cheese,
  coarsely shredded
8 thin slices white bread (½ ounce
  each), lightly toasted and cut
  into 1-inch squares

2 cups skim milk
2 eggs, lightly beaten
½ teaspoon salt
¼ teaspoon each white pepper and
  powdered mustard
Dash ground red pepper

Brush a shallow 2-quart casserole with 1 teaspoon margarine; arrange 8 asparagus spears in casserole, sprinkle with 2 ounces cheese, and top cheese with ⅓ of the bread squares. Repeat layers of asparagus, cheese, and bread 2 more times, ending with bread.

In bowl combine milk, eggs, seasonings, and remaining tablespoon margarine; pour over mixture in casserole. Cover and refrigerate for 1 hour.

Preheat oven to 350°F. Set casserole in larger baking pan and pour boiling water into pan to reach halfway up the sides of casserole; bake for 1¼ hours (until a knife, inserted in center, comes out clean). Remove casserole from water bath and let stand for 10 minutes before cutting.

Each serving provides: 2 Protein Exchanges; 1 Bread Exchange;
  1 Vegetable Exchange; 1 Fat Exchange; ½ Milk Exchange
Per serving: 384 calories; 22 g protein; 22 g fat; 25 g carbohydrate; 520 mg calcium;
  820 mg sodium; 185 mg cholesterol

Eggplant Parmigiana

WEEK 4 ⌒ MAKES 2 SERVINGS

1 medium eggplant (about 1 pound), cut crosswise into 8 rounds, each about ¾ inch thick
1 tablespoon plus 1 teaspoon olive oil, divided
Salt and pepper
2 tablespoons diced onion
1 garlic clove, mashed
½ cup tomato sauce

Dash oregano leaves
4 ounces mozzarella cheese, shredded*
2 teaspoons grated Parmesan cheese

Garnish
1 tablespoon chopped fresh parsley

1. Brush 1 side of each eggplant slice with ¼ teaspoon oil. Transfer slices to nonstick baking sheet, oiled-side up, and sprinkle each with dash each salt and pepper.

2. Bake at 400°F. until browned, about 10 minutes. Turn slices, brush each with ¼ teaspoon oil, and bake 10 minutes longer.

3. While eggplant is baking, in small nonstick skillet combine onion and garlic and cook until onion is tender.

4. In shallow 1-quart casserole spread 3 tablespoons tomato sauce; sprinkle sauce with oregano. Arrange eggplant in casserole, overlapping slices, and pour remaining sauce over eggplant; top with onion mixture, then cheeses.

5. Reduce oven temperature to 350°F. and bake Eggplant Parmigiana until cheese is melted and browned, 25 to 30 minutes; serve garnished with parsley.

Each serving provides: 2 Protein Exchanges; 4⅛ Vegetable Exchanges; 2 Fat Exchanges; 10 calories Optional Exchange
Per serving: 334 calories; 15 g protein; 23 g fat; 20 g carbohydrate; 353 mg calcium; 1,081 mg sodium; 46 mg cholesterol

* Try substituting Cheddar or Swiss cheese for the mozzarella.
Per serving with Cheddar cheese: 403 calories; 19 g protein; 29 g fat; 19 g carbohydrate; 469 mg calcium; 1,221 mg sodium; 61 mg cholesterol
With Swiss cheese: 388 calories; 21 g protein; 26 g fat; 21 g carbohydrate; 605 mg calcium; 1,017 mg sodium; 53 mg cholesterol

Mexican-Style Eggplant

WEEK 4 ⌁ MAKES 4 SERVINGS

Delicious served with a mixed green salad.

1 large eggplant (about 1½ pounds), cut crosswise into ½-inch-thick rounds
1 cup each tomato sauce and canned crushed tomatoes
¼ cup each thinly sliced scallions (green onions) and peeled and chopped drained canned mild green chilies*

8 pitted black olives, sliced
2 garlic cloves, minced
½ teaspoon ground cumin
8 ounces Monterey Jack or sharp Cheddar cheese, shredded
½ cup sour cream

Garnish

Parsley sprigs

On 10 x 15-inch nonstick baking sheet arrange eggplant slices in a single layer; bake at 450°F. until soft, about 20 minutes.

While eggplant is baking, in 1½-quart saucepan combine tomato sauce, tomatoes, scallions, chilies, olives, garlic, and cumin and let simmer for 10 minutes.

Line the bottom of shallow 1½-quart casserole with a single layer of half of the eggplant slices. Spread half the tomato sauce mixture over eggplant and sprinkle with 4 ounces cheese; repeat layers, ending with cheese. Bake at 350°F. until bubbly and hot, about 25 minutes. Serve each portion topped with 2 tablespoons sour cream and garnished with parsley.

Each serving provides: 2 Protein Exchanges; 3¾ Vegetable Exchanges;
  75 calories Optional Exchange
Per serving with Monterey Jack: 369 calories; 18 g protein; 25 g fat;
  21 g carbohydrate; 559 mg calcium; 852 mg sodium; 62 mg cholesterol
With Cheddar cheese: 378 calories; 18 g protein; 27 g fat; 19 g carbohydrate;
  534 mg calcium; 899 mg sodium; 72 mg cholesterol

Variation: Before adding first layer of eggplant, line bottom of casserole with 4 corn tortillas (6-inch diameter each); proceed as directed. Add 1 Bread Exchange to Exchange Information.

Per serving with Monterey Jack and corn tortillas: 411 calories; 19 g protein;
  26 g fat; 30 g carbohydrate; 599 mg calcium; 874 mg sodium; 62 mg cholesterol
With Cheddar cheese and corn tortillas: 420 calories; 19 g protein; 27 g fat;
  28 g carbohydrate; 574 mg calcium; 921 mg sodium; 72 mg cholesterol

* Green chilies make this dish mild to moderately hot; vary the amount according to your taste—up to an additional ¼ cup chilies can be added (adjust Exchange Information accordingly).

Vegetable-Cheese Loaf

WEEK 4 ∼ MAKES 4 SERVINGS

2 tablespoons margarine, divided
1 cup each minced carrots and
  chopped scallions (green onions)
6 ounces pared potatoes, shredded
2 garlic cloves, minced
1 cup cooked chopped broccoli
3 tablespoons all-purpose flour
1 packet instant chicken broth and
  seasoning mix

½ cup skim milk
4 ounces Cheddar cheese, shredded
½ cup part-skim ricotta cheese
½ cup plus 1 tablespoon plain
  dried bread crumbs
2 eggs
Dash each salt and pepper
2 teaspoons sesame seed

In 9-inch nonstick skillet heat 1 tablespoon plus 1 teaspoon margarine; add carrots, scallions, potatoes, and garlic and sauté, stirring occasionally, for about 3 minutes. Reduce heat to lowest setting and cover pan; cook until vegetables are tender, 10 to 15 minutes. Add broccoli, flour, and broth mix and stir to combine thoroughly; gradually stir in milk. Add cheeses and cook, stirring constantly, until mixture is thickened; remove from heat.

Preheat oven to 350°F. In mixing bowl combine cheese mixture with remaining ingredients except sesame seed. Grease 9 x 5 x 3-inch nonstick loaf pan with remaining 2 teaspoons margarine; turn cheese mixture into pan and smooth top. Sprinkle with sesame seed and bake until golden brown, 50 minutes to 1 hour. Remove from oven and let loaf cool in pan for about 10 minutes before serving.

Each serving provides: 2 Protein Exchanges; 1½ Bread Exchanges;
  1½ Vegetable Exchanges; 1½ Fat Exchanges; 25 calories Optional Exchange
Per serving: 418 calories; 21 g protein; 22 g fat; 35 g carbohydrate; 413 mg calcium;
  704 mg sodium; 178 mg cholesterol

Fettuccine and Asparagus in Parmesan Sauce ◐

WEEK 2 ∽ MAKES 4 SERVINGS

1 tablespoon plus 1 teaspoon
  margarine
1 cup sliced mushrooms
1 garlic clove, minced
1 cup diagonally sliced steamed
  asparagus spears
1 egg
¼ cup part-skim ricotta cheese

½ cup skim milk
2 ounces grated Parmesan cheese
Dash each salt and freshly ground
  pepper
2 cups cooked fettucine (hot)
2 tablespoons chopped fresh
  parsley

In 12-inch skillet heat margarine until bubbly and hot; add mushrooms and garlic and sauté briefly, about 2 minutes. Stir in asparagus and set aside.

In small bowl combine egg and ricotta cheese, mixing until smooth; add milk and Parmesan cheese and stir to combine. Sprinkle with salt and pepper and add to skillet; stirring constantly, bring to a slow simmer and cook for about 2 minutes. Add fettucine and toss to combine; serve sprinkled with parsley.

Each serving provides: 1 Protein Exchange; 1 Bread Exchange;
  1 Vegetable Exchange; 1 Fat Exchange; 10 calories Optional Exchange
Per serving: 265 calories; 15 g protein; 12 g fat; 24 g carbohydrate; 205 mg calcium;
  399 mg sodium; 110 mg cholesterol

Fettuccine Supreme ◐

WEEK 2 ∽ MAKES 4 SERVINGS

½ cup part-skim ricotta cheese
¼ cup skim milk
1 tablespoon plus 1 teaspoon
  margarine
3 ounces thinly sliced prosciutto
  (Italian-style ham), diced
1 garlic clove, minced

1 cup cooked chopped broccoli
2 cups cooked fettucine
1 ounce grated Parmesan cheese
Dash white pepper

Garnish

2 tablespoons chopped fresh parsley

In blender container combine ricotta cheese and milk and process until smooth; set aside.

In 9-inch skillet heat margarine until bubbly and hot; add prosciutto and garlic and sauté until garlic is golden, about 1 minute. Add broccoli and cheese mixture and cook over medium heat until sauce begins to bubble. Reduce heat and add remaining ingredients except parsley; cook, stirring and tossing gently, until fettucine is thoroughly coated with sauce. Serve sprinkled with parsley.

Each serving provides: 1½ Protein Exchanges; 1 Bread Exchange;
  ½ Vegetable Exchange; 1 Fat Exchange; 5 calories Optional Exchange
Per serving: 267 calories; 17 g protein; 12 g fat; 24 g carbohydrate; 238 mg calcium;
  424 mg sodium; 59 mg cholesterol

Vegetable-Cheese Burgers ❶

WEEK 4 ∿ MAKES 2 SERVINGS, 2 BURGERS EACH

Delicious served with a mixed green salad.

1 teaspoon margarine
¼ cup each minced onion and
  green bell pepper
⅔ cup cottage cheese
⅓ cup plus 2 teaspoons seasoned
  dried bread crumbs, divided

1 ounce sharp Cheddar cheese,
  shredded
1 egg
Dash each salt, pepper, and paprika
1 tablespoon plus 1 teaspoon
  ketchup

1. Preheat oven to 350°F. In small skillet heat margarine until bubbly and hot; add onion and green pepper and sauté until soft.

2. In medium bowl combine sautéed vegetables, cottage cheese, ¼ cup bread crumbs, and the Cheddar cheese, egg, and seasonings, mixing well (mixture will be soft).

3. Divide cheese mixture into 4 equal portions and roll each into a ball; roll balls in remaining 2 tablespoons bread crumbs and transfer to nonstick baking sheet, leaving a space of about 2 inches between each. Using the palm of your hand, flatten each ball slightly.

4. Bake burgers until golden brown and slightly puffed, about 15 minutes; turn burgers over and bake 3 to 5 minutes longer. Serve each burger topped with 1 teaspoon ketchup.

Each serving provides: 2 Protein Exchanges; 1 Bread Exchange;
  ½ Vegetable Exchange; ½ Fat Exchange; 10 calories Optional Exchange
Per serving: 292 calories; 19 g protein; 14 g fat; 23 g carbohydrate; 197 mg calcium;
  781 mg sodium; 164 mg cholesterol

Pineapple-Berry Cheese Parfait ◑

WEEK 1 ⌒ MAKES 4 SERVINGS, 1 PARFAIT EACH

---

1 cup canned crushed pineapple
  (no sugar added), drain and
  reserve juice
1 cup strawberries, sliced

1¼ cups part-skim ricotta cheese
1 tablespoon plus 1 teaspoon
  granulated sugar, divided
½ teaspoon vanilla extract

Set aside 2 tablespoons crushed pineapple and 12 strawberry slices for garnish.

In bowl combine cheese, reserved pineapple juice, 1 tablespoon sugar, and the vanilla, mixing well; in small bowl combine strawberry slices except garnish with remaining teaspoon sugar.

Into each of 4 parfait glasses spoon 2 tablespoons pineapple; top with 2 tablespoons cheese mixture, then 2 tablespoons sliced strawberries. Repeat layers, using ¼ of the remaining pineapple, 2 tablespoons cheese mixture, and ¼ of the remaining berries for each portion; top berries in each glass with ¼ of remaining cheese mixture and garnish each with 1½ teaspoons reserved pineapple and 3 strawberry slices.

Each serving provides: 1 Protein Exchange; ½ Fruit Exchange;
  50 calories Optional Exchange
Per serving: 174 calories; 9 g protein; 6 g fat; 21 g carbohydrate; 225 mg calcium;
  98 mg sodium; 24 mg cholesterol

Pumpkin-Cheese Pie

WEEK 4 ∽ MAKES 8 SERVINGS

Crust

8 zwieback, made into crumbs
1 tablespoon plus 1 teaspoon
  margarine

Filling

2 eggs, separated
1/4 cup firmly packed light brown
  sugar, divided
1 cup each part-skim ricotta cheese
  and canned pumpkin
2 tablespoons lemon juice
1 teaspoon grated lemon peel

1/2 teaspoon ground cinnamon
1/8 teaspoon each ground ginger
  and ground nutmeg
1/2 cup evaporated skimmed milk
2 tablespoons cornstarch
Dash salt

To Prepare Crust: Preheat oven to 350°F. In bowl combine zwieback crumbs and margarine, mixing thoroughly. Using back of a spoon, press crumb mixture over bottom and up sides of 9-inch pie plate. Bake until crisp and brown, 8 to 10 minutes. Remove from oven to wire rack to cool.

To Prepare Filling and Bake: In large mixing bowl beat egg yolks with 2 tablespoons plus 2 teaspoons brown sugar until well combined; add cheese, pumpkin, lemon juice, lemon peel, and spices and stir to combine. In small bowl or 1-cup measure combine milk and cornstarch, stirring to dissolve cornstarch; stir into pumpkin mixture.

In medium bowl, using electric mixer on high speed, beat egg whites with salt until soft peaks form; beat in remaining 1 tablespoon plus 1 teaspoon sugar and continue beating until stiff peaks form. Gently fold whites into pumpkin mixture; pour filling into cooled crust and bake at 350°F. for 35 to 40 minutes (until a thin-bladed knife, inserted in center, comes out clean). Set on wire rack and let cool completely.

Each serving provides: 1/2 Protein Exchange; 1/2 Bread Exchange;
  1/4 Vegetable Exchange; 1/2 Fat Exchange; 65 calories Optional Exchange
Per serving: 167 calories; 8 g protein; 6 g fat; 20 g carbohydrate; 155 mg calcium;
  199 mg sodium; 80 mg cholesterol

Peanut Butter

Once upon a time you may have believed that peanut butter could only go with jelly in sandwiches. Well, it's no fairy tale to say that peanut butter can be a special treat for kids of all ages. We all need high-protein, high-energy, high-taste-appeal foods. Even the most sophisticated palates will respond to our Nutty Green Beans, Creamy Peanut Dip, or Nutty Chocolate "Ice Cream."

Chicken and Vegetable Sauté with Peanut Sauce ◑

WEEK 4 ～ MAKES 2 SERVINGS

Chicken and Vegetables

8 ounces skinned and boned chicken breast, cut into thin strips
1 teaspoon each cornstarch and peanut or vegetable oil
1 garlic clove, minced
1 medium red bell pepper, seeded and cut into thin strips

¼ cup water
1 teaspoon teriyaki sauce
2 cups broccoli florets, blanched
Dash each salt and pepper

Sauce

¼ cup thinly sliced onion
1 cup water
1 packet instant chicken broth and seasoning mix

2 tablespoons peanut butter
1 teaspoon teriyaki sauce

To Prepare Chicken and Vegetables: Sprinkle chicken with cornstarch. In 12-inch nonstick skillet heat oil; add garlic and chicken and sauté for 2 minutes. Add pepper strips, water, and teriyaki sauce and cook until pepper is tender-crisp, 2 to 3 minutes; add broccoli, salt, and pepper and cook until broccoli is thoroughly heated.

To Prepare Sauce: In 8-inch nonstick skillet cook onion over medium heat, stirring frequently, until translucent; stir in water and broth mix and bring to a boil. Reduce heat, stir in peanut butter and teriyaki sauce, and let simmer until mixture is well blended. Serve over chicken and vegetables.

Each serving provides: 4 Protein Exchanges; 3¼ Vegetable Exchanges;
1½ Fat Exchanges; 10 calories Optional Exchange
Per serving: 324 calories; 37 g protein; 13 g fat; 19 g carbohydrate; 93 mg calcium;
897 mg sodium; 66 mg cholesterol

Nutty Green Beans ❶

WEEK 4 ⬳ MAKES 2 SERVINGS

2 tablespoons each chunky-style
  peanut butter and sherry
2 teaspoons oyster sauce
1 garlic clove, minced

½ teaspoon minced pared ginger
  root
2 cups cooked frozen French-style
  green beans (hot)

In small saucepan combine peanut butter, sherry, oyster sauce, garlic, and ginger; bring to a boil. Reduce heat and let simmer, stirring constantly, until mixture is creamy, about 1 minute. Pour peanut butter mixture over hot green beans and serve immediately.

Each serving provides: 1 Protein Exchange; 2 Vegetable Exchanges;
  1 Fat Exchange; 25 calories Optional Exchange
Per serving: 157 calories; 7 g protein; 8 g fat; 13 g carbohydrate; 68 mg calcium;
  340 mg sodium; 0 mg cholesterol

Creamy Peanut Dip ❶❸

WEEK 4 ⬳ MAKES 4 SERVINGS, ABOUT 3½ TABLESPOONS EACH

Delicious served with fresh fruit (e.g., apples, pears, bananas, etc.) or carrot and celery sticks.

¼ cup smooth peanut butter
3 tablespoons water
2 tablespoons thawed frozen
  concentrated orange juice
  (no sugar added)

1 tablespoon lemon juice
½ cup plain low-fat yogurt
Dash vanilla extract

In small bowl combine peanut butter, water, and juices, mixing until smooth; stir in yogurt and vanilla. Cover and refrigerate until chilled.

Each serving provides: 1 Protein Exchange; 1 Fat Exchange;
  ¼ Milk Exchange; 15 calories Optional Exchange
Per serving: 126 calories; 6 g protein; 8 g fat; 8 g carbohydrate; 65 mg calcium;
  118 mg sodium; 2 mg cholesterol

Gingered Peanut Dressing ◑

WEEK 4 ∽ MAKES 4 SERVINGS, ABOUT 3 TABLESPOONS EACH

A delicious dressing to serve over crisp raw or cooked Oriental vegetables.

¼ cup each rice vinegar, water, and   1 garlic clove, minced
   chunky-style peanut butter   ⅛ teaspoon ground ginger
2 teaspoons soy sauce

In small bowl, using a wire whisk, gradually stir vinegar and water into peanut butter; add remaining ingredients and stir to combine.

Each serving provides: 1 Protein Exchange; 1 Fat Exchange
Per serving: 98 calories; 5 g protein; 8 g fat; 4 g carbohydrate; 235 mg calcium;
   319 mg sodium; 0 mg cholesterol

Peanut Butter Salad Dressing ◑

WEEK 4 ∽ MAKES 2 SERVINGS

Serve over salad greens.

1 tablespoon peanut butter   2 teaspoons each minced scallion
1 teaspoon peanut or vegetable oil   (green onion) and soy sauce
Dash ground red pepper   ½ garlic clove, minced
¼ cup water
1 tablespoon rice vinegar or white
   vinegar

In small saucepan combine peanut butter, oil, and red pepper; heat, stirring constantly, until the consistency of smooth paste. Remove from heat and add remaining ingredients; stir to combine. Serve immediately or cover and refrigerate. Bring to room temperature before serving.

Each serving provides: ½ Protein Exchange; 1 Fat Exchange
Per serving: 74 calories; 3 g protein; 6 g fat; 3 g carbohydrate; 11 mg calcium;
   492 mg sodium; 0 mg cholesterol

Apple-Nut Squares ❶

WEEK 4 〜 MAKES 8 SERVINGS, 2 SQUARES EACH

¾ cup all-purpose flour
1 teaspoon double-acting baking
   powder
1 egg
2 tablespoons plus 2 teaspoons
   firmly packed dark brown sugar

½ cup chunky-style peanut butter
1 teaspoon vanilla extract
½ teaspoon ground cinnamon
¼ cup skim milk
2 small Golden Delicious apples,
   cored, pared, and diced

Preheat oven to 350°F. Onto sheet of wax paper or a paper plate sift together flour and baking powder; set aside.

In medium mixing bowl combine egg and sugar and, using an electric mixer, beat until thick; add peanut butter, vanilla, and cinnamon and beat until combined. Add sifted flour alternately with milk, about ⅓ at a time, beating after each addition; stir in apple.

Spray an 8 x 8 x 2-inch baking pan with nonstick cooking spray; spread batter evenly in pan and bake until top is lightly browned, 30 to 35 minutes. Remove pan to wire rack and let cool for 5 minutes; remove cake from pan and return to rack to cool completely. Cut into sixteen 2-inch squares.

Each serving provides: 1 Protein Exchange; ½ Bread Exchange; 1 Fat Exchange;
   45 calories Optional Exchange
Per serving: 184 calories; 7 g protein; 9 g fat; 21 g carbohydrate; 57 mg calcium;
   163 mg sodium; 34 mg cholesterol

Crunchy Peanut Butter Fudge ◐

WEEK 4 ∽ MAKES 4 SERVINGS, 2 PIECES EACH

²/₃ cup instant nonfat dry milk
  powder
¼ cup chunky-style peanut butter
¼ cup raisins, chopped
2 tablespoons plus 2 teaspoons
  thawed frozen concentrated
  apple juice (no sugar added)

2 tablespoons ice water
¾ ounce ready-to-eat oven-toasted
  rice cereal
1 tablespoon plus 1 teaspoon
  shredded coconut, lightly toasted

In small bowl combine milk powder with peanut butter, blending thoroughly; stir in raisins, apple juice, and water. Add cereal and stir until combined. Press mixture into 7³/₈ x 3⁵/₈ x 2¼-inch nonstick loaf pan; sprinkle with coconut and, using back of spoon, press coconut into mixture. Refrigerate until firm, about 2 hours. To serve, cut into 8 squares.

Each serving provides: 1 Protein Exchange; 1 Fat Exchange; 1 Fruit Exchange;
  ½ Milk Exchange; 30 calories Optional Exchange
Per serving: 211 calories; 9 g protein; 9 g fat; 26 g carbohydrate; 166 mg calcium;
  231 mg sodium; 2 mg cholesterol

Stuffed Dates ◑

WEEK 4 ∽ MAKES 4 SERVINGS, 2 DATES EACH

¼ cup smooth peanut butter
2 teaspoons grated fresh orange
  peel, divided

8 pitted dates, split open lengthwise
½ teaspoon confectioners' sugar

In small bowl combine peanut butter and 1 teaspoon orange peel; spoon ⅛ of mixture into each date. Sift an equal amount of sugar over each filled date, then sprinkle each with ⅛ of the remaining orange peel.

Each serving provides: 1 Protein Exchange; 1 Fat Exchange; 1 Fruit Exchange;
  3 calories Optional Exchange
Per serving: 141 calories; 5 g protein; 8 g fat; 16 g carbohydrate; 17 mg calcium;
  98 mg sodium; 0 mg cholesterol

Nutty Chocolate "Ice Cream" ❸

WEEK 4　◇　MAKES 2 SERVINGS

**6 ounces chocolate dietary frozen
dessert, softened**
**2 tablespoons chunky-style peanut
butter**
**2 teaspoons chocolate fudge
topping**

**1 graham cracker (2½-inch square),
made into crumbs**
**2 teaspoons shredded coconut,
toasted**

In work bowl of food processor or in mixing bowl combine frozen
dessert, peanut butter, and topping and process, or beat with electric mixer, until well blended; transfer mixture to freezer container,
cover, and freeze until firm.

In small bowl combine crumbs and coconut; divide chocolate–
peanut mixture into 2 dessert dishes and sprinkle each portion with
half of the crumb mixture.

Each serving provides: 1 Protein Exchange; 1 Fat Exchange; 1 Fruit Exchange;
½ Milk Exchange; 50 calories Optional Exchange
Per serving: 236 calories; 9 g protein; 11 g fat; 29 g carbohydrate; 169 mg calcium;
197 mg sodium; 2 mg cholesterol

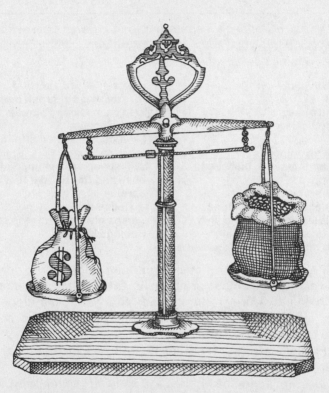

Dry Beans, Lentils, and Peas

If you've ever said "never" to legumes, you'll never say it again once you discover this new world of economical, nutritious cookery. When you add dry beans, peas, lentils, and tofu to your cooking repertoire, you need search no more for thrifty ways to trim your budget and still trim your waistline. Whether you select hearty Vegetarian Casserole or filling Salmon-Garbanzo Salad, you can be sure that the first time you make it certainly won't be the last.

Pasta e Fagioli (Pasta and Bean Soup) ❶

WEEK 3 ∽ MAKES 4 SERVINGS, ABOUT 1½ CUPS EACH

Whether you are Italian, a vegetarian, or just someone who likes a filling bowl of soup, you're sure to enjoy this excellent one-pot meal. Serve with a mixed green salad.

1 tablespoon plus 1 teaspoon
   olive oil
1 cup diced onions
½ cup diced celery (1 large outer
   rib)
1 garlic clove, minced
4 large plum tomatoes, blanched
   and chopped
1 quart plus 1 cup water
6 ounces uncooked white kidney
   (cannellini) beans, rinsed and
   soaked overnight according to
   package directions, then drained

1 cup each sliced zucchini, chopped
   carrots, and cut green beans
½ cup each chopped green and
   red bell peppers
1½ ounces uncooked ditalini (small
   tube macaroni)
1 tablespoon each chopped fresh
   basil and Italian (flat-leaf)
   parsley
1 teaspoon salt
2 ounces grated Parmesan or
   Romano cheese

In 4-quart saucepan heat oil over high heat; add onions, celery, and garlic and sauté until onions are translucent. Add tomatoes and cook, stirring constantly, for 1 to 2 minutes; add water and kidney beans and bring to a boil. Reduce heat to medium, cover, and cook until beans are tender, 20 to 30 minutes.

Add zucchini, carrots, green beans, and peppers to soup and stir to combine; cover and cook until vegetables are tender, about 15 minutes. Stir in ditalini, basil, parsley, and salt; cover and cook until macaroni is just al dente, about 8 minutes. Serve each portion sprinkled with ½ ounce cheese.

Each serving provides: 2½ Protein Exchanges; ½ Bread Exchange;
   3¾ Vegetable Exchanges; 1 Fat Exchange
Per serving with Parmesan cheese: 357 calories; 20 g protein; 10 g fat;
   50 g carbohydrate; 334 mg calcium; 855 mg sodium; 11 mg cholesterol
With Romano cheese: 346 calories; 18 g protein; 10 g fat; 50 g carbohydrate;
   277 mg calcium; 764 mg sodium; 15 mg cholesterol

Hearty Lentil Soup ❶

WEEK 3 ∽ MAKES 2 SERVINGS

Tasty, filling, and inexpensive; serve with a mixed green salad.

3 ounces rinsed uncooked lentils
2 cups water
6 ounces pared potatoes, diced
½ cup each diced onion, celery, and carrot
2 packets instant beef broth and seasoning mix

2 tablespoons chopped fresh parsley
1 garlic clove, minced
1 bay leaf
Dash to ⅛ teaspoon ground cumin

In 2-quart saucepan combine lentils and water and bring to a boil. Reduce heat, cover pan, and let simmer until lentils are tender, about 20 minutes.

Add remaining ingredients to lentils and stir to combine; cover and cook over low heat until potatoes are tender, 20 to 30 minutes. Remove bay leaf before serving.

Each serving provides: 2 Protein Exchanges; 1 Bread Exchange; 1½ Vegetable Exchanges; 10 calories Optional Exchange
Per serving: 258 calories; 15 g protein; 1 g fat; 50 g carbohydrate; 87 mg calcium; 819 mg sodium; 0 mg cholesterol

Minestrone Soup

WEEK 3 ∽ MAKES 2 SERVINGS, ABOUT 2 CUPS EACH

2 teaspoons olive oil
2 cups shredded green cabbage
½ cup sliced onion
4 garlic cloves, minced
1½ cups canned beef broth
1 cup each chopped canned whole
   tomatoes and water
½ cup each sliced carrot and celery
4 ounces drained canned white
   kidney (cannellini) beans

½ cup diced zucchini
1 tablespoon chopped fresh basil or
   2 teaspoons dried
½ teaspoon salt
Dash pepper
1 cup cooked small macaroni shells
   or elbow macaroni
1 tablespoon chopped fresh parsley
2 teaspoons grated Parmesan
   cheese

In 2½- or 3-quart saucepan heat oil over medium heat; add cabbage, onion, and garlic and sauté, stirring occasionally, for about 10 minutes. Add broth, tomatoes, water, carrot, and celery; cook for 15 to 20 minutes longer. Add beans, zucchini, basil, salt, and pepper and let simmer until vegetables are tender, about 15 minutes. Add macaroni and cook until heated; serve sprinkled with parsley and cheese.

Each serving provides: 1 Protein Exchange; 1 Bread Exchange;
   5 Vegetable Exchanges; 1 Fat Exchange; 40 calories Optional Exchange
Per serving: 299 calories; 14 g protein; 7 g fat; 49 g carbohydrate; 194 mg calcium;
   1,579 mg sodium (estimated); 1 mg cholesterol

Black Bean Soup ❶

WEEK 3 ∽ MAKES 2 SERVINGS

2 teaspoons margarine
2 tablespoons diced onion
1 garlic clove, chopped
1¾ cups water
4 ounces drained canned black
  (turtle) beans
¼ cup each chopped carrot and
  celery

1 packet instant chicken broth
  and seasoning mix
½ small bay leaf
1 tablespoon dry sherry
Dash each salt and pepper
1 egg, hard-cooked and chopped

In 1-quart saucepan heat margarine until bubbly and hot; add onion and garlic and sauté until onion is softened. Add water, beans, carrot, celery, broth mix, and bay leaf to saucepan and bring mixture to a boil. Reduce heat, cover, and cook until vegetables are very soft, about 45 minutes. Remove from heat and let cool slightly; remove and discard bay leaf.

Pour mixture into blender container and process at low speed until smooth; return soup to saucepan and stir in sherry, salt, and pepper. Bring to a simmer and let cook until thoroughly heated, about 5 minutes; pour into 2 bowls and sprinkle each portion with half of the chopped egg.

Each serving provides: 1½ Protein Exchanges; ½ Vegetable Exchange;
  1 Fat Exchange; 15 calories Optional Exchange
Per serving: 167 calories; 8 g protein; 7 g fat; 17 g carbohydrate; 56 mg calcium;
  782 mg sodium (estimated); 137 mg cholesterol

Three-Bean Soup ◐❶

2 teaspoons olive or vegetable oil
¼ cup diced onion
1 garlic clove, minced
1 cup each thinly sliced zucchini
  and canned Italian tomatoes
8 ounces drained canned red
  kidney beans (reserve liquid)

4 ounces each drained canned
  chick-peas (garbanzo beans) and
  small white beans (reserve
  liquid)
½ teaspoon basil leaves
⅛ teaspoon each salt and pepper

In 2-quart saucepan heat oil over medium-high heat; add onion and garlic and sauté until onion is softened, about 3 minutes. Add zucchini and cook, stirring constantly, until tender, about 5 minutes. Stir in tomatoes, beans, 1 cup reserved liquid, and the seasonings and bring to a boil. Reduce heat and let simmer for 10 to 15 minutes.

Each serving provides: 2 Protein Exchanges; 1⅛ Vegetable Exchanges;
  ½ Fat Exchange
Per serving: 240 calories; 14 g protein; 4 g fat; 40 g carbohydrate; 93 mg calcium;
  444 mg sodium (estimated); 0 mg cholesterol

White Bean Soup ◐❶

2 teaspoons olive or vegetable oil
½ cup each diced carrot and celery
¼ cup finely diced onion
1 garlic clove, minced
1½ cups water
½ cup tomato sauce
¼ teaspoon each basil leaves and
  salt

⅛ teaspoon each thyme leaves and
  pepper
4 ounces drained canned small
  white beans
2 teaspoons chopped fresh parsley

In 1½- or 2-quart saucepan heat oil; add carrot, celery, onion, and garlic and sauté until vegetables are tender. Stir in water, tomato sauce, and seasonings and bring mixture to a boil. Reduce heat and let simmer for 15 minutes. Stir in beans and cook until thoroughly heated, about 5 minutes longer. Serve each portion sprinkled with 1 teaspoon parsley.

Each serving provides: 1 Protein Exchange; 2¼ Vegetable Exchanges;
1 Fat Exchange
Per serving: 153 calories; 6 g protein; 5 g fat; 22 g carbohydrate; 66 mg calcium;
811 mg sodium (estimated); 0 mg cholesterol

Yellow Split Pea 'n' Ham Soup ❶

WEEK 3   ∽   MAKES 2 SERVINGS, ABOUT 1 CUP EACH

3 ounces uncooked yellow split peas
1 teaspoon margarine
½ cup chopped carrot
¼ cup each chopped onion and celery
2 ounces chopped boiled ham
2 cups water

1½ packets instant chicken broth and seasoning mix
1 small bay leaf, studded with 1 whole clove
Dash each ground cinnamon and white pepper

Sort and rinse peas; set aside. In 2-quart saucepan heat margarine until bubbly and hot; add carrot, onion, celery, and ham and cook, stirring constantly, until onion is translucent. Stir in split peas and remaining ingredients and bring to a boil. Reduce heat, cover, and let simmer until peas and vegetables are soft, about 45 minutes.

Let soup cool slightly; remove and discard bay leaf and clove. Transfer soup to work bowl of food processor and process until pureed; return to saucepan and cook until heated.

Each serving provides: 3 Protein Exchanges; 1 Vegetable Exchange;
½ Fat Exchange; 8 calories Optional Exchange
Per serving: 248 calories; 19 g protein; 5 g fat; 33 g carbohydrate; 41 mg calcium;
955 mg sodium; 25 mg cholesterol

Bean Dip Mexicali ◑❸

WEEK 3 〜 MAKES 4 SERVINGS

8 ounces drained canned pink
 beans (reserve 3 tablespoons
 liquid)
1 tablespoon chopped onion
1 medium garlic clove, mashed
½ teaspoon each chili powder and
 ground cumin

4 ounces sharp Cheddar cheese,
 shredded
2 teaspoons vegetable oil
4 pita breads (1 ounce each),
 each cut into quarters

In blender container or work bowl of food processor combine beans, reserved liquid, onion, garlic, chili powder, and cumin; process until smooth.

Transfer bean mixture to 1-quart saucepan; add cheese and cook over low heat, stirring constantly, until cheese is melted. Stir in oil and serve with pita breads.

Each serving provides: 2 Protein Exchanges; 1 Bread Exchange; ½ Fat Exchange
Per serving: 281 calories; 14 g protein; 13 g fat; 27 g carbohydrate; 231 mg calcium;
 181 mg sodium (estimated); 30 mg cholesterol

Variation: Week 4—Substitute 4 taco shells, broken into pieces, for the pita breads.

Per serving: 255 calories; 12 g protein; 14 g fat; 19 g carbohydrate; 231 mg calcium;
 181 mg sodium (estimated); 30 mg cholesterol

Chick-Pea Salad with Mustard Vinaigrette ◑❸

WEEK 3 〜 MAKES 2 SERVINGS

4 ounces drained canned chick-peas
 (garbanzo beans)
½ cup each chopped celery, tomato,
 and pared cucumber
2 tablespoons wine vinegar
1 tablespoon each chopped fresh
 parsley and lemon juice

2 teaspoons olive or vegetable oil
1 garlic clove, minced, or ⅛
 teaspoon garlic powder
¼ teaspoon spicy brown mustard
Dash each salt, pepper, and oregano
 leaves

In 1-quart bowl combine all ingredients; cover and refrigerate until chilled, tossing occasionally.

Each serving provides: 1 Protein Exchange; 1½ Vegetable Exchanges;
 1 Fat Exchange
Per serving: 136 calories; 5 g protein; 6 g fat; 18 g carbohydrate; 59 mg calcium;
 312 mg sodium (estimated); 0 mg cholesterol

Sesame-Garbanzo Dip ◑

WEEK 4 〰 MAKES 4 SERVINGS, ABOUT 2 TABLESPOONS EACH

Serve with crudités.

6 ounces drained canned chick-peas
  (garbanzo beans)
¼ cup lemon juice
1 tablespoon plus 1 teaspoon
  sesame seed, toasted and
  crushed

2 teaspoons Chinese sesame oil
1 garlic clove, mashed
½ teaspoon salt

In work bowl of food processor combine all ingredients and process until pureed; transfer to serving bowl. Cover and refrigerate until chilled.

Each serving provides: ½ Protein Exchange; ½ Fat Exchange;
  40 calories Optional Exchange
Per serving: 46 calories; 2 g protein; 2 g fat; 5 g carbohydrate; 14 mg calcium;
  208 mg sodium (estimated); 0 mg cholesterol

Marinated Garbanzo Salad ❽

WEEK 3 〰 MAKES 2 SERVINGS

4 ounces drained canned chick-peas
  (garbanzo beans)
1 tablespoon each diced onion,
  diced green bell pepper, and red
  wine vinegar
1½ teaspoons lemon juice
1 teaspoon olive or vegetable oil

½ teaspoon chopped fresh basil
  or ¼ teaspoon dried
½ garlic clove, minced
⅛ teaspoon each salt and oregano
  leaves
Dash pepper

In bowl combine chick-peas, onion, and green pepper. In measuring cup or small bowl combine remaining ingredients, mixing thoroughly. Pour dressing over chick-pea mixture and toss gently to coat; cover and refrigerate overnight or at least 4 hours.

Each serving provides: 1 Protein Exchange; ⅛ Vegetable Exchange;
  ½ Fat Exchange
Per serving: 95 calories; 4 g protein; 3 g fat; 13 g carbohydrate; 38 mg calcium;
  338 mg sodium (estimated); 0 mg cholesterol

Salmon-Garbanzo Salad

WEEK 3 ⬙ MAKES 2 SERVINGS

---

4 ounces skinned and boned drained
   canned salmon
1 cup cooked broccoli florets
2 ounces drained canned chick-peas
   (garbanzo beans)
2 tablespoons chopped scallion
   (green onion)

1 tablespoon plus 1½ teaspoons
   lemon juice
2 teaspoons olive oil
¼ teaspoon Dijon-style mustard
⅛ teaspoon each salt, pepper, and
   basil leaves

In salad bowl combine salmon, broccoli, chick-peas, and scallion. In jar that has a tight-fitting cover or a small bowl combine remaining ingredients; cover and shake well or stir to thoroughly combine. Pour dressing over salad and toss gently to coat.

Each serving provides: 2½ Protein Exchanges; 1⅛ Vegetable Exchanges;
  1 Fat Exchange
Per serving: 181 calories; 16 g protein; 9 g fat; 11 g carbohydrate; 161 mg calcium;
  494 mg sodium (estimated); 20 mg cholesterol

Baked Beans and Rice ◗❸

WEEK 4 ⬙ MAKES 2 SERVINGS

---

4 ounces drained canned pink beans
¼ cup tomato sauce
2 teaspoons ketchup

1 teaspoon dark molasses
½ teaspoon powdered mustard
1 cup cooked long-grain rice

Preheat oven to 350°F. In shallow 2-cup casserole combine beans, tomato sauce, ketchup, molasses, and mustard; mix well. Stir in rice and bake until thoroughly heated, about 15 minutes.

Each serving provides: 1 Protein Exchange; 1 Bread Exchange;
  ½ Vegetable Exchange; 15 calories Optional Exchange
Per serving: 183 calories; 7 g protein; 1 g fat; 38 g carbohydrate; 70 mg calcium;
  404 mg sodium (estimated); 0 mg cholesterol

Vegetarian Eggplant Rolls

WEEK 4 ~ MAKES 4 SERVINGS, 2 ROLLS EACH

1 large eggplant (about 1½ pounds)
2 tablespoons olive or vegetable oil, divided
½ cup each diced onion and green bell pepper
1 tablespoon chopped fresh Italian (flat-leaf) parsley
¼ teaspoon each salt and oregano leaves
10 ounces drained canned chick-peas (garbanzo beans), mashed

1 cup each part-skim ricotta cheese and well-drained cooked chopped spinach
1 egg, beaten
1 cup tomato sauce
4 ounces mozzarella cheese, shredded

Garnish

Chopped fresh Italian (flat-leaf) parsley

1. Cut stem and very thin slice from top of eggplant, then cut eggplant in half lengthwise; starting from cut sides and slicing lengthwise, cut four ¼-inch-thick slices from each half. Reserve remaining eggplant for use at another time.

2. In 12-inch nonstick skillet heat 1¼ teaspoons oil; add 2 eggplant slices and cook, turning once, until soft and lightly browned on both sides. Remove from skillet and set aside. Repeat procedure with remaining eggplant, using 1¼ teaspoons oil for each 2 slices.

3. In same skillet heat remaining teaspoon oil; add onion and green pepper and sauté until onion is translucent. Stir in 1 tablespoon parsley and the salt and oregano; remove from heat.

4. Preheat oven to 350°F. In bowl combine half of sautéed vegetables with chick-peas, ricotta cheese, spinach, and egg, mixing well; spoon ⅛ of mixture onto each eggplant slice and, starting from narrow end, roll eggplant to enclose filling. Arrange rolls seam-side down in a shallow casserole that is just large enough to hold them in a single layer.

5. Combine remaining onion mixture with tomato sauce and pour evenly over eggplant rolls; sprinkle with mozzarella cheese and bake until cheese is melted and lightly browned, about 30 minutes. Serve garnished with chopped parsley.

Each serving provides: 3½ Protein Exchanges; 3 Vegetable Exchanges; 1½ Fat Exchanges
Per serving: 377 calories; 22 g protein; 21 g fat; 28 g carbohydrate; 424 mg calcium; 609 mg sodium (estimated); 110 mg cholesterol

Broccoli-Bean Casserole

WEEK 4 ∾ MAKES 4 SERVINGS

1 tablespoon plus 1 teaspoon
    margarine, divided
¼ cup diced onion
1 medium garlic clove, minced
4 cups broccoli florets, blanched
4 ounces drained canned small
    white beans
½ cup diced drained canned
    pimientos

¼ teaspoon salt
⅛ teaspoon each oregano leaves
    and pepper
4 ounces sharp Cheddar cheese,
    coarsely shredded
3 tablespoons plain dried bread
    crumbs

Preheat oven to 375°F. In small skillet heat 1 teaspoon margarine until bubbly; add onion and garlic and sauté until onion is softened.

In 10 x 6 x 2-inch baking dish spread onion mixture; arrange broccoli florets over onions and top with beans, then pimientos. Sprinkle with salt, oregano, and pepper and top with cheese, then bread crumbs; dot with remaining tablespoon margarine and bake until cheese is melted and crumbs are browned, about 30 minutes.

Each serving provides: 1½ Protein Exchanges; 2¼ Vegetable Exchanges;
    1 Fat Exchange; 20 calories Optional Exchange
Per serving: 251 calories; 15 g protein; 14 g fat; 20 g carbohydrate; 289 mg calcium;
    526 mg sodium (estimated); 30 mg cholesterol

Vegetarian Casserole ❶

WEEK 3 ∾ MAKES 2 SERVINGS

2 teaspoons olive or vegetable oil
¼ cup diced onion
1 medium garlic clove, minced
2 cups thinly sliced zucchini
1 cup canned crushed tomatoes
4 ounces drained canned small red
    beans

¼ teaspoon oregano leaves
⅛ teaspoon each salt and pepper
2 ounces provolone cheese,
    shredded

Preheat oven to 350°F. In 10-inch skillet heat oil; add onion and garlic and sauté until onion is softened. Add zucchini and cook, stirring constantly, until tender-crisp, about 3 minutes. Stir in tomatoes, beans, and seasonings; bring to a boil.

Transfer bean mixture to shallow 1-quart flameproof casserole; sprinkle with cheese and bake until thoroughly heated, 20 to 25 minutes. Turn oven control to broil and broil until cheese is lightly browned.

Each serving provides: 2 Protein Exchanges; 3¼ Vegetable Exchanges;
  1 Fat Exchange
Per serving: 263 calories; 15 g protein; 13 g fat; 25 g carbohydrate; 293 mg calcium;
  740 mg sodium (estimated); 20 mg cholesterol

Variation: Substitute Swiss cheese for provolone cheese and white kidney (cannellini) beans for small red beans.

Per serving: 269 calories; 15 g protein; 13 g fat; 25 g carbohydrate; 347 mg calcium;
  565 mg sodium (estimated); 26 mg cholesterol

Chick-Peas au Gratin ◐ ❸

WEEK 4 ∽ MAKES 2 SERVINGS

---

2 teaspoons olive or vegetable oil
1 garlic clove, sliced
½ cup each diced onion and green
  bell pepper
2 cups shredded green cabbage
1 cup canned Italian tomatoes,
  chopped
1 teaspoon tomato paste
¼ teaspoon each salt and oregano
  leaves

Dash each ground ginger and white
  pepper
8 ounces drained canned chick-peas
  (garbanzo beans)
2 ounces Cheddar cheese, shredded
3 tablespoons plain dried bread
  crumbs

Garnish

Italian (flat-leaf) parsley sprigs

Preheat oven to 450°F. In 9- or 10-inch nonstick skillet heat oil; add garlic and sauté until golden. Using a slotted spoon, remove and discard garlic. Add onion and green pepper to skillet and sauté until onion is translucent; stir in cabbage and cook until cabbage is wilted, about 5 minutes. Add tomatoes and stir to combine; bring mixture to a boil. Stir in tomato paste and seasonings, reduce heat, and let simmer for 5 minutes; stir in chick-peas and remove from heat.

Transfer mixture to shallow 1-quart casserole. In small bowl combine cheese and bread crumbs; sprinkle over chick-pea mixture and bake until thoroughly heated and cheese topping is browned, about 5 minutes. Serve garnished with parsley.

Each serving provides: 3 Protein Exchanges; ½ Bread Exchange;
  4 Vegetable Exchanges; 1 Fat Exchange; 2 calories Optional Exchange
Per serving: 401 calories; 20 g protein; 17 g fat; 47 g carbohydrate; 343 mg calcium;
  1,111 mg sodium (estimated); 30 mg cholesterol

Split Pea Fritters ❶

WEEK 4 ∿ MAKES 4 SERVINGS, 4 FRITTERS EACH

3 ounces uncooked yellow split peas, rinsed and sorted
2 cups water
¼ cup each diced onion and shredded carrot
1 packet instant chicken broth and seasoning mix
⅓ cup plus 2 teaspoons all-purpose flour

1 teaspoon double-acting baking powder
Dash each salt and white pepper
¼ cup skim milk
1 egg, beaten
1 tablespoon plus 1 teaspoon vegetable oil, divided

In 1½-quart saucepan combine peas, water, onion, carrot, and broth mix and bring to a boil. Reduce heat, cover, and let simmer, stirring occasionally, until peas are soft, about 30 minutes; let cool.

In medium bowl combine flour, baking powder, salt, and pepper. Add milk and egg to cooled split pea mixture, stirring to combine; stir into dry ingredients.

In 10-inch nonstick skillet heat 1 teaspoon oil. Spoon 4 heaping tablespoons of batter into skillet, forming 4 small fritters; cook until edges bubble and fritters are browned on bottom. Turn fritters over and cook until browned on other side. Remove to warmed serving plate; set aside and keep warm. Repeat procedure with remaining oil and batter, making a total of 16 fritters and using 1 teaspoon oil for each 4 fritters.

Each serving provides: 1 Protein Exchange; ½ Bread Exchange;
 ¼ Vegetable Exchange; 1 Fat Exchange; 25 calories Optional Exchange
Per serving: 192 calories; 9 g protein; 6 g fat; 25 g carbohydrate; 92 mg calcium;
 384 mg sodium; 69 mg cholesterol

Serving Suggestion: Serve 2 tablespoons sour cream with each portion. Increase Optional Exchange to 90 calories.

Per serving: 253 calories; 10 g protein; 12 g fat; 26 g carbohydrate; 126 mg calcium;
 400 mg sodium; 81 mg cholesterol

Sesame Tofu Sticks ❶

WEEK 4 ～ MAKES 2 SERVINGS, 10 STICKS EACH

**6 ounces firm-style tofu (soybean
curd)**
¼ cup teriyaki sauce
**1 teaspoon shredded pared ginger
root**

1 garlic clove, minced
3 tablespoons all-purpose flour
2 teaspoons sesame seed
1 tablespoon peanut or vegetable oil

Cut tofu into twenty 3 x ½-inch sticks; arrange on paper towels and pat dry. In shallow bowl combine teriyaki sauce, ginger, and garlic; add tofu sticks and toss to coat well. Cover and let stand at room temperature for 30 minutes.

Remove tofu sticks from marinade, place on paper towels, and pat dry. On sheet of wax paper or a paper plate combine flour and sesame seed; roll tofu sticks in flour mixture, coating all sides. In 10-inch nonstick skillet heat oil; add tofu sticks and sauté until browned on all sides.

Each serving provides: 1 Protein Exchange; ½ Bread Exchange;
1½ Fat Exchanges; 20 calories Optional Exchange
Per serving: 219 calories; 10 g protein; 12 g fat; 19 g carbohydrate; 115 mg calcium;
1,205 mg sodium; 0 mg cholesterol

Tofu-Peanut Balls with Sweet 'n' Sour Sauce

WEEK 4 ⌒ MAKES 4 SERVINGS,
4 BALLS AND ABOUT ¼ CUP SAUCE EACH

Tofu-Peanut Balls

15 ounces firm-style tofu (soybean curd)

1 tablespoon plus 1½ teaspoons peanut or vegetable oil, divided

¼ cup each minced onion and red or green bell pepper

1 garlic clove, minced

¼ cup chunky-style peanut butter

¼ cup teriyaki sauce, divided

1 tablespoon sesame seed

Dash each pepper and ground ginger

3 tablespoons all-purpose flour

Sauce

⅔ cup pineapple juice (no sugar added)

1 tablespoon teriyaki sauce

1 teaspoon each cornstarch and rice vinegar

½ teaspoon firmly packed brown sugar

To Prepare Tofu-Peanut Balls: In a medium bowl mash tofu; set aside. In 10-inch nonstick skillet heat ½ teaspoon oil; add onion, bell pepper, and garlic and sauté until onion is golden. Add onion mixture to tofu and stir to combine. Stir in peanut butter, 1 tablespoon teriyaki sauce, and the sesame seed, pepper, and ginger, mixing thoroughly; shape into 16 equal balls. On sheet of wax paper or a paper plate coat tofu balls with flour.

In same skillet heat remaining 1 tablespoon plus 1 teaspoon oil; add balls, 1 at a time, and sauté over medium heat until browned on all sides; pour remaining 3 tablespoons teriyaki sauce into skillet and gently stir balls until glazed. Remove balls to serving plate and keep warm.

To Prepare Sauce: In small saucepan combine all ingredients for sauce and stir to dissolve cornstarch; bring sauce to a boil. Reduce heat and cook, stirring constantly, until mixture thickens. Serve as dipping sauce with tofu-peanut balls.

Each serving provides: 2 Protein Exchanges; ¼ Vegetable Exchange;
2 Fat Exchanges; ½ Fruit Exchange; 65 calories Optional Exchange
Per serving: 305 calories; 15 g protein; 19 g fat; 23 g carbohydrate; 159 mg calcium; 858 mg sodium; 0 mg cholesterol

Poultry

We're taking you on a trip around the world with poultry. Chicken, turkey, and even Cornish hens have earned universal popularity because of the tasty, satisfying, thrifty ways they can be adapted to so many ethnic cuisines. So "weigh anchor" as we set sail to ports that offer such exotic fare as Roast Cornish Hen with Mango Sauce, Chicken Curry, Oriental Stir-Fry, and Chicken Schnitzel. Wherever you go, whatever you choose, we wish you Bon Appétit!

Chicken Oriental Soup ◑

WEEK 4 ✧ MAKES 2 SERVINGS, ABOUT 1 CUP EACH

1 packet instant chicken broth and
  seasoning mix
1½ cups water
1 cup chopped well-washed spinach
  leaves
2 tablespoons sliced scallion (green
  onion)

1 egg white
2 ounces skinned and boned
  cooked chicken, cut into thin
  strips
Dash each ground ginger and pepper

Empty broth mix into small saucepan; add water and bring to a boil. Add spinach and scallion and return to a boil. Reduce heat and slowly add egg white, stirring constantly, until egg white has set. Add chicken and seasonings and cook until thoroughly heated.

Each serving provides: 1 Protein Exchange; 1⅛ Vegetable Exchanges;
  15 calories Optional Exchange
Per serving: 74 calories; 11 g protein; 2 g fat; 3 g carbohydrate; 35 mg calcium;
  486 mg sodium; 25 mg cholesterol

Variation: Substitute instant beef or onion broth mix for the chicken broth mix and use cooked beef or pork, cut into strips.

Per serving with beef: 78 calories; 12 g protein; 2 g fat; 3 g carbohydrate;
  35 mg calcium; 440 mg sodium; 26 mg cholesterol
With pork: 96 calories; 11 g protein; 4 g fat; 3 g carbohydrate; 35 mg calcium;
  448 mg sodium; 25 mg cholesterol

Chicken 'n' Cheese Soup ◑❸

WEEK 4 ✧ MAKES 2 SERVINGS

2 teaspoons margarine
½ cup each finely diced celery,
  onion, and carrot
2 teaspoons all-purpose flour
1 cup water
1 packet instant chicken broth and
  seasoning mix
½ cup each frozen peas and skim
  milk

2 ounces Monterey Jack or Cheddar
  cheese, shredded
4 ounces skinned and boned cooked
  chicken, diced*
½ cup cooked long-grain rice
1 teaspoon Worcestershire sauce
Dash each salt and ground red
  pepper

In 2-quart saucepan heat margarine until bubbly and hot; add celery, onion, and carrot and cook over medium heat, stirring occasionally, until vegetables are tender. Add flour and stir quickly to combine; gradually stir in water. Add broth mix and, stirring constantly, bring to a boil; add peas and cook for 3 minutes. Reduce heat and add milk and cheese; cook, stirring constantly, until cheese is melted. Add remaining ingredients and cook, stirring occasionally, until thoroughly heated.

Each serving provides: 3 Protein Exchanges; 1 Bread Exchange;
  1½ Vegetable Exchanges; 1 Fat Exchange; ¼ Milk Exchange;
  15 calories Optional Exchange
Per serving: 395 calories; 31 g protein; 17 g fat; 29 g carbohydrate; 348 mg calcium;
  893 mg sodium; 52 mg cholesterol

* Diced turkey may be substituted for the chicken.
Per serving: 383 calories; 31 g protein; 15 g fat; 29 g carbohydrate; 354 mg calcium;
  886 mg sodium; 45 mg cholesterol

Gumbo Soup Supper

WEEK 4 ❧ MAKES 4 SERVINGS

1 medium green bell pepper, seeded and diced
¾ cup diced onions
½ cup diced celery
1 packet instant chicken broth and seasoning mix
1 garlic clove, minced
10 ounces skinned and boned chicken breasts, diced

2½ cups canned whole tomatoes, chopped
2 cups each water and drained canned whole-kernel corn
1¼ cups frozen okra, cut into pieces
1½ teaspoons salt
½ teaspoon hot sauce

In 6-quart stockpot combine green pepper, onions, celery, broth mix, and garlic; cook, stirring frequently, until all vegetables are tender. Add chicken, tomatoes, and water to vegetables and bring to a boil. Reduce heat, cover, and let simmer for 30 minutes.

Add corn, okra, salt, and hot sauce to chicken mixture; cook uncovered, stirring frequently, for 45 minutes.

Each serving provides: 2 Protein Exchanges; 1 Bread Exchange;
  3 Vegetable Exchanges; 3 calories Optional Exchange
Per serving: 206 calories; 21 g protein; 2 g fat; 28 g carbohydrate; 96 mg calcium;
  1,338 mg sodium; 41 mg cholesterol

Hot and Sour Soup

WEEK 4 ∽ MAKES 4 SERVINGS

4 large dried black Chinese
  mushrooms
1 teaspoon peanut oil
4 ounces skinned and boned chicken
  breast, cut into thin strips
3 cups plus 2 tablespoons water,
  divided
½ cup each thinly sliced Chinese
  cabbage and drained canned
  sliced bamboo shoots

3 packets instant chicken broth and
  seasoning mix
1 tablespoon plus 1 teaspoon each
  cornstarch and rice vinegar
2 teaspoons soy sauce
3 ounces firm-style tofu (soybean
  curd), cut into 1 x ½-inch pieces
½ teaspoon white pepper

In small bowl combine mushrooms with enough water to cover; let soak for 30 minutes. Drain mushrooms; cut off and discard stems. Thinly slice mushroom caps and squeeze to remove all moisture; set aside.

In 2-quart saucepan heat oil; add chicken and sauté just until meat is no longer pink, about 2 minutes. Add 3 cups water and the mushrooms, cabbage, bamboo shoots, and broth mix; bring mixture to a boil. Reduce heat and let simmer for 5 minutes. In small cup dissolve cornstarch in remaining 2 tablespoons water and stir into chicken mixture; add vinegar and soy sauce and simmer, stirring constantly, until slightly thickened. Add tofu and pepper and stir to blend.

Each serving provides: 1 Protein Exchange; 1 Vegetable Exchange;
  30 calories Optional Exchange
Per serving: 93 calories; 10 g protein; 3 g fat; 13 g carbohydrate; 43 mg calcium;
  872 mg sodium; 16 mg cholesterol

Curried Chicken Salad Sandwich ◑❸

WEEK 4 ∾ MAKES 1 SERVING

¼ cup plain low-fat yogurt
1 tablespoon lemon juice
1½ teaspoons mayonnaise
¼ teaspoon curry powder
⅛ teaspoon each white pepper and
   salt

4 ounces skinned and boned cooked
   chicken, diced
2 tablespoons diced celery
1 tablespoon golden raisins
½ teaspoon sunflower seed
2 slices whole wheat bread, toasted

In medium bowl combine yogurt, lemon juice, mayonnaise, curry powder, pepper, and salt; add chicken, celery, raisins, and sunflower seed and mix to coat with dressing. Spread half of chicken salad on each slice of toast.

Each serving provides: 4 Protein Exchanges; 2 Bread Exchanges;
  ¼ Vegetable Exchange; 1½ Fat Exchanges; ½ Fruit Exchange;
  ½ Milk Exchange; 10 calories Optional Exchange
Per serving: 457 calories; 42 g protein; 17 g fat; 36 g carbohydrate; 185 mg calcium;
  723 mg sodium; 110 mg cholesterol

Chicken Lo Mein ◑

WEEK 4 ∾ MAKES 2 SERVINGS

2 teaspoons peanut oil
¼ cup thinly sliced scallions (green
   onions)
½ teaspoon minced pared ginger
   root
8 ounces skinned and boned chicken
   breasts, cut into thin strips

1 cup thinly sliced mushrooms
¾ cup bean sprouts
1 teaspoon each oyster sauce and
   soy sauce
1 cup cooked vermicelli (very thin
   spaghetti)

In 9- or 10-inch skillet heat oil; add scallions and ginger root and sauté for 1 minute. Add chicken and sauté for 2 minutes; add mushrooms and bean sprouts and cook until vegetables are tender, 3 to 5 minutes. Stir in oyster sauce and soy sauce. Add vermicelli and stir to combine; cook until heated through, about 1 minute.

Each serving provides: 3 Protein Exchanges; 1 Bread Exchange;
  2 Vegetable Exchanges; 1 Fat Exchange; 5 calories Optional Exchange
Per serving: 284 calories; 32 g protein; 7 g fat; 23 g carbohydrate; 38 mg calcium;
  427 mg sodium; 66 mg cholesterol

"Fried" Chinese Chicken

WEEK 4 ～ MAKES 2 SERVINGS

1 tablespoon each cornstarch and rice vinegar
2½ teaspoons teriyaki sauce, divided
1½ teaspoons minced pared ginger root
1 teaspoon dry sherry
½ teaspoon firmly packed brown sugar

12 ounces chicken breasts, skinned and cut into small pieces
1 tablespoon peanut oil
½ cup each Chinese snow peas (stem ends and strings removed),* red bell pepper strips, and scallions (green onions), cut into 2-inch pieces

In small bowl combine cornstarch, vinegar, 1½ teaspoons teriyaki sauce, and the ginger, sherry, and brown sugar; stir well to dissolve cornstarch. Rinse chicken pieces and, using paper towels, pat dry; dip chicken in teriyaki mixture, turning to coat. Place on sheet of wax paper and let stand for about 1 hour to dry.

Brush any liquid that has exuded from chicken over skinned side and let dry. In 12-inch nonstick skillet heat oil; add chicken, 1 piece at a time, and sauté, turning frequently until browned on all sides and, when pierced with a fork, juices run clear. Remove chicken to serving plate and keep warm.

In same skillet combine vegetables and stir-fry until tender-crisp; sprinkle with remaining teaspoon teriyaki sauce and stir to combine. Serve with chicken.

Each serving provides: 3 Protein Exchanges; 1½ Vegetable Exchanges; 1½ Fat Exchanges; 25 calories Optional Exchange
Per serving: 330 calories; 42 g protein; 10 g fat; 17 g carbohydrate; 59 mg calcium; 475 mg sodium; 99 mg cholesterol

* Frozen snow peas may be substituted for the fresh.

Chicken Fontina

WEEK 4 ⌒ MAKES 4 SERVINGS

4 chicken cutlets (3 ounces each), pounded to ¼-inch thickness
4 slices Fontina cheese (1 ounce each)
1 tablespoon plus 1 teaspoon each all-purpose flour and margarine
1 cup thinly sliced mushrooms
1 garlic clove, minced
¾ cup water
1 packet instant chicken broth and seasoning mix

1 teaspoon each tomato paste and salt
¼ teaspoon ground rosemary leaves
Dash pepper
1 tablespoon plus 1 teaspoon white wine

Garnish

Chopped fresh parsley

Top each cutlet with 1 slice cheese and fold chicken to enclose; using meat mallet, pound open edges to seal. Dust each cutlet with 1 teaspoon flour and set aside.

In 9-inch nonstick skillet heat margarine until bubbly and hot; add chicken and brown quickly on both sides. Remove chicken from skillet and set aside.

In same skillet combine mushrooms and garlic and sauté until mushrooms are tender; add water, broth mix, tomato paste, and seasonings and let simmer for 5 minutes. Return chicken to skillet and let simmer for about 5 minutes, basting frequently with sauce; stir in wine and serve sprinkled with parsley.

Each serving provides: 3 Protein Exchanges; ½ Vegetable Exchange; 1 Fat Exchange; 20 calories Optional Exchange
Per serving: 265 calories; 28 g protein; 14 g fat; 4 g carbohydrate; 175 mg calcium; 862 mg sodium; 82 mg cholesterol

Chicken Schnitzel ◑

WEEK 4 ∽ MAKES 2 SERVINGS

3 tablespoons all-purpose flour,
  divided
Dash each salt and pepper
3 tablespoons plain dried bread
  crumbs
Dash each paprika and garlic
  powder
2 chicken cutlets (4 ounces each),
  cut into halves and pounded to
  ⅛-inch thickness
1 egg, lightly beaten
1 tablespoon plus 1 teaspoon
  vegetable oil

½ cup diced onion
1 small apple, cored, pared, and
  thinly sliced
1 packet instant chicken broth and
  seasoning mix, dissolved in ¾
  cup hot water
2 cups drained and rinsed
  sauerkraut*
2 tablespoons raisins

Garnish

1 lemon, thinly sliced, and parsley
  sprigs

On sheet of wax paper or a paper plate combine 2 tablespoons flour with the salt and pepper. On another sheet of wax paper or a paper plate combine bread crumbs, paprika, and garlic powder; dredge each piece of chicken in seasoned flour, dip in beaten egg, and coat with bread crumbs.

In 12-inch nonstick skillet heat oil; add chicken pieces and quickly brown on both sides. Remove chicken to a plate and keep warm.

In same skillet combine onion and apple and sauté over medium heat until softened. Sprinkle remaining tablespoon flour over mixture and stir quickly to combine; cook for 1 minute. Gradually stir in dissolved broth mix and, stirring constantly, bring to a boil. Reduce heat and let simmer until mixture thickens. Stir in sauerkraut and raisins and cook, stirring, until mixture is thoroughly heated. Spoon sauerkraut mixture onto center of serving plate and surround with chicken pieces; garnish chicken with lemon slices and parsley sprigs.

Each serving provides: 3½ Protein Exchanges; 1 Bread Exchange;
  2½ Vegetable Exchanges; 2 Fat Exchanges; 1 Fruit Exchange;
  5 calories Optional Exchange
Per serving: 450 calories; 36 g protein; 15 g fat; 45 g carbohydrate; 144 mg calcium;
  2,404 mg sodium; 203 mg cholesterol

* We suggest that you use the sauerkraut that is packaged in a plastic bag and is stored in the refrigerator section of the supermarket; this is usually crisper and less salty than the canned.

Fruited Ginger Chicken

WEEK 4 ～ MAKES 2 SERVINGS

1 tablespoon each teriyaki sauce and thawed frozen concentrated orange juice (no sugar added)

1 tablespoon minced fresh garlic, divided

2 teaspoons each grated pared ginger root, dry white wine, and chili sauce

10 ounces skinned and boned chicken breasts, cut into thin strips

2 teaspoons peanut or vegetable oil

1 cup sliced onions

1 teaspoon cornstarch

1½ cups canned sliced peaches (no sugar added)

1 cup thawed frozen Chinese snow peas

1. In glass or stainless-steel bowl combine teriyaki sauce, orange juice, 2 teaspoons garlic, ginger, wine, and chili sauce; add chicken and toss to coat thoroughly. Cover and refrigerate for at least 1 hour (may be marinated overnight).

2. Remove chicken from marinade and strain marinade, reserving liquid and discarding garlic and ginger.

3. In 10-inch skillet heat oil; add onions and remaining teaspoon garlic and sauté until onions are translucent. Add chicken and cook until lightly browned on all sides.

4. Combine cornstarch and reserved marinade, stirring to dissolve cornstarch; add to skillet and, stirring constantly, bring to a boil. Reduce heat and let simmer until liquid thickens. Add peaches and snow peas and stir to combine; cook until thoroughly heated.

Each serving provides: 4 Protein Exchanges; 2 Vegetable Exchanges; 1 Fat Exchange; 1½ Fruit Exchanges; 30 calories Optional Exchange
Per serving: 352 calories; 38 g protein; 7 g fat; 35 g carbohydrate; 90 mg calcium; 491 mg sodium; 82 mg cholesterol

Chicken Oriental

WEEK 4 ⌒ MAKES 2 SERVINGS

10 ounces skinned and boned
  chicken breasts, thinly sliced
1 tablespoon plus 1½ teaspoons
  teriyaki sauce
½ teaspoon grated pared ginger
  root
2 teaspoons peanut or vegetable oil
½ cup chopped scallions (green
  onions)

1 garlic clove, minced
1 cup each sliced mushrooms and
  julienne-cut zucchini (thin strips)
⅓ cup water
2 teaspoons cornstarch
½ packet (about ½ teaspoon)
  instant chicken broth and
  seasoning mix
1 cup cauliflower florets, blanched

In bowl combine chicken, teriyaki sauce, and ginger; set aside.

In 12-inch skillet heat oil; add scallions and garlic and sauté until scallions are soft. Add mushrooms and zucchini and sauté, stirring constantly, until vegetables are just tender; add chicken mixture and cook, stirring and turning, until chicken is no longer pink. In measuring cup or small bowl combine water, cornstarch, and broth mix, stirring to dissolve cornstarch; add to chicken mixture and stir to combine. Add cauliflower and cook over medium heat, stirring constantly, until thickened.

Each serving provides: 4 Protein Exchanges; 3½ Vegetable Exchanges;
  1 Fat Exchange; 15 calories Optional Exchange
Per serving: 276 calories; 37 g protein; 7 g fat; 15 g carbohydrate; 68 mg calcium;
  480 mg sodium; 82 mg cholesterol

Sautéed Chicken
in Mushroom-Tarragon Sauce ◑

WEEK 4 ⌒ MAKES 2 SERVINGS

2 teaspoons all-purpose flour
¼ teaspoon salt
⅛ teaspoon pepper
10 ounces skinned and boned
  chicken breasts
2 teaspoons margarine

1 cup sliced mushrooms
¼ cup chopped scallions (green
  onions)
½ teaspoon tarragon leaves
¼ cup each dry white wine and
  water

In small cup or bowl combine flour, salt, and pepper; sprinkle chicken breasts with flour mixture.

In 10-inch skillet heat margarine until bubbly and hot; add chicken and cook, turning once, until lightly browned on both sides. Add mushrooms, scallions, and tarragon and cook until vegetables are softened; stir in wine and bring to a boil. Add water, reduce heat, cover, and let simmer, turning chicken once, until chicken is tender, about 15 minutes.

Each serving provides: 4 Protein Exchanges; 1¼ Vegetable Exchanges;
  1 Fat Exchange; 40 calories Optional Exchange
Per serving: 247 calories; 34 g protein; 6 g fat; 7 g carbohydrate; 36 mg calcium;
  417 mg sodium; 82 mg cholesterol

Oriental Stir-Fry ◑

WEEK 4 ◇ MAKES 2 SERVINGS

2 teaspoons peanut oil
1 teaspoon Chinese sesame oil
10 ounces skinned and boned
  chicken breasts, cut into thin
  strips
1 garlic clove, thinly sliced
¼ teaspoon each grated pared
  ginger root and salt
⅛ teaspoon each pepper and
  paprika

1 cup thinly sliced onions
½ cup each julienne-cut red and
  green bell peppers (thin strips)
½ cup diagonally sliced celery
  (about ¼-inch-thick slices)
¾ cup canned chicken broth,
  divided
1 tablespoon soy sauce
2 teaspoons cornstarch
1 cup cooked long-grain rice (hot)

Heat 12-inch nonstick skillet or a wok; add oils and heat. Add chicken, garlic, and ginger; sprinkle with salt, pepper, and paprika and cook, stirring quickly and frequently, until chicken is no longer pink, 1 to 2 minutes. Add vegetables and half the broth and stir to combine; cover and let cook until vegetables are tender-crisp, 1 to 2 minutes. In measuring cup or small bowl combine remaining broth, soy sauce, and cornstarch, stirring to dissolve cornstarch; add to chicken mixture and cook, stirring constantly, until mixture is thickened.

Arrange rice in a circle around edge of serving platter and spoon chicken mixture onto center of platter.

Each serving provides: 4 Protein Exchanges; 1 Bread Exchange;
  2½ Vegetable Exchanges; 1½ Fat Exchanges; 25 calories Optional Exchange
Per serving: 401 calories; 38 g protein; 9 g fat; 38 g carbohydrate; 75 mg calcium;
  1,458 mg sodium; 82 mg cholesterol

Tropical Chicken Sauté ◑

WEEK 4 ∿ MAKES 2 SERVINGS

⅓ cup plus 2 teaspoons all-purpose
flour
¼ teaspoon each salt and pepper
9 ounces skinned and boned chicken
breasts, cut into 4 pieces
1 egg, beaten
1 tablespoon vegetable oil
1 teaspoon fresh tarragon leaves
or ½ teaspoon dried

¼ cup dry white wine
1 tablespoon lemon juice
1 teaspoon margarine
1 small mango, pared, pitted, and
diced

Garnish

Parsley sprigs

On sheet of wax paper or a paper plate combine flour, salt, and pepper; dip chicken pieces into beaten egg, then dredge in seasoned flour, being sure to use all of egg and flour.

In 12-inch nonstick skillet heat oil over high heat; add chicken and cook until bottom is golden brown. Turn chicken pieces over, sprinkle with tarragon, and brown other side (if necessary, reduce heat). Add wine, lemon juice, and margarine, and bring to a boil; cook until liquid is slightly reduced and thickened. Add mango, cover, and cook until fruit is heated, 1 to 2 minutes; serve garnished with parsley sprigs.

Each serving provides: 4 Protein Exchanges; 1 Bread Exchange; 2 Fat Exchanges;
1 Fruit Exchange; 30 calories Optional Exchange
Per serving: 446 calories; 36 g protein; 14 g fat; 39 g carbohydrate; 55 mg calcium;
417 mg sodium; 211 mg cholesterol

Sesame Chicken Sauté ◑

WEEK 4 ∿ MAKES 4 SERVINGS

1½ ounces (½ cup plus 2
tablespoons) cornflake crumbs
⅓ cup plus 2 teaspoons seasoned
dried bread crumbs
2 teaspoons sesame seed
Dash each salt, onion powder, and
garlic powder

1¼ pounds skinned and boned
chicken breasts, pounded to
¼-inch thickness
½ cup buttermilk
2 tablespoons peanut or vegetable
oil

On sheet of wax paper or a paper plate combine cornflake crumbs, bread crumbs, sesame seed, and seasonings. Dip chicken into buttermilk and then into crumb mixture, turning to coat both sides and using all of milk and crumb mixture.

In 12-inch skillet heat oil; add chicken and cook, turning once, until browned on both sides, 3 to 4 minutes on each side.

Each serving provides: 4 Protein Exchanges; 1 Bread Exchange;
1½ Fat Exchanges; 25 calories Optional Exchange
Per serving: 322 calories; 36 g protein; 11 g fat; 18 g carbohydrate; 67 mg calcium;
366 mg sodium; 84 mg cholesterol

Chicken Gruyère with Sautéed Mushrooms ◑

WEEK 4 ∾ MAKES 1 SERVING

2 teaspoons all-purpose flour
Dash each salt and pepper
1 skinned and boned chicken breast
 (3 ounces), pounded to ¼-inch
 thickness
1½ teaspoons margarine, divided

½ cup sliced mushrooms
1 ounce Gruyère cheese, shredded*

Garnish

Parsley sprigs and 3 cherry
 tomatoes

1. On sheet of wax paper or a paper plate combine flour, salt, and pepper; dredge chicken in seasoned flour, coating all sides.

2. In small nonstick skillet heat 1 teaspoon margarine over medium heat until bubbly and hot; add chicken, sprinkle evenly with any remaining seasoned flour, and cook, turning once, until golden brown on both sides. Remove skillet from heat and transfer chicken to an individual shallow flameproof baking dish; set aside and keep warm.

3. In same skillet heat remaining ½ teaspoon margarine over medium heat until bubbly and hot; add mushrooms and sauté until lightly browned.

4. Top chicken with mushrooms, then cheese; broil 6 inches from heat source until cheese is melted, 3 to 5 minutes. Serve garnished with parsley sprigs and tomatoes.

Each serving provides: 3 Protein Exchanges; 1½ Vegetable Exchanges;
1½ Fat Exchanges; 20 calories Optional Exchange
Per serving: 290 calories; 29 g protein; 16 g fat; 6 g carbohydrate; 302 mg calcium;
351 mg sodium; 81 mg cholesterol

* Swiss or Fontina cheese may be substituted for the Gruyère.
Per serving with Swiss: 279 calories; 29 g protein; 15 g fat; 7 g carbohydrate;
288 mg calcium; 329 mg sodium; 75 mg cholesterol
With Fontina: 283 calories; 28 g protein; 16 g fat; 6 g carbohydrate; 171 mg calcium;
255 mg sodium; 82 mg cholesterol

Herbed Oven-"Fried" Chicken ◑ *good*

WEEK 4 ∽ MAKES 4 SERVINGS

¾ cup seasoned dried bread
  crumbs
1 teaspoon oregano leaves
Dash each salt, pepper, and garlic
  powder

1¼ pounds skinned and boned
  chicken breasts, cut into
  1-inch-wide strips

In small bowl combine crumbs and seasonings; dip chicken strips in water, then into crumb mixture, pressing crumbs to make sure they adhere and chicken is thoroughly coated.

Spray a nonstick baking sheet with nonstick cooking spray; arrange chicken on sheet and sprinkle evenly with any remaining crumb mixture. Bake at 350°F. until tender, about 20 minutes.

Each serving provides: 4 Protein Exchanges; 1 Bread Exchange
Per serving: 239 calories; 35 g protein; 3 g fat; 15 g carbohydrate; 47 mg calcium;
  272 mg sodium; 83 mg cholesterol

Baked Stuffed Chicken Breasts

WEEK 4 ∽ MAKES 2 SERVINGS, 1 STUFFED BREAST EACH

---

2 teaspoons margarine, divided
½ cup finely chopped mushrooms
¼ cup diced onion
2 teaspoons dry vermouth
1 small garlic clove, mashed
½ teaspoon salt
Dash pepper
½ cup cooked long-grain rice
2 skinned and boned chicken
  breasts (5 ounces each), pounded
  to ⅛-inch thickness

3 tablespoons plain dried bread
  crumbs
Dash paprika

Garnish

Parsley sprigs

1. In small nonstick skillet heat 1 teaspoon margarine until bubbly and hot; add mushrooms, onion, vermouth, garlic, salt, and pepper and sauté, stirring occasionally, until onion is tender. Remove from heat and stir in rice.

2. Place chicken breasts skin-side down and spread half of the rice mixture onto each, leaving a border of about ½ inch; fold long

sides over, then roll breast from short end to enclose filling. Secure each roll with wooden toothpicks.

3. Preheat oven to 350°F. In small nonstick skillet melt remaining teaspoon margarine; remove from heat. Spread bread crumbs on sheet of wax paper; roll each stuffed breast in margarine, then in crumbs, coating all sides.

4. Spray 7 x 5½ x 3-inch baking dish with nonstick cooking spray; transfer chicken rolls to dish and sprinkle with any remaining crumbs. Sprinkle with paprika and bake until chicken is tender, 20 to 25 minutes. Serve garnished with parsley sprigs; remove toothpicks before serving.

Each serving provides: 4 Protein Exchanges; 1 Bread Exchange;
    ¾ Vegetable Exchange; 1 Fat Exchange; 5 calories Optional Exchange
Per serving: 310 calories; 36 g protein; 7 g fat; 23 g carbohydrate; 47 mg calcium;
    755 mg sodium; 83 mg cholesterol

Orange Chicken ◐

WEEK 4 ∽ MAKES 4 SERVINGS

2 tablespoons plus 2 teaspoons
    reduced-calorie margarine
1¼ pounds skinned and boned
    chicken breasts
2 cups sliced mushrooms
2 teaspoons all-purpose flour
⅔ cup water
¼ cup thawed frozen concentrated
    orange juice (no sugar added)

2 packets instant chicken broth and
    seasoning mix
½ cup thinly sliced scallions (green
    onions)
1 cup canned mandarin orange
    sections (no sugar added),
    heated

In 10-inch skillet heat margarine until bubbly and hot; add chicken and cook until browned on both sides. Remove from skillet and set aside.

In same skillet cook mushrooms over high heat, stirring occasionally, until all liquid has evaporated; sprinkle mushrooms with flour and stir quickly to combine. Gradually stir in water; add orange juice and broth mix and, stirring constantly, bring to a boil. Reduce heat, add chicken, and let simmer for about 3 minutes to allow flavors to blend; serve sprinkled with scallions and topped with orange sections.

Each serving provides: 4 Protein Exchanges; 1¼ Vegetable Exchanges;
    1 Fat Exchange; 1 Fruit Exchange; 10 calories Optional Exchange
Per serving: 273 calories; 36 g protein; 6 g fat; 18 g carbohydrate; 44 mg calcium;
    616 mg sodium; 82 mg cholesterol

Chicken Gumbo

WEEK 4 ⬯ MAKES 2 SERVINGS

1 tablespoon all-purpose flour
½ teaspoon salt, divided
¼ teaspoon pepper
1 pound 2 ounces chicken parts,
  skinned
2 teaspoons margarine
1 cup diced onions
2 ounces Canadian-style bacon,
  diced

½ cup each sliced fresh or thawed
  frozen okra and diced celery
1 cup each crushed canned Italian
  tomatoes and water
½ cup fresh or frozen whole-kernel
  corn

On sheet of wax paper or a paper plate combine flour, ¼ teaspoon salt, and the pepper; sprinkle seasoned flour over chicken parts and set aside.

In 4-quart saucepan heat margarine until bubbly and hot; add onions and bacon and sauté until onions are softened. Add chicken parts and cook until lightly browned on all sides; add okra and celery and stir to combine. Add tomatoes, water, and remaining ¼ teaspoon salt and bring to a boil. Reduce heat, cover, and let simmer until chicken is almost tender, about 35 minutes; add corn and cook, uncovered, until chicken is tender, about 5 minutes longer.

Each serving provides: 4 Protein Exchanges; ½ Bread Exchange;
  3 Vegetable Exchanges; 1 Fat Exchange; 15 calories Optional Exchange
Per serving: 395 calories; 37 g protein; 15 g fat; 29 g carbohydrate; 104 mg calcium;
  1,543 mg sodium; 97 mg cholesterol

Caper Chicken Sauté

WEEK 2 ⬯ MAKES 2 SERVINGS

2 teaspoons margarine, divided
¼ cup each sliced celery and onion
2 small garlic cloves, minced
½ cup seeded and chopped
  tomatoes
1 tablespoon drained capers, rinsed

10 ounces skinned and boned
  chicken breasts, cut into cubes
Dash pepper
⅓ cup dry vermouth
1 tablespoon chopped fresh parsley
  (optional)

In 9-inch skillet heat 1 teaspoon margarine over medium heat until bubbly and hot; add celery, onion, and garlic and sauté, stirring occasionally, until vegetables are tender. Add tomatoes and capers and continue sautéing until tomatoes begin to soften, about 3 minutes longer. Push vegetables to side of skillet and add remaining teaspoon margarine and the chicken and pepper; brown chicken lightly on all sides. Combine vegetables with chicken, stir in vermouth, and cook until some of the liquid evaporates, about 1 minute. If desired, sprinkle with parsley just before serving.

Each serving provides: 4 Protein Exchanges; 1 Vegetable Exchange;
  1 Fat Exchange; 40 calories Optional Exchange
Per serving: 260 calories; 34 g protein; 6 g fat; 6 g carbohydrate; 37 mg calcium;
  273 mg sodium; 82 mg cholesterol

Brunswick Stew ❶

WEEK 2 ∽ MAKES 2 SERVINGS

---

1 teaspoon margarine
¼ cup chopped onion
12 ounces chicken parts, skinned
1 teaspoon Worcestershire sauce
¼ teaspoon powdered mustard
Dash ground red pepper
½ cup each canned Italian tomatoes
  and hot water

3 ounces peeled cooked potatoes,
  cut into cubes
¼ cup fresh or frozen cut green
  beans
⅛ teaspoon each salt and pepper

In 2-quart saucepan heat margarine until bubbly and hot; add onion and sauté until soft. Add chicken and brown well on all sides; sprinkle with Worcestershire sauce, mustard, and red pepper. Stir in tomatoes and water and bring to a boil. Reduce heat, cover, and let simmer for about 30 minutes. Add potatoes, green beans, salt, and pepper and let simmer uncovered, stirring occasionally, until chicken is tender, 10 to 15 minutes.

Each serving provides: 2 Protein Exchanges; ½ Bread Exchange;
  1 Vegetable Exchange; ½ Fat Exchange
Per serving: 178 calories; 18 g protein; 6 g fat; 12 g carbohydrate; 31 mg calcium;
  319 mg sodium; 49 mg cholesterol

Variation: Week 4—Substitute ¼ cup each fresh or frozen green baby lima beans and whole-kernel corn for the green beans and potatoes; reduce Vegetable Exchange to ¾ Exchange.

Per serving: 187 calories; 19 g protein; 6 g fat; 14 g carbohydrate; 187 mg calcium;
  344 mg sodium; 49 mg cholesterol

Chicken Fricassee ❶

WEEK 4 ∽ MAKES 2 SERVINGS

1 tablespoon plus 1½ teaspoons
  all-purpose flour, divided
¼ teaspoon salt
⅛ teaspoon pepper
Dash ground thyme
12 ounces chicken parts, skinned
1 teaspoon margarine
½ cup diced onion

¾ cup sliced mushrooms
¼ cup diced celery
¾ cup water
½ small bay leaf
¼ cup skim milk

Garnish

2 teaspoons chopped fresh parsley

1. On sheet of wax paper or a paper plate combine 2¼ teaspoons flour with the salt, pepper, and thyme; dredge chicken parts in seasoned flour to coat.

2. In 2-quart saucepan heat margarine until bubbly and hot; add chicken and cook, turning frequently, until browned on all sides. Remove chicken to plate and set aside, reserving pan drippings.

3. In same saucepan sauté onion in pan drippings until softened; add mushrooms and celery and sauté until tender, about 3 minutes. Return chicken to pan; add water and bay leaf and bring to a boil. Reduce heat, cover, and let simmer until chicken is tender, 30 to 35 minutes.

4. In measuring cup or small bowl combine remaining 2¼ teaspoons flour with the milk, stirring to dissolve flour; stir into chicken mixture and cook, stirring constantly, until sauce is thickened, 3 to 5 minutes. Remove and discard bay leaf; serve sprinkled with parsley.

Each serving provides: 2 Protein Exchanges; 1½ Vegetable Exchanges;
  ½ Fat Exchange; 35 calories Optional Exchange
Per serving: 180 calories; 19 g protein; 6 g fat; 12 g carbohydrate; 70 mg calcium;
  381 mg sodium; 49 mg cholesterol

Stuffed Chicken Roll

WEEK 4 ⌁ MAKES 4 SERVINGS

1 tablespoon margarine
½ cup diced onion
1 garlic clove, minced
1 cup each chopped mushrooms and
  well-drained cooked chopped
  spinach
¼ cup part-skim ricotta cheese
3 tablespoons seasoned dried bread
  crumbs
½ teaspoon salt, divided

¼ teaspoon pepper, divided
1 skinned and boned chicken breast
  (14 ounces)
¼ cup dry white wine
1 packet instant chicken broth and
  seasoning mix, dissolved in 1 cup
  hot water
1 tablespoon water
1 teaspoon cornstarch

1. In 10-inch skillet heat margarine until bubbly and hot; add onion and garlic and sauté until softened. Add mushrooms and sauté until browned, about 5 minutes; stir in spinach, cheese, bread crumbs, ¼ teaspoon salt, and ⅛ teaspoon pepper. Remove from heat; set aside and let cool.

2. Between two sheets of plastic wrap pound chicken breast to ¼-inch thickness. Remove top sheet of plastic wrap and sprinkle chicken with remaining ¼ teaspoon salt and ⅛ teaspoon pepper; spread with cooled spinach mixture, leaving a 1-inch border on all sides.

3. Preheat oven to 350°F. Carefully roll chicken breast lengthwise to enclose filling and tie with butcher's twine or secure with small skewers; transfer to 8 x 8 x 2-inch baking pan. Add wine and dissolved broth mix; cover pan with foil and bake for 40 minutes. Remove foil and continue baking, basting with pan juices, until chicken is tender, 10 to 15 minutes longer.

4. Remove chicken roll to a platter and keep warm. In a small saucepan bring pan juices to a boil. Combine water and cornstarch, stirring to dissolve cornstarch; stir into pan juices and cook, stirring constantly, until mixture is slightly thickened. Pour over chicken roll.

Each serving provides: 3 Protein Exchanges; 1¼ Vegetable Exchanges;
  ½ Fat Exchange; 50 calories Optional Exchange
Per serving: 221 calories; 28 g protein; 6 g fat; 11 g carbohydrate; 115 mg calcium;
  662 mg sodium; 63 mg cholesterol

Curried Chicken 'n' Vegetable Sauté ❶

WEEK 4 ✎ MAKES 2 SERVINGS

2 teaspoons all-purpose flour
¼ teaspoon salt
⅛ teaspoon pepper
1½ pounds chicken parts, skinned
2 teaspoons vegetable oil
½ cup diced onion

1 garlic clove, minced
½ cup each diced celery and green
   bell pepper
1½ teaspoons curry powder
1 cup crushed canned Italian
   tomatoes

On sheet of wax paper or a paper plate combine flour, salt, and pepper; sprinkle flour mixture over chicken parts.

In 12-inch skillet heat oil; add chicken and cook until browned on all sides. Remove chicken from skillet and set aside.

In same skillet combine onion and garlic and sauté until onion is softened; add celery, green pepper, and curry powder and sauté until vegetables are softened. Return chicken to skillet and stir in tomatoes; bring mixture to a boil. Reduce heat, cover, and let simmer for 20 minutes; remove cover and let simmer until chicken is tender, 5 to 10 minutes.

Each serving provides: 4 Protein Exchanges; 2½ Vegetable Exchanges;
   1 Fat Exchange; 10 calories Optional Exchange
Per serving: 320 calories; 35 g protein; 13 g fat; 15 g carbohydrate; 61 mg calcium;
   567 mg sodium; 97 mg cholesterol

Chicken Curry ❶

WEEK 1 ✎ MAKES 4 SERVINGS

½ cup plain low-fat yogurt
2 garlic cloves, minced
1 teaspoon curry powder
¼ teaspoon each ground coriander,
   ground ginger, and salt
Dash ground red pepper

1½ pounds chicken parts, skinned
2 teaspoons vegetable oil
½ cup chopped onion
1 cup chopped tomatoes
1 bay leaf

In bowl combine yogurt and seasonings; add chicken parts, turning to coat. Let stand at room temperature for 30 minutes.

In 12-inch skillet heat oil; add onion and sauté until lightly browned. Add tomatoes and bay leaf and let simmer for 5 minutes; add chicken and marinade mixture and stir to combine. Bring mixture to a boil. Reduce heat, cover, and let simmer, turning once or twice, until chicken is tender, about 30 minutes; remove bay leaf before serving.

Each serving provides: 2 Protein Exchanges; ¾ Vegetable Exchange;
½ Fat Exchange; ¼ Milk Exchange
Per serving: 166 calories; 18 g protein; 7 g fat; 7 g carbohydrate; 78 mg calcium;
205 mg sodium; 50 mg cholesterol

Deep-Dish Chicken with "Dumplings" ❶

WEEK 4 ∽ MAKES 2 SERVINGS

---

1 tablespoon margarine
1 cup each thinly sliced carrot and
  mushrooms
½ cup each diced onion and celery
1 tablespoon plus 1 teaspoon
  all-purpose flour
2 packets instant chicken broth and
  seasoning mix

1⅓ cups water
8 ounces skinned and boned cooked
  chicken, diced
⅛ teaspoon each poultry seasoning
  and pepper
2 ready-to-bake refrigerated
  buttermilk flaky biscuits (1 ounce
  each), each cut into 6 wedges

Preheat oven to 375°F. Spray two 1¾-cup casseroles with nonstick cooking spray; set aside.

In 1-quart saucepan heat margarine until bubbly and hot; add vegetables, stirring to coat with margarine. Cover pan and cook over medium heat until vegetables are tender. Sprinkle vegetables with flour and broth mix and stir quickly to combine; cook, uncovered, for 1 minute. Gradually stir in water and, stirring constantly, bring to a boil. Reduce heat and cook, stirring, until mixture thickens; add chicken and seasonings and stir to combine.

Pour half of mixture into each sprayed casserole; top each portion with 6 biscuit wedges and bake until thoroughly heated and "dumplings" are browned, 10 to 15 minutes.

Each serving provides: 4 Protein Exchanges; 1 Bread Exchange;
3 Vegetable Exchanges; 1½ Fat Exchanges; 30 calories Optional Exchange
Per serving: 429 calories; 39 g protein; 16 g fat; 31 g carbohydrate; 82 mg calcium;
1,317 mg sodium; 101 mg cholesterol

Chicken à la King ◐❸

WEEK 4 ～ MAKES 2 SERVINGS

2 teaspoons margarine
½ cup each diced onion and
  mushrooms
1 teaspoon all-purpose flour
½ cup skim milk
6 ounces skinned and boned cooked
  chicken, diced

½ cup peas
2 tablespoons chopped drained
  canned pimientos
¼ teaspoon each salt, white pepper,
  and paprika

In 10-inch skillet heat margarine until bubbly and hot; add onion and mushrooms and sauté, stirring occasionally, until mushrooms are lightly browned. Sprinkle flour over vegetables and stir quickly to combine; gradually stir in milk and, stirring constantly, bring to a boil. Reduce heat and let simmer until mixture thickens. Stir in remaining ingredients and cook until thoroughly heated.

Each serving provides: 3 Protein Exchanges; ½ Bread Exchange;
  1⅛ Vegetable Exchanges; 1 Fat Exchange; ¼ Milk Exchange;
  5 calories Optional Exchange
Per serving: 278 calories; 30 g protein; 11 g fat; 15 g carbohydrate; 116 mg calcium;
  429 mg sodium; 77 mg cholesterol

Creamed Parsley Chicken ◐❸

WEEK 4 ～ MAKES 2 SERVINGS

2 tablespoons each diced carrot
  and celery
1 packet instant chicken broth and
  seasoning mix
¾ cup water
2 teaspoons each margarine and
  all-purpose flour

6 ounces skinned and boned cooked
  chicken, cut into 1-inch cubes
2 tablespoons chopped fresh parsley
3 tablespoons sour cream
⅛ teaspoon pepper

In small saucepan combine carrot, celery, and broth mix; add water and bring to a boil. Cook for 5 minutes.

In 1-quart saucepan heat margarine until bubbly and hot; add flour and cook, stirring constantly, for 2 minutes. Remove from heat and gradually stir in vegetable mixture; return to heat and simmer, stirring constantly, for 5 minutes. Add chicken and parsley and stir to combine. Let simmer until chicken is heated, about 5 minutes; stir in sour cream and season with pepper.

Each serving provides: 3 Protein Exchanges; ¼ Vegetable Exchange;
  1 Fat Exchange; 65 calories Optional Exchange
Per serving: 262 calories; 26 g protein; 15 g fat; 5 g carbohydrate; 50 mg calcium;
  556 mg sodium; 85 mg cholesterol

Variation: Substitute ¼ cup skim milk for the sour cream; reduce Optional Exchange to 25 calories.

Per serving: 227 calories; 27 g protein; 10 g fat; 6 g carbohydrate; 62 mg calcium;
  561 mg sodium; 76 mg cholesterol

Mixed Fruit and Chicken Sauté

WEEK 4 〜 MAKES 4 SERVINGS

3 tablespoons all-purpose flour
½ teaspoon salt
Dash pepper
1½ pounds chicken parts, skinned
1 tablespoon plus 1 teaspoon peanut
  oil
1 cup sliced onions
1 tablespoon minced fresh garlic
1 teaspoon minced pared ginger
  root

2 cups chopped well-washed
  spinach leaves
2 each medium peaches and
  apricots, blanched, peeled, pitted,
  and sliced
⅛ medium pineapple, pared and cut
  into 1-inch pieces
1 teaspoon rice vinegar

On sheet of wax paper or a paper plate combine flour, salt, and pepper. Rinse chicken and, using paper towels, pat dry; dredge chicken pieces in seasoned flour to coat.

In 12-inch nonstick skillet heat oil; add chicken, 1 piece at a time, and cook, turning frequently, until browned on all sides and, when pierced with a fork, juices run clear. Remove chicken to serving plate and keep warm.

In same skillet combine onions, garlic, and ginger and sauté until onion is browned, 2 to 3 minutes; add spinach, fruit, and vinegar and cook, stirring occasionally, until spinach is wilted. Return chicken to skillet and stir to combine.

Each serving provides: 2 Protein Exchanges; 1½ Vegetable Exchanges;
  1 Fat Exchange; 1 Fruit Exchange; 25 calories Optional Exchange
Per serving: 233 calories; 19 g protein; 9 g fat; 21 g carbohydrate; 56 mg calcium;
  341 mg sodium; 49 mg cholesterol

Spanish Chicken and Rice ◑

WEEK 4 ◇ MAKES 2 SERVINGS

2 teaspoons olive oil
½ cup each diced onion and green
  bell pepper
2 garlic cloves, minced
½ cup tomato sauce
⅓ cup water
½ packet (about ½ teaspoon)
  instant chicken broth and
  seasoning mix

¼ teaspoon ground cumin
Dash pepper
6 ounces skinned and boned cooked
  chicken, diced
1 cup cooked long-grain rice
2 ounces drained canned small
  white beans
2 tablespoons chopped fresh
  parsley

In 10-inch skillet heat oil; add onion, green pepper, and garlic and sauté over low heat until vegetables are tender, about 5 minutes. Add tomato sauce, water, broth mix, and seasonings and bring to a boil. Reduce heat and let simmer for 5 minutes; stir in remaining ingredients and cook until thoroughly heated.

Each serving provides: 3½ Protein Exchanges; 1 Bread Exchange;
  2 Vegetable Exchanges; 1 Fat Exchange; 3 calories Optional Exchange
Per serving: 381 calories; 31 g protein; 12 g fat; 38 g carbohydrate; 70 mg calcium;
  685 mg sodium; 76 mg cholesterol

Pressure Cooker Paella

1½ pounds chicken parts, skinned
  and cut into 2-inch pieces
½ teaspoon salt, divided
¼ teaspoon white pepper
1 tablespoon olive oil
½ cup diced onion
2 garlic cloves, minced
1 medium green bell pepper, seeded
  and cut into 1-inch squares
1 cup canned crushed tomatoes
4 ounces uncooked regular
  long-grain rice

¾ cup water
1 packet instant chicken broth and
  seasoning mix
¼ teaspoon marjoram leaves
⅛ teaspoon whole saffron
  (optional)
5 ounces shelled and deveined
  shrimp
12 small clams (in the shell),
  scrubbed, or 4 ounces drained
  canned minced clams

Sprinkle chicken with ¼ teaspoon salt and the white pepper and set aside. In 4-quart pressure cooker heat oil; add onion and garlic and sauté for 2 minutes. Add chicken and continue sautéing for 3 minutes longer; stir in green pepper, tomatoes, and rice. Add water, broth mix, marjoram, saffron if desired, and remaining ¼ teaspoon salt and stir to combine. Close cover securely; place pressure regulator firmly on vent pipe and heat until regulator begins to rock gently. Cook at 15 pounds pressure for 5 minutes.

Hold cooker under running cold water to bring pressure down; remove cover and, using a fork, stir shrimp and clams into rice mixture. Close cooker again and cook at 15 pounds pressure for 3 minutes longer. Bring pressure down under running cold water; using a fork, fluff rice.

Each serving provides: 4 Protein Exchanges; 1 Bread Exchange;
  1¼ Vegetable Exchanges; ½ Fat Exchange; 15 calories Optional Exchange
Per serving: 328 calories; 30 g protein; 9 g fat; 30 g carbohydrate; 68 mg calcium;
  693 mg sodium; 120 mg cholesterol

Honey-Glazed Cornish Hen

WEEK 1 ◇ MAKES 2 SERVINGS, ½ HEN EACH

2 tablespoons finely chopped fresh
  mint
2 teaspoons each honey, heated, and
  olive oil
1 garlic clove, minced
1 Cornish hen (1¼ pounds),
  skinned and cut in half

½ teaspoon salt
2 tablespoons lemon juice

Garnish

Mint sprigs

In small bowl combine chopped mint, honey, oil, and garlic. In 8 x 8 x 2-inch nonstick baking pan sprinkle both sides of hen halves with salt; brush mint-honey mixture over entire hen and sprinkle with lemon juice. Bake cut-side down at 400°F. until tender, 25 to 30 minutes.

Remove baking pan from oven and baste hen with pan juices. Set oven control to broil and broil hen 3 inches from heat source until browned and crisp, about 1 minute. Garnish with mint sprigs before serving.

Each serving provides: 4 Protein Exchanges; 1 Fat Exchange;
  20 calories Optional Exchange
Per serving: 240 calories; 27 g protein; 11 g fat; 7 g carbohydrate; 22 mg calcium;
  619 mg sodium; 81 mg cholesterol

Sautéed Cornish Hen Marsala

WEEK 4 ◇ MAKES 2 SERVINGS

1 Cornish hen (1¼ pounds),
  skinned and cut into pieces
½ teaspoon salt
1 tablespoon plus 1½ teaspoons
  all-purpose flour
1 tablespoon margarine
1 garlic clove, minced

1 cup sliced mushrooms
½ cup canned chicken broth
¼ cup dry Marsala wine
Dash pepper

Garnish

1 tablespoon chopped fresh parsley

Sprinkle hen with salt. On sheet of wax paper or a paper plate dredge hen in flour to coat; set aside.

In 12-inch nonstick skillet heat margarine over medium heat until bubbly and hot; add garlic and sauté briefly, being careful not to burn.

Add hen pieces and brown well on all sides. Reduce heat to low, cover, and cook until hen is tender, 10 to 15 minutes.

Add mushrooms to skillet and cook uncovered, stirring occasionally, for about 3 minutes; add broth, wine, and pepper, cover, and let simmer for about 10 minutes. Serve sprinkled with parsley.

Each serving provides: 4 Protein Exchanges; 1 Vegetable Exchange;
  1½ Fat Exchanges; 65 calories Optional Exchange
Per serving: 308 calories; 29 g protein; 13 g fat; 9 g carbohydrate; 28 mg calcium;
  893 mg sodium; 81 mg cholesterol

Roast Cornish Hen with Mango Sauce

WEEK 4   ⌒   MAKES 4 SERVINGS, ½ HEN AND
ABOUT ¼ CUP SAUCE EACH

Hens

2 Cornish hens (1¼ pounds each),
  cut into halves

¼ teaspoon each salt and pepper

Sauce

2 small mangoes, pared and pitted
¼ cup each lime juice (no sugar
  added) and water
2 teaspoons granulated sugar

⅛ teaspoon ground allspice
2 tablespoons unsalted margarine,
  cut into pieces
2 teaspoons orange marmalade

To Prepare Hens: Preheat oven to 400°F. Place hen halves on rack in roasting pan; lift up skin and season each half with salt and pepper. Replace skin and roast hens until tender, 25 to 30 minutes.

To Prepare Sauce: In blender container combine mangoes, lime juice, water, sugar, and allspice and process until smooth. Transfer mixture to small saucepan; add margarine and marmalade and cook over low heat, stirring constantly, until margarine melts and mixture is heated.

To Serve: Remove and discard skin from hens. Place hen halves skin-side up on rack in broiling pan; broil 2 to 4 inches from heat source until browned and crisp, about 1 minute. Remove to serving plate and pour ¼ of the sauce over each hen half (or serve sauce on the side).

Each serving provides: 4 Protein Exchanges; 1½ Fat Exchanges; 1 Fruit Exchange;
  20 calories Optional Exchange
Per serving: 311 calories; 27 g protein; 13 g fat; 23 g carbohydrate; 30 mg calcium;
  218 mg sodium; 81 mg cholesterol

Chicken Timbales with Mushroom Sauce

WEEK 4 ∾ MAKES 2 SERVINGS

2 teaspoons margarine
1/2 cup chopped onion
10 ounces skinned and boned
chicken breasts, cut into pieces
1 cup skim milk
1 tablespoon chopped fresh parsley,
divided

1/4 teaspoon each salt and pepper,
divided
1/8 teaspoon ground nutmeg
1/2 cup sliced mushrooms
2 tablespoons water
1/2 teaspoon arrowroot

1. In small skillet heat margarine until bubbly and hot; add onion and sauté over low heat until softened, about 5 minutes.

2. Preheat oven to 350°F. Transfer sautéed onion to work bowl of food processor; add chicken and milk and process until smooth. Add 2 teaspoons parsley, 1/8 teaspoon each salt and pepper, and the nutmeg and process to blend; divide mixture into two 10-ounce custard cups and, using back of spoon, smooth surface of each.

3. Cover each cup with foil and bake until a knife, inserted in center, comes out clean, 40 to 45 minutes.

4. Into small skillet carefully drain accumulated liquid from each chicken timbale; set timbales aside and keep warm. Add mushrooms and remaining 1/8 teaspoon each salt and pepper to skillet and cook, stirring occasionally, until mushrooms are tender, about 5 minutes.

5. In small cup combine water and arrowroot, stirring to dissolve arrowroot; add to mushroom mixture and cook, stirring constantly, until thickened. Stir in remaining teaspoon parsley.

6. Unmold each timbale onto a plate and top each with half of the sauce.

Each serving provides: 4 Protein Exchanges; 1 Vegetable Exchange;
1 Fat Exchange; 1/2 Milk Exchange; 3 calories Optional Exchange
Per serving: 264 calories; 38 g protein; 7 g fat; 12 g carbohydrate; 191 mg calcium;
482 mg sodium; 85 mg cholesterol

Skillet Turkey Stew ❶

1 tablespoon plus 1 teaspoon
 all-purpose flour, divided
¼ teaspoon salt
Dash pepper
10 ounces skinned and boned turkey
 breast, cut into 1-inch cubes
2 teaspoons vegetable oil, divided
½ cup each diced onion, diced
 celery, and sliced carrot

½ garlic clove, mashed
½ packet (about ½ teaspoon)
 Instant chicken broth and
 seasoning mix
1 cup skim milk
6 ounces peeled cooked potatoes,
 cut into cubes
½ bay leaf
¼ teaspoon poultry seasoning

On sheet of wax paper or a paper plate combine 1 tablespoon flour with the salt and pepper; dredge turkey in seasoned flour to coat.

In 9- or 10-inch nonstick skillet heat 1½ teaspoons oil; add turkey cubes and sauté until browned on all sides. Remove turkey from skillet; set aside.

In same skillet heat remaining ½ teaspoon oil; add onion, celery, carrot, and garlic and sauté, stirring constantly, until vegetables are tender. Sprinkle remaining 1 teaspoon flour and the broth mix over vegetables, stirring quickly to combine; cook for 1 minute. Gradually stir in milk and, stirring constantly, bring to a boil. Reduce heat and let simmer until mixture thickens. Stir in turkey, potatoes, bay leaf, and poultry seasoning and cook until heated; remove bay leaf before serving.

Each serving provides: 4 Protein Exchanges; 1 Bread Exchange;
 1½ Vegetable Exchanges; 1 Fat Exchange; ½ Milk Exchange;
 25 calories Optional Exchange
Per serving: 357 calories; 41 g protein; 7 g fat; 31 g carbohydrate; 213 mg calcium;
 694 mg sodium; 90 mg cholesterol

Rolled Stuffed Turkey Breasts

WEEK 4 〜 MAKES 8 SERVINGS

2 tablespoons plus 2 teaspoons
  margarine, divided
2 tablespoons minced shallots
2 garlic cloves, minced
1 cup finely chopped mushrooms
1 cup drained cooked chopped
  spinach (or thawed and drained
  frozen chopped spinach)
1 teaspoon salt, divided
1/8 teaspoon ground nutmeg
1 cup each cooked short-grain rice
  and blanched grated carrot
1 tablespoon chopped fresh parsley
1/4 teaspoon celery seed

1/8 teaspoon each ground thyme and
  ground sage
Dash white pepper
6-pound turkey breast,* boned and
  skinned
2 tablespoons honey, mixed with 2
  teaspoons Dijon-style mustard
1/3 cup plus 2 teaspoons plain dried
  bread crumbs

Garnish

Thyme sprigs

In 9-inch skillet heat 1 tablespoon margarine until bubbly and hot; add shallots and garlic and sauté for 1 minute. Add mushrooms and sauté over medium-high heat until all liquid has evaporated. Transfer to mixing bowl and add spinach, dash salt, and nutmeg, mixing well; set aside.

In separate bowl combine rice, carrot, parsley, celery seed, herbs, pepper, and remaining salt; set aside.

Preheat oven to 350°F. Lay turkey breast flat, skin-side down: pull out the tendons from the 2 fillets on each side of the breast and fold the flllets over to the outside. Cover breast with sheet of wax paper and, using a meat mallet, pound to about 1-inch thickness, forming a "butterfly" or free-form rectangle shape. Spread spinach mixture evenly over turkey to about 1 inch from edge of meat, forming a rectangular shape with mixture; top with rice mixture. Fold sides and ends of breast over stuffing to enclose; secure sides and ends with toothpicks or sew with kitchen string. Transfer, seam-side down, to rack in roasting pan; cover pan with a tent of foil and roast for 1½ hours. Remove roast from oven and increase oven temperature to 425°F.

Remove toothpicks or string from turkey. Spread honey mixture over roast and sprinkle with crumbs, making sure top and sides are coated. In metal measuring cup or other small flameproof container melt remaining 1 tablespoon plus 2 teaspoons margarine. Using pastry brush, gently spread melted margarine over roast. Return turkey to oven and roast until topping is lightly browned, 10 to 15 minutes. Garnish with thyme sprigs and serve with any accumulated pan juices.

Each serving provides: 4 Protein Exchanges; ½ Bread Exchange;
  ¾ Vegetable Exchange; 1 Fat Exchange; 15 calories Optional Exchange
Per serving: 290 calories; 36 g protein; 8 g fat; 18 g carbohydrate; 72 mg calcium;
  490 mg sodium; 79 mg cholesterol

* A 6-pound turkey breast will yield about 2 pounds cooked meat.

Vegetable-Turkey Stir-Fry ◑

WEEK 4 ❧ MAKES 2 SERVINGS

Leftover turkey takes on a new dimension in this delicious dish.

1 tablespoon peanut or vegetable oil
1 cup diced onions
½ cup each diagonally sliced celery (¼-inch-thick slices) and julienne-cut red bell pepper (2 x ¼-inch strips)
½ cup cauliflower florets, blanched
8 ounces skinned and boned cooked turkey, cut into thin strips
¾ cup water
1 teaspoon cornstarch
1 packet instant chicken broth and seasoning mix
1 teaspoon each hoisin sauce and teriyaki sauce

In 12-inch nonstick skillet or a wok heat oil over high heat; add vegetables and cook, stirring quickly and frequently, until celery and pepper are tender-crisp, 1 to 2 minutes. Add turkey and stir to combine. In measuring cup or small bowl combine water, cornstarch, and broth mix, stirring to dissolve cornstarch; pour mixture into skillet and, stirring constantly, bring to a boil. Reduce heat and cook, stirring, until mixture thickens. Stir in hoisin and teriyaki sauces; cook for 1 minute longer.

Each serving provides: 4 Protein Exchanges; 2½ Vegetable Exchanges;
  1½ Fat Exchanges; 15 calories Optional Exchange
Per serving: 327 calories; 37 g protein; 12 g fat; 17 g carbohydrate; 78 mg calcium;
  746 mg sodium; 87 mg cholesterol

Turkey-Vegetable Sauté ◑

WEEK 4 ∽ MAKES 2 SERVINGS

2 teaspoons peanut or vegetable oil
1 cup thinly sliced onions
1 garlic clove, minced
10 ounces skinned and boned turkey
breast, cut into 2 x 1-inch strips
2 cups broccoli florets, blanched
1 cup thinly sliced red bell peppers
¾ cup water

1 tablespoon plus 1 teaspoon dry
sherry
1 tablespoon soy sauce
1 packet instant chicken broth and
seasoning mix
2 teaspoons cornstarch, dissolved
in 1½ teaspoons water

In 9- or 10-inch skillet heat oil; add onions and garlic and sauté until
onions are translucent. Add turkey and continue sautéing until turkey
is browned; add broccoli and red peppers and sauté until vegetables
are tender-crisp, about 5 minutes. Add water, sherry, soy sauce, and
broth mix and bring to a boil; stir in dissolved cornstarch and cook,
stirring constantly, until mixture thickens.

Each serving provides: 4 Protein Exchanges; 4 Vegetable Exchanges;
1 Fat Exchange; 25 calories Optional Exchange
Per serving: 334 calories; 41 g protein; 8 g fat; 25 g carbohydrate; 115 mg calcium;
1,226 mg sodium; 88 mg cholesterol

Potted Turkey Patties ❶

WEEK 4 ∽ MAKES 2 SERVINGS, 2 PATTIES EACH

2 teaspoons margarine, divided
2 tablespoons diced onion
1 garlic clove, minced
½ cup chopped mushrooms
8 ounces ground turkey
1 egg
1 slice white bread, made into
crumbs
2 teaspoons chopped fresh parsley,
divided

¼ teaspoon crushed thyme leaves
⅛ teaspoon each salt and pepper
2 teaspoons all-purpose flour,
divided
1 packet instant chicken broth and
seasoning mix, dissolved in
1 cup hot water
¼ cup skim milk

In small nonstick skillet heat 1 teaspoon margarine until bubbly and
hot; add onion and garlic and sauté until onion is translucent, about
2 minutes. Add mushrooms and sauté until softened, about 5 minutes.

Transfer mushroom mixture to a medium bowl and add turkey, egg, bread crumbs, 1 teaspoon parsley, and the thyme, salt, and pepper; stir to combine. Form turkey mixture into 4 equal patties and sprinkle each with ¼ teaspoon flour.

In 10-inch skillet heat remaining teaspoon margarine until bubbly and hot; add turkey patties and cook until browned on both sides. Add dissolved broth mix and bring to a boil. Reduce heat, cover, and let simmer for about 10 minutes. In measuring cup or small bowl combine milk and remaining teaspoon flour, stirring to dissolve flour; gradually stir into pan juices and cook over medium heat, stirring constantly, until mixture becomes slightly thickened. Serve sprinkled with remaining teaspoon parsley.

Each serving provides: 3½ Protein Exchanges; ½ Bread Exchange; ½ Vegetable Exchange; 1 Fat Exchange; 25 calories Optional Exchange
Per serving: 275 calories; 31 g protein; 10 g fat; 13 g carbohydrate; 92 mg calcium; 797 mg sodium; 215 mg cholesterol

Turkey Burgers ◑❸

WEEK 1 ⌒ MAKES 2 SERVINGS, 1 BURGER EACH

8 ounces ground turkey
1 tablespoon plus 1 teaspoon margarine, softened
1½ teaspoons water
1 packet instant chicken broth and seasoning mix

½ cup thinly sliced onion
1 tablespoon plus 1 teaspoon ketchup
2 hamburger rolls (2 ounces each), cut into halves and toasted

In bowl combine turkey, margarine, water, and broth mix; form into 2 equal patties. Spray 9- or 10-inch nonstick skillet with nonstick cooking spray and heat over medium-high heat; add patties and brown on both sides. Reduce heat to low and add onions; cover pan and cook until patties are no longer pink inside, 5 to 8 minutes.

Serve each burger, topped with 2 teaspoons ketchup and half of the cooked onion slices, on a toasted roll.

Each serving provides: 3 Protein Exchanges; 2 Bread Exchanges; ½ Vegetable Exchange; 2 Fat Exchanges; 15 calories Optional Exchange
Per serving: 402 calories; 31 g protein; 14 g fat; 37 g carbohydrate; 74 mg calcium; 998 mg sodium; 81 mg cholesterol

"Porcupines" in Tomato Sauce ❶

WEEK 4 ◇ MAKES 2 SERVINGS

"Porcupines"
10 ounces ground turkey
2 ounces uncooked converted rice
¼ cup diced onion
2 tablespoons chopped fresh parsley
1 teaspoon salt
⅛ teaspoon each marjoram leaves
  and thyme leaves
Dash pepper

Sauce
1 cup tomato sauce
½ cup canned chicken broth
⅛ teaspoon minced fresh garlic

To Prepare "Porcupines": Preheat oven to 350°F. In medium bowl thoroughly combine all ingredients for "porcupines"; shape into 8 equal balls. Spray a 1-quart casserole with nonstick cooking spray and arrange turkey balls in casserole.

To Prepare Sauce and Bake: In small bowl thoroughly combine all ingredients for sauce; pour over "porcupines." Cover casserole and bake for 1 hour, turning "porcupines" once during baking.

Each serving provides: 4 Protein Exchanges; 1 Bread Exchange;
  2¼ Vegetable Exchanges; 10 calories Optional Exchange
Per serving: 331 calories; 36 g protein; 5 g fat; 34 g carbohydrate; 63 mg calcium;
  1,978 mg sodium; 96 mg cholesterol

Turkey-Stuffing Loaf ❶

WEEK 1 ◇ MAKES 4 SERVINGS

1 tablespoon plus 1 teaspoon
  margarine
2 small Granny Smith apples, cored,
  pared, and diced
½ cup each shredded carrot and
  diced onion, celery, and green
  bell pepper

13 ounces ground turkey
4 slices white bread, cut into cubes
½ cup plain low-fat yogurt
2 eggs, beaten
¼ teaspoon each poultry seasoning
  and salt

Preheat oven to 375°F. In 8-inch nonstick skillet heat margarine until bubbly and hot; add apples and vegetables and sauté, stirring constantly, until apples are soft. Remove from heat and stir in remaining ingredients.

Spray a 9 x 5 x 3-inch loaf pan with nonstick cooking spray and transfer turkey mixture to pan; smooth top and bake until set, 35 to 40 minutes (center should be firm). Remove from oven and let stand for 5 minutes; invert onto serving plate.

Each serving provides: 3 Protein Exchanges; 1 Bread Exchange;
  1 Vegetable Exchange; 1 Fat Exchange; ½ Fruit Exchange; ¼ Milk Exchange
Per serving: 310 calories; 27 g protein; 10 g fat; 26 g carbohydrate; 121 mg calcium;
  447 mg sodium; 202 mg cholesterol

Variation: Substitute 3 ounces (1¼ cups) cornflake crumbs for the white bread.

Per serving: 330 calories; 27 g protein; 10 g fat; 33 g carbohydrate; 102 mg calcium;
  594 mg sodium; 201 mg cholesterol

Turkey-Rice Salad ❶

WEEK 3 ∾ MAKES 2 SERVINGS

Turn leftover turkey into a delicious quick and easy salad for two.

6 ounces skinned and boned cooked
  turkey, chilled and diced
½ cup cooked long-grain rice,
  chilled
¼ cup diced celery
2 tablespoons each diced onion and
  red bell pepper
1 tablespoon each mayonnaise and
  sour cream
1½ teaspoons each chopped fresh
  parsley and lemon juice

¼ teaspoon Dijon-style mustard
Dash each salt, pepper, and garlic
  powder
2 iceberg, romaine, or loose-leafed
  lettuce leaves

Garnish

Radish rose

In 1-quart bowl combine turkey, rice, celery, onion, and red pepper. In small bowl thoroughly combine mayonnaise, sour cream, parsley, lemon juice, mustard, and seasonings; pour dressing over salad and toss well to coat. Cover and refrigerate until chilled; toss again just before serving. Serve on lettuce leaves, garnished with radish rose.

Each serving provides: 3 Protein Exchanges; ½ Bread Exchange;
  ¾ Vegetable Exchange; 1½ Fat Exchanges; 15 calories Optional Exchange
Per serving: 275 calories; 27 g protein; 11 g fat; 15 g carbohydrate; 53 mg calcium;
  206 mg sodium; 73 mg cholesterol

Turkey Cutlets in Mushroom Sauce ◗◓

WEEK 4 ～ MAKES 2 SERVINGS

2 teaspoons margarine
10 ounces turkey cutlets, cut ¼ inch thick
1 cup thinly sliced mushrooms
½ cup diced onion
2 teaspoons all-purpose flour, divided

3 tablespoons sour cream
1 tablespoon chopped fresh parsley
1 teaspoon paprika
½ teaspoon salt
⅛ teaspoon pepper

In 10-inch nonstick skillet heat margarine until bubbly and hot; add turkey and cook until lightly browned on both sides. Remove from skillet and keep warm.

To same skillet add mushrooms and onion and cook, stirring occasionally, until liquid has evaporated; sprinkle with 1 teaspoon flour and cook, stirring constantly, for 1 minute. Remove from heat.

In small bowl stir sour cream until creamy; add remaining teaspoon flour and stir to combine. Stir 2 tablespoons vegetable mixture into sour cream mixture, then add sour cream mixture to skillet and stir to combine. Place skillet over low heat and stir in parsley and seasonings; add turkey and cook just until heated (*do not boil*).

Each serving provides: 4 Protein Exchanges; 1½ Vegetable Exchanges;
  1 Fat Exchange; 60 calories Optional Exchange
Per serving: 278 calories; 36 g protein; 11 g fat; 8 g carbohydrate; 64 mg calcium;
  701 mg sodium; 97 mg cholesterol

Variation: Substitute ½ cup plain low-fat yogurt for the sour cream. Add ½ Milk Exchange to Exchange Information and reduce Optional Exchange to 10 calories.

Per serving: 267 calories; 38 g protein; 7 g fat; 11 g carbohydrate; 143 mg calcium;
  730 mg sodium; 91 mg cholesterol

Turkey-Cheddar Muffins ❶

WEEK 1 ∽ MAKES 4 SERVINGS, 2 MUFFINS EACH

2 ready-to-bake refrigerated
  buttermilk flaky biscuits (1 ounce
  each) *
2 teaspoons margarine
1/2 cup each diced onion and green
  bell pepper
4 ounces skinned and boned cooked
  turkey, diced
2 ounces Cheddar cheese, shredded

2 eggs, lightly beaten
1/4 cup chopped drained canned
  pimientos
1 teaspoon Worcestershire sauce
1/2 teaspoon Dijon-style mustard
Dash pepper

Garnish

Parsley sprigs

Carefully separate each biscuit into 4 thin layers of dough.* Spray 8 cups (2 1/2-inch diameter each) of a 12-cup muffin pan with nonstick cooking spray and place 1 layer of dough in bottom of each sprayed cup; set aside.

Preheat oven to 450°F. In small nonstick skillet heat margarine until bubbly and hot; add onion and green pepper and sauté until onion is golden and pepper is soft. Remove skillet from heat and add remaining ingredients except parsley; stir to combine. Spoon 1/8 of mixture over each layer of dough and partially fill empty cups with water (this will prevent pan from burning and/or warping). Bake until muffins are golden brown and set, 15 to 20 minutes. Before removing muffins from pan, carefully drain off water (remember, it will be boiling hot); serve muffins warm, garnished with parsley sprigs.

Each serving provides: 2 Protein Exchanges; 1/2 Bread Exchange;
  1/2 Vegetable Exchange; 1/2 Fat Exchange
Per serving: 218 calories; 17 g protein; 12 g fat; 11 g carbohydrate; 140 mg calcium;
  329 mg sodium; 174 mg cholesterol

* Separate dough into layers as soon as it is removed from refrigerator; it will be difficult to work with if allowed to come to room temperature.

Turkey Kabobs with Pineapple-Teriyaki Sauce

WEEK 4 ～ MAKES 2 SERVINGS, 2 SKEWERS EACH

½ cup diced onion
⅓ cup pineapple juice (no sugar added)
2 tablespoons each teriyaki sauce and lemon juice
2 teaspoons each spicy brown mustard and dry sherry
1 garlic clove, sliced
1-inch piece pared ginger root, sliced
10 ounces skinned and boned turkey, cut into 1-inch cubes

½ medium red bell pepper, seeded and cut into 1-inch squares
8 medium mushroom caps (about 1½-inch diameter each)
8 scallions (green onions), white portion only (2-inch pieces)
1 tablespoon vegetable oil
½ cup canned crushed pineapple (no sugar added)
1 teaspoon cornstarch

1. In glass or stainless-steel bowl combine onion, pineapple juice, teriyaki sauce, lemon juice, mustard, sherry, garlic, and ginger; add turkey and remaining vegetables to marinade and toss to coat. Cover and refrigerate for 1 hour.

2. Using slotted spoon, remove turkey, pepper squares, mushrooms, and scallions from marinade. Onto each of four 8-inch wooden skewers, alternating ingredients, thread ¼ of the turkey cubes, ¼ of the pepper squares, 2 mushroom caps, and 2 scallions. Arrange kabobs in a shallow flameproof casserole that is large enough to hold them in a single layer; set aside.

3. Strain marinade, reserving liquid and onion and discarding garlic and ginger. In small skillet heat oil; add reserved onion and sauté until softened. Stir in crushed pineapple. Add cornstarch to reserved marinade liquid, stirring to dissolve cornstarch; add to skillet and, stirring constantly, bring mixture to a boil. Reduce heat and let simmer until mixture thickens. Pour pineapple sauce into blender container and process at low speed until smooth.

4. Preheat broiler. Lightly brush kabobs with some of the pineapple sauce and broil, turning once and brushing again with some of the sauce, until turkey is browned, about 5 minutes on each side. Reheat remaining sauce and serve with kabobs.

Each serving provides: 4 Protein Exchanges; 2¼ Vegetable Exchanges;
  1½ Fat Exchanges; 1 Fruit Exchange; 10 calories Optional Exchange
Per serving: 384 calories; 35 g protein; 11 g fat; 35 g carbohydrate; 76 mg calcium;
  779 mg sodium; 96 mg cholesterol

Veal

When an artist creates a painting, it's designed to be pleasing to the eye; when our chefs create recipes, they plan to please both the eye and the palate. In this collection of culinary masterpieces—from Veal Stew to Skillet Ground Veal 'n' Cabbage, they've drawn on the subtle flavor of veal and blended it superbly with a variety of sauces and seasonings.

Veal Steaks Piccata ◐

WEEK 4 ～ MAKES 2 SERVINGS, 1 VEAL STEAK EACH

3 tablespoons all-purpose flour
½ teaspoon salt
Dash pepper
2 boneless veal shoulder cube
  steaks (5 ounces each)
1 tablespoon margarine
1 cup thinly sliced mushrooms

1 garlic clove, minced
¼ cup dry white wine
2 tablespoons each chopped fresh
  Italian (flat-leaf) parsley and
  lemon juice
1 small lemon, thinly sliced

On sheet of wax paper or a paper plate combine flour, salt, and pepper. Dredge steaks in seasoned flour, turning to coat all sides; set aside remaining flour mixture.

In 12-inch nonstick skillet heat margarine until bubbly and hot; add veal steaks and, over high heat, brown quickly on both sides. Remove to warmed serving plate; set aside and keep warm.

In same skillet combine mushrooms and garlic; sauté over medium-high heat, stirring constantly, until mushrooms are browned, about 1 minute. Sprinkle with remaining flour mixture and stir quickly to combine. Gradually stir in wine; add parsley and lemon juice and, stirring constantly, bring to a boil. Reduce heat and let simmer until slightly thickened; add lemon slices and stir to combine. To serve, pour sauce over veal steaks.

Each serving provides: 4 Protein Exchanges; ½ Bread Exchange;
  1 Vegetable Exchange; 1½ Fat Exchanges; 30 calories Optional Exchange
Per serving: 390 calories; 31 g protein; 20 g fat; 18 g carbohydrate; 63 mg calcium;
  714 mg sodium; 101 mg cholesterol

Broiled Veal Chops ◐

WEEK 1 ～ MAKES 2 SERVINGS, 1 CHOP EACH

2 veal loin chops (6 ounces each)
¼ teaspoon crushed rosemary
  leaves, divided
⅛ teaspoon pepper, divided

2 teaspoons margarine, divided
1 teaspoon lemon juice, divided
¼ teaspoon salt (optional)

Sprinkle 1 side of each veal chop with ¼ each of the rosemary and pepper; place in jelly-roll pan. Dot each chop with ½ teaspoon margarine and sprinkle each with ¼ teaspoon lemon juice; broil 6 inches from heat source for 5 minutes.

Turn chops over and sprinkle with remaining rosemary, pepper, and lemon juice; dot each with ½ teaspoon margarine and broil until lightly browned, 4 to 5 minutes. If desired, sprinkle with salt; serve topped with any accumulated pan juices.

Each serving provides: 4 Protein Exchanges; 1 Fat Exchange
Per serving without salt: 300 calories; 30 g protein; 19 g fat; 0.4 g carbohydrate;
  17 mg calcium; 119 mg sodium; 115 mg cholesterol
With salt: 300 calories; 30 g protein; 19 g fat; 0.4 g carbohydrate; 18 mg calcium;
  387 mg sodium; 115 mg cholesterol

Veal Stew

WEEK 4 ◇ MAKES 4 SERVINGS

Noodles are a perfect accompaniment.

2 tablespoons all-purpose flour
¼ teaspoon each salt and pepper
1¼ pounds boneless veal shoulder,
  cut into 1-inch cubes
1 tablespoon plus 1 teaspoon
  margarine
¼ cup diced shallots or onion
2 tablespoons plus 2 teaspoons dry
  white wine

1 cup quartered mushrooms
½ cup each sliced celery and carrot
1½ teaspoons chopped fresh
  parsley
1 cup water
1 packet instant chicken broth and
  seasoning mix
1 bay leaf

On sheet of wax paper or a paper plate combine flour, salt, and pepper; dredge veal cubes in seasoned flour, coating all sides.

In 2-quart saucepan heat margarine until bubbly and hot; add veal cubes and sauté until lightly browned on all sides. Add shallots (or onion) and any remaining flour mixture; sauté until shallots (or onion) are translucent. Gradually stir in wine; stirring constantly, bring to a boil. Add mushrooms, celery, carrot, and parsley and cook for 3 minutes. Stir in water, broth mix, and bay leaf and return mixture to a boil. Reduce heat, cover, and cook until veal is tender, 45 to 50 minutes; remove bay leaf before serving.

Each serving provides: 4 Protein Exchanges; 1⅛ Vegetable Exchanges;
  1 Fat Exchange; 30 calories Optional Exchange
Per serving: 326 calories; 29 g protein; 18 g fat; 8 g carbohydrate; 36 mg calcium;
  505 mg sodium; 101 mg cholesterol

Veal Birds

WEEK 2 ∿ MAKES 4 SERVINGS, 2 "BIRDS" EACH

This one-skillet entrée may look complicated, but it's actually an easy-to-prepare treat; most of the ingredients are probably on your pantry shelves, and cooking time for the entire dish is less than 30 minutes.

2 tablespoons plus 2 teaspoons
 margarine, divided
2 cups thinly sliced onions
¼ cup minced celery
4 garlic cloves, minced, or 1
 teaspoon garlic powder
2 cups thinly sliced mushrooms
⅛ teaspoon each salt and pepper
1 cup cooked long-grain rice

¼ cup chopped fresh parsley,
 divided
1 tablespoon plus 1 teaspoon grated
 Parmesan cheese
8 veal cutlets (3 ounces each),
 pounded to ¼-inch thickness
1 cup dry Marsala wine
½ cup canned chicken broth

In 12-inch nonstick skillet heat 1 tablespoon plus 1 teaspoon margarine over medium heat until bubbly and hot; add onions, celery, and garlic and sauté for 2 minutes (*do not brown*). Add mushrooms, salt, and pepper and continue cooking until most of liquid has evaporated, about 5 minutes. Transfer mixture to bowl; add rice, 2 tablespoons parsley, and the cheese and stir to combine. Mound an equal amount of rice mixture onto each cutlet (about 3 heaping tablespoons) and roll veal to enclose filling, folding in edges; secure each with a toothpick.

In same skillet heat remaining 1 tablespoon plus 1 teaspoon margarine over medium heat until bubbly and hot; add veal birds and cook, turning occasionally, until browned on all sides. Remove veal birds to a warmed serving platter; remove and discard toothpicks and keep "birds" warm.

In same skillet combine wine and broth; cook over high heat, stirring occasionally and scraping particles from sides and bottom of pan, until sauce is slightly thickened. Pour over veal birds, garnish with remaining 2 tablespoons parsley, and serve immediately.

Each serving provides: 4 Protein Exchanges; ½ Bread Exchange;
 2⅛ Vegetable Exchanges; 2 Fat Exchanges; 75 calories Optional Exchange
Per serving: 535 calories; 38 g protein; 24 g fat; 25 g carbohydrate; 85 mg calcium;
 436 mg sodium; 122 mg cholesterol

Veal Stew Marsala

This stew freezes well, so prepare ahead and freeze for future use. If you freeze the stew in individual portions, the exact number of servings that you require will be readily available.

1 tablespoon vegetable oil
1 pound 14 ounces veal cubes
1 cup chopped onions
1 tablespoon minced fresh garlic
2 tablespoons all-purpose flour
2 cups sliced mushrooms
1½ cups each thinly sliced carrots
   and water

¾ cup dry Marsala wine
½ cup chopped fresh or canned
   crushed tomatoes
2 packets instant chicken broth and
   seasoning mix
1 teaspoon salt
Dash pepper
½ cup frozen peas

In 3-quart saucepan heat oil; add veal and brown on all sides. Add onions and garlic and sauté briefly, about 3 minutes (*do not brown*). Add flour and stir until thoroughly combined; add remaining ingredients except peas and bring to a boil, stirring occasionally. Reduce heat, cover, and let simmer until meat is tender, about 40 minutes. Add peas, cover, and cook for 10 minutes longer. Serve immediately or let cool, then freeze for future use.

Each serving provides: 4 Protein Exchanges; 1¾ Vegetable Exchanges;
   ½ Fat Exchange; 55 calories Optional Exchange
Per serving with fresh tomatoes: 364 calories; 31 g protein; 17 g fat;
   14 g carbohydrate; 46 mg calcium; 771 mg sodium; 101 mg cholesterol
With canned tomatoes: 364 calories; 31 g protein; 17 g fat; 14 g carbohydrate;
   45 mg calcium; 797 mg sodium; 101 mg cholesterol

Serving Suggestion—Serve each portion of stew over ½ cup cooked long-grain rice and sprinkle with 1 teaspoon chopped fresh parsley; add 1 Bread Exchange to Exchange Information.

Per serving with fresh tomatoes: 478 calories; 33 g protein; 17 g fat;
   39 g carbohydrate; 59 mg calcium; 772 mg sodium; 101 mg cholesterol
With canned tomatoes: 478 calories; 33 g protein; 17 g fat; 39 g carbohydrate;
   58 mg calcium; 797 mg sodium; 101 mg cholesterol

Sautéed Veal Marsala ◑

WEEK 4 〜 MAKES 2 SERVINGS

1 tablespoon plus 1 teaspoon
  margarine
10 ounces thinly sliced veal
1 cup sliced mushrooms
1 garlic clove, minced

½ cup dry Marsala wine
¼ cup canned chicken broth
1 teaspoon all-purpose flour
¼ teaspoon salt
Dash freshly ground pepper

In 9-inch nonstick skillet heat margarine until bubbly and hot; add veal and quickly sauté on both sides. Remove veal from pan and set aside.

In same skillet combine mushrooms and garlic; cook over high heat, stirring constantly, until liquid evaporates. Add wine and cook, stirring occasionally, for 3 to 4 minutes. Combine broth and flour, stirring to dissolve flour; add to skillet and cook, stirring constantly, until sauce thickens. Add veal, any juices remaining from veal, and salt and pepper and cook until heated; serve immediately.

Each serving provides: 4 Protein Exchanges; 1 Vegetable Exchange;
  2 Fat Exchanges; 70 calories Optional Exchange
Per serving: 402 calories; 30 g protein; 21 g fat; 8 g carbohydrate; 29 mg calcium;
  564 mg sodium; 101 mg cholesterol

Skillet Ground Veal 'n' Cabbage

WEEK 4 〜 MAKES 4 SERVINGS

1 tablespoon plus 1 teaspoon
  margarine
1 cup chopped onions
2 garlic cloves, minced
1¼ pounds ground veal
1 teaspoon paprika
½ teaspoon salt
¼ teaspoon pepper
2 cups shredded green cabbage

1½ cups plus 2 tablespoons water,
  divided
1 cup canned whole tomatoes,
  chopped
1 packet instant chicken broth and
  seasoning mix
2 teaspoons all-purpose flour
2 cups cooked elbow macaroni

In 12-inch skillet heat margarine until bubbly and hot; add onions and garlic and sauté until softened. Add veal, paprika, salt, and pepper and sauté until veal is lightly browned. Add cabbage, 1½ cups water, and the tomatoes and broth mix and stir to combine; cover and cook over medium heat, stirring occasionally, for 30 minutes.

Dissolve flour in remaining 2 tablespoons water and stir into veal mixture; stirring constantly, bring to a boil and cook until thickened. Stir in macaroni and cook until thoroughly heated.

Each serving provides: 4 Protein Exchanges; 1 Bread Exchange;
2 Vegetable Exchanges; 1 Fat Exchange; 10 calories Optional Exchange
Per serving: 409 calories; 32 g protein; 19 g fat; 27 g carbohydrate; 63 mg calcium;
710 mg sodium; 101 mg cholesterol

Veal and Pepper Sauté ◑

WEEK 4 ∾ MAKES 4 SERVINGS

2 teaspoons olive or vegetable oil, divided
2 garlic cloves, sliced
2 cups each thinly sliced onions, red bell pepper strips, and green bell pepper strips (3 x ¼-inch strips)
3 tablespoons all-purpose flour
½ teaspoon salt

⅛ teaspoon pepper
1¼ pounds veal cutlets, cut into 6 x 1-inch strips
1 tablespoon plus 1 teaspoon margarine
½ cup dry white wine
2 tablespoons chopped fresh basil
¼ teaspoon oregano leaves

In 12-inch nonstick skillet heat 1 teaspoon oil; add garlic and sauté until browned (*be careful not to burn*). Using a slotted spoon, remove and discard garlic. To same skillet add onions and sauté, stirring occasionally, until onions are browned; remove to bowl and set aside. Add bell peppers to skillet and sauté until tender-crisp; remove to bowl with onions and set aside.

In large plastic bag combine flour, salt, and pepper; add veal and shake until pieces are lightly coated.

In same skillet combine remaining teaspoon oil with the margarine and heat until margarine is bubbly and hot; add veal, several pieces at a time, and sauté until browned on both sides. Return onions and peppers to skillet, stirring to combine. Add wine and seasonings and bring to a boil. Reduce heat and let simmer for 2 to 3 minutes to blend flavors; serve immediately.

Each serving provides: 4 Protein Exchanges; 3 Vegetable Exchanges;
1½ Fat Exchanges; 55 calories Optional Exchange
Per serving: 409 calories; 32 g protein; 19 g fat; 23 g carbohydrate; 76 mg calcium;
440 mg sodium; 101 mg cholesterol

Sautéed Veal Patties ◐

WEEK 4 〜 MAKES 2 SERVINGS, 1 PATTY EACH

---

1 tablespoon margarine, divided
½ cup diced onion
1 garlic clove, minced
9 ounces ground veal
⅓ cup plus 2 teaspoons plain dried
bread crumbs, divided
1 egg
1 tablespoon each chopped fresh
Italian (flat-leaf) parsley and
lemon juice

½ teaspoon salt
⅛ teaspoon each ground nutmeg
and pepper
1 teaspoon all-purpose flour
1 packet instant chicken broth and
seasoning mix, dissolved in ¾
cup hot water

In small nonstick skillet heat 1 teaspoon margarine until bubbly and hot; add onion and garlic and sauté until onion is translucent. Transfer to medium bowl; add veal, 3 tablespoons bread crumbs, and the egg, parsley, lemon juice, and seasonings. Mix thoroughly and shape into 2 patties; dredge patties in remaining 3 tablespoons bread crumbs to coat.

In same skillet heat remaining 2 teaspoons margarine until bubbly and hot; add patties and cook over medium heat, turning once, until browned on both sides and done to taste (*do not overcook*). Remove patties to serving platter; set aside and keep warm. Stir flour into remaining pan juices; gradually stir in dissolved broth mix and cook, stirring constantly, until mixture comes to a boil. Reduce heat and let simmer until thickened; pour over patties and serve immediately.

Each serving provides: 4 Protein Exchanges; 1 Bread Exchange;
½ Vegetable Exchange: 1½ Fat Exchanges; 10 calories Optional Exchange
Per serving: 420 calories; 32 g protein; 22 g fat; 22 g carbohydrate; 75 mg calcium;
1,293 mg sodium; 229 mg cholesterol

Baked Veal-Stuffed Eggplant

WEEK 2 ∽ MAKES 4 SERVINGS, 1 EGGPLANT HALF EACH

2 medium eggplants (about 1¼
  pounds each)
1 tablespoon plus 1 teaspoon olive
  or vegetable oil
1 cup chopped onions
1 tablespoon minced fresh garlic
2 cups sliced mushrooms
10 ounces ground veal
1 cup canned crushed tomatoes

1 teaspoon basil leaves
½ teaspoon salt
⅛ teaspoon freshly ground pepper
1½ cups cooked elbow macaroni
4 ounces mozzarella cheese,
  shredded
1 tablespoon plus 1 teaspoon grated
  Parmesan cheese

1. Cut each eggplant in half lengthwise; blanch halves in boiling water for 1 to 2 minutes, then drain. Let eggplant halves cool slightly.

2. Using a spoon, scoop pulp from each half, leaving about a ¼-inch-thick shell; set shells cut-side down on paper towels and set aside. Chop pulp and reserve.

3. In 3-quart saucepan heat oil; add onions and garlic and sauté over medium heat just until onions soften, about 1 minute. Increase heat to high, add mushrooms, and sauté, stirring constantly, until all liquid evaporates, about 3 minutes. Add veal and stir quickly to break up large pieces; cook, stirring constantly, until veal loses pink color and begins to brown. Stir in tomatoes, seasonings, and reserved eggplant pulp. Reduce heat to low and cook until mixture is slightly thickened, 5 to 8 minutes.

4. Preheat oven to 375°F. Remove pan from heat and stir in macaroni. Fill each reserved eggplant shell with ¼ of the veal mixture; top each with 1 ounce mozzarella cheese, then sprinkle with 1 teaspoon Parmesan cheese. Bake until cheese is bubbly, 20 to 25 minutes.

Each serving provides: 3 Protein Exchanges; ½ Bread Exchange;
  5 Vegetable Exchanges; 1 Fat Exchange; 30 calories Optional Exchange
Per serving: 424 calories; 28 g protein; 19 g fat; 38 g carbohydrate; 244 mg calcium;
  548 mg sodium; 74 mg cholesterol

Ground Veal Rouladen

WEEK 4 ～ MAKES 2 SERVINGS, 2 ROLLS EACH

1 tablespoon margarine, divided
¼ cup minced onion
10 ounces ground veal
⅔ cup instant mashed potato
 flakes, divided
2 teaspoons each imitation bacon
 bits, crushed, and spicy brown
 mustard

1 tablespoon sour cream
4 thin scallions (green onions),
 white portion only (each about
 3 inches long), blanched
1 teaspoon all-purpose flour
¾ cup water
1 packet instant chicken broth and
 seasoning mix

In 8-inch nonstick skillet heat 1 teaspoon margarine until bubbly and hot; add onion and sauté until translucent. Transfer to a bowl and add veal, ½ cup potato flakes, and the bacon bits, mustard, and sour cream; mix until thoroughly combined. Divide veal mixture into 4 equal portions.

On sheet of wax paper flatten 1 portion of veal mixture into a circle and top with a scallion; roll circle to enclose scallion, using a metal spatula to lift meat if it should stick to wax paper. Repeat procedure with remaining 3 portions of veal and scallions. On paper plate coat veal rolls evenly in remaining potato flakes; arrange on a plate, cover, and refrigerate for 30 minutes.

In same skillet heat remaining 2 teaspoons margarine until bubbly and hot; add chilled veal rolls and cook over medium heat until rolls are browned on all sides. Remove veal rolls to warmed serving plate and keep warm. Sprinkle flour into pan drippings and stir quickly to combine; gradually stir in water. Add broth mix and, stirring constantly, bring to a boil. Reduce heat and let simmer until mixture thickens slightly. Pour gravy over veal rolls and serve immediately.

Each serving provides: 4 Protein Exchanges; 1 Bread Exchange;
 ½ Vegetable Exchange; 1½ Fat Exchanges; 35 calories Optional Exchange
Per serving: 591 calories; 35 g protein; 23 g fat; 62 g carbohydrate; 77 mg calcium;
 821 mg sodium; 104 mg cholesterol

Variation: Substitute plain low-fat yogurt for the sour cream; reduce Optional Exchange to 25 calories.

Per serving: 580 calories; 36 g protein; 21 g fat; 62 g carbohydrate; 82 mg calcium;
 822 mg sodium; 101 mg cholesterol

Stuffed Spaghetti Squash

WEEK 1 ～ MAKES 2 SERVINGS

**1 spaghetti squash (1¼ to 1½
  pounds) ***
2 teaspoons olive or vegetable oil
**½ cup each diced onion and red
  bell pepper**
1 garlic clove, minced
8 ounces ground veal
**1 cup canned whole tomatoes,
  chopped**

¼ teaspoon oregano leaves
Dash each salt and pepper
**2 ounces shredded mozzarella or
  Cheddar cheese**
**1 tablespoon chopped Italian
  (flat-leaf) parsley**

Preheat oven to 400°F. Using tines of a fork, pierce squash in several places; place whole squash on baking sheet and bake for 45 minutes. Remove from oven and let cool. Reduce oven temperature to 350°F.

Cut squash in half lengthwise and remove and discard seeds; scoop out pulp, reserving shells. Set aside shells and pulp.

In small skillet heat oil; add onion, red pepper, and garlic and sauté until onion is translucent. Stir in veal and sauté until veal is no longer pink; add tomatoes, seasonings, and reserved squash pulp and cook, stirring occasionally, until liquid has been absorbed. Spoon half of mixture into each reserved shell; place each shell in individual flameproof baking dish and bake for 20 minutes. Sprinkle each portion with 1 ounce cheese and broil until cheese is melted and browned. Serve sprinkled with parsley.

Each serving provides: 4 Protein Exchanges; 4 Vegetable Exchanges;
  1 Fat Exchange
Per serving with mozzarella cheese: 409 calories; 31 g protein; 23 g fat;
  21 g carbohydrate; 216 mg calcium; 414 mg sodium; 103 mg cholesterol
With Cheddar cheese: 443 calories; 33 g protein; 26 g fat; 21 g carbohydrate;
  274 mg calcium; 484 mg sodium; 110 mg cholesterol

* A 1¼- to 1½-pound spaghetti squash will yield about 2 cups cooked squash.

Veal-Stuffed Cabbage in Wine Sauce

WEEK 4 ⮑ MAKES 2 SERVINGS, 2 CABBAGE ROLLS EACH

¼ cup minced shallots or onion
9 ounces ground veal
1 egg, lightly beaten with 1
  tablespoon water
3 tablespoons seasoned dried
  bread crumbs
¼ teaspoon salt
Dash each white pepper and ground
  nutmeg

4 medium green cabbage leaves,
  blanched
½ cup tomato sauce
¼ cup canned chicken broth
2 tablespoons dry red wine
Dash each garlic powder and onion
  powder

In small nonstick skillet cook shallots (or onion) until softened. In medium bowl combine cooked shallots (or onion), veal, egg, bread crumbs, salt, pepper, and nutmeg; mix well.

Remove about 1 inch from core end of each blanched cabbage leaf. Place ¼ of meat mixture in center of each leaf; roll tightly, tucking in sides to enclose filling. In same skillet arrange filled leaves seam-side down. In small bowl combine remaining ingredients; pour over cabbage rolls, bring to a boil, and cook for 10 minutes. Reduce heat to low, cover, and let simmer until cabbage is tender, about 25 minutes.

Each serving provides: 4 Protein Exchanges; ½ Bread Exchange;
  2¼ Vegetable Exchanges; 20 calories Optional Exchange
Per serving with shallots: 377 calories; 32 g protein; 17 g fat; 22 g carbohydrate;
  105 mg calcium; 883 mg sodium; 228 mg cholesterol
With onion: 371 calories; 32 g protein; 17 g fat; 20 g carbohydrate; 103 mg calcium;
  883 mg sodium; 228 mg cholesterol

Sausage and Onion Parmigiana Hero ◐

WEEK 1 ⮑ MAKES 4 SERVINGS

1 loaf (8 ounces) Italian bread
1 tablespoon plus 1 teaspoon olive
  oil, divided
1 cup each sliced onions, green
  bell peppers, and red bell peppers

1 garlic clove, minced
15 ounces veal sausage
2 ounces mozzarella cheese,
  shredded

1. Cut bread in half lengthwise and place bottom half, cut-side up, on piece of foil; set aside.

2. In 12-inch nonstick skillet heat 2 teaspoons oil; add onions, peppers, and garlic and sauté, stirring occasionally, until onions are lightly browned. Remove from skillet and set aside.

3. In same skillet heat remaining 2 teaspoons oil; add sausage and cook, turning, until browned on all sides. Remove from skillet and slice sausage diagonally, then stir into onion-pepper mixture.

4. Preheat broiler. Spoon sausage mixture over bottom half of loaf; sprinkle evenly with mozzarella cheese and broil just until cheese melts, about 1 minute. Remove from broiler and top with remaining half of loaf to form a sandwich; to serve, cut into 4 equal sections.

Each serving provides: 3½ Protein Exchanges; 2 Bread Exchanges;
 1½ Vegetable Exchanges; 1 Fat Exchange
Per serving: 463 calories; 33 g protein; 19 g fat; 38 g carbohydrate; 107 mg calcium;
 1,354 mg sodium (estimated); 98 mg cholesterol

Veal Balls in Beer Sauce

WEEK 2 ∽ MAKES 4 SERVINGS, 4 VEAL BALLS EACH

4 slices white bread, torn into small pieces	1 garlic clove, minced
1 cup beer, divided	1 pound 3 ounces ground veal
½ cup water	1 egg
2 teaspoons honey	1 tablespoon chopped fresh parsley
2 tablespoons margarine, divided	½ teaspoon salt
1 cup diced onions	Dash pepper

In mixing bowl combine bread pieces and ¼ cup beer; set aside and let soak. In small bowl combine remaining ¾ cup beer with the water and honey; set aside.

In 12-inch nonstick skillet heat 1 teaspoon margarine until bubbly and hot; add onions and garlic and sauté until onions are translucent. Add sautéed onions to soaked bread; add veal, egg, parsley, salt, and pepper and mix until thoroughly combined. Shape into 16 balls, each about 2 inches in diameter.

In same skillet heat remaining 1 tablespoon plus 2 teaspoons margarine over medium-high heat until bubbly and hot; add meatballs, 1 at a time, and quickly brown on all sides (*be careful not to burn; if necessary, reduce heat to medium*). Add reserved honey mixture to skillet and bring to a boil. Reduce heat to low; let simmer 1 minute.

Each serving provides: 4 Protein Exchanges; 1 Bread Exchange;
 ½ Vegetable Exchange; 1½ Fat Exchanges; 35 calories Optional Exchange
Per serving: 419 calories; 31 g protein; 21 g fat; 21 g carbohydrate; 62 mg calcium;
 570 mg sodium; 165 mg cholesterol

Veal and Spinach Canneloni

WEEK 4 ～ MAKES 4 SERVINGS, 2 CANNELONI EACH

1 tablespoon plus 1 teaspoon
  margarine
2 tablespoons minced shallots or
  onion
4 garlic cloves, minced
1 pound 2 ounces ground veal
2 cups well-drained cooked chopped
  spinach
1 cup chopped mushrooms

1 cup tomato sauce, divided
1/2 teaspoon salt
1/4 teaspoon each ground nutmeg
  and pepper
8 crêpes (see "Crêpes Suzette,"
  page 433)
White Sauce (see page 172)
1 tablespoon plus 1 teaspoon
  grated Parmesan cheese

In 12-inch skillet heat margarine until bubbly and hot; add shallots (or onion) and garlic and sauté until translucent, about 3 minutes. Add veal and cook, stirring constantly, until veal loses its pink color, about 5 minutes; stir in spinach and mushrooms and cook for 5 minutes longer. Add 1/2 cup tomato sauce and the salt, nutmeg, and pepper; stir to combine and remove from heat.

Preheat oven to 400°F. Spoon 1/8 of veal mixture onto center of each crêpe and fold sides of crêpe to enclose; place crêpes seam-side down in shallow 4-quart casserole. Combine White Sauce with remaining 1/2 cup tomato sauce and spoon over crêpes; sprinkle with Parmesan cheese and bake until thoroughly heated and bubbly, 20 to 25 minutes.

Each serving provides (includes crêpes and White Sauce): 4 Protein Exchanges;
  1 Bread Exchange; 2½ Vegetable Exchanges; 2½ Fat Exchanges;
  ¾ Milk Exchange; 35 calories Optional Exchange
Per serving: 583 calories; 43 g protein; 27 g fat; 43 g carbohydrate; 381 mg calcium;
  1,044 mg sodium; 233 mg cholesterol

Duchess Veal Loaf

WEEK 4 ∽ MAKES 2 SERVINGS

Veal Mixture

2 teaspoons margarine
2 tablespoons each minced celery, onion, and green bell pepper
5 ounces ground veal
1/4 cup part-skim ricotta cheese
1 egg, beaten
3 tablespoons plain dried bread crumbs

2 tablespoons chopped fresh parsley
1 tablespoon water
1 teaspoon Worcestershire sauce
1/4 teaspoon salt
Dash pepper

Topping

6 ounces peeled cooked potatoes (hot)
2 tablespoons each grated Parmesan cheese and skim milk

1 tablespoon chopped chives
2 teaspoons margarine
Dash each salt and pepper

Garnish

Pimiento strips (about 2 tablespoons)

To Prepare Veal Mixture: In small skillet heat margarine over medium heat until bubbly and hot; add celery, onion, and green pepper and sauté until vegetables are tender, about 3 minutes.

In medium bowl combine sautéed vegetables with remaining ingredients for veal mixture; shape into a loaf. Transfer to roasting pan and bake at 375°F. until browned, 30 to 35 minutes.

To Prepare Topping: In small mixing bowl combine all ingredients for topping and, using electric mixer, beat until smooth. Set baked loaf into an 8 x 8 x 2-inch baking dish and top with potato mixture, covering entire loaf. Bake at 425°F. until topping is browned, about 15 minutes; garnish with pimiento strips.

Each serving provides: 3 Protein Exchanges; 1½ Bread Exchanges;
   ½ Vegetable Exchange; 2 Fat Exchanges; 35 calories Optional Exchange
Per serving: 395 calories; 26 g protein; 21 g fat; 25 g carbohydrate; 233 mg calcium;
   737 mg sodium; 199 mg cholesterol

Veal Chili

WEEK 4 ∾ MAKES 4 SERVINGS, ABOUT 1¼ CUPS EACH

1 tablespoon plus 1 teaspoon olive
or vegetable oil
1 cup each diced onions and green
bell peppers
4 garlic cloves, minced
12 ounces ground veal
2½ cups canned whole tomatoes,
drained and coarsely chopped
(reserve liquid)
¼ cup tomato puree
1 teaspoon each chili powder and
crushed red pepper, or to taste

½ teaspoon salt
¼ teaspoon pepper
1½ ounces (about ¼ cup) uncooked
cornmeal
8 ounces drained canned red kidney
beans
3 ounces extra-sharp Cheddar
cheese, shredded
2 taco shells, broken into quarters

In 4-quart saucepan heat oil; add onions, green peppers, and garlic and sauté until onions are translucent. Add veal and cook, stirring constantly, until meat loses its pink color, 3 to 5 minutes; stir in tomatoes, reserved liquid, tomato puree, and seasonings and bring to a boil. Reduce heat, cover, and let simmer, stirring occasionally, for 20 minutes.

Stir cornmeal into veal mixture; cover pan and let simmer for 5 minutes longer. Add beans and cook until thoroughly heated. To serve, transfer mixture to a 1½-quart serving bowl; sprinkle with cheese and arrange taco shell quarters around edge of bowl.

Each serving provides: 4 Protein Exchanges; 1 Bread Exchange;
2½ Vegetable Exchanges; 1 Fat Exchange
Per serving: 442 calories; 29 g protein; 21 g fat; 34 g carbohydrate; 242 mg calcium;
970 mg sodium (estimated); 83 mg cholesterol

Serving Suggestion: Top each portion with 2 tablespoons sour cream. Add 65 calories Optional Exchange to Exchange Information.

Per serving: 504 calories; 29 g protein; 27 g fat; 36 g carbohydrate; 276 mg calcium;
985 mg sodium (estimated); 95 mg cholesterol

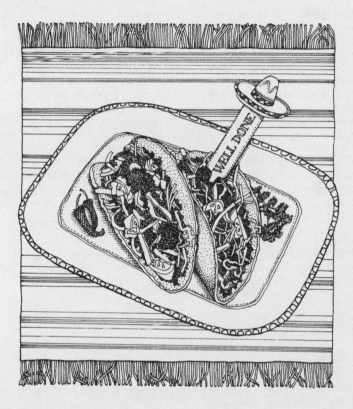

Meats

Meat can be the best choice for the prime of your life. If your taste runs to rare, we suggest our Veal Kidney 'n' Bacon Sauté, and for a meal that's sure to bring cries of "well-done," try Beef Tacos.

There's no need to get yourself into a stew or to cut your budget down to the bare bone when planning meat dishes. Because any way you slice it, sauté it, marinate it, pot it, or chop it, meat offers a variety of ways to meet your needs.

Beef-Barley Soup ❶

WEEK 4 ∽ MAKES 4 SERVINGS

4 packets instant beef broth and
    seasoning mix
3 cups water
12 ounces cubed cooked beef
2 cups cooked barley
1 cup each sliced mushrooms,
    diced onions, and shredded green
    cabbage
½ cup each diced celery, diced
    carrot, and tomato sauce

1 bay leaf
1 teaspoon salt
½ teaspoon thyme leaves
Dash pepper

Garnish

Chopped fresh parsley

In 3-quart saucepan combine broth mix and water and heat; add remaining ingredients except parsley, partially cover pan, and let simmer until vegetables are tender, about 40 minutes. Remove and discard bay leaf; serve soup sprinkled with parsley.

Each serving provides: 3 Protein Exchanges; 1 Bread Exchange;
   2½ Vegetable Exchanges; 10 calories Optional Exchange
Per serving: 323 calories; 31 g protein; 9 g fat; 29 g carbohydrate; 58 mg calcium;
   1,514 mg sodium; 77 mg cholesterol

Beef Stir-Fry

WEEK 4 ∽ MAKES 2 SERVINGS

2 teaspoons peanut or vegetable oil
1 cup thinly sliced onions
½ cup each thinly sliced
    mushrooms, diagonally sliced
    carrot, and canned beef broth
2 tablespoons each dry sherry and
    soy sauce
1 teaspoon cornstarch

¼ teaspoon five spice powder
8 ounces broiled top or bottom
    round steak, thinly sliced
    diagonally across the grain
2 cups torn well-washed spinach
    leaves
1 cup cooked long-grain rice (hot)

In 10-inch skillet or a wok heat oil; add onions, mushrooms, and carrot and cook, stirring quickly and frequently, until carrot is tender. In measuring cup or small bowl combine broth, sherry, soy sauce, cornstarch, and spice, stirring to dissolve cornstarch; pour over vegetables and, stirring constantly, bring to a boil. Reduce heat and stir in beef and spinach; let simmer, stirring occasionally, until thoroughly heated. Serve over hot rice.

Each serving provides: 4 Protein Exchanges; 1 Bread Exchange;
  4 Vegetable Exchanges; 1 Fat Exchange; 30 calories Optional Exchange
Per serving: 452 calories; 43 g protein; 12 g fat; 38 g carbohydrate; 137 mg calcium;
  1,676 mg sodium; 103 mg cholesterol

Oriental Beef with Teriyaki Vegetables

WEEK 4 ∽ MAKES 2 SERVINGS

1 beef top or bottom round steak
  (10 ounces)
2 tablespoons each teriyaki sauce
  and dry sherry
1 tablespoon hoisin sauce
1 teaspoon minced pared ginger
  root

1 garlic clove, mashed
2 teaspoons peanut or vegetable oil
1 cup each shredded carrots,
  shredded green cabbage, and
  thinly sliced onions

1. Chill steak in freezer until slightly firm, 10 to 15 minutes (this makes slicing easier). Remove to cutting board and slice diagonally across the grain into 1/4-inch-thick strips. In large bowl combine teriyaki sauce, sherry, hoisin sauce, ginger, and garlic; add beef and toss to coat. Let stand at room temperature for 1 hour.

2. In 10-inch nonstick skillet heat oil; add vegetables and sauté, stirring, until carrots are soft. Remove skillet from heat.

3. Preheat broiler. Remove meat from marinade, reserving marinade. Onto each of eight 8-inch wooden skewers thread 1/8 of the steak strips; set on rack in broiling pan and broil until done to taste.

4. While steak is broiling, add reserved marinade to sautéed vegetables and cook until mixture is thoroughly heated. Transfer vegetables to serving platter and top with skewers of steak.

Each serving provides: 4 Protein Exchanges; 3 Vegetable Exchanges;
  1 Fat Exchange; 30 calories Optional Exchange
Per serving: 372 calories; 39 g protein; 12 g fat; 23 g carbohydrate; 83 mg calcium;
  992 mg sodium; 103 mg cholesterol

Swiss Steaks in Tomato Sauce

WEEK 4 ⬙ MAKES 4 SERVINGS

2 teaspoons olive or vegetable oil
1/2 cup each diced onion and celery
2 teaspoons all-purpose flour
3/4 cup water
1 cup canned whole tomatoes,
  chopped
1/2 cup tomato puree
2 packets instant beef broth and
  seasoning mix

1 cup green bell pepper strips
  (3 x 1/2-inch strips)
4 beef top or bottom round steaks
  (5 ounces each), broiled until
  rare
2 tablespoons chopped fresh
  Italian (flat-leaf) parsley

Preheat oven to 350°F. In 10-inch nonstick skillet heat oil; add onion and celery and sauté until onion is translucent. Sprinkle flour over vegetables and cook, stirring constantly, for 1 minute; gradually stir in water. Stir in tomatoes, puree, and broth mix and, stirring constantly, bring to a boil; remove from heat and stir in pepper strips.

In 2-quart casserole arrange steaks and top with vegetable mixture; cover and bake until steaks are tender, about 45 minutes. Serve sprinkled with parsley.

Each serving provides: 4 Protein Exchanges; 2 Vegetable Exchanges;
  1/2 Fat Exchange; 10 calories Optional Exchange
Per serving: 288 calories; 38 g protein; 10 g fat; 12 g carbohydrate; 41 mg calcium;
  689 mg sodium; 103 mg cholesterol

Steak Provençale ◑

WEEK 2 ⬙ MAKES 4 SERVINGS

4 boneless beef top loin steaks
  (5 ounces each)
1 tablespoon plus 1 teaspoon
  margarine
1/2 cup thinly sliced scallions (green
  onions)

1 garlic clove, minced
2 tablespoons dry vermouth
2 medium tomatoes, cut into
  1/4-inch-thick slices
1 tablespoon chopped fresh basil

Preheat broiler. On rack in broiling pan broil steaks until browned on both sides, about 5 minutes on each side, or until done to taste.

While steaks are broiling, in 8-inch nonstick skillet heat margarine until bubbly and hot; add scallions and garlic and sauté until scallions are softened, 1 to 2 minutes. Add vermouth and cook, stirring constantly, for 1 minute; add tomato slices and basil and cook, stirring gently, until heated. To serve, spoon tomato mixture over broiled steaks.

Each serving provides: 4 Protein Exchanges; 1¼ Vegetable Exchanges;
  1 Fat Exchange; 10 calories Optional Exchange
Per serving: 298 calories; 38 g protein; 13 g fat; 5 g carbohydrate; 36 mg calcium;
  137 mg sodium; 103 mg cholesterol

Pepper Steak with Onions and Mushrooms ◑

WEEK 4 ∽ MAKES 4 SERVINGS

1¼ pounds beef top or bottom
  round steak
1 tablespoon plus 1 teaspoon
  vegetable oil
2 garlic cloves, sliced
1-inch piece ginger root, pared and
  sliced
2 cups green bell pepper strips
  (3 x ½-inch strips)

1 cup each sliced onions and
  mushrooms
1 cup canned beef broth
2 tablespoons dry sherry
1 tablespoon oyster sauce
2 teaspoons cornstarch

Preheat broiler. Place steak on rack in broiling pan and broil, turning once, until rare, about 5 minutes on each side. Slice steak diagonally across the grain and cut each strip in half lengthwise; set aside.

In 12-inch nonstick skillet heat oil; add garlic and ginger and sauté until garlic is browned (*be careful not to burn*). Remove and discard garlic and ginger. Add vegetables to skillet and sauté, stirring constantly, until tender-crisp. In 2-cup measure or small bowl combine broth, sherry, oyster sauce, and cornstarch, stirring to dissolve cornstarch; add to vegetables and, stirring constantly, bring to a boil. Reduce heat, stir in steak slices, and let simmer until mixture is thoroughly heated.

Each serving provides: 4 Protein Exchanges; 2 Vegetable Exchanges;
  1 Fat Exchange; 30 calories Optional Exchange
Per serving: 319 calories; 39 g protein; 12 g fat; 11 g carbohydrate; 40 mg calcium;
  480 mg sodium; 103 mg cholesterol

Pot Roast Italienne

WEEK 4 〜 MAKES 10 SERVINGS

Prepare this on a day when you have some time for cooking, then freeze pot roast in premeasured portions. On a less leisurely occasion, reheat the pot roast, prepare the spaghetti, and presto—a delicious meal in minutes.

3 pounds 2 ounces boneless beef
    rump roast
1 tablespoon plus 2 teaspoons
    vegetable oil
2 cups each chopped onions and
    red or green bell peppers
2 garlic cloves, chopped
1 cup each tomato sauce and red
    Burgundy wine

2 tablespoons each chopped fresh
    basil and Italian (flat-leaf)
    parsley
1 teaspoon salt
½ teaspoon each oregano leaves
    and pepper
4 cups chopped carrots
5 cups cooked spaghetti (hot)

Preheat oven to 325°F. Place meat on rack in roasting pan and roast until rare, about 1 hour.

In Dutch oven or 6-quart saucepot heat oil over medium-high heat; add roast, onions, peppers, and garlic and sear meat on all sides, stirring vegetables to prevent burning. Add remaining ingredients except carrots and spaghetti and stir to combine. Reduce heat to low, cover pot, and let simmer for 1 hour, turning meat occasionally. Add carrots, cover, and cook until tender, about 30 minutes. Remove meat from pot and keep warm.

Remove half of the liquid and half of the vegetables from pot; in blender container, in batches (no more than 2 cups at a time), process liquid and vegetables until smooth. Combine with mixture remaining in pot and, if necessary, reheat. Slice roast and pour sauce over meat; serve each portion with ½ cup cooked spaghetti.

Each serving provides: 4 Protein Exchanges; 1 Bread Exchange;
    2 Vegetable Exchanges; ½ Fat Exchange; 25 calories Optional Exchange
Per serving: 406 calories; 37 g protein; 13 g fat; 29 g carbohydrate; 61 mg calcium;
    445 mg sodium; 103 mg cholesterol

Note: If pot roast is to be frozen, to make future serving easier, slice meat and divide into 10 portions; combine each portion with an equal amount of sauce and transfer to freezer containers. Label containers and freeze for future use. When ready to serve, reheat as many portions as needed.

Top: Veal Stew (page 293)
Middle: Apple, Onion, and Chops (page 338)
Bottom: Lamb Primavera (page 330)

Deluxe Burgers (page 318)

Top: Gumbo Soup Supper (page 255)
Bottom: Pasta e Fagioli—Pasta and
Bean Soup (page 238)

Orange Chicken (page 267)

Top left: Ricotta-Parmesan Torte (page 204)
Top right: Cottage-Cheddar Puff (page 212)
Bottom: Blueberry-Cheese Blintzes with
Blueberry Sauce (page 214)

Top: Chilled Eggplant Relish (page 426)
Middle: Vegetable Sauté (page 101)
Bottom: Nutty Green Beans (page 231)

Top: Fillet Diable (page 384)
Bottom: Portuguese Cod Fillets (page 377)

Strawberry-Cream Log (page 55)

Swiss Steak with Sour Cream en Casserole

WEEK 4   ⤳   MAKES 4 SERVINGS

2 teaspoons olive or vegetable oil
1 cup each diced onions and sliced
  mushroom caps
2 teaspoons all-purpose flour
1½ cups water
2 packets instant beef broth and
  seasoning mix
1 tablespoon grated Parmesan
  cheese

1 teaspoon Worcestershire sauce
¼ teaspoon paprika
Dash pepper
4 beef top or bottom round steaks
  (5 ounces each), broiled until
  rare
⅓ cup plus 2 teaspoons sour cream
1 tablespoon chopped fresh parsley

Preheat oven to 350°F. In 10-inch nonstick skillet heat oil; add onions and mushrooms and sauté, stirring, until onions are translucent. Sprinkle flour over vegetables and cook, stirring constantly, for 1 minute; gradually stir in water. Add broth mix and, stirring constantly, bring to a boil. Reduce heat and let simmer until mixture thickens. Stir in cheese, Worcestershire sauce, paprika, and pepper and remove from heat.

Transfer steaks to 2-quart casserole and pour vegetable sauce over meat; cover and bake until steaks are tender, about 45 minutes.

Remove steaks from casserole and set aside. Spoon 2 tablespoons of vegetable sauce into sour cream and stir to combine; pour sour cream mixture into casserole and stir until well blended. Return steaks to casserole and serve sprinkled with parsley.

Each serving provides: 4 Protein Exchanges; 1 Vegetable Exchange;
  ½ Fat Exchange; 70 calories Optional Exchange
Per serving: 316 calories; 38 g protein; 14 g fat; 7 g carbohydrate; 70 mg calcium;
  510 mg sodium; 114 mg cholesterol

Variation: Substitute ½ cup plain low-fat yogurt for the sour cream. Add ¼ Milk Exchange to Exchange Information and reduce Optional Exchange to 20 calories.

Per serving: 287 calories; 39 g protein; 10 g fat; 8 g carbohydrate; 97 mg calcium;
  519 mg sodium; 106 mg cholesterol

Oriental Steak 'n' Pepper ◑

WEEK 4 ∽ MAKES 2 SERVINGS

10 ounces boneless sirloin steak
2 teaspoons peanut or vegetable oil
1 medium green bell pepper, seeded
  and thinly sliced
1/2 cup sliced onion
1 garlic clove, minced
3/4 cup water

1 packet instant beef broth and
  seasoning mix
1 tablespoon soy sauce
2 teaspoons cornstarch
1 medium tomato, cut into eighths
1/8 teaspoon pepper

On rack in broiling pan broil steak, 2 to 4 inches from heat source, until rare, about 3 minutes on each side (broil thicker steak farther away from heat); cut steak across the grain into thin slices and set aside.

In 10-inch skillet heat oil; add green pepper, onion, and garlic and sauté until onion is translucent and pepper is tender-crisp. Add steak slices and sauté for 1 minute; add water and broth mix and bring liquid to a boil. In small bowl combine soy sauce and cornstarch, stirring to dissolve cornstarch; stir into steak mixture. Add tomatoes and cook, stirring constantly, until tomatoes are just cooked and mixture is slightly thickened; sprinkle with pepper and serve immediately.

Each serving provides: 4 Protein Exchanges; 2½ Vegetable Exchanges;
  1 Fat Exchange; 15 calories Optional Exchange
Per serving: 340 calories; 40 g protein; 14 g fat; 14 g carbohydrate; 48 mg calcium;
  1,140 mg sodium; 103 mg cholesterol

Broiled Marinated Chuck Steak ◐

WEEK 2 ∽ MAKES 4 SERVINGS

1 cup each beer and sliced onions
1 tablespoon grated lemon peel
1 garlic clove, sliced
1/2 teaspoon each salt and pepper
1½ pounds chuck steak (about 2
  inches thick)

1 medium tomato, thinly sliced
  (about 1/8-inch-thick slices)
1 tablespoon chopped fresh parsley

In self-sealing plastic bag or a glass or stainless-steel bowl combine beer, onions, lemon peel, and seasonings; add steak, turning to coat with marinade. Seal bag or cover bowl and refrigerate for at least 8 hours, turning meat several times in marinade (if bag is used, simply turn bag over).

Preheat broiler. Transfer steak to rack in broiling pan, discarding marinade; broil 3 inches from heat source until steak is browned on both sides, 5 to 7 minutes on each side, or until done to taste. Arrange tomato slices over surface of steak and broil until tomatoes are lightly browned; serve sprinkled with parsley.

Each serving provides: 4 Protein Exchanges; ½ Vegetable Exchange
Per serving: 301 calories; 33 g protein; 16 g fat; 3 g carbohydrate; 27 mg calcium; 195 mg sodium; 103 mg cholesterol

Hoisin Beef and Vegetables ◐

WEEK 4 ◇ MAKES 2 SERVINGS

---

2 teaspoons peanut or vegetable oil
1 cup each thinly sliced onions and
   red bell peppers
2 garlic cloves, minced
½ teaspoon minced pared ginger
   root
¾ cup water

1 tablespoon hoisin sauce
1 teaspoon cornstarch
1 packet instant beef broth and
   seasoning mix
1 cup broccoli florets, blanched
10 ounces beef tenderloin or
   boneless sirloin steak

In 10-inch skillet heat oil; add onions, red peppers, garlic, and ginger and sauté over medium heat until vegetables are tender-crisp, about 4 minutes. In small bowl combine water, hoisin sauce, and cornstarch, stirring to dissolve cornstarch; add to vegetable mixture, along with broth mix and, stirring constantly, bring to a boil. Continue stirring and cook until thickened; add broccoli and stir to combine. Reduce heat to lowest possible setting, just hot enough to keep mixture warm while beef is cooking.

On rack in broiling pan broil beef for 4 to 5 minutes on each side, depending on thickness of meat; remove from rack and slice across the grain into thin strips. Transfer vegetable mixture to serving platter and top with beef.

Each serving provides: 4 Protein Exchanges; 3 Vegetable Exchanges; 1 Fat Exchange; 25 calories Optional Exchange
Per serving: 376 calories; 42 g protein; 14 g fat; 22 g carbohydrate; 78 mg calcium; 754 mg sodium; 103 mg cholesterol

Beef Curry ❶

WEEK 4 ∽ MAKES 2 SERVINGS

10 ounces boneless chuck steak,
 cut into 1-inch cubes
2 teaspoons vegetable oil
1 cup chopped onions
1 garlic clove, minced
1 to 1½ teaspoons curry powder

¾ cup water
¼ cup tomato sauce
1 packet instant beef broth and
 seasoning mix
½ cup frozen peas
Dash salt

On rack in broiling pan broil beef cubes, turning to brown all sides, until rare, about 6 minutes; set aside.

In 1½-quart saucepan heat oil; add onions and garlic and sauté until onions are translucent. Add beef and curry powder and stir to combine; stir in water, tomato sauce, and broth mix. Cover and let simmer, stirring occasionally, for about 1 hour. Add peas and salt and cook for 5 minutes longer.

Each serving provides: 4 Protein Exchanges; ½ Bread Exchange;
 1½ Vegetable Exchanges; 1 Fat Exchange; 5 calories Optional Exchange
Per serving: 365 calories; 39 g protein; 16 g fat; 17 g carbohydrate; 53 mg calcium;
 705 mg sodium; 103 mg cholesterol

Beef and Kraut Stew ❶

WEEK 4 ∽ MAKES 2 SERVINGS

10 ounces boneless chuck steak,
 cut into 1-inch cubes
1 tablespoon margarine
½ cup each sliced green bell pepper
 and onion
¼ cup water
1 tablespoon paprika

½ teaspoon salt
1 cup drained sauerkraut*
2 teaspoons firmly packed brown
 sugar
1 teaspoon cornstarch, dissolved in
 1 tablespoon water

Preheat broiler. On rack in broiling pan broil steak cubes, turning to brown all sides, until rare, about 6 minutes; remove from broiler and set aside.

In 1½-quart nonstick saucepan heat margarine until bubbly and hot; add green pepper and onion and sauté until onion is golden. Add meat, water, paprika, and salt and, stirring to combine, bring to a boil. Reduce heat, cover, and let simmer until meat is tender, 25 to 30 minutes.

Add remaining ingredients to pan and, stirring constantly, bring to a boil. Reduce heat and cook, stirring, until mixture thickens.

Each serving provides: 4 Protein Exchanges; 2 Vegetable Exchanges;
  1½ Fat Exchanges; 25 calories Optional Exchange
Per serving: 411 calories; 36 g protein; 22 g fat; 18 g carbohydrate; 87 mg calcium;
  1,539 mg sodium; 103 mg cholesterol

* We recommend that you use the sauerkraut that is packaged in plastic bags and is stored in the refrigerator section of the market; this is usually crisper and less salty than the canned.

Beef and Pasta Casserole ❸

WEEK 2 ∽ MAKES 2 SERVINGS

9 ounces ground beef
2 teaspoons vegetable or olive oil
½ cup diced onion
2 garlic cloves, minced
1 cup sliced mushrooms
1 tablespoon chopped fresh parsley
2 cups canned crushed tomatoes

¼ teaspoon each basil leaves, salt, and pepper
⅛ teaspoon oregano leaves
1 cup cooked ziti
1 ounce thinly sliced provolone cheese, cut into strips

1. Shape beef into a patty; on rack in broiling pan broil meat, turning once, for about 7 minutes. Crumble beef and set aside.

2. In 1½-quart saucepan heat oil; add onion and garlic and sauté until onion is softened. Add mushrooms, parsley, and crumbled beef and sauté for about 5 minutes; stir in tomatoes and seasonings and let simmer, stirring occasionally, for 15 minutes.

3. Preheat oven to 350°F. Stir ziti into beef mixture and spoon mixture into shallow 1-quart flameproof casserole; top with cheese strips and bake until mixture is heated through, 20 to 25 minutes.

4. Turn oven control to broil and broil until cheese is lightly browned, about 2 minutes.

Each serving provides: 4 Protein Exchanges; 1 Bread Exchange;
  3½ Vegetable Exchanges; 1 Fat Exchange
Per serving: 518 calories; 37 g protein; 26 g fat; 33 g carbohydrate; 166 mg calcium;
  783 mg sodium; 103 mg cholesterol

Deluxe Burgers ◐❸

WEEK 4 ∽ MAKES 2 SERVINGS

½ teaspoon vegetable oil
¼ cup diced onion
10 ounces ground chuck
1 tablespoon each chopped fresh
  parsley and plain low-fat yogurt
¼ teaspoon Worcestershire sauce
Dash each salt, pepper, and ground
  thyme

1 ounce sliced Cheddar or American
  cheese
2 hamburger rolls (2 ounces each)
2 iceberg lettuce leaves
½ medium tomato, sliced
½ medium dill pickle, sliced

In small nonstick skillet heat oil; add onion and sauté until golden. Transfer onion to a bowl and add ground chuck, parsley, yogurt, Worcestershire sauce, and seasonings; combine thoroughly. Shape into 2 equal patties and place on rack in broiling pan; broil, turning once, for 7 to 10 minutes on each side or until done to taste. Top each patty with ½ ounce cheese and broil just until cheese is melted.

To serve, line bottom half of each roll with a lettuce leaf. Top each with half of the tomato and pickle slices, a cheese-topped patty, and top half of roll.

Each serving provides: 4½ Protein Exchanges; 2 Bread Exchanges;
  1½ Vegetable Exchanges; 15 calories Optional Exchange
Per serving with Cheddar cheese: 622 calories; 40 g protein; 35 g fat;
  35 g carbohydrate; 193 mg calcium; 764 mg sodium; 125 mg cholesterol
With American cheese: 618 calories; 40 g protein; 35 g fat; 35 g carbohydrate;
  178 mg calcium; 879 mg sodium; 124 mg cholesterol

Beef and Vegetable Sauté ❸

WEEK 4 ∽ MAKES 4 SERVINGS

1¼ pounds ground chuck
1 tablespoon plus 1 teaspoon
  vegetable oil
1 cup chopped onions
2 garlic cloves, minced
2 cups thinly sliced green bell
  peppers

1 cup thinly sliced carrots
2½ cups water, divided
4 cups shredded Chinese cabbage
2 tablespoons plus 2 teaspoons soy
  sauce
1 tablespoon plus 1 teaspoon
  cornstarch

Shape chuck into 4 patties; transfer to rack in broiling pan and broil, turning once, until rare.

In 12-inch nonstick skillet heat oil; add onions and garlic and sauté until onions are translucent. Crumble beef into skillet; add green peppers and carrots and sauté for 5 minutes. Stir in 2 cups water; cover skillet and let simmer for 5 minutes. Add cabbage, cover, and let simmer for 10 minutes longer, stirring occasionally.

In measuring cup combine remaining ½ cup water with the soy sauce and cornstarch, stirring to dissolve cornstarch; add to beef mixture and cook, stirring constantly, until slightly thickened.

Each serving provides: 4 Protein Exchanges; 4 Vegetable Exchanges;
  1 Fat Exchange; 10 calories Optional Exchange
Per serving: 357 calories; 38 g protein; 16 g fat; 16 g carbohydrate; 85 mg calcium;
  991 mg sodium; 103 mg cholesterol

Spicy Skillet Beef Crumble ◐❶

WEEK 4 〰 MAKES 2 SERVINGS

You'll find that most of the ingredients in this recipe are probably already in your pantry—combine them into this delicious 30-minute dish.

10 ounces ground beef
1 teaspoon margarine
½ cup diced onion
1 garlic clove, minced
½ cup sliced mushrooms
1 cup tomato sauce
1 tablespoon chopped fresh parsley,
  divided

½ teaspoon Dijon-style mustard
¼ teaspoon each oregano leaves
  and Worcestershire sauce
⅛ teaspoon salt
Dash hot sauce
1 cup cooked long-grain rice (hot)

Form beef into patties and place on rack in broiling pan; broil, turning once, for about 5 minutes. Let cool slightly, then crumble.

In 9- or 10-inch skillet heat margarine until bubbly and hot; add onion and garlic and sauté until onion is softened. Stir in crumbled meat and mushrooms and sauté for 5 minutes; stir in tomato sauce, 1½ teaspoons parsley, and the mustard, oregano, Worcestershire sauce, salt, and hot sauce. Cover pan and let simmer for 10 to 15 minutes. Serve over hot rice and sprinkle with remaining 1½ teaspoons parsley.

Each serving provides: 4 Protein Exchanges; 1 Bread Exchange;
  2 Vegetable Exchanges; ½ Fat Exchange; 25 calories Optional Exchange
Per serving: 552 calories; 35 g protein; 28 g fat; 38 g carbohydrate; 61 mg calcium;
  1,024 mg sodium; 107 mg cholesterol

Beef in Creamy Mushroom Sauce ◖

WEEK 4 ∾ MAKES 2 SERVINGS

10 ounces beef tenderloin, cut into
  1-inch-thick slices
1 tablespoon margarine
2 tablespoons minced onion
½ garlic clove, minced
1 cup thinly sliced mushrooms
1 tablespoon all-purpose flour

¾ cup canned beef broth
2 teaspoons tomato paste
⅓ cup plus 2 teaspoons sour cream
Dash freshly ground pepper
1 tablespoon chopped fresh parsley
1 cup cooked noodles or long-grain
  rice (hot)

On rack in broiling pan broil tenderloin slices 2 to 4 inches from heat source, turning once, until rare.

While meat is broiling, in 9-inch skillet heat margarine until bubbly and hot; add onion and garlic and sauté until onion is translucent, about 2 minutes. Add mushrooms and cook, stirring occasionally, for 3 minutes. Sprinkle flour over vegetables and stir quickly to combine; gradually stir in broth. Add tomato paste and cook, stirring constantly, until mixture is slightly thickened.

Remove skillet from heat and stir in sour cream, pepper, and parsley; add meat and cook just until heated through (*do not boil*). Serve over hot noodles or rice.

Each serving provides: 4 Protein Exchanges; 1 Bread Exchange;
  1⅛ Vegetable Exchanges; 1½ Fat Exchanges; 135 calories Optional Exchange
Per serving with noodles: 557 calories; 39 g protein; 32 g fat; 28 g carbohydrate;
  84 mg calcium; 563 mg sodium; 147 mg cholesterol
With rice: 569 calories; 38 g protein; 31 g fat; 34 g carbohydrate; 87 mg calcium;
  562 mg sodium; 122 mg cholesterol

Variation: Substitute ½ cup plain low-fat yogurt for the sour cream. Add ½ Milk Exchange to Exchange Information and reduce Optional Exchange to 35 calories.

Per serving with noodles: 501 calories; 41 g protein; 24 g fat; 30 g carbohydrate;
  138 mg calcium; 580 mg sodium; 131 mg cholesterol
With rice: 513 calories; 39 g protein; 23 g fat; 36 g carbohydrate; 141 mg calcium;
  578 mg sodium; 107 mg cholesterol

Creamed Shepherd's Pie ❶

WEEK 4 ⌇ MAKES 4 SERVINGS

1¼ pounds ground beef
2 tablespoons margarine, divided
2 cups each thinly sliced carrots
  and mushrooms
1 cup diced onions
2 packets instant beef broth and
  seasoning mix

2 teaspoons all-purpose flour
1½ cups skim milk, divided
12 ounces peeled cooked potatoes,
  cut into cubes
½ teaspoon paprika

Preheat broiler. Form beef into 4 patties and place on rack in broiling pan; broil, turning once, until meat is rare, about 5 minutes. Remove from broiler and set aside.

Spray 2-quart flameproof casserole with nonstick cooking spray and set aside. In 12-inch nonstick skillet heat 1 tablespoon margarine until bubbly and hot; add carrots, mushrooms, and onions and sauté, stirring, until onion is translucent. Sprinkle broth mix and flour over vegetables and stir quickly to combine; cook, stirring constantly, for 1 minute. Gradually stir in 1 cup milk and, stirring constantly, bring to a boil. Reduce heat and let simmer until mixture thickens. Crumble beef into vegetable mixture and stir to combine; transfer to sprayed casserole and set aside.

Preheat oven to 375°F. In small saucepan combine potatoes with remaining ½ cup milk and 1 tablespoon margarine; bring to a boil, stirring until margarine is melted. Remove from heat and, using electric mixer, beat until smooth. Spread whipped potatoes over meat mixture, sprinkle with paprika, and bake until heated, 10 to 15 minutes. Turn oven control to broil and broil until potatoes are browned, 1 to 2 minutes.

Each serving provides: 4 Protein Exchanges; 1 Bread Exchange;
  2½ Vegetable Exchanges; 1½ Fat Exchanges; ¼ Milk Exchange;
  20 calories Optional Exchange
Per serving: 504 calories; 39 g protein; 26 g fat; 30 g carbohydrate; 170 mg calcium;
  601 mg sodium; 108 mg cholesterol

Hearty Beef Stew ❶

WEEK 4 ⌇ MAKES 4 SERVINGS

1¼ pounds beef for stew, cut into
 1½-inch cubes
3 tablespoons all-purpose flour,
 divided
1 tablespoon plus 1 teaspoon
 vegetable oil
2 cups diagonally sliced celery
1 cup chopped onions
2 garlic cloves, minced
3 cups water
1 cup canned beef broth

1 tablespoon each chopped fresh
 parsley, Worcestershire sauce,
 and Dijon-style mustard
2 bay leaves, broken into halves
1 teaspoon salt
½ teaspoon pepper
2 cups sliced carrots (2-inch-long
 sticks)
9 ounces pared potatoes, cut into
 cubes
½ cup frozen peas

1. Preheat broiler. On rack in broiling pan broil meat, turning once, until rare, about 6 minutes. Transfer meat to a bowl; add 2 tablespoons flour and toss to combine.

2. In Dutch oven or 6-quart saucepot heat oil; add meat, a few pieces at a time, and cook, stirring constantly, until seared on all sides. Remove meat to a bowl and set aside.

3. In same pot combine celery, onions, and garlic and cook, stirring constantly, until onions are translucent; return meat to pot and stir to combine. Sprinkle remaining tablespoon flour over mixture and stir quickly to combine; gradually stir in water. Add broth and seasonings and, stirring constantly, bring to a boil. Reduce heat, cover, and let simmer until meat is tender, 45 to 60 minutes.

4. Add carrots and potatoes to meat mixture, cover, and let simmer for 30 minutes. Stir in peas and cook until heated, about 5 minutes. Remove and discard bay leaves before serving.

Each serving provides: 4 Protein Exchanges; 1 Bread Exchange;
 2½ Vegetable Exchanges; 1 Fat Exchange; 35 calories Optional Exchange
Per serving: 435 calories; 40 g protein; 16 g fat; 32 g carbohydrate; 95 mg calcium;
 1,081 mg sodium; 103 mg cholesterol

Glazed Meat Loaf Ring ❶

½ cup buttermilk
1 egg
4 slices whole wheat bread, cut
  into cubes
1 teaspoon vegetable oil
½ cup each diced onion, diced
  celery, diced red bell pepper, and
  shredded carrot
1 garlic clove, minced

1 pound 3 ounces ground chuck
½ teaspoon salt
⅛ teaspoon each pepper, oregano
  leaves, basil leaves, and crushed
  thyme leaves
3 tablespoons chili sauce
2½ teaspoons firmly packed brown
  sugar
½ teaspoon powdered mustard

1. In large bowl combine milk and egg; add bread cubes and toss to coat. Set aside.

2. In 8-inch nonstick skillet heat oil; add vegetables and garlic and sauté, stirring constantly, until vegetables are tender. Add sautéed vegetables to bread mixture, then add meat, salt, pepper, and herbs and combine thoroughly.

3. In small bowl combine chili sauce, sugar, and mustard, mixing well; set aside.

4. Preheat oven to 350°F. Spray roasting rack with nonstick cooking spray; set meat mixture on rack and shape into a ring. Place rack in roasting pan and bake until loaf is browned, 35 to 40 minutes.

5. Brush chili sauce mixture over entire surface of meat and bake for 15 minutes longer.

Each serving provides: 4 Protein Exchanges; 1 Bread Exchange;
  1 Vegetable Exchange; 50 calories Optional Exchange
Per serving: 434 calories; 35 g protein; 22 g fat; 24 g carbohydrate; 108 mg calcium;
  714 mg sodium; 170 mg cholesterol

Serving Suggestion—Using 2 cups each cooked broccoli and cauliflower florets, decoratively arrange vegetables around and in center of ring; increase Vegetable Exchange to 3 Exchanges.

Per serving: 477 calories; 39 g protein; 22 g fat; 33 g carbohydrate; 157 mg calcium;
  746 mg sodium; 170 mg cholesterol

Taco Salad

WEEK 4 ⌢ MAKES 2 SERVINGS

Besides being a marvelous way to use up leftovers, this dish is particularly well suited to a hot summer's day. Initial preparations can be completed in the morning so you can serve up a delicious dinner while remaining cool and unfrazzled.

4 ounces cooked ground beef, crumbled and chilled
2 ounces drained canned red kidney beans
1 very ripe medium tomato, diced
3 tablespoons lemon juice
2 tablespoons diced onion
2 teaspoons olive oil
⅛ teaspoon each salt, chili powder, and ground cumin
1 to 2 drops hot sauce
4 iceberg lettuce leaves
1 ounce Cheddar cheese, shredded
2 taco shells, broken into pieces
¼ cup sour cream

In 1-quart bowl combine all ingredients except lettuce, cheese, and taco shells; cover and refrigerate until ready to serve (at least 30 minutes).

Chill 2 bowls. Line each chilled bowl with 2 lettuce leaves; spoon an equal amount of beef mixture over each portion of lettuce, then sprinkle each with ½ ounce cheese. Surround each portion with half of the taco shell pieces and top with 2 tablespoons sour cream.

Each serving provides: 3 Protein Exchanges; 1 Bread Exchange; 1½ Vegetable Exchanges; 1 Fat Exchange; 65 calories Optional Exchange
Per serving: 448 calories; 23 g protein; 31 g fat; 19 g carbohydrate; 179 mg calcium; 391 mg sodium (estimated); 81 mg cholesterol

Beef Tacos ◑❸

WEEK 4 ⌢ MAKES 2 SERVINGS

2 teaspoons vegetable oil
½ cup chopped onion
¼ cup chopped green bell pepper
2 garlic cloves, minced
1 teaspoon chili powder
½ cup each tomato sauce and chopped tomato
Dash each oregano leaves and hot sauce
4 ounces cooked ground beef, crumbled
2 taco shells
2 ounces Cheddar cheese, shredded
½ cup shredded lettuce

In 9-inch skillet heat oil; add onion, green pepper, garlic, and chili powder and sauté until vegetables are tender, about 5 minutes. Add tomato sauce, tomato, and seasonings and cook over medium heat for about 3 minutes to blend flavors; add beef and cook until heated.

On baking sheet bake taco shells at 350°F. until heated, about 2 minutes.* Fill each shell with half of beef mixture; top each with 1 ounce cheese and ¼ cup lettuce and serve hot.

Each serving provides: 3 Protein Exchanges; 1 Bread Exchange;
2¾ Vegetable Exchanges; 1 Fat Exchange
Per serving: 418 calories; 25 g protein; 26 g fat; 20 g carbohydrate; 239 mg calcium;
532 mg sodium; 83 mg cholesterol

* May be heated in conventional oven or toaster-oven.

Chili-Cheese Pie ❸

WEEK 4 ～ MAKES 4 SERVINGS

An easy, economical dish for informal get-togethers. Serve with a tossed salad to complete the menu.

1 tablespoon plus 1 teaspoon
  margarine, divided
1 cup chopped onions
½ cup chopped red bell pepper
1 garlic clove, minced
8 ounces cooked ground beef,
  crumbled
2 canned mild green chilies,
  chopped
1 tablespoon plus 1 teaspoon tomato
  paste

1 teaspoon chili powder
Salt
Dash freshly ground pepper
2 ounces Cheddar cheese, shredded
¾ cup all-purpose flour
½ cup buttermilk
2 large eggs
¼ teaspoon baking soda

Preheat oven to 425°F. In 8-inch nonstick skillet heat 1 teaspoon margarine over medium heat until bubbly and hot; add onions, red pepper, and garlic and sauté until pepper is tender, about 3 minutes. Add beef, chilies, tomato paste, chili powder, ½ teaspoon salt, and the ground pepper; cook, stirring occasionally, for about 5 minutes to blend flavors. Transfer mixture to a 9-inch pie plate and sprinkle with cheese.

In blender container combine remaining tablespoon margarine with the flour, milk, eggs, baking soda, and dash salt; process until smooth. Pour batter over beef mixture and bake until crust is golden brown, about 30 minutes.

Each serving provides: 3 Protein Exchanges; 1 Bread Exchange;
1 Vegetable Exchange; 1 Fat Exchange; 20 calories Optional Exchange
Per serving: 417 calories; 27 g protein; 22 g fat; 28 g carbohydrate; 185 mg calcium;
651 mg sodium; 206 mg cholesterol

Mexican Cornmeal Casserole

WEEK 4 ◇ MAKES 4 SERVINGS

3 cups freshly cooked yellow
cornmeal (hot)
2 teaspoons vegetable oil
1 cup chopped onions
3 garlic cloves, minced
8 ounces cooked ground beef,
crumbled
1 cup tomato sauce

¼ cup chopped drained canned
mild green chilies
1 packet instant chicken broth and
seasoning mix
1 teaspoon each chili powder and
oregano leaves
4 ounces Cheddar cheese, shredded
¾ cup sour cream

Spray a baking sheet with nonstick cooking spray; pour cornmeal onto sheet and, using a spatula, spread in an even layer, about ½-inch thick. Allow to cool; cut into 2½-inch squares and set aside.

Preheat oven to 400°F. In 10-inch skillet heat oil; add onions and garlic and sauté until onions are translucent, about 2 minutes. Add remaining ingredients except cornmeal, cheese, and sour cream and cook, stirring constantly, for about 5 minutes to blend flavors.

In bottom of a 2-quart casserole arrange a layer of half of the cornmeal squares; top with meat mixture, then 2 ounces cheese, then sour cream, then remaining cornmeal squares. Sprinkle remaining 2 ounces cheese over cornmeal and bake until cheese is thoroughly melted, about 20 minutes. Remove from oven and let stand for 10 minutes before serving.

Each serving provides: 3 Protein Exchanges; 1½ Bread Exchanges; 1½ Vegetable Exchanges; ½ Fat Exchange; 105 calories Optional Exchange
Per serving: 560 calories; 28 g protein; 34 g fat; 35 g carbohydrate; 292 mg calcium; 821 mg sodium; 102 mg cholesterol

Variation: Substitute 1 cup plain low-fat yogurt for the sour cream. Add ½ Milk Exchange to Exchange Information and reduce Optional Exchange to 3 calories.

Per serving: 503 calories; 30 g protein; 26 g fat; 37 g carbohydrate; 346 mg calcium; 838 mg sodium; 86 mg cholesterol

Spaghetti with Italian Meat Sauce ❶

WEEK 4 ◇ MAKES 4 SERVINGS

1 tablespoon plus 1 teaspoon olive
  or vegetable oil
1 cup each diced onions and red or
  green bell peppers
2 garlic cloves, minced
4 cups canned whole tomatoes,
  pureed in blender
1 pound broiled ground beef,
  crumbled
¼ cup dry red wine

2 tablespoons each chopped fresh
  Italian (flat-leaf) parsley and
  tomato paste
1 bay leaf
¼ teaspoon each oregano leaves,
  anise seed, salt, and pepper
4 cups cooked spaghetti (hot)
2 tablespoons plus 2 teaspoons
  grated Parmesan cheese, divided

In 12-inch nonstick skillet or 4-quart saucepan heat oil over medium-high heat; add onions, bell peppers, and garlic and sauté until onion is translucent. Add remaining ingredients except spaghetti and cheese; stir to combine. Reduce heat and let simmer, stirring occasionally, until sauce is thick, 1½ to 2 hours. Remove and discard bay leaf before serving. For each serving, top 1 cup hot spaghetti with ¼ of the sauce and sprinkle with 2 teaspoons cheese.

Each serving provides: 4 Protein Exchanges; 2 Bread Exchanges;
  3⅛ Vegetable Exchanges; 1 Fat Exchange; 35 calories Optional Exchange
Per serving: 622 calories; 41 g protein; 26 g fat; 53 g carbohydrate; 114 mg calcium;
  663 mg sodium; 109 mg cholesterol

Variations:
  1. Substitute 1 pound broiled cubed beef (small cubes) for the ground beef.
  2. Substitute 1¼ pounds cubed skinned chicken breasts (small cubes) for the beef. Sauté vegetables as directed, then remove vegetables from skillet and brown chicken; return vegetables to skillet and proceed as directed.

Per serving with beef cubes: 559 calories; 44 g protein; 18 g fat; 53 g carbohydrate;
  115 mg calcium; 647 mg sodium; 106 mg cholesterol
With chicken: 513 calories; 45 g protein; 12 g fat; 53 g carbohydrate;
  117 mg calcium; 675 mg sodium; 99 mg cholesterol

Marinated Lamb Kabobs

WEEK 2 ⌇ MAKES 2 SERVINGS

½ cup lemon juice
1 tablespoon water
2 teaspoons ketchup
1 teaspoon honey
1 garlic clove, chopped
½ teaspoon each onion flakes,
  grated lemon peel, and oregano
  leaves

¼ teaspoon mint flakes
⅛ teaspoon salt
10 ounces lamb cubes (about 1-inch
  cubes)
2 cups cubed and blanched eggplant
  (1-inch cubes)
1 medium green bell pepper, seeded
  and cut into 1-inch squares

In blender container combine lemon juice, water, ketchup, honey, and seasonings and process until smooth; transfer to shallow dish. Add lamb and eggplant and toss to coat. Cover dish and refrigerate for at least 1 hour, turning meat and eggplant occasionally.

Soak 4 bamboo skewers in water for 10 minutes. Preheat broiler. Onto each skewer, alternating ingredients, thread ¼ of the lamb, eggplant cubes, and pepper squares; reserve marinade. Transfer skewers to rack in broiling pan and broil, turning skewers often and basting with reserved marinade, until vegetables are tender and meat is done, about 8 minutes.

Each serving provides: 4 Protein Exchanges; 3 Vegetable Exchanges;
  15 calories Optional Exchange
Per serving: 315 calories; 34 g protein; 12 g fat; 20 g carbohydrate; 57 mg calcium;
  297 mg sodium; 113 mg cholesterol

Apricot-Glazed Lamb Steaks ◑

WEEK 1 ⌇ MAKES 2 SERVINGS

1 tablespoon plus 1 teaspoon
  reduced-calorie apricot spread
  (16 calories per 2 teaspoons)
1 teaspoon each Dijon-style mustard,
  honey, and teriyaki sauce

½ garlic clove, finely mashed to
  form paste
12 ounces lamb steaks

In small bowl thoroughly combine all ingredients except lamb steaks. On rack in broiling pan broil steaks 2 to 5 inches from heat source (depending on thickness of steaks; thinner steaks should be closer to heat) for 1 to 2 minutes; brush steaks with half the apricot mixture and broil for 5 to 7 minutes longer. Turn steaks over and broil for 1 to 2 minutes; brush with remaining apricot mixture and broil for 5 to 7 minutes longer or until done to taste.

Each serving provides: 4 Protein Exchanges; 25 calories Optional Exchange
Per serving: 266 calories; 31 g protein; 12 g fat; 8 g carbohydrate; 14 mg calcium;
   251 mg sodium; 113 mg cholesterol

Marinated Sweet 'n' Sour Lamb

WEEK 4 ～ MAKES 2 SERVINGS

½ cup lemon juice
2 teaspoons chili sauce
1¼ teaspoons grated orange peel
1 teaspoon Worcestershire sauce
¾ teaspoon grated lemon peel

½ teaspoon each granulated sugar and honey
1 garlic clove, minced
10 ounces lamb cubes (about 1-inch cubes)

In medium bowl combine all ingredients except lamb; add lamb and toss to coat well. Cover and refrigerate for at least 1 hour, turning lamb occasionally.

Transfer meat to rack in broiling pan, reserving marinade; broil for 6 minutes. Turn cubes over and brush with marinade; broil 6 minutes longer or until done to taste.

Each serving provides: 4 Protein Exchanges; 15 calories Optional Exchange
Per serving: 267 calories; 31 g protein; 12 g fat; 9 g carbohydrate; 25 mg calcium;
   193 mg sodium; 113 mg cholesterol

Lamb Primavera

WEEK 4 ⌒ MAKES 2 SERVINGS

12 ounces lamb steaks
2 teaspoons olive or vegetable oil
½ cup sliced onion
2 garlic cloves, minced
½ cup quartered mushrooms
2 medium tomatoes, blanched,
  peeled, seeded, and chopped
¾ cup water

2 teaspoons tomato paste
1 packet instant chicken broth and
  seasoning mix
½ teaspoon rosemary leaves,
  ground with ½ teaspoon salt
½ cup thawed frozen peas
½ cup cooked cut-up asparagus
¼ cup rosé wine

On rack in broiling pan broil lamb, turning once, until done, 6 to 8 minutes on each side depending on thickness of steaks.

While meat is broiling, in 10-inch skillet heat oil; add onion and garlic and sauté until onion is translucent. Add mushrooms and cook, stirring occasionally, until mushrooms are just tender, about 3 minutes; add tomatoes, water, tomato paste, broth mix, and ground rosemary and cook over medium heat, stirring occasionally, until mixture thickens, about 5 minutes. Stir in peas, asparagus, and wine and continue cooking until thoroughly heated, about 3 minutes.

Transfer lamb steaks to serving platter and surround with vegetable mixture.

Each serving provides: 4 Protein Exchanges; ½ Bread Exchange;
  3½ Vegetable Exchanges; 1 Fat Exchange; 40 calories Optional Exchange
Per serving: 398 calories; 37 g protein; 17 g fat; 20 g carbohydrate; 67 mg calcium;
  1,137 mg sodium; 113 mg cholesterol

Lamb and Eggplant Stew

WEEK 2 ᴥ MAKES 2 SERVINGS

---

10 ounces boned leg of lamb, cut into 1-inch cubes
2 teaspoons vegetable oil
½ cup chopped onion
2 garlic cloves, minced
1 cup drained canned whole tomatoes, chopped

¾ cup water
¼ teaspoon each salt and ground cumin
⅛ teaspoon pepper
2 cups cubed eggplant (1-inch cubes)
2 teaspoons chopped fresh parsley

On rack in broiling pan broil lamb cubes 2 to 4 inches from heat source, turning, until browned on all sides; set aside.

In 2-quart saucepan heat oil; add onion and garlic and sauté until onion is lightly browned. Add lamb, tomatoes, water, salt, cumin, and pepper and bring to a boil. Reduce heat, cover, and let simmer until meat is fork-tender, 50 minutes to 1 hour.

Add eggplant to saucepan; cover and cook until eggplant is soft, about 20 minutes. Serve sprinkled with parsley.

Each serving provides: 4 Protein Exchanges; 3½ Vegetable Exchanges; 1 Fat Exchange
Per serving: 330 calories; 36 g protein; 14 g fat; 15 g carbohydrate; 52 mg calcium; 512 mg sodium; 113 mg cholesterol

Lamb Chops Oriental ◐

WEEK 4 ～ MAKES 2 SERVINGS

4 lamb loin chops (3 ounces each)*
1½ teaspoons peanut oil
½ teaspoon Chinese sesame oil
½ cup each thinly sliced onion
   (thin wedges), diced celery, and
   sliced green bell pepper (3 x
   ½-inch strips)
1 small garlic clove, minced
⅛ teaspoon ground ginger

1 tablespoon soy sauce
2 teaspoons dry sherry
2 teaspoons cornstarch, dissolved
   in 2 teaspoons water
1 medium tomato, blanched, peeled,
   and cut into 8 wedges
½ cup drained canned or fresh bean
   sprouts
Dash each salt and pepper

On rack in broiling pan broil chops, turning once, until rare, at least 3 minutes on each side. Remove from broiler and keep warm.

In 9- or 10-inch nonstick skillet combine oils and heat over medium-high heat; add onion, celery, green pepper, garlic, and ginger and sauté, stirring constantly, until onion is translucent and vegetables are tender-crisp. Reduce heat and add soy sauce and sherry; stir dissolved cornstarch, add to vegetable mixture, and cook, stirring constantly, until mixture thickens. Add lamb chops, tomato wedges, and bean sprouts and cook, stirring occasionally, until thoroughly heated, about 3 minutes. Season with salt and pepper and serve immediately.

Each serving provides: 4 Protein Exchanges; 3 Vegetable Exchanges;
   1 Fat Exchange; 15 calories Optional Exchange
Per serving: 316 calories; 34 g protein; 14 g fat; 12 g carbohydrate; 50 mg calcium;
   850 mg sodium; 113 mg cholesterol

* Two 6-ounce chops may be substituted; broil for 3 to 5 minutes on each side.

Lamb Burgers à la Grecque

WEEK 4 ～ MAKES 2 SERVINGS

2 teaspoons olive oil
½ cup diced onion
1 garlic clove, minced
1 cup each canned whole tomatoes
   and frozen artichoke hearts
¼ cup water

½ teaspoon salt, divided
¼ teaspoon each pepper, divided,
   and oregano leaves
10 ounces ground lamb
4 pitted black olives, cut into
   quarters

In 10-inch skillet heat oil; add onion and garlic and sauté until onion is translucent. Add tomatoes, artichoke hearts, water, ¼ teaspoon salt, ⅛ teaspoon pepper, and the oregano; cover and let simmer, stirring occasionally, for about 15 minutes.

While sauce is simmering, in small bowl mix lamb with remaining ¼ teaspoon salt and ⅛ teaspoon pepper; shape into 4 equal patties. On rack in broiling pan broil patties, turning once, for about 7 minutes. Add lamb burgers and olives to skillet; cover and let simmer for 5 minutes.

Each serving provides: 4 Protein Exchanges; 2½ Vegetable Exchanges;
  1 Fat Exchange; 10 calories Optional Exchange
Per serving: 365 calories; 35 g protein; 18 g fat; 16 g carbohydrate; 65 mg calcium;
  873 mg sodium; 113 mg cholesterol

Lamb Chops with Vegetable-Wine Sauce

WEEK 4 ➷ MAKES 2 SERVINGS

1 tablespoon olive or vegetable oil
½ cup sliced onion
2 garlic cloves, minced
½ cup drained canned or frozen artichoke hearts
2 medium tomatoes, blanched, peeled, seeded, and chopped
¾ cup canned chicken broth
2 teaspoons tomato paste

½ teaspoon rosemary leaves, ground
¼ cup dry vermouth
½ teaspoon salt
Dash freshly ground pepper
12 ounces lamb loin chops

Garnish

1 tablespoon chopped fresh parsley

In 9-inch skillet heat oil; add onion and garlic and sauté until onion slices are translucent. Add artichoke hearts, cover, and cook over medium heat for 5 minutes; stir in tomatoes, broth, tomato paste, and rosemary. Cover and let simmer, stirring occasionally, for about 10 minutes; add vermouth, salt, and pepper and cook uncovered, over medium heat, until mixture thickens slightly.

While vegetable sauce is cooking, on rack in broiling pan broil chops 2 to 5 inches from heat source (depending on thickness of chops; thinner chops should be closer to heat) for 6 to 9 minutes on each side or until done to taste. Transfer to warmed serving platter, top with vegetable sauce, and sprinkle with parsley.

Each serving provides: 4 Protein Exchanges; 3 Vegetable Exchanges;
  1½ Fat Exchanges; 50 calories Optional Exchange
Per serving: 391 calories; 37 g protein; 17 g fat; 16 g carbohydrate; 64 mg calcium;
  993 mg sodium; 113 mg cholesterol

Potted Lamb Chops in Apricot Sauce

WEEK 1 ∾ MAKES 2 SERVINGS

2 lamb shoulder chops (6 ounces each)
2 teaspoons vegetable oil
2 tablespoons diced onion
1 garlic clove, minced
1 tablespoon plus 1 teaspoon reduced-calorie apricot spread (16 calories per 2 teaspoons)

1 teaspoon each minced pared ginger root and soy sauce
Dash each salt and pepper
1/2 cup water

On rack in broiling pan broil lamb chops until rare, at least 3 minutes on each side; set aside.

In 10-inch skillet heat oil; add onion and garlic and sauté until onion is softened. Add apricot spread, ginger, and soy sauce and bring to a boil. Sprinkle lamb chops with salt and pepper; add chops and water to apricot sauce. Reduce heat, cover, and let simmer, turning once, until meat is fork-tender, about 30 minutes.

Each serving provides: 4 Protein Exchanges; 1/8 Vegetable Exchange; 1 Fat Exchange; 16 calories Optional Exchange
Per serving: 299 calories; 31 g protein; 16 g fat; 6 g carbohydrate; 20 mg calcium; 363 mg sodium; 113 mg cholesterol

Teriyaki Lamb Burger ◑

WEEK 1 ∾ MAKES 1 SERVING

2 tablespoons diced onion
5 ounces ground lamb
1 tablespoon chopped fresh parsley

1 teaspoon Worcestershire sauce
1/2 teaspoon teriyaki sauce
1/8 teaspoon pepper

Heat a small nonstick skillet; add onion and cook, stirring constantly, until lightly browned. In small bowl mix browned onion with remaining ingredients and shape into a patty. On rack in broiling pan broil patty, turning once, about 7 minutes or until done to taste.

Each serving provides: 4 Protein Exchanges; 1/4 Vegetable Exchange
Per serving: 251 calories; 31 g protein; 11 g fat; 4 g carbohydrate; 29 mg calcium; 236 mg sodium; 113 mg cholesterol

Braised Caraway Pork Chops

WEEK 4 ~ MAKES 4 SERVINGS

4 center-cut pork loin chops (6 ounces each)
1 tablespoon plus 1 teaspoon margarine
1 cup each chopped onions and sliced mushrooms

½ teaspoon each caraway seed and salt
¼ teaspoon pepper
1½ cups water
1 tablespoon plus 1 teaspoon chopped fresh parsley

On rack in broiling pan broil chops, turning once, until rare.

In 12-inch skillet heat margarine until bubbly and hot; add onions and sauté until softened. Add pork chops, mushrooms, caraway seed, salt, and pepper and cook for 5 minutes; add water, cover, and let simmer until meat is tender, about 45 minutes. Serve sprinkled with parsley.

Each serving provides: 4 Protein Exchanges; 1 Vegetable Exchange;
  1 Fat Exchange; 3 calories Optional Exchange
Per serving: 345 calories; 35 g protein; 20 g fat; 5 g carbohydrate; 36 mg calcium;
  402 mg sodium; 100 mg cholesterol

Pork Salad ◑ ❸

WEEK 1 ~ MAKES 1 SERVING

3 ounces boned cooked pork, cut into 1-inch strips
¼ cup each diced celery and red bell pepper
1 tablespoon chopped scallion (green onion)
2 tablespoons rice vinegar

1 teaspoon mayonnaise
½ teaspoon Dijon-style mustard
1 small garlic clove, minced
¼ teaspoon salt
⅛ teaspoon pepper
2 iceberg, romaine, or loose-leafed lettuce leaves

In small bowl combine pork, celery, red pepper, and scallion. In another small bowl combine vinegar, mayonnaise, mustard, garlic, salt, and pepper, mixing well; pour over salad and toss to coat thoroughly. Serve on lettuce leaves.

Each serving provides: 3 Protein Exchanges; 1½ Vegetable Exchanges;
  1 Fat Exchange
Per serving: 282 calories; 26 g protein; 16 g fat; 8 g carbohydrate; 40 mg calcium;
  745 mg sodium: 78 mg cholesterol

Apricot-Glazed Roast Pork

WEEK 2 ⋄ MAKES 6 SERVINGS

2¼-pound pork center loin roast
Dash salt
1 tablespoon vegetable oil
2 garlic cloves, minced
3 medium peaches, blanched,
   peeled, pitted, and sliced

¾ cup dry sherry
¼ cup reduced-calorie apricot
   spread (16 calories per 2
   teaspoons)
1 tablespoon each granulated sugar
   and teriyaki sauce

Set pork loin on rack in roasting pan and sprinkle with salt. Insert meat thermometer into center of roast, being careful thermometer does not touch bone. Roast at 325°F. until thermometer registers 170°F., about 1½ hours. Remove pan from oven.

In 1-quart saucepan heat oil; add garlic and sauté briefly. Add remaining ingredients and bring to a boil. Reduce heat and let simmer until sauce is thickened, about 5 minutes. Spread over pork and return meat to oven; roast until sauce is bubbly and pork is glazed, about 5 minutes.

Each serving provides: 4 Protein Exchanges; ½ Fat Exchange;
   ½ Fruit Exchange; 55 calories Optional Exchange
Per serving: 400 calories; 34 g protein; 18 g fat; 15 g carbohydrate; 20 mg calcium;
   205 mg sodium; 100 mg cholesterol

Spicy Pork and Bean Casserole ❶

WEEK 4 ⋄ MAKES 4 SERVINGS

15 ounces pork cubes (1-inch cubes)
2 teaspoons vegetable oil
½ cup diced onion
2 garlic cloves, minced
1 medium green bell pepper, seeded
   and cut into 1-inch squares
1 tablespoon plus 1 teaspoon chili
   powder

½ teaspoon ground cumin
1 cup each tomato sauce and water
¼ teaspoon salt
Dash ground red pepper
8 ounces drained canned white
   kidney (cannellini) beans
2 ounces sharp Cheddar cheese,
   coarsely shredded

On rack in broiling pan broil pork cubes until rare; set aside.

In 1½-quart saucepan heat oil; add onion and garlic and sauté until onion is translucent. Stir in pork cubes, green pepper, chili powder, and cumin; add tomato sauce, water, salt, and red pepper and stir to combine. Cover and let simmer, stirring occasionally, until pork is fork-tender, about 45 minutes. Add beans and let simmer, uncovered, for 10 minutes longer.

Transfer pork mixture to 1½-quart flameproof casserole; sprinkle with cheese and broil until cheese is bubbly, about 3 minutes.

Each serving provides: 4 Protein Exchanges; ½ Bread Exchange;
   1¾ Vegetable Exchanges; ½ Fat Exchange
Per serving: 402 calories; 35 g protein; 20 g fat; 21 g carbohydrate; 153 mg calcium;
   802 mg sodium (estimated); 90 mg cholesterol

Apple-Pork Chop Bake ❶

WEEK 2 ∿ MAKES 4 SERVINGS

4 pork shoulder chops (5 ounces each)
½ teaspoon salt, divided
¼ teaspoon each pepper, divided, and ground sage
2 teaspoons vegetable oil

½ cup diced onion
12 ounces yams, parboiled, peeled, and cut into ¼-inch-thick slices
2 small apples, cored, pared, and cut into ¼-inch-thick wedges
½ cup water

On rack in broiling pan broil pork chops, turning once, until rare. Sprinkle chops with ¼ teaspoon salt, ⅛ teaspoon pepper, and the sage; set aside.

Preheat oven to 350°F. In small skillet heat oil; add onion and sauté until translucent. Spread sautéed onion over bottom of shallow square 2-quart casserole; top with sliced yams and sprinkle with remaining ¼ teaspoon salt and ⅛ teaspoon pepper. Top yams with apple wedges, then pork chops; add water and cover casserole. Bake for 45 minutes. Remove cover and bake until pork is fork-tender, about 15 minutes longer.

Each serving provides: 3 Protein Exchanges; 1 Bread Exchange;
   ¼ Vegetable Exchange; ½ Fat Exchange; ½ Fruit Exchange
Per serving: 356 calories; 25 g protein; 15 g fat; 30 g carbohydrate; 42 mg calcium;
   368 mg sodium; 75 mg cholesterol

Apple, Onion, and Chops ◑

WEEK 1 ∾ MAKES 2 SERVINGS, 1 CHOP EACH

2 pork loin chops (6 ounces each)
2 teaspoons each spicy brown
   mustard and margarine
1 small apple, cored, pared, and
   thinly sliced

½ cup sliced onion
½ teaspoon ground savory

Garnish
Parsley sprigs

Preheat broiler. Spread each side of each pork chop with ½ teaspoon mustard; set chops on rack in broiling pan and broil, turning once, until browned and done to taste.

While chops are broiling, in small nonstick skillet heat margarine over medium heat until bubbly and hot; add apple and onion slices and sauté until onion is lightly browned. Reduce heat to low and sprinkle with savory; cover pan and cook, stirring occasionally, until apples are soft.

To serve, transfer pork chops to warmed serving plate; top with apple mixture and garnish with parsley.

Each serving provides: 4 Protein Exchanges; ½ Vegetable Exchange;
   1 Fat Exchange; ½ Fruit Exchange
Per serving: 344 calories; 37 g protein; 16 g fat; 11 g carbohydrate; 27 mg calcium;
   184 mg sodium; 111 mg cholesterol

Baked Pork Chops 'n' Stuffing

WEEK 1 ∾ MAKES 2 SERVINGS

2 pork loin chops (6 ounces each)
¼ teaspoon each salt, pepper, and
   thyme leaves, divided
½ cup canned chicken broth
1 teaspoon margarine
2 tablespoons diced onion

1 garlic clove, minced
½ cup chopped mushrooms
2 tablespoons diced celery
2 thin slices white bread (½ ounce
   each), lightly toasted and cut
   into ¼-inch cubes

1. On rack in broiling pan broil pork chops, turning once, until rare.

2. Preheat oven to 325°F. Arrange chops in casserole that is large enough to hold them in 1 layer and sprinkle with ⅛ teaspoon each

salt, pepper, and thyme; add broth, cover casserole, and bake for about 45 minutes.

3. While pork chops are baking, in small skillet heat margarine until bubbly and hot; add onion and garlic and sauté until onion is translucent. Add mushrooms, celery, and remaining 1/8 teaspoon each salt, pepper, and thyme; sauté for 5 minutes. Stir in bread cubes.

4. Spoon an equal amount of stuffing mixture onto each baked pork chop; bake, uncovered, for 15 minutes longer.

Each serving provides: 4 Protein Exchanges; 1/2 Bread Exchange;
3/4 Vegetable Exchange; 1/2 Fat Exchange; 10 calories Optional Exchange
Per serving: 373 calories; 37 g protein; 19 g fat; 11 g carbohydrate; 46 mg calcium;
673 mg sodium; 100 mg cholesterol

Baked Pork Chops in Wine Sauce

WEEK 4 ⁓ MAKES 2 SERVINGS

1 teaspoon vegetable oil
1/4 cup each sliced onion and diced celery
1 garlic clove, minced
2 pork loin chops (6 ounces each), broiled until rare
1 cup sliced mushrooms
1/4 cup dry white wine
1/4 teaspoon each basil leaves and salt

1/8 teaspoon pepper
1 cup plus 2 tablespoons water, divided
1 medium tomato, blanched, peeled, seeded, and chopped
1 packet instant chicken broth and seasoning mix
1 teaspoon cornstarch
2 teaspoons chopped fresh parsley

Preheat oven to 325°F. In 10-inch nonstick skillet that has an oven-safe or removable handle heat oil; add onion, celery, and garlic and sauté until translucent. Add pork chops, mushrooms, wine, basil, salt, and pepper and bring liquid to a boil; cook for 2 minutes. Stir in 1 cup water and the tomato and broth mix and return mixture to a boil. Remove skillet from heat, cover, and transfer to oven; bake for 45 to 50 minutes.

In small cup or bowl combine remaining 2 tablespoons water with the cornstarch, stirring to dissolve cornstarch. Return skillet to burner and stir in dissolved cornstarch; stirring constantly, bring to a boil and cook until mixture is thickened. Serve sprinkled with parsley.

Each serving provides: 4 Protein Exchanges; 2 1/2 Vegetable Exchanges;
1/2 Fat Exchange; 40 calories Optional Exchange
Per serving: 382 calories; 36 g protein; 19 g fat; 11 g carbohydrate; 49 mg calcium;
798 mg sodium; 100 mg cholesterol

Oriental Pork 'n' Cabbage Sauté ◑❸

WEEK 4 ❧ MAKES 2 SERVINGS

2 teaspoons peanut or vegetable oil
¼ cup diced onion
1 garlic clove, minced
8 ounces boned cooked pork, cut
   into 2 x 1-inch strips
2 cups shredded Chinese cabbage
½ cup each drained canned sliced
   bamboo shoots and canned
   chicken broth

2 teaspoons soy sauce
⅛ teaspoon each pepper and
   ground ginger
½ teaspoon cornstarch, dissolved
   in 1 tablespoon water

In 12-inch skillet heat oil; add onion and garlic and sauté until onion is translucent. Add pork strips, cabbage, and bamboo shoots and sauté for 2 minutes. Stir in chicken broth, soy sauce, pepper, and ginger and bring to a boil; cook, stirring constantly, for 2 minutes. Stir in dissolved cornstarch and cook, stirring constantly, until mixture is slightly thickened.

Each serving provides: 4 Protein Exchanges; 2¾ Vegetable Exchanges;
   1 Fat Exchange; 15 calories Optional Exchange
Per serving: 372 calories; 37 g protein; 21 g fat; 17 g carbohydrate; 65 mg calcium;
   750 mg sodium; 100 mg cholesterol

Pork "Fried" Rice ◑❸

WEEK 2 ❧ MAKES 2 SERVINGS

An easy way to turn leftovers into an Oriental culinary delight!

2 teaspoons peanut or vegetable oil
1 cup cooked long-grain rice
1 tablespoon soy sauce
¼ cup sliced scallions (green
   onions)

6 ounces diced cooked pork
1 egg, beaten

In small nonstick skillet heat oil; add rice and soy sauce and cook, stirring constantly, until rice is hot. Add scallions and continue cooking and stirring until scallions are soft; add pork and cook, stirring constantly, until entire mixture is hot. Slowly stir in egg, a little at a time, and cook just until egg is set; serve immediately.

Each serving provides: 3½ Protein Exchanges; 1 Bread Exchange;
¼ Vegetable Exchange; 1 Fat Exchange
Per serving: 401 calories; 31 g protein; 20 g fat; 23 g carbohydrate; 54 mg calcium; 761 mg sodium; 212 mg cholesterol

Variation: Diced cooked beef, skinned and diced cooked chicken, or shelled and deveined cooked shrimp may be substituted for the pork (or a combination of these ingredients to total 6 ounces may be used).

Per serving with beef: 367 calories; 31 g protein; 16 g fat; 23 g carbohydrate;
54 mg calcium; 744 mg sodium; 214 mg cholesterol
With chicken: 346 calories; 30 g protein; 14 g fat; 23 g carbohydrate;
56 mg calcium; 773 mg sodium; 213 mg cholesterol
With shrimp: 284 calories; 26 g protein; 8 g fat; 24 g carbohydrate; 141 mg calcium;
819 mg sodium; 265 mg cholesterol

Pork Chow Mein ❶❸

WEEK 4 ◇ MAKES 4 SERVINGS

1 tablespoon plus 1 teaspoon peanut
  or vegetable oil
2 cups sliced onions
2 garlic cloves, minced
1 cup each sliced celery, julienne-cut
  red or green bell pepper (thin
  strips), sliced mushrooms, and
  bean sprouts
12 ounces julienne-cut cooked
  pork (thin strips)

2 teaspoons soy sauce
1 packet instant chicken broth and
  seasoning mix
¾ cup water
1 teaspoon cornstarch
2 tablespoons chopped scallion
  (green onion)
2 cups cooked long-grain rice (hot)

In 10-inch nonstick skillet heat oil; add onions and garlic and sauté briefly (*do not brown*). Add celery and pepper strips and sauté until tender-crisp, about 3 minutes; add mushrooms and bean sprouts and sauté, stirring occasionally, for 3 minutes. Add pork, soy sauce, and broth mix and stir to combine. Combine water and cornstarch, stirring to dissolve cornstarch; add to skillet and cook, stirring constantly, until mixture is thickened. Sprinkle with scallion and serve over rice.

Each serving provides: 3 Protein Exchanges; 1 Bread Exchange;
3 Vegetable Exchanges; 1 Fat Exchange; 5 calories Optional Exchange
Per serving: 423 calories; 31 g protein; 17 g fat; 36 g carbohydrate; 77 mg calcium;
547 mg sodium; 75 mg cholesterol

Sweet and Sour Pineapple Pork ◑

WEEK 4 ∽ MAKES 2 SERVINGS

2 teaspoons peanut oil
½ cup green bell pepper strips
¼ cup each thinly sliced carrot
   and scallions (green onions)
2 garlic cloves, minced
8 ounces boned cooked pork, cut
   into 1-inch cubes
½ cup canned chicken broth

2 teaspoons each red wine vinegar
   and soy sauce
1 teaspoon firmly packed brown
   sugar
1 tablespoon water
2 teaspoons cornstarch
½ cup canned pineapple chunks
   (no sugar added)

In 10-inch skillet heat oil; add pepper, carrot, scallions, and garlic and sauté until vegetables are tender-crisp, about 5 minutes. Stir in pork cubes, chicken broth, vinegar, soy sauce, and sugar and bring to a boil. Reduce heat and let simmer for 5 minutes. In small cup or bowl combine water and cornstarch, stirring to dissolve cornstarch; add to skillet, along with pineapple, and cook, stirring constantly, until mixture is slightly thickened.

Each serving provides: 4 Protein Exchanges; 1 Vegetable Exchange;
   1 Fat Exchange; ½ Fruit Exchange; 30 calories Optional Exchange
Per serving: 423 calories; 36 g protein; 21 g fat; 21 g carbohydrate; 48 mg calcium;
   743 mg sodium; 100 mg cholesterol

Creamed Glazed Apple and Pork Sauté ◑❸

WEEK 4 ∽ MAKES 2 SERVINGS

2 teaspoons margarine
¼ cup diced onion
1 small apple, cored, pared, and
   cut into ¼-inch-thick slices
1 teaspoon granulated brown sugar
2 teaspoons all-purpose flour
⅓ cup apple juice (no sugar
   added)

¼ cup dry sherry
8 ounces boned cooked pork, cut
   into strips
¼ teaspoon salt
⅛ teaspoon white pepper
¼ cup plain low-fat yogurt

In 9- or 10-inch nonstick skillet heat margarine until bubbly and hot; add onion and sauté until translucent. Add apple slices and brown sugar and stir to combine; sprinkle with flour and stir quickly to combine. Cook, stirring constantly, for 2 minutes; gradually stir in apple juice. Add sherry and bring to a boil. Add pork, salt, and pepper and cook over medium heat, stirring constantly, until mixture thickens. Stir in yogurt and heat thoroughly (*do not boil*).

Each serving provides: 4 Protein Exchanges; ¼ Vegetable Exchange;
1 Fat Exchange; 1 Fruit Exchange; ¼ Milk Exchange;
50 calories Optional Exchange
Per serving: 453 calories; 36 g protein; 21 g fat; 23 g carbohydrate; 85 mg calcium;
419 mg sodium; 101 mg cholesterol

Potted Pork Balls ❶

WEEK 3   ◡   MAKES 2 SERVINGS

½ cup diced onion, divided
1½ garlic cloves, minced, divided
10 ounces ground pork
1 slice white bread, cut into cubes
2 tablespoons sour cream
1 tablespoon chopped fresh parsley

¼ teaspoon each salt and crushed
   rosemary leaves
⅛ teaspoon pepper
1 teaspoon vegetable oil
1 cup canned crushed tomatoes
1 teaspoon Worcestershire sauce

In small nonstick skillet combine ¼ cup onion and ¼ teaspoon garlic and cook, stirring constantly, until onion is soft but not brown. Transfer to medium bowl and add pork, bread cubes, sour cream, parsley, salt, rosemary, and pepper; stir to combine. Form mixture into 8 pork balls, about 2½-inch diameter each; arrange pork balls on rack in broiling pan and broil 6 inches from heat source, turning once, until browned.

In 10-inch skillet heat oil; add remaining ¼ cup onion and remaining garlic and sauté until onion is soft. Add pork balls and toss with onion; stir in crushed tomatoes and Worcestershire sauce. Cover and let simmer for 30 minutes, turning pork balls once.

Each serving provides: 4 Protein Exchanges; ½ Bread Exchange;
1½ Vegetable Exchanges; ½ Fat Exchange; 35 calories Optional Exchange
Per serving: 418 calories; 31 g protein; 25 g fat; 16 g carbohydrate; 86 mg calcium;
647 mg sodium; 118 mg cholesterol

Variation: Week 1—Substitute plain low-fat yogurt for the sour cream; reduce Optional Exchange to 10 calories.

Per serving: 397 calories; 31 g protein; 22 g fat; 17 g carbohydrate; 96 mg calcium;
649 mg sodium; 112 mg cholesterol

Creamy Pork and Apple Stew ❸

WEEK 4 ∽ MAKES 2 SERVINGS

A delicious way to use up leftover pork.

2 teaspoons margarine
¼ cup sliced onion
1 garlic clove, minced
¾ cup water
1 packet instant chicken broth and
　seasoning mix
8 ounces cubed cooked pork
¼ teaspoon each salt and ground
　sage

1 small apple, cored, pared, and cut
　into ½-inch-thick slices
2 tablespoons golden raisins
2 teaspoons cornstarch
¼ cup plain low-fat yogurt
1 cup cooked long-grain rice (hot)

In 2-quart saucepan heat margarine over medium heat until bubbly and hot; add onion and garlic and sauté, stirring constantly, until onion is translucent, about 3 minutes. Add water and broth mix and stir to combine; bring to a boil. Reduce heat to a simmer and add pork and seasonings; cover and cook until pork is fork-tender, about 1 hour.

Stir apple slices and raisins into pork mixture; cover and cook until apple slices are tender, about 15 minutes. Add cornstarch to yogurt and stir until thoroughly combined; stir into pork mixture and immediately remove from heat. Serve over cooked rice.

Each serving provides: 4 Protein Exchanges; 1 Bread Exchange;
　¼ Vegetable Exchange; 1 Fat Exchange; 1 Fruit Exchange; ¼ Milk Exchange;
　15 calories Optional Exchange
Per serving: 513 calories; 38 g protein; 21 g fat; 42 g carbohydrate; 100 mg calcium;
　834 mg sodium; 101 mg cholesterol

Spicy "Fried" Pork 'n' Vegetables ❶❸

WEEK 1 ∽ MAKES 2 SERVINGS

1 tablespoon peanut or vegetable oil
2 garlic cloves, sliced
1 cup each thinly sliced onions and
　mushroom caps
8 ounces boned cooked pork, cut
　into 3 x 1-inch strips

2 to 3 drained canned mild green
　chilies, seeded and thinly sliced
2 tablespoons each lime juice (no
　sugar added) and teriyaki sauce
1 tablespoon firmly packed dark
　brown sugar

In 12-inch nonstick skillet heat oil; add garlic and sauté until browned (*be careful not to burn*). Using a slotted spoon, remove and discard garlic. Add onions and mushrooms to skillet and sauté until lightly browned; add pork and chilies and stir to combine. Cook until thoroughly heated. In small cup or bowl combine remaining ingredients; pour over pork mixture, stir to combine, and bring to a boil. Reduce heat and let simmer until mixture is thoroughly heated, about 3 minutes.

Each serving provides: 4 Protein Exchanges; 2½ Vegetable Exchanges; 1½ Fat Exchanges; 30 calories Optional Exchange
Per serving: 455 calories; 37 g protein; 23 g fat; 25 g carbohydrate; 52 mg calcium; 704 mg sodium; 100 mg cholesterol

Variation: Substitute 10 ounces skinned and boned chicken breasts, cut into 3 x 1-inch strips, for the pork. After sautéing onions and mushrooms remove from pan and set aside. Add chicken to skillet and sauté until browned. Return cooked vegetables to skillet and proceed as directed for pork.

Per serving: 329 calories; 36 g protein; 9 g fat; 25 g carbohydrate; 55 mg calcium; 718 mg sodium; 82 mg cholesterol

Prosciutto and Honeydew Appetizer ◑

WEEK 2 ～ MAKES 2 SERVINGS

For an attractive buffet, arrange 8 to 10 servings of Prosciutto and Honeydew Appetizer on a round serving platter, with the melon wedges radiating out like the spokes of a wheel; garnish with a lemon crown in the center of the platter and ask guests to help themselves.

2 honeydew wedges (each 2 inches wide)
2 lemon wedges

2 ounces prosciutto (Italian-style ham), cut into 4 equal slices

Using sharp knife, cut fruit from rind, leaving wedge of fruit intact. Leaving wedge on rind, cut pulp in half lengthwise, then crosswise into bite-size pieces. Using decorative toothpicks secure a lemon wedge, rind down, crosswise across center of each melon wedge. Tightly roll each slice of prosciutto; secure 2 rolls crosswise across each melon wedge, 1 on each side of lemon wedge. Cover with plastic wrap and refrigerate until ready to serve.

Each serving provides: 1 Protein Exchange; 1 Fruit Exchange
Per serving: 95 calories; 8 g protein; 3 g fat; 12 g carbohydrate; 26 mg calcium; 268 mg sodium; 25 mg cholesterol

Ham Patties in Orange-Mustard Sauce ◖●◗

WEEK 4 ∽ MAKES 2 SERVINGS

8 ounces "fully cooked" smoked
 ham patties
2 teaspoons margarine
½ cup diced onion
1 teaspoon all-purpose flour
½ cup orange juice (no sugar
 added)

2 teaspoons Dijon-style mustard
½ cup canned mandarin orange
 sections (no sugar added)

Garnish

Parsley sprigs

In 12-inch nonstick skillet cook patties over medium heat until browned on both sides; remove from pan and keep warm.

In same skillet heat margarine until bubbly and hot; add onion and sauté until lightly browned. Sprinkle with flour and cook, stirring constantly, for 1 minute; gradually stir in juice and, continuing to stir, bring to a boil. Reduce heat and simmer, stirring constantly, until mixture thickens; stir in mustard. Add ham patties and orange sections and cook until heated; transfer patties to serving platter, top with sauce, and garnish with parsley.

Each serving provides: 4 Protein Exchanges; ½ Vegetable Exchange;
 1 Fat Exchange; 1 Fruit Exchange; 5 calories Optional Exchange
Per serving: 551 calories; 29 g protein; 40 g fat; 19 g carbohydrate; 40 mg calcium;
 1,617 mg sodium; 88 mg cholesterol

Baked Smoked Ham with Pineapple Rings ●

WEEK 2 ∽ MAKES 8 SERVINGS

Although this recipe serves eight, a 3-pound ham will actually yield about twelve 4-ounce portions; remaining ham can be wrapped and refrigerated for future use. Serve with Pickle-Mustard Relish (see page 95).

3-pound "fully cooked" boneless
 smoked ham
20 whole cloves
4 canned pineapple slices (no sugar
 added)

½ cup diet ginger ale (0 calories)
Ground cinnamon

Preheat oven to 325°F. Remove and discard casing from ham. Using a sharp pointed knife, score top of ham in a diamond pattern (cut long diagonal slashes, about 1½ inches apart, in 1 direction, then cut across these slashes in other direction); stud the intersection of each "diamond" with a clove.

Transfer ham to a 1-quart casserole and arrange pineapple slices on top of meat; pour ginger ale over ham and sprinkle each pineapple slice with dash cinnamon. Bake until heated through, 25 to 30 minutes. Serve 4 ounces sliced ham and ½ pineapple slice per portion.

Each serving provides: 4 Protein Exchanges; 15 calories Optional Exchange
Per serving: 458 calories; 28 g protein; 36 g fat; 5 g carbohydrate; 21 mg calcium;
   1,416 mg sodium; 88 mg cholesterol

Potato-Ham Hash ◖❸

WEEK 2 〜 MAKES 2 SERVINGS

1 teaspoon margarine
2 tablespoons each diced onion and
   green bell pepper
6 ounces peeled cooked potatoes,
   diced

6 ounces ground boiled ham
Dash ground cinnamon

In 8-inch nonstick skillet heat margarine until bubbly and hot; add onion and pepper and sauté, stirring occasionally, until tender. Add potatoes, ham, and cinnamon and cook until all ingredients are heated through; serve hot.

Each serving provides: 3 Protein Exchanges; 1 Bread Exchange;
   ¼ Vegetable Exchange; ½ Fat Exchange
Per serving: 238 calories; 23 g protein; 9 g fat; 14 g carbohydrate; 20 mg calcium;
   797 mg sodium; 75 mg cholesterol

Variation: Eggs 'n' Hash—Cook ingredients as directed above, then make 2 wells in hash. Break 1 large egg into a small bowl; carefully slide egg into 1 of the wells. Repeat with another egg and second well. Cover skillet and cook over low heat until eggs are done; increase Protein Exchange to 4 Exchanges.

Per serving: 317 calories; 30 g protein; 15 g fat; 14 g carbohydrate; 48 mg calcium;
   866 mg sodium; 349 mg cholesterol

Zucchini-Ham Frittata ◑

WEEK 2 ∽ MAKES 4 SERVINGS

4 eggs
¼ cup water
Dash each pepper and garlic powder
1 tablespoon plus 1 teaspoon
  margarine
½ cup chopped onion
1 cup sliced zucchini (¼-inch-thick
  slices)

2 ounces chopped prosciutto
  (Italian-style ham) or cooked
  smoked ham
2 ounces mozzarella or Fontina
  cheese, shredded

In small bowl combine eggs, water, and seasoning; set aside.

In 9-inch nonstick skillet that has a metal or removable handle heat margarine until bubbly and hot; add onion and sauté until translucent. Add zucchini and sauté until fork-tender, 5 to 7 minutes; add meat and cook over medium heat, stirring occasionally, for about 2 minutes. Pour egg mixture over zucchini mixture, stirring quickly to combine before eggs begin to set; sprinkle with cheese and cook until bottom of frittata begins to set.

Transfer skillet to broiler and broil until frittata is puffed and lightly browned; slide frittata onto warmed platter and serve immediately.

Each serving provides: 2 Protein Exchanges; ¾ Vegetable Exchange;
  1 Fat Exchange
Per serving with prosciutto and mozzarella cheese: 222 calories; 13 g protein;
  17 g fat; 4 g carbohydrate; 120 mg calcium; 346 mg sodium; 296 mg cholesterol
With ham and mozzarella cheese: 193 calories; 13 g protein; 14 g fat;
  4 g carbohydrate; 120 mg calcium; 297 mg sodium; 298 mg cholesterol
With prosciutto and Fontina cheese: 237 calories; 13 g protein; 18 g fat;
  4 g carbohydrate; 125 mg calcium; 293 mg sodium; 302 mg cholesterol
With ham and Fontina cheese: 208 calories; 14 g protein; 15 g fat;
  4 g carbohydrate; 124 mg calcium; 244 mg sodium; 303 mg cholesterol

Ham Spread or Dip ◖❸

WEEK 2 ∽ MAKES 4 SERVINGS

²/₃ cup cottage cheese
1 tablespoon plus 1 teaspoon
  margarine
6 ounces ground boiled ham

2 tablespoons chopped scallion
  (green onion)
1 tablespoon spicy brown mustard

In blender container combine cheese and margarine and process until smooth; add remaining ingredients and process until combined.

Each serving provides: 2 Protein Exchanges; 1 Fat Exchange
Per serving: 157 calories; 16 g protein; 9 g fat; 2 g carbohydrate; 30 mg calcium;
  619 mg sodium; 43 mg cholesterol

Serving Suggestions:
  1. Spread each of 16 melba toast slices with an equal amount of mixture and garnish each with a parsley sprig. Add 1 Bread Exchange to Exchange Information; change nutrition information to 221 calories; 18 g protein; 10 g fat; 14 g carbohydrate; 33 mg calcium; 619 mg sodium; 43 mg cholesterol.
  2. Serve mixture in a bowl with cut-up raw vegetables to be used as dippers. Count vegetables toward Vegetable Exchange.

Ham and Cheese Roll Appetizers ◖❸

WEEK 2 ∽ MAKES 2 SERVINGS, 2 ROLLS EACH

1 iceberg lettuce leaf
1 slice boiled ham (1 ounce)
1 slice Muenster cheese (1 ounce)

½ teaspoon Dijon-style mustard
4 Italian (flat-leaf) parsley leaves

Lay lettuce leaf flat; place ham on lettuce and top with cheese. Trim any excess lettuce so that all slices are even. Spread mustard over surface of cheese; starting from narrow end of leaf, roll lettuce tightly to enclose ham and cheese. Secure with 4 toothpicks, evenly spaced. Cut into 4 rolls, each ¾ to 1 inch long; arrange rolls cut-side down on serving platter and top each with a parsley leaf.

Each serving provides: 1 Protein Exchange; ⅛ Vegetable Exchange
Per serving: 82 calories; 7 g protein; 6 g fat; 1 g carbohydrate; 109 mg calcium;
  258 mg sodium; 26 mg cholesterol

Open-Face Ham Salad Sandwich ◑ ❸

WEEK 4 ∽ MAKES 2 SERVINGS, 1 OPEN-FACE SANDWICH EACH

5 ounces ground boiled ham
1 egg, hard-cooked and mashed
1 tablespoon each minced celery,
   minced onion, and sour cream
2 teaspoons each pickle relish and
   mayonnaise

½ teaspoon Dijon-style mustard
2 slices rye bread, toasted
2 iceberg or romaine lettuce leaves
1 medium tomato, sliced

In small bowl combine ham, egg, minced vegetables, sour cream, relish, mayonnaise, and mustard, mixing well; cover and refrigerate until chilled.

Top each slice of toast with a lettuce leaf; stir salad again, then spoon half of salad onto each lettuce leaf. Serve with tomato slices.

Each serving provides: 3 Protein Exchanges; 1 Bread Exchange;
   1¼ Vegetable Exchanges; 1 Fat Exchange; 25 calories Optional Exchange
Per serving: 277 calories; 21 g protein; 12 g fat; 20 g carbohydrate; 63 mg calcium;
   1,139 mg sodium; 203 mg cholesterol

Variation: Substitute plain low-fat yogurt for the sour cream; reduce Optional Exchange to 15 calories.

Per serving: 266 calories; 21 g protein; 11 g fat; 21 g carbohydrate; 67 mg calcium;
   1,140 mg sodium; 178 mg cholesterol

Reuben Rounds ❸

WEEK 4 ∽ MAKES 2 SERVINGS, 6 ROUNDS EACH

Delicious served with mustard.

1 cup drained canned sauerkraut
½ cup water, divided
¼ cup minced onion
1 tablespoon plus 1½ teaspoons
   all-purpose flour, divided
½ packet (about ½ teaspoon)
   instant chicken broth and
   seasoning mix

4 ounces finely chopped boiled ham
1 ounce Swiss cheese, shredded
1 egg
¼ cup plus 1½ teaspoons plain
   dried bread crumbs
1 tablespoon plus 1 teaspoon
   vegetable oil

Finely chop sauerkraut and set aside. In 10-inch nonstick skillet combine 2 tablespoons water and the onion and cook over low heat until onion is translucent; sprinkle with 2 teaspoons flour and, stirring constantly, cook until flour is dissolved. Increase heat to high and add broth mix and remaining water; stirring constantly, bring mixture to a boil and cook until thickened. Reduce heat and add sauerkraut, ham, and cheese; continue cooking and stirring until cheese is melted. Transfer mixture to a bowl and let cool slightly; cover and refrigerate until thoroughly chilled, at least 30 minutes.

In small bowl lightly beat egg; add remaining 2½ teaspoons flour and stir to combine. On sheet of wax paper or a paper plate spread bread crumbs. Divide chilled cheese mixture into 12 equal portions and roll each into a ball; roll each ball in egg mixture, then in crumbs, being sure to use all of mixture and crumbs.

In 10-inch nonstick skillet heat oil over medium-high heat. Add balls and cook, turning, until browned on all sides; serve immediately.

Each serving provides: 3 Protein Exchanges; 1 Bread Exchange;
 1¼ Vegetable Exchanges; 2 Fat Exchanges; 3 calories Optional Exchange
Per serving: 393 calories; 26 g protein; 22 g fat; 23 g carbohydrate; 223 mg calcium;
 1,770 mg sodium; 201 mg cholesterol

Skillet Ham 'n' Beans ◑❶

WEEK 4 ∽ MAKES 2 SERVINGS

2 teaspoons vegetable oil
¼ cup diced onion
1 garlic clove, minced
6 ounces julienne-cut boiled ham
 (thin strips)
½ cup tomato sauce

¼ cup water
¼ teaspoon Worcestershire sauce
⅛ teaspoon each salt, pepper, and
 ground thyme
4 ounces drained cooked or canned
 dry lima beans

In 9- or 10-inch skillet heat oil; add onion and garlic and sauté until onion is softened. Add ham and sauté for about 3 minutes; stir in tomato sauce, water, and seasonings and let simmer, stirring occasionally, for 15 minutes. Add beans and let simmer until beans are heated, about 5 minutes.

Each serving provides: 4 Protein Exchanges; 1¼ Vegetable Exchanges;
 1 Fat Exchange
Per serving with cooked lima beans: 295 calories; 27 g protein; 13 g fat;
 18 g carbohydrate; 46 mg calcium; 1,215 mg sodium; 75 mg cholesterol
With canned lima beans: 286 calories; 26 g protein; 13 g fat; 17 g carbohydrate;
 35 mg calcium; 1,348 mg sodium; 75 mg cholesterol

Glazed Ham Steak ◐ ❶

WEEK 2 ∽ MAKES 4 SERVINGS

2 tablespoons each pineapple
  preserves and dry vermouth
1 teaspoon each firmly packed dark
  brown sugar and Dijon-style
  mustard

1 pound "fully cooked" boneless
  ham steak
12 whole cloves

In a small saucepan combine preserves, vermouth, sugar, and mustard; cook over low heat until sugar is melted and mixture is hot.

Preheat broiler. Score one side of ham steak in a crisscross pattern and stud with cloves; transfer to a shallow flameproof casserole that is just large enough to hold steak flat. Pour glaze over entire surface and broil until glaze is bubbly and browned, about 3 minutes.

Each serving provides: 4 Protein Exchanges; 40 calories Optional Exchange
Per serving: 254 calories; 29 g protein; 10 g fat; 9 g carbohydrate; 17 mg calcium;
  1,067 mg sodium; 100 mg cholesterol

BLT Sandwich with Spicy Russian Dressing ◐

WEEK 4 ∽ MAKES 4 SERVINGS, 1 SANDWICH EACH

Dressing

2 tablespoons plus 2 teaspoons
  each mayonnaise and ketchup
1 tablespoon plus 1 teaspoon spicy
  brown mustard

Sandwich

12 ounces Canadian-style bacon,
  sliced
8 slices whole wheat bread, toasted
2 medium tomatoes, thinly sliced
8 iceberg lettuce leaves

To Prepare Dressing: In small bowl combine mayonnaise, ketchup, and mustard, mixing well; cover and refrigerate until chilled.

To Prepare Sandwiches: In 12-inch nonstick skillet cook bacon until browned. Divide bacon onto 4 slices of toast; top each portion with ¼ of the tomato slices, 2 lettuce leaves, and 1 of the remaining toast slices. Cut each sandwich into quarters and serve each portion with ¼ of the chilled dressing.

Each serving provides: 3 Protein Exchanges; 2 Bread Exchanges;
  1½ Vegetable Exchanges; 2 Fat Exchanges; 10 calories Optional Exchange
Per serving: 445 calories; 29 g protein; 24 g fat; 29 g carbohydrate; 82 mg calcium;
  2,657 mg sodium; 78 mg cholesterol

Bacon-Artichoke Bake

WEEK 4 ～ MAKES 2 SERVINGS

1 cup skim milk
3 eggs
3 ounces Swiss cheese, shredded
2 teaspoons margarine
½ cup chopped onion

2 ounces Canadian-style bacon,
  diced
1 cup thawed frozen artichoke
  hearts, chopped
Dash pepper

In large bowl beat together milk and eggs; add cheese and stir to combine. Set aside. Spray a 1-quart casserole with nonstick cooking spray and set aside.

Preheat oven to 375°F. In small skillet heat margarine until bubbly and hot; add onion and sauté briefly (*do not brown*). Add bacon and continue sautéing until onion is soft; add artichokes and cook until thoroughly heated, stirring occasionally. Sprinkle with pepper and add to milk mixture, stirring to combine; transfer mixture to sprayed casserole and bake until eggs are set, 35 to 40 minutes.

Each serving provides: 4 Protein Exchanges; 1½ Vegetable Exchanges;
  1 Fat Exchange; ½ Milk Exchange
Per serving: 481 calories; 36 g protein; 29 g fat; 19 g carbohydrate; 638 mg calcium;
  1,091 mg sodium; 476 mg cholesterol

Sautéed Franks 'n' Beans ◖●❸

WEEK 4 ～ MAKES 4 SERVINGS

1 tablespoon plus 1 teaspoon
  margarine
12 ounces frankfurters, cut into
  1-inch pieces
1 cup each diced onions and green
  bell peppers

8 ounces drained canned pink beans
2 tablespoons plus 2 teaspoons
  extra-spicy ketchup
2 teaspoons firmly packed brown
  sugar
½ teaspoon garlic powder

In 12-inch nonstick skillet heat margarine over medium heat until bubbly and hot; add frankfurters and diced vegetables and sauté until meat is browned. Reduce heat to low and add remaining ingredients; cook, stirring occasionally, until thoroughly heated.

Each serving provides: 4 Protein Exchanges; 1 Vegetable Exchange;
  1 Fat Exchange; 20 calories Optional Exchange
Per serving: 417 calories; 15 g protein; 29 g fat; 25 g carbohydrate; 58 mg calcium;
  1,320 mg sodium (estimated); 43 mg cholesterol

Skillet Franks 'n' Vegetables ◐❸

WEEK 4 ᔐ MAKES 2 SERVINGS

2 teaspoons vegetable oil
½ cup each sliced onion, sliced
  carrot, and thinly sliced green
  bell pepper
1 small garlic clove, minced, or ⅛
  teaspoon garlic powder

1 cup shredded green cabbage
6 ounces frankfurters, cut crosswise
  into ¼-inch-thick slices
¼ cup canned chicken broth
1 teaspoon each soy sauce and
  cornstarch

In 9- or 10-inch nonstick skillet heat oil; add onion, carrot, green pepper, and garlic (or garlic powder) and sauté until onion is translucent, about 5 minutes. Stir in cabbage. Reduce heat, cover, and cook, stirring occasionally, until cabbage is soft, about 10 minutes. Add frankfurters and cook, uncovered, until thoroughly heated.

In measuring cup combine broth, soy sauce, and cornstarch, stirring to dissolve cornstarch; pour over frankfurter mixture and cook, stirring constantly, until slightly thickened.

Each serving provides: 3 Protein Exchanges; 2½ Vegetable Exchanges;
  1 Fat Exchange; 10 calories Optional Exchange
Per serving: 374 calories; 12 g protein; 30 g fat; 15 g carbohydrate; 60 mg calcium;
  1,307 mg sodium; 43 mg cholesterol

Quick Franks 'n' Kraut ◐❸

WEEK 4 ᔐ MAKES 2 SERVINGS

We suggest that you use the sauerkraut that is packaged in a plastic bag and is stored in the refrigerator section of the supermarket; this is usually crisper and less salty than the canned.

2 teaspoons margarine
¼ cup each diced celery, onion,
  and green bell pepper
6 ounces frankfurters, cut diagonally
  into ½-inch pieces
⅓ cup water

2 teaspoons white wine vinegar
1 teaspoon each granulated sugar
  and cornstarch
Dash pepper
1 cup drained sauerkraut

In 10-inch nonstick skillet heat margarine until bubbly and hot; add celery, onion, and green pepper and sauté until vegetables are soft and lightly browned. Remove vegetables to a plate and set aside.

Add frankfurters to same skillet and sauté until browned; remove franks to plate with vegetables.

In measuring cup or small bowl combine water, vinegar, sugar, cornstarch, and pepper, stirring to dissolve cornstarch; add to skillet, along with sauerkraut, and bring to a boil. Reduce heat and simmer, stirring constantly, until mixture thickens; return vegetables and franks to skillet and cook, stirring, until heated.

Each serving provides: 3 Protein Exchanges; 1¾ Vegetable Exchanges;
  1 Fat Exchange; 15 calories Optional Exchange
Per serving: 355 calories; 11 g protein; 29 g fat; 14 g carbohydrate; 66 mg calcium;
  1,888 mg sodium; 43 mg cholesterol

Skillet Cabbage 'n' Wurst ❶

WEEK 4 ∼ MAKES 2 SERVINGS

---

2 knockwurst, 3 ounces each
2 teaspoons vegetable oil
1 cup sliced onions
½ cup thinly sliced carrot
1 garlic clove, minced
1 cup shredded green cabbage
½ cup water
¼ cup dry white wine

½ packet (about ½ teaspoon) instant chicken broth and seasoning mix
½ bay leaf
¼ teaspoon salt
1 whole clove
1 cup cooked long-grain rice (hot)

In small skillet brown knockwurst on all sides; set aside and keep warm.

In same skillet heat oil over medium heat; add onions, carrot, and garlic and sauté, stirring occasionally, until carrot slices are tender. Add cabbage and continue sautéing until cabbage begins to wilt, about 5 minutes. Reduce heat and stir in remaining ingredients except rice and knockwurst; cover and cook, stirring occasionally, for about 15 minutes. Add knockwurst and cook until thoroughly heated; remove bay leaf and clove.

To serve, arrange hot rice on serving platter; spoon vegetable mixture over rice and top with knockwurst.

Each serving provides: 3 Protein Exchanges; 1 Bread Exchange;
  2½ Vegetable Exchanges; 1 Fat Exchange; 35 calories Optional Exchange
Per serving: 492 calories; 14 g protein; 29 g fat; 39 g carbohydrate; 73 mg calcium;
  1,357 mg sodium; 49 mg cholesterol

Cheddar Dogs ◐❸

WEEK 4 ∽ MAKES 4 SERVINGS

4 ready-to-bake refrigerated
   buttermilk flaky biscuits (1 ounce
   each)
4 frankfurters (1½ ounces each)

6 ounces Cheddar cheese, shredded
1 tablespoon plus 1 teaspoon each
   pickle relish and spicy brown
   mustard

Preheat oven to 350°F. Roll each biscuit between 2 sheets of wax paper, forming 4 circles, each about 6 inches in diameter; carefully remove paper. Set 1 frankfurter in center of each circle; top each frank with 1½ ounces cheese and fold dough around frankfurter and cheese to enclose. Transfer wrapped franks to baking sheet, seam-side up; at open ends of each, pinch up bottom portion of dough so that cheese does not melt onto baking sheet. Bake until biscuits are golden brown and cheese is melted, about 15 minutes.

   In small cup combine relish and mustard; serve with Cheddar Dogs.

Each serving provides: 3 Protein Exchanges; 1 Bread Exchange;
   10 calories Optional Exchange
Per serving: 395 calories; 18 g protein; 29 g fat; 16 g carbohydrate; 327 mg calcium;
   1,052 mg sodium; 66 mg cholesterol

Frank 'n' Bean Casserole ❸

WEEK 4 ∽ MAKES 2 SERVINGS

2 teaspoons vegetable oil
½ cup each diced onion and
   chopped green bell pepper
1 garlic clove, minced
½ cup chopped canned Italian
   tomatoes
2 teaspoons each Worcestershire
   sauce and red wine vinegar
1 teaspoon firmly packed brown
   sugar

½ teaspoon paprika
¼ teaspoon powdered mustard
6 ounces frankfurters, cut diagonally
   into 1-inch pieces
4 ounces drained canned small
   white beans
2 tablespoons shredded Cheddar
   cheese

In 2-quart saucepan heat oil; add onion, green pepper, and garlic and sauté until vegetables are lightly browned. Stir in tomatoes, Worcestershire sauce, vinegar, sugar, paprika, and mustard; bring to a boil.

Reduce heat, cover, and let simmer, stirring occasionally, for 15 minutes.

Preheat oven to 450°F. Add frankfurters and beans to saucepan and stir to combine; transfer mixture to 1-quart casserole. Sprinkle with cheese and bake until cheese is melted, about 15 minutes.

Each serving provides: 4 Protein Exchanges; 1½ Vegetable Exchanges;
  1 Fat Exchange; 40 calories Optional Exchange
Per serving: 461 calories; 18 g protein; 32 g fat; 26 g carbohydrate; 110 mg calcium;
  1,335 mg sodium (estimated); 50 mg cholesterol

Sautéed Lamb Kidneys in Sherry-Mushroom Sauce ❶

WEEK 4 ⌒ MAKES 2 SERVINGS

2 teaspoons margarine, divided
½ cup each finely chopped onion and sliced mushrooms
10 ounces trimmed lamb kidneys (tubes and fat removed), cut into quarters, soaked in water for 1 hour, and drained
2 teaspoons all-purpose flour
⅛ teaspoon pepper

1 packet instant beef broth and seasoning mix, dissolved in ¼ cup hot water
1 tablespoon plus 1 teaspoon dry sherry
2 slices white bread, toasted and cut diagonally into halves
2 teaspoons chopped fresh parsley

In 8-inch skillet heat 1 teaspoon margarine until bubbly and hot; add onion and sauté until translucent. Add mushrooms and sauté until lightly browned. Transfer mushroom mixture to 1-quart casserole.

Preheat oven to 350°F. In small bowl sprinkle drained kidneys with flour and pepper; using a fork, toss to coat. In same skillet heat remaining teaspoon margarine until bubbly and hot; add kidneys and sauté until lightly browned.

Arrange sautéed kidneys over mushroom mixture in casserole; add dissolved broth mix and sherry and stir to combine. Cover casserole and bake until kidneys are tender, about 45 minutes. To serve, place 2 toast triangles on each of 2 plates and spoon half of kidney mixture over each portion of toast; sprinkle with parsley.

Each serving provides: 4 Protein Exchanges; 1 Bread Exchange;
  1 Vegetable Exchange; 1 Fat Exchange; 25 calories Optional Exchange
Per serving: 296 calories; 28 g protein; 9 g fat; 21 g carbohydrate; 56 mg calcium;
  827 mg sodium; 532 mg cholesterol

Veal Kidney 'n' Bacon Sauté

WEEK 4 ⟋ MAKES 4 SERVINGS

1 pound 2 ounces trimmed veal
kidneys (tubes and fat removed),
cut into halves lengthwise,
soaked in water for 1 hour, and
drained
2 teaspoons vegetable oil
1 cup diced onions
1 garlic clove, minced
2 ounces diced Canadian-style
bacon

1 tablespoon all-purpose flour
½ cup each dry red wine and
canned beef broth
2 tablespoons chopped fresh
parsley
Dash each salt and pepper
2 cups cooked long-grain rice
(hot)

Chop drained kidneys and set aside. In 10-inch nonstick skillet heat oil; add onions and garlic and sauté until onions are translucent. Stir in bacon and sauté until onions and bacon are browned. Transfer mixture to a bowl and set aside.

In same skillet sauté kidneys until browned; return onion mixture to skillet and stir to combine. Sprinkle mixture with flour and stir quickly to combine; cook, stirring constantly, for 1 minute. Gradually stir in wine; add broth and, stirring constantly, bring to a boil. Reduce heat, cover skillet, and let simmer until kidneys are tender, 30 to 35 minutes. Stir in parsley, salt, and pepper and serve over hot rice.

Each serving provides: 4 Protein Exchanges; 1 Bread Exchange;
½ Vegetable Exchange; ½ Fat Exchange; 45 calories Optional Exchange
Per serving: 349 calories; 28 g protein; 11 g fat; 28 g carbohydrate; 54 mg calcium;
724 mg sodium; 492 mg cholesterol

Fresh Tongue with Horseradish Sauce ◑ ❸

WEEK 4 ～ MAKES 2 SERVINGS

⅓ cup plus 2 teaspoons sour cream
1 tablespoon each chopped fresh
  parsley and prepared horseradish
2 teaspoons Dijon-style mustard

1 teaspoon minced shallots or onion
¼ teaspoon granulated sugar
8 ounces sliced cooked fresh beef
  tongue, chilled

In small bowl combine all ingredients except tongue. Arrange tongue on serving platter and serve with sauce.

Each serving provides: 4 Protein Exchanges; 105 calories Optional Exchange
Per serving: 382 calories; 26 g protein; 28 g fat; 5 g carbohydrate; 66 mg calcium;
  249 mg sodium; 126 mg cholesterol

Variation: Substitute ½ cup plain low-fat yogurt for the sour cream. Add ½ Milk Exchange to Exchange Information and reduce Optional Exchange to 3 calories.

Per serving: 325 calories; 28 g protein; 20 g fat; 7 g carbohydrate; 119 mg calcium;
  266 mg sodium; 110 mg cholesterol

Boiled Fresh Tongue ❸

WEEK 4 ～ YIELDS ABOUT 1½ POUNDS COOKED TONGUE

1 fresh beef tongue (about 2¾
  pounds), washed and drained
3 quarts water
2 medium tomatoes, cut into
  quarters
2 large carrots, trimmed and
  scraped
1 large onion, cut into quarters

2 celery ribs
3 garlic cloves, crushed
2 parsley sprigs
1½ teaspoons salt
½ teaspoon thyme leaves
6 whole peppercorns
3 whole cloves
2 bay leaves

Place tongue in 5- or 6-quart saucepot; add remaining ingredients and bring to a boil. Reduce heat, cover, and let simmer until tongue is fork-tender, 2½ to 3 hours. Allow meat to cool in broth.

Remove tongue from broth. On underside of tongue, slit skin lengthwise from root to tip and peel off skin. Cut off root end, any small bones, and gristle. Starting at large end, thinly slice diagonally across the grain; serve hot or chilled.

One ounce cooked tongue provides: 1 Protein Exchange
Per 1 ounce: 69 calories; 6 g protein; 5 g fat; 0.1 g carbohydrate; 2 mg calcium;
  62 mg sodium; 27 mg cholesterol

Chilled Tongue and Vegetable Medley

WEEK 4 ∽ MAKES 4 SERVINGS

1 medium eggplant (about 1 pound), sliced into ½-inch-thick rounds
12 ounces julienne-cut cooked pickled tongue (thin strips)
2 medium tomatoes, blanched, peeled, seeded, and chopped
1 cup thinly sliced red bell peppers
¼ cup chopped scallions (green onions)
2 tablespoons each red wine vinegar and lemon juice
1 tablespoon plus 1 teaspoon olive oil
1 garlic clove, minced
¼ teaspoon pepper
⅛ teaspoon salt
1 tablespoon chopped fresh parsley

Spray a cookie sheet with nonstick cooking spray; arrange eggplant slices on sheet and bake at 350°F., turning once, until soft, about 30 minutes. Cut eggplant into ½-inch cubes.

In salad bowl combine eggplant, tongue, tomatoes, red peppers, and scallions; in small bowl combine remaining ingredients except parsley, mixing well. Pour dressing over salad and toss to combine; cover and refrigerate until chilled. Just before serving, toss again and sprinkle with parsley.

Each serving provides: 3 Protein Exchanges; 3⅛ Vegetable Exchanges; 1 Fat Exchange
Per serving: 310 calories; 21 g protein; 19 g fat; 14 g carbohydrate; 40 mg calcium; 135 mg sodium; 80 mg cholesterol

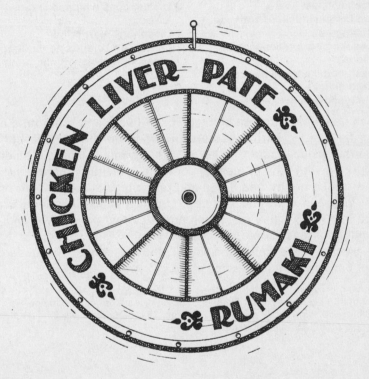

Liver

Liver can become a winning mealtime selection that's not only low in cost but high in nutrition. Whether you spin the wheel of fortune and land on Chicken Liver Pâté or take a chance on Rumaki, we bet you'll hit the jackpot.

So be adventurous, because even on a weight-control program gaining can be as rewarding as losing, if what you're gaining are new ideas for meal appeal and what you're losing is that old bugaboo against liver.

Chicken Liver Pâté ●

WEEK 3 ❧ MAKES 2 SERVINGS

10 ounces chicken livers
1 packet instant chicken broth and seasoning mix
1 tablespoon plus 1 teaspoon dry vermouth
6 ounces peeled cooked potatoes, cut into chunks
¼ cup minced onion
3 tablespoons whipped cream cheese
2 teaspoons margarine
½ teaspoon Dijon-style mustard
¼ teaspoon each salt and ground nutmeg
Dash pepper

In 9-inch nonstick skillet combine chicken livers and broth mix; cook, stirring frequently, until livers are browned on the outside but still pink on the inside, about 5 minutes. Add vermouth and set aside.

In work bowl of food processor combine remaining ingredients and process until smooth; add livers and pan juices and, using an on–off motion, process until just blended. Using a rubber scraper, scrape mixture into a 7⅜ x 3⅝ x 2¼-inch nonstick loaf pan; cover and chill overnight or at least 3 hours.

To serve, using a knife or spatula, loosen edges of pâté around sides of pan; invert onto serving plate.

Each serving provides: 4 Protein Exchanges; 1 Bread Exchange;
¼ Vegetable Exchange; 1 Fat Exchange; 65 calories Optional Exchange
Per serving: 359 calories; 29 g protein; 15 g fat; 25 g carbohydrate; 43 mg calcium;
927 mg sodium; 638 mg cholesterol

Chopped Chicken Livers ●

WEEK 1 ❧ MAKES 2 SERVINGS

1 tablespoon margarine, divided
¼ cup diced onion
4 ounces chicken livers
1 egg, hard-cooked and chopped
⅛ teaspoon salt
Dash white pepper
4 iceberg, romaine, or loose-leafed lettuce leaves
1 medium tomato, cut into 8 wedges
1 medium carrot, cut into 6 sticks
¼ cup sliced onion (separated into rings)

In small nonstick skillet heat ½ teaspoon margarine until bubbly and hot; add diced onion and sauté until translucent. Add livers and cook, stirring frequently, until livers are browned on the outside but still pink on the inside, about 5 minutes. Transfer mixture to work bowl of food processor; process until smooth. Using a rubber scraper, scrape mixture into a small bowl; stir in remaining 2½ teaspoons margarine and the egg, salt, and pepper. Cover and refrigerate until chilled.

Chill 2 salad plates. When ready to serve, line each chilled plate with 2 lettuce leaves. Mound half of liver mixture (about ⅓ cup) on each portion of lettuce; garnish each with 4 tomato wedges, 3 carrot sticks, and half of the onion rings.

Each serving provides: 2 Protein Exchanges; 3 Vegetable Exchanges;
   1½ Fat Exchanges
Per serving: 210 calories; 16 g protein; 11 g fat; 13 g carbohydrate; 60 mg calcium;
   293 mg sodium; 454 mg cholesterol

Liver 'n' Cheese Spread ❶

WEEK 4   ∽   MAKES 4 SERVINGS

A festive dish to serve when company's coming or to treat the family. Serve with melba rounds and saltines.

2 teaspoons margarine
½ cup diced onion
8 ounces chicken livers
⅓ cup plus 2 teaspoons whipped
   cream cheese

1 tablespoon plus 1 teaspoon pickle
   relish
4 iceberg or romaine lettuce leaves

1. In small nonstick skillet heat margarine until bubbly and hot; add onion and sauté until translucent. Add livers and sauté, stirring frequently, until browned on the outside but still pink on the inside.

2. Transfer liver mixture to work bowl of food processor; process until smooth. Using a rubber scraper, scrape mixture into a medium bowl; add cream cheese and relish and stir until well combined.

3. Transfer mixture to sheet of wax paper and, rolling mixture in the wax paper, form into a cylinder about 6 inches long and 2 inches in diameter; refrigerate wrapped, until firm, at least 2 hours.

4. When ready to serve, line a serving plate with lettuce leaves; unwrap liver and serve on lettuce.

Each serving provides: 1½ Protein Exchanges; ½ Vegetable Exchange;
   ½ Fat Exchange; 60 calories Optional Exchange
Per serving: 153 calories; 12 g protein; 9 g fat; 6 g carbohydrate; 31 mg calcium;
   147 mg sodium; 265 mg cholesterol

Oriental Liver and Vegetables ◐ ❸

WEEK 4 ⌒ MAKES 2 SERVINGS

2 teaspoons peanut or vegetable oil
½ cup chopped onion
1 garlic clove, minced
10 ounces chicken livers
1 cup sliced mushrooms
½ cup cut-up green bell pepper
   (½-inch squares) or sliced celery

⅓ cup water
2 teaspoons soy sauce
1 teaspoon cornstarch
Dash pepper

In 10-inch skillet heat oil; add onion and garlic and sauté until onion is translucent. Add livers, mushrooms, and green pepper (or celery) and sauté over medium-high heat for 5 minutes. In measuring cup combine water, soy sauce, and cornstarch, stirring to dissolve cornstarch; stir into liver mixture and sprinkle with pepper. Stirring constantly, cook until mixture thickens.

Each serving provides: 4 Protein Exchanges; 2 Vegetable Exchanges;
   1 Fat Exchange; 5 calories Optional Exchange
Per serving with green pepper: 273 calories; 33 g protein; 10 g fat;
   13 g carbohydrate; 35 mg calcium; 527 mg sodium; 846 mg cholesterol
With celery: 270 calories; 32 g protein; 10 g fat; 12 g carbohydrate; 43 mg calcium;
   560 mg sodium; 846 mg cholesterol

Chicken Livers in Creamy Mushroom Sauce ◖❶

WEEK 4 ⌖ MAKES 2 SERVINGS

2 teaspoons margarine
10 ounces chicken livers
2 cups sliced mushrooms
1 packet instant onion broth and
  seasoning mix
¼ teaspoon each paprika and salt
Dash pepper
1 tablespoon water

1 teaspoon all-purpose flour
2 tablespoons sour cream
2 slices white bread, toasted and
  cut into 4 triangles each

Garnish
2 tablespoons chopped fresh parsley

In small skillet heat margarine until bubbly and hot. Add chicken livers, mushrooms, broth mix, paprika, salt, and pepper; cover and cook for 5 minutes, stirring occasionally.

In small cup combine water and flour, stirring to dissolve flour; stir into liver mixture. Stirring constantly, cook over medium heat until mixture thickens. Remove skillet from heat and stir in sour cream.

On each of 2 plates arrange 4 toast triangles; spoon half of the liver mixture over each portion of toast and sprinkle each serving with 1 tablespoon chopped parsley.

Each serving provides: 4 Protein Exchanges; 1 Bread Exchange;
  2 Vegetable Exchanges; 1 Fat Exchange; 45 calories Optional Exchange
Per serving: 336 calories; 30 g protein; 13 g fat; 23 g carbohydrate; 65 mg calcium;
  943 mg sodium; 629 mg cholesterol

Variation: Substitute plain low-fat yogurt for the sour cream; reduce Optional Exchange to 20 calories.

Per serving: 314 calories; 31 g protein; 11 g fat; 23 g carbohydrate; 74 mg calcium;
  945 mg sodium; 624 mg cholesterol

Polynesian Chicken Livers ◐❸

WEEK 4 ⌇ MAKES 2 SERVINGS

1 teaspoon Chinese sesame oil
10 ounces chicken livers
1/4 cup each diced green bell pepper and thinly sliced scallions (green onions)
1/2 cup canned pineapple chunks (no sugar added), drain and reserve juice

1 tablespoon each rice vinegar and teriyaki sauce
1 1/2 teaspoons granulated brown sugar
1 teaspoon cornstarch

1. In 9-inch skillet heat oil over medium heat. Increase heat to high, add livers, green pepper, and scallions and cook, stirring constantly, until livers are browned; remove from heat and set aside.

2. In small saucepan combine pineapple chunks, vinegar, teriyaki sauce, and sugar; heat.

3. While fruit mixture is heating, dissolve cornstarch in reserved pineapple juice; add to heated fruit and cook, stirring constantly, until mixture is thickened.

4. Pour fruit mixture over liver mixture in skillet; return skillet to medium heat and cook for 1 minute.

Each serving provides: 4 Protein Exchanges; 1/2 Vegetable Exchange;
   1/2 Fat Exchange; 1/2 Fruit Exchange; 20 calories Optional Exchange
Per serving: 282 calories; 31 g protein; 7 g fat; 22 g carbohydrate; 31 mg calcium;
   376 mg sodium; 846 mg cholesterol

Italian-Style Liver and Onions ◐❸

WEEK 4 ⌇ MAKES 2 SERVINGS

1/2 cup plus 1 tablespoon plain dried bread crumbs
1 tablespoon plus 1 teaspoon grated Parmesan cheese
1 tablespoon chopped fresh parsley
1/2 teaspoon oregano leaves
1/4 teaspoon garlic powder

Dash each salt and pepper
10 ounces chicken livers, cut into chunks
3 tablespoons buttermilk
2 teaspoons margarine
1 cup sliced onions

In shallow dish combine bread crumbs, cheese, parsley, oregano, garlic powder, salt, and pepper; dip liver, 1 piece at a time, into milk, then into crumb mixture, being sure to use all of milk and crumb mixture.

Spray a baking sheet with nonstick cooking spray; transfer liver to sheet and bake at 350°F. until lightly browned, 15 to 20 minutes.

While liver is baking, in 9-inch nonstick skillet heat margarine until bubbly and hot; add onions and sauté until golden. Serve with breaded liver.

Each serving provides: 4 Protein Exchanges; 1½ Bread Exchanges;
  1 Vegetable Exchange; 1 Fat Exchange; 30 calories Optional Exchange
Per serving: 396 calories; 37 g protein; 11 g fat; 34 g carbohydrate; 157 mg calcium;
  492 mg sodium; 851 mg cholesterol

Pepper 'n' Livers Sauté ◑❸

WEEK 2 ◇ MAKES 2 SERVINGS

2 teaspoons margarine
¼ cup diced onion
1 small garlic clove, minced
10 ounces chicken livers
1 medium green bell pepper, seeded
  and cut into slivers

1 tablespoon plus 1 teaspoon dry
  sherry
¼ cup canned chicken broth
⅛ teaspoon pepper
Dash ground thyme

In 10-inch skillet heat margarine until bubbly and hot; add onion and garlic and sauté until onion is soft, about 2 minutes. Add livers and sauté, turning occasionally, until browned, about 3 minutes; add green pepper and sherry and sauté for 1 minute longer. Stir in remaining ingredients and bring to a boil; reduce heat, cover, and let simmer for 2 mInutes.

Each serving provides: 4 Protein Exchanges; 1¼ Vegetable Exchanges;
  1 Fat Exchange; 15 calories Optional Exchange
Per serving: 260 calories; 32 g protein; 9 g fat; 9 g carbohydrate; 28 mg calcium;
  225 mg sodium; 846 mg cholesterol

Rumaki

WEEK 4 ∽ MAKES 4 SERVINGS

4 ounces Canadian-style bacon
5 ounces chicken livers, cut into
  chunks
1½ ounces drained canned water
  chestnuts
¼ cup teriyaki sauce

1 teaspoon vegetable oil
½ teaspoon firmly packed brown
  sugar
1-inch piece ginger root, pared and
  sliced

Cut bacon into 3 x 1 x ⅛-inch strips; there should be the same number of bacon strips as liver chunks and water chestnuts (if necessary, cut water chestnuts into halves).

Onto each strip of bacon place 1 liver chunk and 1 water chestnut; roll bacon around liver and water chestnuts and secure each with a toothpick. Place in shallow bowl. In small cup combine teriyaki sauce, oil, sugar, and ginger root; pour over bacon rolls and toss gently to coat. Cover and refrigerate for about 1 hour, tossing occasionally.

Preheat broiler. Transfer bacon rolls to nonstick baking sheet, reserving marinade. Broil, turning frequently and brushing with reserved marinade, until livers are no longer pink. Transfer to serving platter and serve piping hot.

Each serving provides: 2 Protein Exchanges; 25 calories Optional Exchange
Per serving: 163 calories; 16 g protein; 7 g fat; 7 g carbohydrate; 10 mg calcium;
  1,343 mg sodium; 235 mg cholesterol

Sautéed Livers 'n' Vegetables ◗❸

WEEK 1 ∽ MAKES 2 SERVINGS

2 teaspoons margarine
½ cup diced onion
1 garlic clove, minced
10 ounces chicken livers

½ cup sliced green bell pepper
1 medium tomato, cut into 8 wedges
Dash salt

In 9-inch skillet heat margarine until bubbly and hot; add onion and garlic and sauté until softened. Add livers and sauté over medium-high heat for 3 minutes; add green pepper and sauté for 2 minutes longer. Add tomato and sauté until just heated through; season with salt and serve.

Each serving provides: 4 Protein Exchanges; 2 Vegetable Exchanges;
1 Fat Exchange
Per serving: 262 calories; 32 g protein; 9 g fat; 13 g carbohydrate; 38 mg calcium;
189 mg sodium; 846 mg cholesterol

Fruit 'n' Rice-Filled Liver

WEEK 4 ∽ MAKES 2 SERVINGS

1 tablespoon margarine, divided
½ cup sliced onion
¼ cup minced celery
1 garlic clove, minced
¼ cup dry sherry
1 small apple, cored, pared, and diced
2 tablespoons raisins
½ teaspoon salt

Dash each white pepper, ground sage, and ground nutmeg
½ cup cooked long-grain rice
2 slices calf or beef liver (5 ounces each)
2 tablespoons buttermilk
3 tablespoons plain dried bread crumbs

1. In 9-inch skillet heat 2 teaspoons margarine until bubbly and hot; add onion, celery, and garlic and sauté until onion is translucent, about 5 minutes. Add sherry, then apple, raisins, and seasonings; cover and cook, stirring occasionally, until most of liquid evaporates, about 5 minutes. Add rice and stir to combine; remove from heat and set aside.

2. Dip each slice of liver into buttermilk, coating both sides, then into bread crumbs, being sure to use all of the milk and crumbs.

3. Spray an 8 x 8 x 2-inch baking pan with nonstick cooking spray. Place 1 slice of breaded liver in pan; top with fruit mixture, then second liver slice. Secure with toothpicks (some stuffing may fall into pan). Dot liver with remaining teaspoon margarine.

4. Bake at 375°F. until liver is cooked but, when pierced with a fork, still slightly pink on the inside, about 20 minutes.

Each serving provides: 4 Protein Exchanges; 1 Bread Exchange;
¾ Vegetable Exchange; 1½ Fat Exchanges; 1 Fruit Exchange;
40 calories Optional Exchange
Per serving with calf liver: 457 calories; 31 g protein; 13 g fat; 46 g carbohydrate;
86 mg calcium; 822 mg sodium; 426 mg cholesterol
With beef liver: 457 calories; 32 g protein; 12 g fat; 47 g carbohydrate;
84 mg calcium; 911 mg sodium; 426 mg cholesterol

Herbed Liver-Vegetable Medley ◐

WEEK 4 ∾ MAKES 2 SERVINGS

2 teaspoons vegetable oil
1 cup sliced mushrooms
½ cup each julienne-cut carrot and
 green bell pepper (thin strips)
1 garlic clove, minced
10 ounces calf liver, cut into
 1-inch-wide strips
½ cup canned chicken broth, divided
2 teaspoons all-purpose flour

2 medium tomatoes, blanched,
 peeled, seeded, and chopped
¼ teaspoon rosemary leaves,
 crushed
Dash each salt and pepper

Garnish
1 tablespoon chopped fresh parsley

In 9-inch skillet heat oil; add mushrooms, carrot, green pepper, and garlic and sauté until vegetables are tender-crisp, about 5 minutes. Add liver and cook, stirring quickly, until all pink has disappeared, about 5 minutes. In small cup combine 1 tablespoon broth with the flour, stirring to dissolve flour; add to liver mixture along with remaining ingredients except parsley. Cook, stirring constantly, until sauce is thickened; serve sprinkled with parsley.

Each serving provides: 4 Protein Exchanges; 4 Vegetable Exchanges;
 1 Fat Exchange; 20 calories Optional Exchange
Per serving: 321 calories; 32 g protein; 12 g fat; 21 g carbohydrate; 54 mg calcium;
 399 mg sodium; 425 mg cholesterol

Skillet Liver, Peppers, and Onions ◐

WEEK 4 ∾ MAKES 2 SERVINGS

1 cup each sliced onions (separated
 into rings) and green bell peppers
 (rings)
½ teaspoon marjoram leaves
3 tablespoons all-purpose flour
½ teaspoon salt

Dash freshly ground pepper
10 ounces calf liver, thinly sliced
1 tablespoon plus 1 teaspoon
 reduced-calorie margarine
1½ cups cooked long-grain rice
 (hot)

Spray 10-inch nonstick skillet with nonstick cooking spray; add onion and pepper rings and cook, stirring occasionally, just until tender.

Remove vegetables from skillet and sprinkle with marjoram; set aside and keep warm.

On sheet of wax paper or a paper plate combine flour, salt, and pepper; dredge liver in seasoned flour, using the entire mixture to coat all sides of liver slices.

In same skillet heat margarine until bubbly and hot; add liver and sauté briefly (just until golden brown on both sides). Remove liver to serving platter and top with onion and pepper rings. Serve with rice.

Each serving provides: 4 Protein Exchanges; 2 Bread Exchanges;
2 Vegetable Exchanges; 1 Fat Exchange
Per serving: 495 calories; 34 g protein; 11 g fat; 64 g carbohydrate; 70 mg calcium;
753 mg sodium; 425 mg cholesterol

Beef or Calf Liver in Wine Sauce ◐❸

WEEK 2 ❧ MAKES 2 SERVINGS

This dish is also delicious with chicken livers.

2 teaspoons margarine
1/2 cup chopped onion
1 small garlic clove, minced
10 ounces beef or calf liver, thinly
  sliced
2 tablespoons plus 2 teaspoons
  white wine

1/8 teaspoon ground thyme
2 slices white bread, toasted and
  cut diagonally into halves
2 teaspoons chopped fresh parsley

In 9- or 10-inch skillet heat margarine until bubbly and hot; add onion and garlic and sauté until onion is softened. Add liver and cook, turning once, until slices are firm, 5 to 7 minutes; add wine and thyme and cook for 2 minutes longer. On each of 2 plates arrange 2 toast triangles; top each portion of toast with half of the liver mixture and sprinkle each with 1 teaspoon parsley.

Each serving provides: 4 Protein Exchanges; 1 Bread Exchange;
1/2 Vegetable Exchange; 1 Fat Exchange; 20 calories Optional Exchange
Per serving with beef liver: 330 calories; 31 g protein; 10 g fat; 24 g carbohydrate;
51 mg calcium; 361 mg sodium; 426 mg cholesterol
With calf liver: 330 calories; 31 g protein; 12 g fat; 23 g carbohydrate;
49 mg calcium; 272 mg sodium; 426 mg cholesterol

Calf Liver Jardinière ◐

WEEK 4 ∽ MAKES 2 SERVINGS

1 tablespoon all-purpose flour
Dash each salt and pepper
2 slices calf liver (5 ounces each)
1 tablespoon vegetable oil
1 cup thinly sliced onions

½ cup each julienne-cut carrot and
  celery (3 x ¼-inch strips)
1 cup canned Italian tomatoes,
  drained and chopped (reserve
  liquid)

1. On paper plate combine flour, salt, and pepper. Dredge liver In flour mixture, coating both sides.

2. In 10-inch nonstick skillet heat oil over high heat; add liver and brown quickly on both sides. Remove liver from skillet to a plate and set aside.

3. Reduce heat to medium and add onions, carrot, and celery to same skillet; sauté, stirring to prevent sticking, until onions are browned. Add reserved tomato liquid, reduce heat to low, cover, and let simmer until vegetables are tender, about 5 minutes.

4. Stir tomatoes into vegetable mixture; top with liver, cover, and let simmer until mixture is thoroughly heated, about 5 minutes.

Each serving provides: 4 Protein Exchanges; 3 Vegetable Exchanges;
  1½ Fat Exchanges; 15 calories Optional Exchange
Per serving: 342 calories; 31 g protein; 14 g fat; 25 g carbohydrate; 68 mg calcium;
  383 mg sodium; 425 mg cholesterol

Deviled Calf Liver ◐

WEEK 4 ∽ MAKES 2 SERVINGS

⅓ cup plus 2 teaspoons sour cream
½ teaspoon Dijon-style mustard
¼ teaspoon Worcestershire sauce
2 teaspoons margarine
½ cup diced onion

10 ounces calf liver, cut into
  ½-inch-wide strips
2 teaspoons all-purpose flour
⅛ teaspoon thyme leaves
Dash each pepper and salt

In small bowl combine sour cream, mustard, and Worcestershire sauce; set aside.

In 9-inch skillet heat margarine until bubbly and hot; add onion and sauté until softened. Add liver and sprinkle with flour; add thyme and pepper and sauté over medium-high heat until liver strips are browned on the outside but still pink on the inside, about 5 minutes. Reduce heat to low and stir in sour cream mixture; heat but *do not boil.* Season with salt.

Each serving provides: 4 Protein Exchanges; ½ Vegetable Exchange;
  1 Fat Exchange; 110 calories Optional Exchange
Per serving: 350 calories; 29 g protein; 20 g fat; 13 g carbohydrate; 76 mg calcium;
  282 mg sodium; 444 mg cholesterol

Variation: Substitute ½ cup plain low-fat yogurt for the sour cream. Add ½ Milk Exchange to Exchange Information and reduce Optional Exchange to 10 calories.

Per serving: 294 calories; 31 g protein; 12 g fat; 15 g carbohydrate; 129 mg calcium;
  298 mg sodium; 429 mg cholesterol

Easy Beef Liver Sauté ◑❸

WEEK 1 ✎ MAKES 2 SERVINGS

2 teaspoons margarine
10 ounces beef liver, cut into 3 x
  1-inch strips
1 cup thinly sliced onions
2 medium tomatoes, blanched,
  peeled, and cut into wedges

1 teaspoon salt
¼ teaspoon pepper

Garnish

Chopped fresh parsley

In 12-inch nonstick skillet heat margarine over medium heat until bubbly and hot. Increase heat, add liver and onions, and sauté, stirring occasionally, until liver is browned and onions are tender, about 5 minutes. Reduce heat and add tomatoes, salt, and pepper; cook, stirring occasionally, until tomatoes are thoroughly heated. Serve garnished with parsley.

Each serving provides: 4 Protein Exchanges; 3 Vegetable Exchanges;
  1 Fat Exchange
Per serving: 295 calories; 31 g protein; 10 g fat; 21 g carbohydrate; 62 mg calcium;
  1,324 mg sodium; 425 mg cholesterol

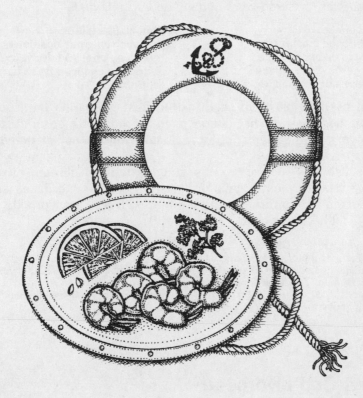

Fish

You don't have to be an outdoor-sports lover to enjoy the lure of fish, for what can be better than casting for economical, wholesome, flavorful meals and catching some compliments at the same time? Seafood is delicious in combination with other ingredients, as in our Quick Jambalaya, but it can swim exquisitely on its own, as in Butterfly Shrimp with Honey Sauce.

Remember, if you use the freshest fish available and never overcook it, you'll be hooked on some unforgettable dishes.

Baked Fish with Mushroom-Wine Sauce ◐

WEEK 2 ∽ MAKES 2 SERVINGS

Cod, haddock, or scrod work equally well in this dish.

2 teaspoons margarine
1 cup chopped mushrooms
2 tablespoons lemon juice
1 small garlic clove, minced
Dash each salt and pepper

10 ounces fish fillets
¼ cup each chopped scallions
  (green onions) and dry vermouth
1 tablespoon chopped fresh parsley
  (optional)

Preheat oven to 400°F. In small skillet heat margarine until bubbly and hot; add mushrooms, lemon juice, garlic, and seasonings and sauté over high heat, stirring occasionally, until most of liquid has evaporated.

Place fish in 1-quart casserole and top with mushroom mixture, scallions, and vermouth; bake until fish is opaque and flakes easily when tested with a fork, about 10 minutes. If desired, sprinkle with parsley just before serving.

Each serving provides: 4 Protein Exchanges; 1¼ Vegetable Exchanges;
  1 Fat Exchange; 30 calories Optional Exchange
Per serving with cod or scrod: 196 calories; 26 g protein; 4 g fat; 5 g carbohydrate;
  26 mg calcium; 218 mg sodium; 71 mg cholesterol
With haddock: 197 calories; 27 g protein; 4 g fat; 5 g carbohydrate; 44 mg calcium;
  205 mg sodium; 85 mg cholesterol

Baked Cod Livornese

WEEK 2 ∽ MAKES 2 SERVINGS

2 teaspoons olive oil
¼ cup chopped onion
1 garlic clove, minced
½ cup chopped mushrooms
¼ cup white wine
½ cup canned Italian tomatoes,
  chopped

¼ teaspoon each basil leaves,
  oregano leaves, and salt
Dash pepper
10 ounces cod fillets
2 teaspoons grated Parmesan
  cheese
1 tablespoon chopped fresh parsley

Preheat oven to 400°F. In 10-inch skillet heat oil; add onion and garlic and sauté until onion is translucent, about 1 minute. Add mush-

FISH · 377

rooms and cook until mushrooms are just tender, about 2 minutes; add wine and bring to a boil. Add tomatoes and seasonings and cook, stirring occasionally, until sauce thickens, about 2 minutes.

In shallow 1-quart flameproof casserole arrange fillets and top with sauce; sprinkle with cheese and bake until fish flakes easily at the touch of a fork, 15 to 20 minutes.

Using slotted pancake turner, carefully remove fish from casserole to serving platter; keep fish warm. Place casserole over medium heat and cook remaining pan juices until reduced and thickened, about 2 minutes; pour over fish and serve sprinkled with parsley.

Each serving provides: 4 Protein Exchanges; 1¼ Vegetable Exchanges;
  1 Fat Exchange; 40 calories Optional Exchange
Per serving: 213 calories; 27 g protein; 6 g fat; 7 g carbohydrate; 64 mg calcium;
  485 mg sodium; 72 mg cholesterol

Portuguese Cod Fillets ◑

WEEK 4 ～ MAKES 2 SERVINGS

1 tablespoon olive oil, divided
¼ cup diced onion
1 garlic clove, minced
½ cup diced green bell pepper
¾ cup canned crushed tomatoes
2 tablespoons white wine

4 pitted black olives, sliced
10 ounces cod fillets
Dash each salt and pepper

Garnish
2 teaspoons chopped fresh parsley

In 1-quart saucepan heat 1 teaspoon oil; add onion and garlic and sauté until onion is softened. Add green pepper and sauté for 3 minutes longer. Add tomatoes, wine, and olives; cover and let simmer, stirring occasionally, for 10 minutes.

Sprinkle both sides of cod fillets with salt and pepper. In 9-inch skillet heat remaining 2 teaspoons oil; add fish and cook for 3 to 4 minutes. Turn fish over and top with vegetable mixture; let simmer until fish flakes easily when tested with a fork and vegetables are hot, about 3 minutes. Transfer to platter and serve.

Each serving provides: 4 Protein Exchanges; 1½ Vegetable Exchanges;
  1½ Fat Exchanges; 25 calories Optional Exchange
Per serving: 229 calories; 26 g protein; 9 g fat; 8 g carbohydrate; 56 mg calcium;
  368 mg sodium; 71 mg cholesterol

Flounder Florentine

WEEK 1 ❤ MAKES 2 SERVINGS

¼ cup chopped onion
1 garlic clove, minced
1 cup sliced mushrooms
¾ cup well-drained cooked chopped
   spinach
Dash each salt and pepper

2 flounder fillets (5 ounces each)
2 teaspoons mayonnaise
1 teaspoon Dijon-style mustard
1 tablespoon each lemon juice and
   chopped fresh parsley

1. In 10-inch nonstick skillet combine onion and garlic; cover and cook until onion is soft. Add mushrooms and cook, stirring constantly, until all liquid has evaporated; add spinach, salt, and pepper and stir to combine.

2. Preheat oven to 400°F. Spoon half of spinach mixture onto center of each fillet; roll fillets to enclose fillings and place seam-side down in shallow 1-quart casserole.

3. In small cup combine mayonnaise and mustard; spread mixture evenly over fish rolls and sprinkle with lemon juice.

4. Bake until fish is lightly browned, 15 to 20 minutes. Serve sprinkled with parsley.

Each serving provides: 4 Protein Exchanges; 2 Vegetable Exchanges;
   1 Fat Exchange
Per serving: 187 calories; 27 g protein; 5 g fat; 8 g carbohydrate; 96 mg calcium;
   321 mg sodium; 74 mg cholesterol

Variation: Add 2 teaspoons grated Parmesan cheese to mayonnaise mixture and proceed as directed; add 10 calories Optional Exchange to Exchange Information.

Per serving: 195 calories; 28 g protein; 6 g fat; 8 g carbohydrate; 119 mg calcium;
   353 mg sodium; 75 mg cholesterol

Mushroom-Stuffed Flounder Roll-Ups

WEEK 1 ⟡ MAKES 2 SERVINGS

2 teaspoons olive oil, divided
1/2 cup chopped scallions (green
  onions)
1 garlic clove, minced
1 cup chopped mushrooms
1 teaspoon salt, divided

1/8 teaspoon each pepper and ground
  thyme
2 flounder fillets (5 ounces each)
1 teaspoon each lemon juice and
  chopped fresh parsley
1/2 teaspoon grated lemon peel

In small skillet heat 1 teaspoon oil; add scallions and garlic and sauté until softened. Add mushrooms, 1/4 teaspoon salt, and the pepper and thyme and sauté for 5 minutes.

Preheat oven to 400°F. Sprinkle fillets with lemon juice and remaining 3/4 teaspoon salt. Spoon half of mushroom mixture onto center of each fillet and roll to enclose filling; secure each with a toothpick. Transfer rolls seam-side down to shallow 1-quart flameproof casserole; sprinkle each roll with 1/2 teaspoon parsley and 1/4 teaspoon lemon peel, then 1/2 teaspoon oil. Bake until fish flakes easily when tested with a fork, about 15 minutes. Carefully remove rolls to serving plate; remove toothpicks before serving.

Each serving provides: 4 Protein Exchanges; 1½ Vegetable Exchanges;
  1 Fat Exchange
Per serving: 178 calories; 25 g protein; 6 g fat; 5 g carbohydrate; 42 mg calcium;
  1,191 mg sodium; 71 mg cholesterol

Variation: Week 4—Stir 1 tablespoon plus 1½ teaspoons plain dried bread crumbs into sauteed mushroom mixture; roll fillets as directed. Combine the lemon peel and parsley with an additional 1 tablespoon plus 1½ teaspoons crumbs and sprinkle over fish, then sprinkle with oil and bake as directed. Add 1/2 Bread Exchange to Exchange Information.

Per serving: 216 calories; 26 g protein; 6 g fat; 12 g carbohydrate; 54 mg calcium;
  1,265 mg sodium; 71 mg cholesterol

Salmon with Asparagus Sauce ◐

WEEK 2 ∽ MAKES 2 SERVINGS

---

2 teaspoons olive oil
1 tablespoon minced shallots
1 garlic clove, minced
½ cup cooked chopped asparagus
½ teaspoon salt, divided
¼ teaspoon white pepper, divided

2 teaspoons mayonnaise
¼ teaspoon Dijon-style mustard
1 salmon fillet, 10 ounces
¼ cup dry white wine
2 teaspoons grated Parmesan
 cheese

1. In 9-inch skillet heat oil; add shallots and garlic and sauté until shallots are translucent, being careful not to burn garlic.

2. Transfer shallot mixture to blender container. Add asparagus, ¼ teaspoon salt, and ⅛ teaspoon pepper and process until smooth; set aside.

3. Preheat oven to 400°F. In small bowl combine mayonnaise and mustard; spread on fillet and sprinkle with remaining ¼ teaspoon salt and ⅛ teaspoon pepper. Transfer salmon to 8 x 8 x 2-inch non-stick baking pan; add wine and bake until fish flakes easily when tested with a fork, about 15 minutes (exact timing will depend upon thickness of fillet).

4. Remove pan from oven and turn oven control to broil. Spread asparagus puree over fish and sprinkle with cheese. Broil just until heated through.

Each serving provides: 4 Protein Exchanges; ½ Vegetable Exchange;
 2 Fat Exchanges; 40 calories Optional Exchange
Per serving: 431 calories; 34 g protein; 28 g fat; 5 g carbohydrate; 155 mg calcium;
 722 mg sodium; 59 mg cholesterol

Batter "Fried" Fish
with Sweet 'n' Sour Medley ❸

WEEK 4 ◇ MAKES 2 SERVINGS

Sweet 'n' Sour Medley

½ cup diagonally sliced carrot
  (thin slices)
¼ cup water
½ cup canned pineapple chunks
  (no sugar added), drain and
  reserve juice
¼ cup each diced red and green
  bell peppers
2 teaspoons each firmly packed
  brown sugar and teriyaki sauce
1 teaspoon each cornstarch and
  rice wine vinegar
⅛ teaspoon salt

Batter and Fish

3 tablespoons all-purpose flour
¼ teaspoon double-acting baking
  powder
⅛ teaspoon salt
3 tablespoons water
10 ounces scrod fillets, cut into
  1-inch pieces
1 tablespoon plus 1 teaspoon
  vegetable oil

To Prepare Sweet 'n' Sour Medley: In 1-quart saucepan combine carrot and water; bring to a boil. Reduce heat, cover, and let simmer until carrot slices are tender, about 3 minutes; stir in pineapple chunks and red and green peppers and cook until mixture is heated. In measuring cup or small bowl combine reserved pineapple juice with remaining ingredients for sweet 'n' sour medley, stirring to dissolve cornstarch; pour over carrot mixture and cook, stirring constantly, until mixture thickens and is thoroughly heated. Set aside.

To Prepare Fish: In small bowl, using fork, combine dry ingredients; add water and stir until batter is smooth. Add fish pieces to batter and turn until thoroughly coated.

In 10-inch nonstick skillet heat oil over medium-high heat; add fish and cook until golden brown on bottom, 3 to 4 minutes. Carefully turn pieces over and cook until other side is browned; remove to a serving platter and top with warm sweet 'n' sour medley.

Each serving provides: 4 Protein Exchanges; ½ Bread Exchange;
  1 Vegetable Exchange; 2 Fat Exchanges, ½ Fruit Exchange;
  25 calories Optional Exchange
Per serving: 323 calories; 27 g protein; 9 g fat; 31 g carbohydrate; 71 mg calcium;
  652 mg sodium; 71 mg cholesterol

Variation: Substitute flounder or sole fillets for the scrod.

Per serving: 324 calories; 26 g protein; 11 g fat; 31 g carbohydrate; 73 mg calcium;
  663 mg sodium; 71 mg cholesterol

Salmon-Cheese Ball

WEEK 1 ∽ MAKES 4 SERVINGS

1 cup pot cheese, forced through a sieve
5 ounces skinned and boned drained canned salmon, flaked
2 tablespoons each finely chopped scallion (green onion) and lemon juice
1 tablespoon plus 1 teaspoon mayonnaise
2 teaspoons each prepared horseradish and Dijon-style mustard
8 iceberg, romaine, or loose-leafed lettuce leaves
1 medium tomato, thinly sliced
2 tablespoons chopped fresh dill (optional)

In medium bowl combine cheese, salmon, scallion, lemon juice, mayonnaise, horseradish, and mustard; stir until thoroughly combined. Place cheese mixture in 2-cup measure, cover, and refrigerate for at least 2 hours.

To serve, line serving plate with lettuce leaves and top with tomato slices, arranged in a circular pattern with slices overlapping; invert measuring cup on tomato slices (mixture will slide out). If desired, sprinkle dill evenly over surface of cheese ball and gently pat down.

Each serving provides: 2 Protein Exchanges; 1 Vegetable Exchange; 1 Fat Exchange
Per serving: 145 calories; 17 g protein; 6 g fat; 5 g carbohydrate; 382 mg calcium; 465 mg sodium; 5 mg cholesterol

Scrod Florentine ◑❸

WEEK 1 ∽ MAKES 2 SERVINGS

If frozen fish is used, reduce salt to 1/4 teaspoon.

10 ounces scrod fillets
1/2 teaspoon salt, divided
1 teaspoon margarine
1/2 garlic clove, minced
1 cup well-drained cooked chopped spinach
1 tablespoon lemon juice
Dash pepper

Preheat oven to 350°F. Spray a shallow 1-quart casserole with non-stick cooking spray; arrange fillets in casserole and sprinkle with half of the salt. Bake until fish flakes easily when tested with a fork, 10 to 12 minutes.

While fish is baking, in small nonstick skillet heat margarine until bubbly and hot; add garlic and sauté briefly (*do not brown*). Add spinach, lemon juice, pepper, and remaining salt; cook for 2 to 3 minutes.

When fish is done, spoon spinach mixture over fillets; return to oven and bake until thoroughly heated, 3 to 5 minutes.

Each serving provides: 4 Protein Exchanges; 1 Vegetable Exchange;
½ Fat Exchange
Per serving: 151 calories; 28 g protein; 3 g fat; 4 g carbohydrate; 105 mg calcium;
706 mg sodium; 71 mg cholesterol

Variation: Week 2—Add 1 tablespoon plus 1 teaspoon white wine to skillet with spinach and other ingredients; proceed as directed. Add 10 calories Optional Exchange to Exchange Information.

Per serving: 161 calories; 28 g protein; 3 g fat; 5 g carbohydrate; 106 mg calcium;
707 mg sodium; 71 mg cholesterol

Artichoke-Stuffed Red Snapper

WEEK 4 ∽ MAKES 6 SERVINGS

1 tablespoon vegetable oil	1 teaspoon salt
¾ cup finely chopped onions	½ teaspoon pepper
1½ cups frozen artichoke hearts, thawed and chopped	1 red snapper, 3 pounds dressed with head and tail left on*
3 slices white bread, toasted and made into fine crumbs	1 cup mixed vegetable juice
¼ cup each chopped fresh parsley and lemon juice	

Preheat oven to 350°F. In 9-inch skillet heat oil; add onions and sauté until translucent. Add artichoke hearts and sauté for 3 minutes longer. Stir in bread crumbs, parsley, lemon juice, salt, and pepper; remove from heat and allow mixture to cool slightly.

Stuff fish with artichoke mixture, using toothpicks or wooden skewers to close cavity. Spray baking dish that is large enough to hold fish flat with nonstick cooking spray; transfer stuffed snapper to dish and pour vegetable juice over fish. Bake, basting frequently with pan juices, until fish flakes easily at the touch of a fork, 40 to 50 minutes.

Each serving provides: 4 Protein Exchanges; ½ Bread Exchange;
¾ Vegetable Exchange; ½ Fat Exchange; 10 calories Optional Exchange
Per serving: 218 calories; 31 g protein; 4 g fat; 13 g carbohydrate; 61 mg calcium;
617 mg sodium; 78 mg cholesterol

* A 3-pound dressed red snapper will yield about 1½ pounds cooked fish.

Fillet Diable ⬗❸

WEEK 4 ～ MAKES 2 SERVINGS

2 teaspoons margarine
1 teaspoon all-purpose flour
¼ cup water
2 tablespoons dry white wine
1 teaspoon Dijon-style mustard
1 teaspoon drained capers
½ teaspoon grated lemon rind
⅛ teaspoon white pepper, divided

2 fillets of sole (5 ounces each)
1 teaspoon lemon juice
⅛ teaspoon salt

Garnish

2 thin lemon slices, chopped fresh
  parsley, and parsley sprigs

In small saucepan heat margarine until bubbly and hot. Sprinkle with flour and stir quickly to combine; cook over low heat, stirring constantly, for 1 minute. Remove from heat; stir in water, wine, and mustard. Return to heat and bring mixture to a boil; reduce heat and let simmer, stirring constantly, until sauce is thickened. Stir in capers, lemon rind, and dash pepper; remove from heat and keep warm.

Sprinkle sole fillets with lemon juice and remaining pepper. Spray rack of broiling pan with nonstick cooking spray; transfer fish to rack and broil until fish flakes easily when tested with a fork, about 5 minutes. Sprinkle fillets with salt, then transfer to serving platter. Spoon sauce over fish; garnish with lemon and parsley.

Each serving provides: 4 Protein Exchanges; 1 Fat Exchange;
  20 calories Optional Exchange
Per serving: 167 calories; 24 g protein; 5 g fat; 2 g carbohydrate; 22 mg calcium;
  406 mg sodium; 71 mg cholesterol

Fish au Gratin ⬗❸

WEEK 4 ～ MAKES 4 SERVINGS

15 ounces sole fillets
½ teaspoon each salt and pepper
1 tablespoon plus 1 teaspoon
  margarine
1 teaspoon all-purpose flour ·
1 cup skim milk

4 ounces extra-sharp Cheddar
  cheese, shredded

Garnish

Parsley sprigs

Preheat oven to 350°F. Spray shallow 2-quart flameproof casserole with nonstick cooking spray. Arrange fillets in casserole and sprinkle evenly with salt and pepper; bake until fish flakes easily when tested with a fork, 10 to 15 minutes.

While fish is baking, prepare sauce. In 1-quart nonstick saucepan melt margarine; add flour and cook, stirring constantly, for 1 minute. Using wire whisk, gradually stir in milk and, stirring constantly, heat just to the boiling point. Reduce heat, add cheese, and simmer, stirring constantly, until mixture thickens and cheese is melted.

Pour cheese sauce over fish and broil until sauce is browned, 1 to 2 minutes. Serve garnished with parsley.

Each serving provides: 4 Protein Exchanges; 1 Fat Exchange;
¼ Milk Exchange; 3 calories Optional Exchange
Per serving: 257 calories; 27 g protein; 14 g fat; 4 g carbohydrate; 298 mg calcium;
604 mg sodium; 84 mg cholesterol

Rice-Stuffed Fish Rolls with Lemon Sauce ❶

WEEK 4 ~ MAKES 2 SERVINGS, 1 FISH ROLL EACH

1 tablespoon margarine, divided	2 fish fillets (5 ounces each)
½ cup cooked long-grain rice	Paprika
¼ cup minced carrot	1 teaspoon all-purpose flour
2 tablespoons chopped fresh parsley	¼ cup skim milk (at room
¼ teaspoon salt	temperature)
Dash pepper	2 teaspoons lemon juice

Preheat oven to 350°F. In small flameproof container melt 1 teaspoon margarine; set aside remaining margarine. In small bowl combine ½ teaspoon melted margarine with the rice, carrot, parsley, salt, and pepper, mixing well; spoon an equal amount of mixture onto each fillet and roll fish to enclose filling. Place rolls seam-side down in shallow 1-quart casserole and drizzle with remaining melted margarine; sprinkle each roll with dash paprika and bake until fish flakes easily at the touch of a fork, 15 to 20 minutes.

While fish is baking, in small nonstick saucepan heat remaining 2 teaspoons margarine over medium-low heat until bubbly and hot; add flour and stir until combined. Gradually stir in milk and cook, stirring constantly, until mixture thickens, 2 to 3 minutes; stir in lemon juice and dash paprika and cook until heated (do not boil). Carefully transfer fish rolls to serving platter and top with sauce.

Each serving provides: 4 Protein Exchanges; ½ Bread Exchange;
¼ Vegetable Exchange; 1½ Fat Exchanges; 15 calories Optional Exchange
Per serving: 242 calories; 27 g protein; 6 g fat; 17 g carbohydrate; 71 mg calcium;
460 mg sodium; 71 mg cholesterol

Lemon Ring Mold
with Tuna-Cheddar Salad ❶

WEEK 1 ～ MAKES 4 SERVINGS

An attractive light summer meal; perfect for dining in the garden or on the patio. All items can be prepared ahead of time and assembled just before serving.

Mold

1 envelope (four ½-cup servings)
   low-calorie lemon-flavored
   gelatin (8 calories per ½ cup)
1 cup each boiling water and
   canned crushed tomatoes
½ cup diced green bell pepper
2 tablespoons minced onion
½ teaspoon salt
¼ teaspoon Worcestershire sauce
3 drops hot sauce

Salad

8 ounces drained canned chunk
   white tuna, flaked
2 tablespoons each diced onion and
   celery
2 tablespoons mayonnaise
Dash each salt and pepper
1 cup shredded iceberg lettuce
4 ounces Cheddar cheese, cut into
   four 1-ounce squares

To Prepare Mold: Spray 3-cup ring mold with nonstick cooking spray and set aside. In medium heatproof bowl sprinkle gelatin over boiling water and stir until dissolved; add remaining ingredients for mold to gelatin mixture and stir until combined. Pour mixture into sprayed mold, cover with plastic wrap, and refrigerate until set, at least 3 hours.

To Prepare Salad and Serve: In bowl combine tuna, onion, celery, mayonnaise, salt, and pepper, mixing thoroughly. Unmold gelatin ring onto large serving platter and fill center of ring with tuna mixture; arrange lettuce around ring. Cut each Cheddar square in half diagonally, forming 8 triangles; arrange triangles on shredded lettuce.

Each serving provides: 3 Protein Exchanges; 1½ Vegetable Exchanges;
   1½ Fat Exchanges; 8 calories Optional Exchange
Per serving: 307 calories; 23 g protein; 22 g fat; 5 g carbohydrate; 243 mg calcium;
   903 mg sodium; 49 mg cholesterol

Variations:

   1. Substitute 8 ounces chopped skinned cooked chicken or chopped shelled and deveined cooked shrimp for the tuna.

Per serving with chicken: 295 calories; 25 g protein; 19 g fat; 5 g carbohydrate;
   246 mg calcium; 680 mg sodium; 84 mg cholesterol
With shrimp: 253 calories; 22 g protein; 16 g fat; 6 g carbohydrate; 303 mg calcium;
   710 mg sodium; 119 mg cholesterol

2. For a less sweet mold, substitute 1 envelope unflavored gelatin for the lemon-flavored gelatin; add 2 tablespoons lemon juice with "remaining ingredients" and increase salt to 1 teaspoon. Eliminate Optional Exchange from Exchange Information. Increase sodium for tuna salad to 1,152 mg; for chicken salad to 928 mg; for shrimp salad to 951 mg.

Tuna Canapés ◑❸

WEEK 4 ～ MAKES 4 SERVINGS, 1 CANAPÉ EACH

2 ounces drained canned chunk white tuna, finely ground in food processor
3 tablespoons whipped cream cheese
1 tablespoon chopped drained canned pimiento

2 teaspoons each mayonnaise and pickle relish
Dash each salt and Worcestershire sauce
2 thin slices each white and whole wheat or rye bread (½ ounce each slice), lightly toasted

In small bowl combine all ingredients except toast and mix to a smooth spread. Onto each of 3 slices of toast spread ⅓ of the tuna mixture, spreading to ¼ inch from edge of bread; stack slices, alternating white bread with whole wheat (or rye) bread, and top with remaining slice of toast. Cut stack diagonally into quarters.

Each serving provides: ½ Protein Exchange; ½ Bread Exchange; ½ Fat Exchange; 30 calories Optional Exchange
Per serving with white and whole wheat bread: 112 calories; 6 g protein; 6 g fat; 8 g carbohydrate; 21 mg calcium; 228 mg sodium; 13 mg cholesterol
With white and rye bread: 112 calories; 5 g protein; 6 g fat; 9 g carbohydrate; 20 mg calcium; 230 mg sodium; 13 mg cholesterol

Tuna Salad with Lemon-French Dressing ◐

WEEK 1 ⌒ MAKES 2 SERVINGS

2 medium tomatoes, chopped
8 romaine lettuce leaves, torn into
 ½-inch pieces
4 ounces drained canned tuna, flaked
1 tablespoon chopped scallion
 (green onion)
2 teaspoons olive oil

½ teaspoon Dijon-style mustard
1 tablespoon lemon juice
1½ teaspoons each red wine
 vinegar and water
⅛ teaspoon each salt and pepper
2 teaspoons chopped fresh parsley

In salad bowl combine tomatoes, lettuce, tuna, and scallion. In small bowl combine oil and mustard and whip until creamy; add lemon juice, vinegar, water, salt, and pepper and stir to combine. Pour dressing over tuna mixture and toss; sprinkle with parsley.

Each serving provides: 2 Protein Exchanges; 3 Vegetable Exchanges;
 1 Fat Exchange
Per serving: 199 calories; 16 g protein; 12 g fat; 9 g carbohydrate; 36 mg calcium;
 459 mg sodium; 15 mg cholesterol

Variation: Substitute 2 medium Belgian endives (about 3 ounces each), sliced into ½-inch pieces, for the lettuce.

Per serving: 208 calories; 17 g protein; 12 g fat; 11 g carbohydrate; 45 mg calcium;
 462 mg sodium; 15 mg cholesterol

Tuna Tacos ◐❸

WEEK 4 ⌒ MAKES 4 SERVINGS, 1 TACO EACH

1 tablespoon plus 1 teaspoon
 vegetable oil
1 cup sliced onions
3 garlic cloves, minced
1 cup each chopped tomatoes and
 tomato sauce
⅛ teaspoon each oregano leaves,
 salt, and pepper

Dash hot sauce
8 ounces drained canned tuna, flaked
4 taco shells
4 ounces Cheddar cheese, shredded
1 cup shredded lettuce

In 10-inch skillet heat oil; add onions and garlic and sauté until onions are translucent, about 5 minutes. Add tomatoes, tomato sauce, and seasonings; cook, stirring occasionally, for 5 minutes. Stir in tuna and cook until heated through.

Fill each taco shell with ¼ of tuna mixture and top each portion with 1 ounce cheese and ¼ cup lettuce.

Each serving provides: 3 Protein Exchanges; 1 Bread Exchange;
  2½ Vegetable Exchanges; 1 Fat Exchange
Per serving: 375 calories; 24 g protein; 23 g fat; 18 g carbohydrate; 233 mg calcium;
  821 mg sodium; 45 mg cholesterol

Variation: Just before serving, top each taco with 1 tablespoon plain low-fat yogurt; add 10 calories Optional Exchange to Exchange Information.

Per serving: 384 calories; 24 g protein; 23 g fat; 19 g carbohydrate; 259 mg calcium;
  830 mg sodium; 45 mg cholesterol

Spinach Pasta with Tuna Sauce ❶❸

WEEK 4 ∽ MAKES 4 SERVINGS

---

2 tablespoons margarine
1 garlic clove, sliced
1 cup thinly sliced mushrooms
½ cup each diced onion and green
  bell pepper
2 teaspoons all-purpose flour
1 cup skim milk
¾ cup water
2 packets instant chicken broth and
  seasoning mix

12 ounces drained canned chunk
  white tuna, flaked
1 tablespoon each chopped fresh
  basil and Italian (flat-leaf) parsley
2 cups cooked spinach pasta (hot)
1 tablespoon plus 1 teaspoon grated
  Parmesan cheese

In 12-inch nonstick skillet heat margarine until bubbly and hot; add garlic and sauté until golden. Using slotted spoon, remove and discard garlic.

To same skillet add mushrooms, onion, and green pepper and sauté until onion is lightly browned. Sprinkle vegetables with flour and stir quickly to combine; cook, stirring constantly, for 1 minute. Gradually stir in milk; add water and broth mix and, stirring constantly, bring to a boil. Reduce heat and simmer, stirring, until mixture thickens. Stir in tuna, basil, and parsley and cook until thoroughly heated. Pour sauce over hot pasta and sprinkle with cheese.

Each serving provides: 3 Protein Exchanges; 1 Bread Exchange;
  1 Vegetable Exchange; 1½ Fat Exchanges; ¼ Milk Exchange;
  20 calories Optional Exchange
Per serving: 370 calories; 29 g protein; 18 g fat; 24 g carbohydrate; 135 mg calcium;
  964 mg sodium; 45 mg cholesterol

Quick-and-Easy Tuna Pot Pie ◐ ❸

WEEK 4 ∿ MAKES 4 SERVINGS

1 tablespoon plus 1 teaspoon
  margarine
1 cup diced carrots
½ cup each diced onion and celery
1 teaspoon all-purpose flour
1 cup skim milk
1 pound drained canned chunk
  white tuna, flaked

½ teaspoon salt
⅛ teaspoon each ground thyme
  and white pepper
4 ready-to-bake refrigerated
  buttermilk flaky biscuits (1 ounce
  each)

In 10-inch nonstick skillet heat margarine until bubbly and hot; add carrots, onion, and celery and sauté until onion is translucent. Sprinkle vegetables with flour and stir quickly to combine; cook, stirring constantly, for 1 minute. Gradually stir in milk and, stirring constantly, bring to a boil. Reduce heat and simmer, stirring, until mixture thickens. Add tuna and seasonings and stir to combine; remove from heat.

Preheat oven to 400°F. Spray four 4½ x 1¼-inch foil tart pans with nonstick cooking spray; spoon ¼ of tuna mixture into each pan. Roll each biscuit between 2 sheets of wax paper, forming four 5-inch circles; set 1 circle over each portion of tuna mixture and seal by pressing edges of dough under lip of pan. Prick dough of each "pie" in several places to allow steam to escape; bake until crust is browned and filling is hot, about 10 minutes.

Each serving provides: 4 Protein Exchanges; 1 Bread Exchange;
  1 Vegetable Exchange; 1 Fat Exchange; ¼ Milk Exchange;
  3 calories Optional Exchange
Per serving: 397 calories; 34 g protein; 19 g fat; 22 g carbohydrate; 129 mg calcium;
  1,170 mg sodium; 31 mg cholesterol

Tuna-Stuffed Potato ❶

1 baking potato (6 ounces), cut in half lengthwise
6 ounces drained canned chunk white tuna
2 teaspoons margarine
¼ cup minced onion
2 teaspoons all-purpose flour, divided

½ cup plain low-fat yogurt
2 ounces Cheddar cheese, shredded, divided
2 tablespoons chopped drained canned pimiento
½ teaspoon salt
Dash each pepper and paprika

1. Preheat oven to 350°F. On nonstick baking sheet set potato halves cut-side down and bake until tender but not soft, 20 to 25 minutes. Remove from oven and let cool.

2. Scoop pulp from each potato half into work bowl of food processor, leaving ¼-inch-thick shell; reserve shells. Add tuna to potato pulp and, using an on–off motion, process until finely ground (*do not puree*); set aside.

3. In small nonstick skillet heat margarine until bubbly and hot; add onion and sauté for about 1 minute. Sprinkle with 1 teaspoon flour and stir quickly to combine; cook, stirring constantly, for about 1 minute. Remove skillet from heat.

4. In small bowl stir yogurt until creamy; stir in remaining teaspoon flour. Stir 2 tablespoons onion mixture into yogurt mixture, then add yogurt mixture to skillet and stir to combine. Add 1 ounce cheese and the pimiento, salt, pepper, paprika, and reserved tuna mixture to yogurt mixture and combine thoroughly.

5. Spoon half of tuna mixture into each reserved potato shell, mounding mixture; sprinkle each stuffed half with ½ ounce cheese and set on baking sheet. Bake at 350°F. until cheese is melted and potato is thoroughly heated, 10 to 15 minutes.

Each serving provides: 4 Protein Exchanges; 1 Bread Exchange;
  ¼ Vegetable Exchange; 1 Fat Exchange; ½ Milk Exchange;
  10 calories Optional Exchange
Per serving: 448 calories; 34 g protein; 24 g fat; 24 g carbohydrate; 334 mg calcium;
  1,212 mg sodium; 55 mg cholesterol

Tuna Provençale

WEEK 2 ✣ MAKES 4 SERVINGS

---

4 cups diced pared eggplant
   (½-inch dice)
1 teaspoon salt
1 tablespoon plus 1 teaspoon olive
   oil
2 cups sliced onions
2 garlic cloves, minced
4 cups canned crushed tomatoes

2 cups each thinly sliced green
   bell peppers and water
1 teaspoon basil leaves
½ teaspoon oregano leaves
¼ teaspoon pepper
1 pound drained canned tuna,
   flaked
1 tablespoon chopped fresh parsley

On paper towels arrange eggplant in single layer and sprinkle with salt; let stand 30 minutes, then pat dry and set aside.

In 4-quart saucepan heat oil; add onions and garlic and sauté until onions are translucent. Add eggplant, tomatoes, green peppers, water, basil, oregano, and pepper; cover and let simmer, stirring occasionally, for 35 minutes. Stir in tuna and cook for 5 minutes longer. Serve sprinkled with parsley.

Each serving provides: 4 Protein Exchanges; 6 Vegetable Exchanges;
   1 Fat Exchange
Per serving: 406 calories; 35 g protein; 19 g fat; 28 g carbohydrate; 83 mg calcium;
   1,146 mg sodium; 29 mg cholesterol

Quick-and-Easy Baked Clam Appetizers ◑ ❸

WEEK 4 ✣ MAKES 4 SERVINGS

---

4 ounces drained canned minced
   clams
⅓ cup plus 2 teaspoons seasoned
   dried bread crumbs
2 tablespoons diced onion
1 tablespoon each olive or vegetable
   oil and lemon juice
⅛ teaspoon each garlic powder
   and thyme leaves

Dash each salt and pepper
1 tablespoon chopped fresh parsley
   or ½ teaspoon dried
¼ teaspoon paprika

Garnish

Lemon wedges and parsley sprigs

In small bowl combine all ingredients except parsley, paprika, and garnish; spoon ¼ of mixture onto each of 4 flameproof scallop shells.

Preheat broiler. Sprinkle each portion of clams with an equal amount of chopped (or dried) parsley, then paprika; transfer shells to broiling pan and broil until clam mixture is browned on top, 3 to 5 minutes. Remove shells to serving platter, garnish, and serve immediately, 1 shell per portion.

Each serving provides: 1 Protein Exchange; ½ Bread Exchange;
 ½ Fat Exchange; 10 calories Optional Exchange
Per serving: 101 calories; 6 g protein; 5 g fat; 9 g carbohydrate; 34 mg calcium;
 275 mg sodium; 18 mg cholesterol

Variation: Substitute 4 ounces drained canned chunk white tuna, flaked, for the clams.

Per serving: 132 calories; 9 g protein; 7 g fat; 8 g carbohydrate; 21 mg calcium;
 377 mg sodium; 8 mg cholesterol

Crab Meat Puff Hors d'Oeuvres

WEEK 4 ～ MAKES 8 SERVINGS, 3 PUFFS EACH

2 teaspoons margarine
1 cup minced scallions (green onions)
½ cup each minced celery and red bell pepper
1 cup minced mushrooms
5 ounces cooked fresh or thawed and drained frozen crab meat, flaked
1 slice white bread, made into crumbs

2 tablespoons chopped fresh parsley
1 tablespoon plus 1 teaspoon reduced-calorie mayonnaise
1 tablespoon lemon juice
1 teaspoon each Worcestershire sauce and spicy brown mustard
½ teaspoon each salt and white pepper
24 puff shells (see Vegetable-Cheese Appetizer Puffs, page 184)

In 10-inch nonstick skillet heat margarine until bubbly and hot; add scallions, celery, and red pepper and sauté until vegetables are soft. Add mushrooms and cook over medium heat until most of liquid has evaporated, about 5 minutes. Transfer mixture to a bowl; add remaining ingredients except puff shells and mix thoroughly.

Using a sharp knife, slice off top of each puff shell and spoon an equal amount of filling (about 2 tablespoons) into each; replace tops and keep puffs warm until ready to serve.

Each serving provides: 1 Protein Exchange; ¾ Vegetable Exchange;
 2 Fat Exchanges; 40 calories Optional Exchange
Per serving: 160 calories; 7 g protein; 10 g fat; 11 g carbohydrate; 36 mg calcium;
 332 mg sodium; 109 mg cholesterol

Crab-Stuffed Artichoke Appetizer

WEEK 4 ⟳ MAKES 4 SERVINGS

Artichokes

2 small artichokes (about 8 ounces each),* prepared for cooking as directed in Parmesan-Stuffed Artichokes (see page 72)

1 tablespoon lemon juice
½ teaspoon salt

Filling

2 tablespoons sour cream
1 tablespoon plus 1 teaspoon mayonnaise
1 tablespoon chopped fresh or frozen chives
2 teaspoons chili sauce

1 teaspoon each prepared horseradish and Worcestershire sauce
½ teaspoon Dijon-style mustard
Dash hot sauce
4 ounces drained thawed frozen or canned crab meat

To Prepare Artichokes: Pour about 3 inches water into saucepan (not aluminum or cast-iron) that is just large enough to hold artichokes snugly; add lemon juice and salt and stand artichokes upright in pan. Cover pan and let simmer until bases of artichokes can be pierced easily with a fork, about 35 minutes. Remove artichokes from liquid and stand upside down to drain. When artichokes have drained thoroughly, cut each in half lengthwise; remove and discard choke and tough outer leaves.

To Prepare Filling: In medium bowl combine all ingredients for filling except crab meat; stir in crab meat, stirring until thoroughly coated with dressing. Stuff each artichoke half with ¼ of the filling; transfer to serving plate, cover with plastic wrap, and refrigerate until well chilled.

Each serving provides: 1 Protein Exchange; ½ Vegetable Exchange;
    1 Fat Exchange; 20 calories Optional Exchange
Per serving with frozen crab meat: 104 calories; 7 g protein; 6 g fat;
    7 g carbohydrate; 47 mg calcium; 474 mg sodium; 34 mg cholesterol
With canned crab meat: 106 calories; 7 g protein; 6 g fat; 8 g carbohydrate;
    48 mg calcium; 696 mg sodium; 34 mg cholesterol

* 1 cup thawed frozen artichoke hearts, cooked, may be substituted; cut each heart in half and top each with an equal amount of filling.

Variation: Substitute plain low-fat yogurt for the sour cream; reduce Optional Exchange to 10 calories.

Per serving with frozen crab meat: 93 calories; 7 g protein; 4 g fat;
  8 g carbohydrate; 52 mg calcium; 475 mg sodium; 31 mg cholesterol
With canned crab meat: 96 calories; 7 g protein; 5 g fat; 8 g carbohydrate;
  52 mg calcium; 697 mg sodium; 32 mg cholesterol

Crab and Potato-Stuffed Peppers

WEEK 2 ∾ MAKES 2 SERVINGS, 2 PEPPER HALVES EACH

2 medium green bell peppers, cut
  lengthwise into halves, seeded,
  and blanched
4 ounces thawed and thoroughly
  drained frozen crab meat, flaked
3 ounces Cheddar cheese, shredded,
  divided
1 cup each diced onions, steamed,
  and skim milk

⅔ cup instant mashed potato flakes
1 egg, beaten
2 teaspoons margarine, melted

Garnish
Parsley sprigs

1. Set pepper halves on paper towels and let drain and cool.

2. In small bowl combine crab meat, 1 ounce cheese, and remaining ingredients except parsley, stirring to thoroughly combine; let stand for 5 minutes.

3. Preheat oven to 375°F. Spoon ¼ of crab mixture into each pepper half; sprinkle each with ½ ounce shredded cheese.

4. Spray 2-quart casserole with nonstick cooking spray; set pepper halves in casserole and bake until stuffing is firm and cheese is browned, 25 to 30 minutes. Serve garnished with parsley sprigs.

Each serving provides: 4 Protein Exchanges; 1 Bread Exchange;
  3 Vegetable Exchanges; 1 Fat Exchange; ½ Milk Exchange
Per serving: 453 calories; 31 g protein; 22 g fat; 33 g carbohydrate; 536 mg calcium;
  562 mg sodium; 241 mg cholesterol

Hot Deviled Crab

WEEK 4 ∽ MAKES 4 SERVINGS

---

2 tablespoons margarine, divided
2 tablespoons each diced onion
  and red bell pepper
1 teaspoon all-purpose flour
1 cup skim milk
11 ounces thawed and thoroughly
  drained frozen crab meat
1 egg, beaten
3 tablespoons lemon juice, divided

1 tablespoon chopped fresh parsley
2 teaspoons Dijon-style mustard
4 drops hot sauce
⅓ cup plus 2 teaspoons plain dried
  bread crumbs

Garnish

Lemon crowns and dill sprigs

1. In 10-inch nonstick skillet heat 2 teaspoons margarine until bubbly and hot; add onion and pepper and sauté until onion is golden. Sprinkle vegetables with flour and stir quickly to combine; cook, stirring constantly, for 1 minute. Gradually stir in milk and, stirring constantly, bring to a boil. Reduce heat and simmer, stirring, until mixture thickens; stir in crab meat and remove from heat.

2. In small bowl combine egg with 2 tablespoons lemon juice and the parsley, mustard, and hot sauce; add ¼ cup hot crab mixture to egg mixture, stirring to combine. Pour egg mixture into skillet containing remaining crab mixture and cook over low heat, stirring constantly, until thoroughly heated (*do not boil*); remove from heat.

3. Preheat broiler. Spray 4 large or 16 small flameproof scallop shells with nonstick cooking spray; spoon an equal amount of crab mixture into each shell.

4. In small bowl combine remaining 1 tablespoon plus 1 teaspoon margarine with bread crumbs and remaining tablespoon lemon juice; sprinkle an equal amount of crumb mixture around edge of each shell and broil until crumbs are browned and crab mixture is thoroughly heated, 1 to 2 minutes. Serve garnished with lemon and dill.

Each serving provides: 3 Protein Exchanges; ½ Bread Exchange;
  ⅛ Vegetable Exchange; 1½ Fat Exchanges; ¼ Milk Exchange;
  3 calories Optional Exchange
Per serving: 214 calories; 19 g protein; 9 g fat; 13 g carbohydrate; 139 mg calcium;
  389 mg sodium; 148 mg cholesterol

Shrimp Quiche with Rice Crust

WEEK 4 ⌒ MAKES 4 SERVINGS

Crust

1½ cups cooked long-grain rice
1 egg, beaten

1 ounce Cheddar cheese, shredded
Dash each salt and pepper

Filling

2 teaspoons margarine, divided
1 cup each diced red bell peppers
  and onions
1 garlic clove, minced
6 ounces thawed frozen "ready-to-
  serve" shrimp

3 eggs, beaten
1 ounce Cheddar cheese, shredded
1 tablespoon chopped fresh parsley

Topping

2 teaspoons margarine

3 tablespoons plain dried bread
  crumbs

To Prepare Crust: Preheat oven to 425°F. Spray 9-inch quiche dish
or pie plate with nonstick cooking spray. In medium bowl combine
all ingredients for crust and press mixture over bottom and up sides
of sprayed dish; bake until firm and lightly browned, about 25 minutes. Remove from oven and set aside; reduce oven temperature to
375°F.

To Prepare Filling: In small skillet heat margarine until bubbly and
hot; add peppers, onions, and garlic and sauté, stirring occasionally,
until vegetables are tender. Transfer to medium bowl; add remaining
ingredients for filling and stir to combine. Spoon into prepared crust.

To Prepare Topping and Bake: In same skillet heat margarine until
bubbly and hot; add bread crumbs and stir to combine. Sprinkle
crumbs evenly over filling and bake until filling has set, 30 to 35 minutes (if crumb topping browns too fast, cover top of quiche with
foil). Remove quiche from oven and let stand for 10 minutes before
cutting.

Each serving provides: 3 Protein Exchanges; 1 Bread Exchange;
  1 Vegetable Exchange; 1 Fat Exchange
Per serving: 338 calories; 23 g protein; 15 g fat; 27 g carbohydrate; 218 mg calcium;
  339 mg sodium; 353 mg cholesterol

Shrimp Scampi ◑

WEEK 1 ❤ MAKES 4 SERVINGS

1¼ pounds shelled and deveined
medium shrimp
3 tablespoons lemon juice
1 tablespoon plus 1 teaspoon
margarine, melted
2 large or 4 small garlic cloves,
mashed

½ teaspoon each salt, pepper, and
paprika

Garnish
Parsley sprigs

Preheat broiler. In each of 4 individual flameproof casseroles* arrange 5 ounces shrimp. In small bowl combine remaining ingredients except parsley; pour ¼ of mixture over each portion of shrimp and toss to coat. Broil 3 to 4 inches from heat source until shrimp are golden brown, 1 to 2 minutes. Serve garnished with parsley.

Each serving provides: 4 Protein Exchanges; 1 Fat Exchange
Per serving: 169 calories; 26 g protein; 5 g fat; 4 g carbohydrate; 96 mg calcium;
514 mg sodium; 213 mg cholesterol

* If preferred, 1 shallow 2-quart flameproof casserole may be used.

Butterfly Shrimp with Honey Sauce ◑

WEEK 4 ❤ MAKES 2 SERVINGS

Shrimp
12 ounces jumbo shrimp (under
10s)
1 tablespoon plus 1½ teaspoons
all-purpose flour
1 tablespoon uncooked white
cornmeal

2 teaspoons cornstarch
1 teaspoon double-acting baking
powder
¼ cup skim milk
1 tablespoon plus 1 teaspoon
vegetable oil

Sauce
2 tablespoons teriyaki sauce
2 teaspoons dry sherry

1 teaspoon honey
½ small garlic clove, mashed

Garnish
Scallion brushes

To Prepare Shrimp: Shell and devein shrimp, leaving tail "feathers" attached. Butterfly shrimp by cutting each lengthwise along back down to tail, cutting as deep as possible without going through to other side; spread shrimp open so they lie flat.

In shallow bowl combine flour, cornmeal, cornstarch, and baking powder; add milk and stir until smooth. Add shrimp and toss to coat evenly.

In 9- or 10-inch nonstick skillet heat oil over medium-high heat; add shrimp in a single layer and cook until browned on bottom. Reduce heat to medium, turn shrimp over, and brown other side. Remove to serving platter and keep warm.

To Prepare Sauce and Serve: In small saucepan combine all ingredients for sauce and bring to a boil. Reduce heat and let simmer for 2 to 3 minutes; strain sauce into small bowl and serve with shrimp. Garnish with scallion brushes.

Each serving provides: 4 Protein Exchanges; ½ Bread Exchange;
  2 Fat Exchanges; 35 calories Optional Exchange
Per serving: 330 calories; 33 g protein; 11 g fat; 22 g carbohydrate; 249 mg calcium;
  1,063 mg sodium; 256 mg cholesterol

Quick Jambalaya ◑

WEEK 2 ⬭ MAKES 4 SERVINGS

1 tablespoon plus 1 teaspoon each vegetable oil and margarine	2 cups cooked long-grain rice
1 cup each diced celery, onions, and green bell peppers	4 ounces boiled ham, diced
4 small garlic cloves, mashed	2 bay leaves
4 cups canned crushed tomatoes	½ teaspoon each chili powder, pepper, and ground thyme
12 ounces shelled and devcined cooked shrimp	

In 12-inch nonstick skillet combine oil and margarine and heat until margarine is bubbly and hot; add diced vegetables and garlic and sauté over medium heat until vegetables are soft. Reduce heat to low, add remaining ingredients, and let simmer, stirring occasionally, until thoroughly heated. Remove bay leaves before serving.

Each serving provides: 4 Protein Exchanges; 1 Bread Exchange;
  3½ Vegetable Exchanges; 2 Fat Exchanges
Per serving: 424 calories; 34 g protein; 13 g fat; 44 g carbohydrate; 160 mg calcium;
  783 mg sodium; 153 mg cholesterol

Sautéed Shrimp with Green Sauce ◖

WEEK 2 ⌇ MAKES 2 SERVINGS

2 teaspoons olive oil
2 garlic cloves, minced
½ cup fresh basil, processed in
   blender
2 tablespoons fresh parsley,
   processed in blender
10 ounces shelled and deveined
   shrimp

¾ cup water
1 packet instant chicken broth and
   seasoning mix
Dash freshly ground pepper
1 cup cooked long-grain rice (hot)
2 teaspoons grated Parmesan
   cheese

In 9-inch skillet heat oil; add garlic and sauté briefly (*do not brown*). Stir in basil and parsley; add shrimp and sauté just until shrimp turn pink. Add water, broth mix, and pepper and cook until thoroughly heated, 3 to 5 minutes. Spoon shrimp mixture over rice and sprinkle with Parmesan cheese.

Each serving provides: 4 Protein Exchanges; 1 Bread Exchange; 1 Fat Exchange;
   15 calories Optional Exchange
Per serving: 312 calories; 30 g protein; 6 g fat; 32 g carbohydrate; 227 mg calcium;
   650 mg sodium; 214 mg cholesterol

Shrimp and Mushrooms au Gratin ◖

WEEK 4 ⌇ MAKES 2 SERVINGS

½ cup skim milk
¼ cup bottled clam juice
1 tablespoon plus 1 teaspoon dry
   sherry
¼ teaspoon salt
⅛ teaspoon each white pepper and
   powdered mustard
Dash ground red pepper

1 tablespoon margarine, divided
8 ounces shelled and deveined
   medium shrimp
1 cup sliced mushrooms
2 tablespoons chopped scallion
   (green onion)
2 teaspoons all-purpose flour
1 ounce grated Parmesan cheese

In measuring cup or small bowl combine milk, clam juice, sherry, and seasonings; set aside.

In 9-inch skillet heat 1 teaspoon margarine over medium-high heat until bubbly and hot; add shrimp and sauté until shrimp turn pink, about 3 minutes. Divide shrimp into two 1½-cup flameproof ramekins or shallow baking dishes; keep warm.

To same skillet add remaining 2 teaspoons margarine and heat until bubbly and hot; add mushrooms and scallion and sauté until most of liquid has evaporated, about 5 minutes. Sprinkle flour over vegetables and cook, stirring constantly, for 2 minutes longer. Gradually stir milk mixture into vegetable mixture and cook, stirring constantly, until thickened, about 3 minutes. Pour half of the sauce over each portion of shrimp; sprinkle each with ½ ounce cheese and broil until cheese is lightly browned, about 3 minutes.

Each serving provides: 3½ Protein Exchanges; 1⅛ Vegetable Exchanges; 1½ Fat Exchanges; ¼ Milk Exchange; 25 calories Optional Exchange
Per serving: 281 calories; 30 g protein; 11 g fat; 11 g carbohydrate; 353 mg calcium; 914 mg sodium; 185 mg cholesterol

Gazpacho Shrimp Cocktail

WEEK 4 ∽ MAKES 4 SERVINGS

½ cup each chopped green bell pepper and pared, seeded, and chopped cucumber
½ medium tomato, blanched, peeled, seeded, and chopped
2 tablespoons plus 2 teaspoons chili sauce
2 tablespoons chopped onion
1 tablespoon plus 1 teaspoon ketchup

1 tablespoon olive or vegetable oil
2 teaspoons prepared horseradish
1 teaspoon cider vinegar
¼ teaspoon Worcestershire sauce
1 small garlic clove, crushed
12 small romaine or iceberg lettuce leaves
8 ounces shelled and deveined cooked shrimp, chilled

In work bowl of food processor, or blender container, combine all ingredients except lettuce and shrimp and process until vegetables are finely chopped (*do not puree*); pour into a container, cover, and refrigerate until chilled.

Chill 4 cocktail glasses. In each glass place 3 lettuce leaves, then arrange 2 ounces of shrimp around rim of each glass. Stir dressing and ladle ¼ of mixture into center of each portion.

Each serving provides: 2 Protein Exchanges; 1½ Vegetable Exchanges; ½ Fat Exchange; 25 calories Optional Exchange
Per serving: 133 calories; 15 g protein; 4 g fat; 9 g carbohydrate; 95 mg calcium; 304 mg sodium; 85 mg cholesterol

Golden Broiled Scallops ◗

WEEK 4 ∾ MAKES 4 SERVINGS

1¼ pounds bay scallops (or sea
   scallops, cut into 1-inch pieces)
¼ cup lemon juice
2 tablespoons plus 2 teaspoons
   margarine, melted
½ teaspoon each paprika and
   pepper
¼ cup tartar sauce

Garnish
4 each lemon wedges and parsley
   sprigs

Preheat broiler. In each of 4 shallow individual flameproof casseroles* arrange 5 ounces scallops in a single layer; pour 1 tablespoon lemon juice and ¼ of the margarine over each portion and toss to coat. Sprinkle evenly with seasonings and broil until golden, about 2 minutes. Serve with tartar sauce on the side and garnish with lemon and parsley.

Each serving provides: 4 Protein Exchanges; 2 Fat Exchanges;
   75 calories Optional Exchange
Per serving: 264 calories; 22 g protein; 16 g fat; 7 g carbohydrate; 46 mg calcium;
   556 mg sodium; 57 mg cholesterol

* If preferred, 1 shallow 4-quart flameproof casserole can be used.

Scallops en Brochette

good used zucchini instead of grn pepper

WEEK 2 ∾ MAKES 2 SERVINGS, 3 SKEWERS EACH

Serve over rice.

10 ounces bay scallops (or sea
   scallops, cut into 1-inch pieces)
¼ cup dry white wine
12 small mushroom caps (about
   1-inch diameter each)
½ each medium green and red bell
   peppers, seeded and cut into
   1-inch squares

2 teaspoons margarine, melted
¼ teaspoon paprika

Garnish
Lemon slices and parsley sprigs

In 1-quart glass or stainless-steel bowl soak scallops in wine for 30 minutes; drain, reserving wine.

Onto each of six 8- or 9-inch wooden skewers, thread 1 mushroom cap; alternating ingredients, thread ⅙ of the scallops and pepper squares onto each skewer, then thread each with 1 of the remaining mushroom caps.

Preheat broiler. In 13 x 9 x 2-inch baking pan arrange skewers in a single layer and pour wine over skewers; drizzle margarine over scallops only. Dust all ingredients with paprika and broil until scallops turn opaque white, 4 to 5 minutes; serve immediately with pan juices and garnished with lemon slices and parsley sprigs.

Each serving provides: 4 Protein Exchanges; 1¾ Vegetable Exchanges;
  1 Fat Exchange; 30 calories Optional Exchange
Per serving: 198 calories; 23 g protein; 4 g fat; 11 g carbohydrate; 46 mg calcium;
  419 mg sodium; 50 mg cholesterol

Calamari Salad

WEEK 1 ◇ MAKES 2 SERVINGS

1½ pounds cleaned squid*
½ lemon
1 cup diced celery
½ cup thinly sliced red onion
3 tablespoons lemon juice
2 tablespoons each drained capers
  and chopped fresh parsley
1 tablespoon olive oil

1 garlic clove, minced
½ teaspoon each oregano leaves
  and salt
Dash freshly ground pepper

Garnish

2 lemon wedges

Remove tentacles from each squid and set aside; turn body section (mantle) inside-out, wash thoroughly to remove all grit, and return to right side. Cut mantles into bite-size pieces; place tentacles and mantle pieces in small saucepan. Add the lemon half and water to cover; bring to a boil. Reduce heat, cover, and cook until squid are tender, about 20 minutes; drain, cover, and refrigerate until chilled.

To serve, in salad bowl combine remaining ingredients except lemon wedges. Weigh 8 ounces chilled squid; add to salad and toss to combine. Serve garnished with lemon wedges.

Each serving provides: 4 Protein Exchanges; 1½ Vegetable Exchanges;
  1½ Fat Exchanges
Per serving: 217 calories; 25 g protein; 8 g fat; 13 g carbohydrate; 85 mg calcium;
  933 mg sodium; 78 mg cholesterol

* 1½ pounds cleaned squid will yield 8 to 12 ounces boiled seafood.

Baked Cheese-Stuffed Squid

WEEK 4 ◇ MAKES 2 SERVINGS

12 ounces cleaned squid*
¼ cup part-skim ricotta cheese
1 egg, beaten
3 tablespoons seasoned dried bread
  crumbs
2 tablespoons minced onion
1 garlic clove, minced
½ teaspoon salt
¼ teaspoon each oregano leaves
  and pepper

½ cup tomato sauce
2 teaspoons dry red wine
1 tablespoon grated Parmesan
  cheese

Garnish

1 tablespoon chopped fresh parsley

Remove tentacles from each squid and set aside; turn body section (mantle) inside-out, wash thoroughly to remove all grit, and return to right side.

Preheat oven to 375°F. Cut tentacles into small pieces; in small bowl combine tentacles with ricotta cheese, egg, bread crumbs, onion, and seasonings, mixing well. Stuff each squid with an equal amount of crumb mixture and secure open end with toothpicks; transfer squid to shallow 1-quart casserole.

In small bowl combine tomato sauce and wine; pour over stuffed squid, cover casserole, and bake for 30 minutes. Sprinkle squid with Parmesan cheese and bake, uncovered, until sauce reduces slightly and cheese is golden, 10 to 15 minutes. Serve sprinkled with parsley.

Each serving provides: 4 Protein Exchanges; ½ Bread Exchange;
  1⅛ Vegetable Exchanges; 20 calories Optional Exchange
Per serving: 306 calories; 38 g protein; 8 g fat; 18 g carbohydrate; 177 mg calcium;
  1,152 mg sodium; 243 mg cholesterol

* 12 ounces cleaned squid will yield about 6 ounces baked seafood.

The Optional Exchange

HAVE you ever been on a diet where you wished you could wave a magic wand or rub Aladdin's lamp to add some new tricks to your menu planning? Well, on our Food Plan, you don't need any magic; just juggle your allotted calories for a spellbinding Wine Spritzer or Caramel Sauce. You can even enjoy sugar, sherry, wine, honey, or chili sauce and still not need a trick mirror to see a new slim you appear right before your eyes.

◗ Pointers on the Optional Exchange

◗ This Exchange has been included to enhance your enjoyment of the Food Plan and to provide you with variety. Using these flavorful items can turn reduced-calorie eating into a taste adventure.

	WEEK 1	WEEK 2	WEEK 3	WEEK 4
Weekly Total	up to 150 calories	up to 200 calories	up to 250 calories	up to 550 calories

◗ The Optional Exchange is comprised of the following groups: 10-Calorie Foods; 50-Calorie Foods; 100-Calorie Foods; and Additional Items (Beverages and Seasonings/Condiments). If you are following Week 1, you are limited to 150 calories per week; if following Week 2, you are limited to 200 calories per week. For Week 3, the limit is 250 calories per week, and when you reach Week 4 you are allowed up to 550 calories per week. Starting with Week 1, you may use all of the items listed under Beverages and Seasonings/ Condiments.

◗ Spend your Optional Exchange calories wisely. You may put them in a "bank account" and spend them little by little throughout the week, or you may "cash" them in and spend them all at once. If all your Optional Exchange calories are not spent within the one-week time frame, they cannot be carried over; that is, Optional Exchange calories may not be saved from week to week.

◗ In calculating the Optional Exchange Information for recipes, calories have been rounded to the nearest 5 (e.g., round 7.5 or 8 calories to 10 calories; 11 or 12 calories to 10 calories; 12.5 or 13 calories to 15 calories; etc.). Additionally, Exchange Information on recipes has been given in whole and half Exchanges for items from the Fruit, Bread, Fat, and Protein Exchanges; whole, half, and quarter Exchanges for items from the Milk Exchange; and no less than 1/8 Exchange for Vegetable Exchanges. When Exchanges for a recipe result in other than those fractions indicated above, the foods involved have been calculated as Optional Exchange calories. In these cases, the following caloric values have been used.

Exchanges	Optional Calories per 1 Exchange
Fruit	50
Milk	90
Bread	80
Fat	40
Protein	70
Vegetables	30

Therefore, if a recipe provides (per serving):	Count as:
⅛ Bread Exchange	80 calories per Bread Exchange ÷ 8 = 10 calories Optional Exchange
¼ Fat Exchange	40 calories per Fat Exchange ÷ 4 = 10 calories Optional Exchange
¼ Fruit Exchange	50 calories per Fruit Exchange ÷ 4 = 12.5 calories, rounded up to 15 calories Optional Exchange

▶ *Bouillon cubes and broth and seasoning mixes* may contain up to 12 calories per serving.

▶ You may prepare *homemade broth* by boiling meat, fish, or skinned poultry or game in water, with or without vegetables; refrigerate the liquid until fat congeals on top, then remove and discard congealed fat (this step is not necessary for fish broth).

▶ All varieties of *flour and cornstarch* are permitted; they need not be enriched.

▶ Check labels of *diet foods* carefully for caloric count; do not use if the label does not indicate calories. Any item is permitted as a diet food if it falls within one of the following categories and the label indicates that it is calorie-reduced, low-calorie, low-fat, low-sugar, reduced-calorie, reduced-sugar, or sugar-free:

> beverages, carbonated and noncarbonated
> fruit-flavored spreads, jams, jellies, and preserves
> gelatin, flavored
> ketchup
> salad dressings
> syrups and toppings

You may use diet foods that contain sugar such as sucrose, fructose, or sorbitol as long as they meet the above guidelines.

▶ *Coffees and teas* may contain only those ingredients that are not restricted (e.g., seasonings, condiments, flavorings or extracts, etc.).

▶ It is recommended that you drink at least 6 to 8 glasses of *water* or *mineral water* daily.

▶ All *seasonings and condiments* are permitted. You may use all types of dehydrated vegetable flakes as a seasoning, except potato flakes; potato flakes are listed under the Bread Exchange.

OPTIONAL EXCHANGE LISTS

Week 1—Up to 150 calories weekly
10-calorie foods

Selections	Amounts
Bouillon	1 cube, packet, or teaspoon
Broth and Seasoning Mix	1 packet or teaspoon
Broth or Consommé, canned or fat-free homemade	¼ cup
Carob powder, unsweetened	2 teaspoons
Cheese:	
Cottage	2 teaspoons
Hard, grated	1 teaspoon
Ricotta, part-skim	1 teaspoon
Chewing Gum	1 stick or piece
Cocoa, unsweetened	2 teaspoons
Fructose	½ teaspoon
Honey	½ teaspoon
Ketchup	2 teaspoons
Molasses	½ teaspoon
Sugar, all varieties	½ teaspoon
Syrup (Cane, Chocolate, Corn [light and dark], Maple, Sorghum, etc.)	½ teaspoon
Toppings (Butterscotch, Chocolate Fudge, etc.)	½ teaspoon

50-Calorie Foods

Selections	Amounts
Bread	½ Exchange
Fat	1 Exchange
Fruit	1 Exchange
Milk	½ Exchange
Protein	1 Exchange
Jams, Jellies, and Preserves	1 tablespoon

Diet Foods

Check labels for calories.

Week 2—Up to 200 calories weekly

You may use all of the items listed under Week 1 and may add the following to your Exchange List.

10-Calorie Foods

Selections	Amounts
Bacon Bits, imitation	1 teaspoon
Wine, any type	2 teaspoons

50-Calorie Foods

Selections	Amounts
Cream, any type	1 tablespoon
Half-and-Half	2 tablespoons
Whipped Cream, aerosol instant	¼ cup
Whipped Topping, dairy or nondairy	¼ cup prepared

100-Calorie Foods

Selections	Amounts
Beer	8 fluid ounces (1 cup)
light	12 fluid ounces (1½ cups)
Milk, whole	½ cup
Wine or Champagne	4 fluid ounces (½ cup)
light	6 fluid ounces (¾ cup)

Week 3—Up to 250 calories weekly

You may use all of the items listed under Weeks 1 and 2 and may add the following to your Exchange List.

100-Calorie Foods

Selections	Amounts
Cream Cheese	2 tablespoons
Cream Cheese, whipped	3 tablespoons
Sour Cream	3 tablespoons

Week 4—Up to 550 calories weekly

You may use all of the items listed under Weeks 1, 2, and 3 and may add the following to your Exchange List.

10-Calorie Foods

Selections	Amounts
Anchovies	2 fillets or 1 teaspoon mashed
Arrowroot	1 teaspoon
Black Bean Sauce	1 teaspoon
Bran	1 teaspoon
Bread Crumbs, dried (plain or seasoned)	1 teaspoon
Clam Juice	¼ cup
Coconut, shredded (sweetened or unsweetened)	1 teaspoon
Coffee Substitute or Cereal Beverage Powder	1 teaspoon
Concentrated Yeast Extract	1 teaspoon
Cornstarch	1 teaspoon
Creamer, nondairy (powder or liquid)	1 teaspoon
Egg White	½
Flour	1 teaspoon
Hoisin Sauce	1 teaspoon
Matzo Cake Meal	1 teaspoon
Matzo Meal	1 teaspoon
Miso (Fermented Soybean Paste)	1 teaspoon
Olives, all varieties and sizes	2
Oyster Sauce	1 teaspoon
Pickle Relish	1 teaspoon
Potato Starch	1 teaspoon
Seeds (Caraway, Poppy, Pumpkin, Sesame, Sunflower)	½ teaspoon
Sweet Relish	1 teaspoon
Tapioca, uncooked	1 teaspoon
Wheat Germ	1 teaspoon

50-Calorie Foods

Selections	Amounts
Sauces (Barbecue, Chili, Oriental Chili, Seafood Cocktail, Steak)	3 tablespoons
Tartar Sauce	2 teaspoons
Tomato Paste	¼ cup
Tomato Puree or Sauce	½ cup

100-Calorie Foods

Selections	Amounts
Avocado	¼ (2 ounces with skin)
Coleslaw	½ cup
Gelatin, fruit-flavored	½ cup prepared

Additional Items

The following items may be consumed in all weeks in reasonable amounts; nonstick cooking spray may be used in moderation.

Beverages

Club Soda
Coffee
Mineral Water, flavored and unflavored

Seltzer, flavored and unflavored
Tea
Water

Seasonings/Condiments

Aromatic Bitters
Baking Powder
Baking Soda
Browning Sauce
Capers
Cream of Tartar
Dehydrated Vegetable Flakes
Extracts
Flavorings
Herbs
Horseradish
Hot Sauce (Pepper Sauce)
Lemon Juice
Lime Juice (no sugar added)
Mustard
Nori Sheets (dried seaweed)
Pectin

Pepper
Picante Sauce
Rennin Tablets
Salt
Seasonings
Seaweed
Soy Sauce
Spices
Sugar Substitutes
Tamari
Teriyaki Sauce
Unflavored Gelatin
Vinegar, all types
Worcestershire Sauce
Yeast

Blender Cream of Tomato Soup ◑❶

WEEK 4 ∿ MAKES 4 SERVINGS

1 tablespoon margarine	**½ bay leaf**
½ cup chopped onion	**1 cup evaporated skimmed milk**
1 tablespoon all-purpose flour	**½ teaspoon Worcestershire sauce**
2 cups tomato juice	**⅛ teaspoon each salt and pepper**

In 2-quart saucepan heat margarine until bubbly and hot; add onion and sauté until softened. Sprinkle with flour and stir quickly to combine; cook, stirring constantly, for 2 minutes. Gradually stir in tomato juice; add bay leaf and, stirring constantly, bring mixture to a boil. Reduce heat and let simmer for 5 minutes; remove from heat and let cool slightly.

Remove bay leaf. Pour mixture into blender container and process at low speed until smooth. Return mixture to saucepan and gradually stir in milk; add Worcestershire sauce, salt, and pepper; cook over low heat, stirring occasionally, until thoroughly heated (*do not boil*).

Each serving provides: ¼ Vegetable Exchange; ½ Fat Exchange;
  ½ Milk Exchange; 45 calories Optional Exchange
Per serving: 114 calories; 7 g protein; 3 g fat; 16 g carbohydrate; 202 mg calcium;
  426 mg sodium; 3 mg cholesterol

Chicken Broth ❶

WEEK 1 ∿ MAKES ABOUT 8½ CUPS

1½ pounds skinned chicken necks and backs	**1 large celery rib, sliced**
2 quarts water	**3 each parsley stems and peppercorns**
1 medium onion, quartered	**1 bay leaf**
1 medium carrot, sliced	**1 teaspoon salt**

In 4-quart saucepan combine all ingredients and bring to a boil. Reduce heat to low, partially cover pan, and cook for about 1 hour.

Strain liquid, discarding solids. Cover broth and refrigerate until fat congeals on top; remove and discard congealed fat.

Each ¼ cup broth provides: 10 calories Optional Exchange
Per ¼ cup: 12 calories; 0.2 g protein; 0.5 g fat; 2 g carbohydrate; 3 mg calcium;
  92 mg sodium; 0 mg cholesterol

"Sour Cream" ◑

WEEK 1 ∽ MAKES 2 SERVINGS

Great on baked potatoes or a mixed green salad.

2 tablespoons part-skim ricotta
  cheese
1 tablespoon buttermilk

2 teaspoons lemon juice
Dash each salt and white pepper

In blender container combine all ingredients and process at low speed until smooth.

Each serving provides: 35 calories Optional Exchange
Per serving: 26 calories; 2 g protein; 1 g fat; 2 g carbohydrate; 53 mg calcium;
  93 mg sodium; 5 mg cholesterol

Variation: Add dash Worcestershire sauce before processing; process as directed, then stir in 1 tablespoon chopped chives.

Per serving: 28 calories; 2 g protein; 1 g fat; 2 g carbohydrate; 56 mg calcium;
  97 mg sodium; 5 mg cholesterol

Sweet 'n' Sour Salad Dressing

WEEK 4 ∽ MAKES 4 SERVINGS, ABOUT ¼ CUP EACH

This salad dressing is also a delicious marinade for cooked vegetables such as broccoli, cauliflower, and green beans.

1 tablespoon cornstarch
1 cup water
2 tablespoons each lemon juice
  and rice vinegar
1 tablespoon finely chopped fresh
  parsley

2 teaspoons chili sauce
1 teaspoon each honey and
  Worcestershire sauce
1 garlic clove, minced
Dash each granulated sugar
  substitute, salt, and pepper

In small saucepan stir cornstarch into water and, stirring constantly, bring to a boil; continue cooking and stirring for 1 minute longer. Transfer to heatproof bowl and add remaining ingredients; stir well. Cover and refrigerate until chilled. Stir again just before serving.

Each serving provides: 15 calories Optional Exchange
Per serving: 22 calories; 1 g protein; trace fat; 5 g carbohydrate; 4 mg calcium;
  87 mg sodium; 0 mg cholesterol

Creamy Onion Dip ◐❸

WEEK 3 ∽ MAKES 4 SERVINGS, ABOUT 2 TABLESPOONS EACH

In small bowl combine ½ **cup sour cream, 1 packet instant onion broth and seasoning mix,** and **2 teaspoons chopped chives;** cover and refrigerate until chilled.

Each serving provides: 70 calories Optional Exchange
Per serving: 64 calories; 1 g protein; 6 g fat; 2 g carbohydrate; 34 mg calcium;
   207 mg sodium; 13 mg cholesterol

Variation: Week 1—Substitute plain low-fat yogurt for the sour cream. Add ¼ Milk Exchange and decrease Optional Exchange to 3 calories.

Per serving: 21 calories; 2 g protein; 0.4 g fat; 2 g carbohydrate; 52 mg calcium;
   211 mg sodium; 2 mg cholesterol

Guacamole

WEEK 4 ∽ MAKES 8 SERVINGS, ABOUT ¼ CUP EACH

Serve with taco shells, broken into bite-size pieces.

**1 ripe avocado (8 ounces), pared
   and pitted
3 tablespoons lemon juice
4 ounces Canadian-style bacon,
   sautéed and diced
1 medium tomato, blanched, peeled,
   seeded, and chopped
2 tablespoons each minced onion
   and drained canned mild green
   chilies**

**1 tablespoon chopped fresh Italian
   (flat-leaf) parsley or 1 teaspoon
   parsley flakes
1 tablespoon chopped fresh
   coriander or ½ teaspoon ground
½ teaspoon salt
1 small garlic clove, mashed
Dash pepper**

In medium bowl, using a fork, mash avocado with lemon juice into a smooth pulp; stir in remaining ingredients. Cover with plastic wrap and refrigerate for at least 1 hour.

Each serving provides: ½ Protein Exchange; ¼ Vegetable Exchange;
   50 calories Optional Exchange
Per serving: 83 calories; 4 g protein; 6 g fat; 4 g carbohydrate; 11 mg calcium;
   408 mg sodium; 9 mg cholesterol

Zucchini-Onion Dip ❸

WEEK 3 ∾ MAKES 8 SERVINGS, ABOUT 3 TABLESPOONS EACH

Serve with platter of crudités (e.g., blanched broccoli and cauliflower florets, carrot and bell pepper strips, cucumber and mushroom slices, and cherry tomatoes).

2 teaspoons olive or vegetable oil
½ cup diced onion
1 garlic clove, sliced
2 cups chopped zucchini

1 teaspoon salt
Dash each pepper and lemon juice
½ cup sour cream

In 8-inch nonstick skillet heat oil; add onion and garlic and sauté until onion is translucent. Add zucchini and sauté, stirring constantly, until softened, about 5 minutes.

Transfer onion mixture to work bowl of food processor; add salt, pepper, and lemon juice and process until pureed. Pour mixture into bowl and stir In sour cream; cover and refrigerate until chilled.

Each serving provides: ½ Vegetable Exchange; 45 calories Optional Exchange
Per serving: 49 calories; 1 g protein; 4 g fat; 2 g carbohydrate; 27 mg calcium;
  284 mg sodium; 6 mg cholesterol

Variation: Week 1—Substitute plain low-fat yogurt for the sour cream and decrease Optional Exchange to 20 calories.

Per serving: 27 calories; 1 g protein; 1 g fat; 3 g carbohydrate; 36 mg calcium;
  286 mg sodium; 1 mg cholesterol

Sherry Marinade ◑

WEEK 2 ∽ MAKES 4 SERVINGS

Use as a marinade with poultry or fish.

¼ cup each dry sherry and lemon
  juice
1 teaspoon firmly packed dark
  brown sugar

1 garlic clove, chopped
½ bay leaf, crushed
½ teaspoon basil leaves
Dash each salt and pepper

In blender container combine all ingredients and process until smooth.

Each serving provides: 20 calories Optional Exchange
Per serving: 29 calories; 0.2 g protein; 0.1 g fat; 4 g carbohydrate; 9 mg calcium;
  37 mg sodium; 0 mg cholesterol

Anise Rusks ❶

WEEK 4 ∽ MAKES 16 SERVINGS, 2 COOKIES EACH

These cookies can be stored in a covered container for up to 1 month.

4 eggs, separated
⅓ cup granulated sugar, divided
1 teaspoon anise extract

½ teaspoon grated orange peel
¾ cup self-rising flour
¼ cup ice water

1. Preheat oven to 375°F. Line bottom of 13 x 9 x 2-inch baking pan with wax paper or parchment paper; set aside.

2. In medium mixing bowl combine egg yolks and half of the sugar; using electric mixer, beat until thick and lemon colored, about 3 minutes. Beat in extract and orange peel; set mixer on low speed and gradually beat in flour and water, beating just until combined. Set aside.

3. In separate bowl, using clean beaters, beat egg whites until foamy; gradually add remaining sugar and beat until stiff peaks form. Spoon 2 heaping tablespoons of beaten whites into yolk mixture to loosen batter, then fold in remaining whites, ⅓ at a time.

4. Pour batter into paper-lined pan and, using a spatula, smooth top; bake until top is browned, 20 to 25 minutes.

5. Remove pan from oven and reduce oven temperature to 250°F. Using a knife or metal spatula, loosen edges of cake from pan; invert cake onto wire rack. Peel off paper and set cake right-side up on cutting board; cut into 4 equal sections, then cut each section in half and each half into 4 equal slices.

6. Arrange slices on cookie sheet and bake until golden and crisp, 1 to 1½ hours.

Each serving provides: 60 calories Optional Exchange
Per serving: 58 calories; 2 g protein; 1 g fat; 9 g carbohydrate; 23 mg calcium;
    82 mg sodium; 69 mg cholesterol

Caramel Sauce ❶❸

WEEK 4   ∽   MAKES 4 SERVINGS, ABOUT 2 TABLESPOONS EACH

In small saucepan combine **¼ cup firmly packed brown sugar** with **1 tablespoon plus 1 teaspoon unsalted margarine;** cook over medium heat, stirring constantly, until melted. Gradually stir in **2 tablespoons evaporated skimmed milk** and cook, stirring constantly, until mixture is thick and syrupy, about 1 minute.

Each serving provides: 1 Fat Exchange; 65 calories Optional Exchange
Per serving: 92 calories; 1 g protein; 3 g fat; 14 g carbohydrate; 36 mg calcium;
    14 mg sodium; 0.3 mg cholesterol

Kiwi-Lemon Chiffon Pie

WEEK 4 ∽ MAKES 8 SERVINGS

Crust

¾ cup all-purpose flour
¼ teaspoon salt

2 tablespoons plus 2 teaspoons
   margarine
¼ cup plain low-fat yogurt

Filling

1 envelope (four ½-cup servings)
   low-calorie lemon-flavored gelatin
   (8 calories per ½ cup)
1 cup each boiling and cold water
1 cup thawed frozen dairy whipped
   topping

2 egg whites (at room temperature)
⅛ teaspoon cream of tartar
1 medium kiwi fruit, pared and
   thinly sliced

Garnish

1 thin lemon slice

To Prepare Crust: In mixing bowl combine flour and salt; with pastry blender, or 2 knives used scissors-fashion, cut in margarine until mixture resembles coarse meal. Add yogurt and mix thoroughly to form dough; form dough into a ball, wrap in plastic wrap, and refrigerate for at least 1 hour (may be kept in refrigerator for up to 3 days).

Preheat oven to 400°F. Between 2 sheets of wax paper, roll dough to form a 10-inch circle, about ⅛ inch thick; carefully remove paper and fit dough into an 8-inch pie plate. Fold under any dough that extends beyond edge of plate and flute or crimp edge. Using a fork, prick bottom and sides of pie shell; bake until lightly browned, 15 to 20 minutes. Remove pie plate to wire rack and let cool. While crust is cooling, prepare filling.

To Prepare Filling: In medium heatproof bowl sprinkle gelatin over boiling water and stir until dissolved; let cool slightly. Add cold water and whipped topping, stirring until completely blended. Cover and refrigerate until partially set, about 30 minutes.

In medium mixing bowl using an electric mixer on medium-high speed, beat egg whites until foamy; add cream of tartar and continue beating until stiff peaks form. Fold beaten whites into lemon gelatin mixture and pour into cooled pie crust; decoratively arrange kiwi slices over filling. Cover and refrigerate until set.

To Serve: Garnish with lemon slice.

Each serving provides: ½ Bread Exchange; 1 Fat Exchange;
 45 calories Optional Exchange
Per serving: 119 calories; 3 g protein; 6 g fat; 13 g carbohydrate; 20 mg calcium;
 133 mg sodium; 0.4 mg cholesterol

Lady Fingers ❶

WEEK 4 〜 MAKES 8 SERVINGS, 2 LADY FINGERS EACH

⅓ cup sifted cake flour
½ teaspoon double-acting baking
 powder
2 eggs, separated

1 tablespoon granulated sugar
¼ teaspoon each grated lemon peel
 and vanilla extract
⅛ teaspoon cream of tartar

1. Preheat oven to 350°F. Onto sheet of wax paper or a paper plate sift together flour and baking powder; set aside.

2. In small mixing bowl combine egg yolks, sugar, lemon peel, and vanilla and, using electric mixer, beat until thick and lemon colored, about 3 minutes; beat in half of flour mixture.

3. In another bowl, using clean beaters, beat egg whites with cream of tartar until stiff peaks form; gently fold whites, alternately with remaining flour mixture, into yolk mixture.

4. Spray a baking sheet with nonstick cooking spray. Fit a pastry bag with a No. 6 plain ½-inch-wide tube and spoon batter into bag; pipe out batter onto sheet, forming 16 strips, each about 3 inches long and 1 inch wide. Bake for 10 to 12 minutes.

5. Using a spatula, immediately remove lady fingers to a wire rack; let cool.

Each serving provides: 45 calories Optional Exchange
Per serving: 40 calories; 2 g protein; 1 g fat; 5 g carbohydrate; 20 mg calcium;
 43 mg sodium; 69 mg cholesterol

Melba Snowballs 🌓

WEEK 4 ∽ MAKES 2 SERVINGS, 2 SNOWBALLS EACH

1 tablespoon plus 1 teaspoon
   reduced-calorie raspberry spread
   (16 calories per 2 teaspoons)
6 ounces vanilla dietary frozen
   dessert, slightly softened

3 zwieback, made into crumbs
1 tablespoon plus 1 teaspoon
   shredded coconut, toasted

Force raspberry spread through sieve into small bowl to remove seeds; add frozen dessert and, using a fork, stir spread slightly through dessert to create swirl effect (do not thoroughly combine). Using small ice cream scoop, form 4 balls and place on baking sheet; cover lightly with plastic wrap and freeze until hard.

On sheet of wax paper combine crumbs and coconut; roll each ball in mixture until well coated on all sides. Serve immediately or cover and freeze for future use.

Each serving provides: ½ Bread Exchange; 1 Fruit Exchange; ½ Milk Exchange; 55 calories Optional Exchange
Per serving: 174 calories; 6 g protein; 3 g fat; 32 g carbohydrate; 147 mg calcium; 84 mg sodium; 4 mg cholesterol

Wine Spritzer 🌗

WEEK 2 ∽ MAKES 2 SERVINGS, ABOUT 10 FLUID OUNCES EACH

Recipe may be easily doubled or tripled for a party.

¾ cup chilled club soda
½ cup chilled dry white wine

4 to 6 ice cubes
2 strips lemon peel

Chill 2 tall glasses. In 2-cup glass measure or pitcher stir together soda and wine. Divide mixture into chilled glasses; add 2 or 3 ice cubes and 1 strip lemon peel to each glass and serve immediately.

Each serving provides: 50 calories Optional Exchange
Per serving: 50 calories; 0.1 g protein; 0 g fat; 3 g carbohydrate; 6 mg calcium; 3 mg sodium; 0 mg cholesterol

Personal Choice

NOW you can orchestrate magnificent meals with the symphony of sweets and savories we call Personal Choice Selections. Jazz up brunch with Crêpes Suzette or Puffy Brandied Apple Omelet. Let Pesto-Parmesan Sauce harmonize with a pasta course. End dinner on a high note with Frozen Strawberry Soufflé. Whatever you choose, you're sure to cheer "bravo" as you and Weight Watchers make beautiful music together.

▶ Pointers On Personal Choice Food Selections

▶ Personal Choice food selections are offered to help customize the Food Plan to fit your life-style, thereby making your weight-control efforts easier and more enjoyable. With Week 5, you can begin making some exciting new choices that will add variety, interest, and flexibility to your recipes and meal planning.

▶ Personal Choice selections are divided into the following categories: Cheers; Sweet Dreams; Eye Openers; and Holiday Magic. On Week 5 you may choose items from one of these categories. Thereafter, on alternate weeks, you may add another category to your repertoire. Therefore, by the eleventh week, you can make selections from all of the categories.

▶ Since everyone's life-style is different, you may choose to use the Personal Choice food selections at times when they are most appropriate to you. For example, if you are preparing a special dinner party to celebrate a birthday, you may use some of the items from the Holiday Magic list; you needn't save them specifically for a holiday.

▶ Some of the Personal Choice food selections provide Exchanges from the first 6 food categories only (Fruit, Vegetables, Milk, Bread, Fat, and Protein); some also include Optional Exchange calories, and some provide Optional Exchange calories only. This determination is based on the nutrient composition of the particular food selection and how it best fits into the Food Plan.

▶ Some selections may contain ingredients which may not appear to be accounted for in the Exchange Information. For example, pound cake is made with egg, yet the Exchange Information does not indicate any Protein Exchanges. This is because there is not enough egg per serving to contribute the nutrients necessary to be considered a Protein Exchange. The calories from the egg have been counted toward the Optional Exchange.

▶ When a serving size is listed by amount and weight, if possible use the weight as the primary guide. For example, when selecting potato chips, try to use the 1-ounce serving size rather than the count.

PERSONAL CHOICE
FOOD SELECTIONS LISTS

Cheers

Selections	Serving	Exchange
SNACKS		
Corn Chips	1 ounce	160 calories Optional
Crackers (any type)	1 ounce	1 Bread; 1½ Fat
Dip (any type)	2 tablespoons	70 calories Optional
Potato Chips	14 (1 ounce)	160 calories Optional
NUTS		
Almonds	22 nuts (1 oz shelled)	170 calories Optional
Brazil Nuts	7 nuts (1 oz shelled)	190 calories Optional
Cashews	14 large (1 oz shelled)	170 calories Optional
Hazelnuts	20 nuts (1 oz shelled)	180 calories Optional
Macadamia Nuts	12 nuts (1 oz shelled)	220 calories Optional
Peanuts	15 nuts (1 oz shelled)	170 calories Optional
Pecans	25 halves (1 oz shelled)	190 calories Optional
Pignolias (pine nuts)	1 ounce	160 calories Optional
Pistachios	25 nuts (1 oz shelled)	180 calories Optional
Walnuts	25 halves (1 oz shelled)	190 calories Optional
BEVERAGES		
Brandy or Cognac	2 fluid ounces	150 calories Optional
Gin, Rum, Scotch, Vodka, Whiskey	2 fluid ounces	140 calories Optional
Liqueurs (any type)	1 fluid ounce	100 calories Optional
Soda (any type)	8 fluid ounces	120 calories Optional

Sweet Dreams

Selections	Serving	Exchange
Chocolate (any type)	1 ounce	150 calories Optional
Cookie (any type)	1 medium (½ ounce)	70 calories Optional
Ice Cream (any flavor)	½ cup	250 calories Optional*
Ice Milk (any flavor)	½ cup	120 calories Optional
Pound Cake	1 slice (2 ounces)	260 calories Optional
Pudding (any flavor)	½ cup	150 calories Optional
Sherbet (any flavor)	½ cup	140 calories Optional

* Ice cream ranges from 150 to 400 calories per ½ cup based on the percent fat and added ingredients. If nutrition information is available, use the caloric value that appears on the label.

Eye Openers

Selections	Serving	Exchange
Bacon, crisp	2 slices	90 calories Optional
Sausages (brown-and-serve)	2 links (1 ounce)	1 Protein†; 70 calories Optional

† Count Protein Exchange as pork.

Holiday Magic

Selections	Serving	Exchange
Cranberry Sauce	¼ cup	90 calories Optional
Dip (any type)	2 tablespoons	70 calories Optional
Gravy (for roast beef, lamb, or turkey)	¼ cup	50 calories Optional
Hollandaise Sauce	¼ cup	2 Fat; 90 calories Optional
Ice Cream (any flavor)	½ cup	250 calories Optional*
Marshmallows	2 medium (½ ounce)	50 calories Optional

* Ice cream ranges from 150 to 400 calories per ½ cup based on the percent fat and added ingredients. If nutrition information is available, use the caloric value that appears on the label.

Shredded Carrot Salad

CHEERS ∾ MAKES 2 SERVINGS

2 cups shredded carrots
24 large seedless green grapes,
   cut into halves
2 teaspoons mayonnaise

½ teaspoon poppy seed
¼ teaspoon salt
4 iceberg or romaine lettuce leaves
½ ounce walnut pieces

In bowl combine all ingredients except lettuce leaves and walnuts; cover and refrigerate for at least 2 hours. Serve on lettuce leaves; top with walnuts.

Each serving provides: 2½ Vegetable Exchanges; 1 Fat Exchange; 1 Fruit Exchange; 55 calories Optional Exchange
Per serving: 192 calories; 3 g protein; 9 g fat; 28 g carbohydrate; 66 mg calcium; 339 mg sodium; 3 mg cholesterol

Variation: Substitute ¼ cup raisins for the grapes.

Per serving: 188 calories; 3 g protein; 9 g fat; 28 g carbohydrate; 72 mg calcium; 340 mg sodium; 3 mg cholesterol

Pesto-Parmesan Sauce

CHEERS ∾ MAKES 2 SERVINGS, ABOUT ¼ CUP EACH

Serve over cooked vegetables.

2 cups firmly packed fresh basil
   leaves, chopped
1 ounce pignolias (pine nuts)
1 tablespoon plus 1 teaspoon olive
   oil

½ teaspoon salt
⅛ teaspoon pepper
1 garlic clove, minced
1 ounce grated Parmesan cheese

In blender container combine all ingredients except cheese and process until smooth, stopping motor when necessary to scrape mixture down from sides of container. Transfer sauce to small bowl and stir in cheese; serve immediately or cover and refrigerate. When ready to use, bring to room temperature.

Each serving provides: ½ Protein Exchange; 2 Fat Exchanges; 80 calories Optional Exchange
Per serving: 265 calories; 12 g protein; 21 g fat; 14 g carbohydrate; 586 mg calcium; 818 mg sodium; 11 mg cholesterol

Chilled Eggplant Relish

CHEERS ～ MAKES 4 SERVINGS

3 cups cubed eggplant
1 teaspoon salt
1 tablespoon plus 1 teaspoon olive oil
1 cup thinly sliced onions
2 garlic cloves, minced
1 cup each diced celery and chopped tomatoes

2 teaspoons wine vinegar
1 teaspoon granulated sugar
8 black olives, pitted and cut into halves
1 tablespoon drained capers
1 ounce pignolias (pine nuts), lightly toasted

On paper towels arrange eggplant in a single layer; sprinkle with salt and let stand for at least 1 hour. Pat dry and set aside.

In 9- or 10-inch skillet heat oil over medium heat; add onions and garlic and sauté until onions are translucent, 3 to 5 minutes. Add eggplant and cook, stirring occasionally, until eggplant begins to soften, about 5 minutes; stir in celery and tomatoes, cover pan, and let simmer until celery is tender, about 15 minutes. Stir in vinegar and sugar and cook, uncovered, for 5 minutes longer. Remove from heat and add olives, capers, and pignolias, tossing to combine; transfer to a glass, plastic, or stainless-steel container, cover, and refrigerate until chilled.

Each serving provides: 3 Vegetable Exchanges; 1 Fat Exchange; 55 calories Optional Exchange
Per serving: 138 calories; 4 g protein; 10 g fat; 13 g carbohydrate; 61 mg calcium; 687 mg sodium; 0 mg cholesterol

Velvet Chicken and Vegetables

CHEERS ⌒ MAKES 4 SERVINGS

2 tablespoons cornstarch
1 tablespoon soy sauce
1 egg white
1¼ pounds skinned and boned
  chicken breasts, cut into
  2-inch-long strips
2 cups water
2 packets instant chicken broth
  and seasoning mix
1 tablespoon vegetable oil
1 teaspoon Chinese sesame oil

½ cup each thinly sliced red and
  green bell peppers (thin strips)
2 garlic cloves, minced
1 teaspoon minced pared ginger
  root
1 cup each broccoli florets,
  blanched, and drained canned
  straw mushrooms*
2 cups cooked long-grain rice (hot)
1 ounce unsalted shelled cashews

In medium bowl combine cornstarch, soy sauce, and egg white, mixing well; add chicken and toss to coat evenly. Refrigerate, uncovered, for 30 minutes so that coating will adhere to chicken.

In 9-inch skillet combine water and broth mix and bring to a boil; gradually add chicken, stirring gently to separate chicken pieces. Return mixture to a boil; remove from heat and drain chicken, reserving 1 cup broth. Set aside chicken and broth.

In same skillet combine oils and heat; add peppers, garlic, and ginger and sauté over medium-low heat until peppers are tender, about 5 minutes. Add broccoli, mushrooms, chicken, and reserved broth to skillet and cook, stirring occasionally, until ingredients are thoroughly heated and mixture is slightly thickened; serve over rice and top with cashews.

Each serving provides: 4 Protein Exchanges; 1 Bread Exchange;
  1½ Vegetable Exchanges; 1 Fat Exchange; 70 calories Optional Exchange
Per serving: 406 calories; 40 g protein; 10 g fat; 38 g carbohydrate; 56 mg calcium;
  973 mg sodium; 82 mg cholesterol

* Button mushrooms may be substituted.

Creamy Broccoli-Chicken Casserole

CHEERS ∾ MAKES 2 SERVINGS

2 teaspoons margarine
1/4 cup diced onion
1 tablespoon plus 1 1/2 teaspoons
all-purpose flour
1 cup skim milk
2 ounces Cheddar cheese, shredded
Dash each salt and pepper

6 ounces skinned and boned cooked
chicken, diced
1 cup cooked chopped broccoli
3/4 cup cooked macaroni shells
1/4 cup chopped drained canned
pimientos
1/2 ounce slivered almonds

Preheat oven to 375°F. In small saucepan heat margarine until bubbly and hot; add onion and sauté briefly (*do not brown*). Add flour and stir quickly to thoroughly combine; remove from heat and gradually stir in milk, stirring until thoroughly blended. Return to heat and cook, stirring constantly, until slightly thickened; add cheese and cook over low heat, stirring occasionally, until sauce is thick and creamy, about 2 minutes. Remove from heat and stir in salt and pepper.

In 2-quart casserole combine remaining ingredients; pour cheese sauce over chicken mixture and stir to combine. Sprinkle with almonds and bake for 30 minutes.

Each serving provides: 4 Protein Exchanges; 1 Bread Exchange;
1 1/2 Vegetable Exchanges; 1 Fat Exchange; 1/2 Milk Exchange;
45 calories Optional Exchange
Per serving: 510 calories; 42 g protein; 24 g fat; 31 g carbohydrate; 490 mg calcium;
439 mg sodium; 108 mg cholesterol

Soft-Shell Crab Sauté ◑

CHEERS 〜 MAKES 4 SERVINGS

1¼ pounds cleaned soft-shell blue
 crabs
2 tablespoons all-purpose flour
Dash each salt and white pepper
2 tablespoons margarine
2 garlic cloves, minced
½ cup dry white wine or dry
 vermouth

2 tablespoons each lemon juice and
 chopped fresh parsley
1 ounce sliced almonds, lightly
 toasted

Garnish
Lemon wedges

Using paper towels, dry crabs thoroughly. On sheet of wax paper or
a paper plate combine flour, salt, and pepper; dredge crabs in seasoned flour.

In 12-inch nonstick skillet heat margarine until bubbly and hot;
add crabs, top-side up, and sauté over medium to low heat for about
6 minutes on each side. Remove from pan and keep warm. Add garlic
to same skillet and sauté briefly (*do not brown*); add wine (or vermouth) and lemon juice and bring to a boil. Return crabs to skillet
and baste with pan juices; serve immediately, sprinkled with parsley
and almonds and garnished with lemon wedges.

Each serving provides: 4 Protein Exchanges; 1½ Fat Exchanges;
 90 calories Optional Exchange
Per serving with wine; 242 calories; 22 g protein; 12 g fat; 7 g carbohydrate;
 79 mg calcium; 343 mg sodium; 114 mg cholesterol
With vermouth: 248 calories; 22 g protein; 12 g fat; 6 g carbohydrate;
 79 mg calcium; 343 mg sodium; 114 mg cholesterol

Puffy Brandied Apple Omelet

CHEERS 〜 MAKES 4 SERVINGS

1 tablespoon plus 1 teaspoon
  margarine, divided
2 small apples, cored, pared, and
  thinly sliced
2 tablespoons apple brandy
1 teaspoon each firmly packed light
  brown sugar and grated orange
  peel

Dash ground cinnamon
Water
4 eggs, separated
1 tablespoon granulated sugar
¼ teaspoon vanilla extract
Dash salt

1. In small nonstick skillet heat 1 teaspoon margarine until bubbly and hot; add apple slices, brandy, brown sugar, orange peel, and cinnamon and sauté over medium heat, turning apple slices until apples are glazed and tender, about 5 minutes (if necessary, add 2 to 3 teaspoons water to prevent burning). Remove from heat and keep warm.

2. Preheat oven to 350°F. In small mixing bowl combine egg yolks, granulated sugar, and vanilla and, using electric mixer, beat until thick and lemon colored. In large mixing bowl, using clean beaters, beat egg whites with ¼ cup water and the salt until stiff peaks form. Fold a few spoonfuls of beaten whites into yolk mixture, then quickly fold yolk mixture into whites.

3. In 10-inch skillet that has an oven-safe or removable handle heat remaining tablespoon margarine until bubbly and hot; tilt skillet to coat entire bottom with melted margarine. Pour in egg mixture, spread lightly to smooth top, and cook until light and puffy and underside is lightly browned, about 3 minutes.

4. Transfer skillet to upper-third section of oven and bake for 10 to 12 minutes (until a sharp knife, inserted in center, comes out clean). Using a spatula, loosen omelet around edges; spoon apples onto half of omelet and, using a pancake turner, fold omelet in half and slide onto warmed platter. Serve immediately.

Each serving provides: 1 Protein Exchange; 1 Fat Exchange; ½ Fruit Exchange;
  40 calories Optional Exchange
Per serving: 179 calories; 6 g protein; 10 g fat; 15 g carbohydrate; 34 mg calcium;
  147 mg sodium; 274 mg cholesterol

Apple-Raisin Cake ❶

CHEERS ⌒ MAKES 12 SERVINGS

This cake may be frozen for future use; to make serving easier, slice cake into individual portions, then wrap each portion in plastic freezer wrap and freeze. When ready to use, thaw the number of portions needed at room temperature.

2¼ cups self-rising flour
1 teaspoon ground cinnamon
½ teaspoon ground cloves
⅓ cup plus 2 teaspoons unsalted margarine
¼ cup granulated sugar
1 teaspoon baking soda

1½ cups applesauce (no sugar added)
2 small Golden Delicious apples, cored, pared, and shredded
1 cup less 2 tablespoons raisins
2 ounces shelled walnuts, chopped

Spray an 8 x 8 x 2-inch baking pan with nonstick cooking spray and set aside. Into medium bowl sift together flour, cinnamon, and cloves; set aside.

Preheat oven to 350°F. In medium mixing bowl, using electric mixer, cream margarine; add sugar and stir to combine. Stir baking soda into applesauce, then add to margarine mixture and stir to combine; add sifted ingredients and, using electric mixer on medium speed, beat until thoroughly combined. Fold in apples, raisins, and walnuts; pour batter into sprayed pan and bake for 45 to 50 minutes (until cake is browned and a cake tester or toothpick, inserted in center, comes out dry). Remove cake from pan and cool on wire rack.

Each serving provides: 1 Bread Exchange; 1½ Fat Exchanges; 1 Fruit Exchange; 50 calories Optional Exchange
Per serving: 235 calories; 3 g protein; 9 g fat; 37 g carbohydrate; 78 mg calcium; 324 mg sodium; 0 mg cholesterol

Cinnamon Crumb Coffee Cake ❶

CHEERS ∽ MAKES 8 SERVINGS

2¼ cups all-purpose flour, divided
3 tablespoons granulated sugar
2 teaspoons double-acting baking
   powder
1 teaspoon baking soda
¼ teaspoon salt
⅓ cup margarine, divided
2 eggs
1 cup buttermilk

1 teaspoon vanilla extract
½ teaspoon grated lemon peel
1 tablespoon firmly packed brown
   sugar
1 ounce shelled pecans or walnuts,
   chopped
½ teaspoon ground cinnamon

Preheat oven to 400°F. Spray an 8-inch square or round nonstick baking pan with nonstick cooking spray and set aside. Into mixing bowl sift together 2 cups flour and the granulated sugar, baking powder, baking soda, and salt; with pastry blender, or 2 knives used scissors-fashion, cut in ¼ cup margarine until mixture resembles coarse meal. Add eggs, buttermilk, vanilla, and lemon peel and, using electric mixer, beat just until smooth; pour batter into sprayed pan.

In small bowl combine remaining 1 tablespoon plus 1 teaspoon margarine and the brown sugar; add remaining ¼ cup flour, the nuts, and cinnamon and mix until all ingredients are thoroughly combined and crumbly. Sprinkle nut-crumb mixture evenly over batter and bake for 25 to 30 minutes (until cake pulls away slightly from sides of pan). Transfer pan to wire rack and let cake cool in pan. To serve, cut into 8 equal pieces.

Each serving provides: 1½ Bread Exchanges; 2 Fat Exchanges;
   85 calories Optional Exchange
Per serving: 278 calories; 7 g protein; 12 g fat; 36 g carbohydrate; 109 mg calcium;
   416 mg sodium; 70 mg cholesterol

Crêpes Suzette

CHEERS 〜 MAKES 4 SERVINGS, 2 CRÊPES EACH

Crêpes may be prepared in advance and frozen for future use. To freeze, stack cooled crêpes, using 2 sheets of wax paper between each to separate; wrap stack in moisture- and vapor-resistant wrapping and label. Freeze until needed. When ready to use, thaw at room temperature for 10 to 15 minutes.

Crêpes

1 cup skim milk
¾ cup all-purpose flour
2 eggs

Sauce

2 tablespoons unsalted margarine
1 tablespoon granulated sugar
1 cup orange juice (no sugar added)
¼ cup thawed frozen concentrated
   orange juice (no sugar added)
2 tablespoons orange liqueur

To Prepare Crêpes: In blender container combine milk, flour, and eggs and process until smooth; let stand for 15 minutes so that bubbles will subside.

Lightly spray 6-inch nonstick skillet or crêpe pan with nonstick cooking spray and heat (to test, sprinkle pan with drop of water; if water sizzles, pan is hot enough). Pour ¼ cup of batter into pan and quickly swirl batter so that it covers entire bottom of pan; cook over medium-high heat until edges and underside are dry. Using pancake turner, carefully turn crêpe over; cook other side briefly just to dry, about 30 seconds. Slide crêpe onto a plate. Repeat procedure 7 more times using remaining batter and making 7 more crêpes.

To Prepare Sauce: In 12-inch nonstick skillet melt margarine; add sugar and stir until dissolved. Stir in orange juice, concentrated orange juice, and liqueur and bring mixture to a boil. Reduce heat to low.

To Prepare Crêpes Suzette: Add 1 crêpe to skillet, coating both sides with sauce; fold crêpe in half, then fold again to create triangular shape. Slide to side of skillet and repeat procedure with remaining crêpes; serve immediately.

Each serving provides: ½ Protein Exchange; 1 Bread Exchange; 1½ Fat Exchanges;
   1 Fruit Exchange; ¼ Milk Exchange; 40 calories Optional Exchange
Per serving: 286 calories; 8 g protein; 9 g fat; 40 g carbohydrate; 106 mg calcium;
   68 mg sodium; 138 mg cholesterol

Tofu-Peach "Shortcake" ◐ ❸

SWEET DREAMS ∿ MAKES 2 SERVINGS

½ cup canned sliced peaches (no sugar added)
3 ounces firm-style tofu (soybean curd)
1 tablespoon thawed frozen concentrated orange juice (no sugar added)

1 teaspoon each firmly packed light brown sugar and lemon juice
¼ teaspoon vanilla extract
2 slices pound cake (1 ounce each)

Reserve 4 peach slices for garnish; dice remaining peaches and set aside.

In blender container or work bowl of food processor combine tofu, orange juice, sugar, lemon juice, and vanilla and process until smooth, scraping down sides of container as necessary.

On serving plate place 1 slice pound cake; spread with half of tofu mixture and top with diced peaches. Top peaches with remaining slice pound cake and spread remaining tofu mixture over top and sides of "shortcake"; garnish with reserved peach slices. Cover and refrigerate for at least 10 minutes before serving.

Each serving provides: ½ Protein Exchange; ½ Fruit Exchange;
 155 calories Optional Exchange
Per serving: 204 calories; 5 g protein; 10 g fat; 24 g carbohydrate; 67 mg calcium;
 37 mg sodium; 42 mg cholesterol

Sugar-Glazed Cinnamon Wedges ❸

CHEERS ∿ MAKES 4 SERVINGS, 3 WEDGES EACH

⅓ cup plus 2 teaspoons all-purpose flour
Dash salt
1 tablespoon plus 1 teaspoon margarine
2 tablespoons plain low-fat yogurt

2 teaspoons thawed frozen dairy whipped topping
½ ounce shelled pecans, chopped
1 tablespoon firmly packed light brown sugar
Dash cinnamon

In mixing bowl combine flour and salt; with pastry blender, or 2 knives used scissors-fashion, cut in margarine until mixture resembles coarse meal. Add yogurt and mix thoroughly. Form dough into a ball; wrap in plastic wrap and refrigerate for at least 1 hour (may be kept in the refrigerator for up to 3 days).

Preheat oven to 425°F. Between 2 sheets of wax paper roll dough, forming a circle about ¼ inch thick; remove paper and fit dough into a 7-inch tart pan that has a removable bottom, or a 7-inch pie plate. Using a fork, prick bottom of dough; spread whipped topping over dough and sprinkle entire surface with pecans, sugar, and cinnamon. Bake until sugar is melted and no longer bubbles, 10 to 15 minutes. To serve, cut into 12 equal wedges.

Each serving provides: ½ Bread Exchange; 1 Fat Exchange;
  45 calories Optional Exchange
Per serving: 120 calories; 2 g protein; 7 g fat; 14 g carbohydrate; 21 mg calcium;
  84 mg sodium; 0.4 mg cholesterol

Belgian Waffles

SWEET DREAMS and HOLIDAY MAGIC ⌣ MAKES 2 SERVINGS

If you have a waffle iron with a special design, these will look extra special, but a regular waffle iron will work just as well.

⅓ cup plus 2 teaspoons all-purpose
  flour
1 teaspoon each double-acting
  baking powder and granulated
  sugar
½ teaspoon baking soda
½ cup buttermilk

1 egg, separated
2 teaspoons vegetable oil
1 teaspoon vanilla extract
1 cup vanilla or strawberry ice
  cream
¾ cup sliced strawberries

1. Onto sheet of wax paper or a paper plate sift together dry ingredients; set aside.

2. In small mixing bowl combine milk, egg yolk, oil, and vanilla; add sifted ingredients and, using electric mixer, beat until smooth.

3. Spray nonstick waffle iron with nonstick cooking spray and heat. In separate bowl, using clean beaters, beat egg white until stiff but not dry; fold into batter. Pour batter onto waffle iron and cook according to manufacturer's directions.

4. Separate cooked waffle into 4 sections; onto each of 2 dessert plates place 2 sections and top with ½ cup ice cream and half of the strawberries.

Each serving provides: ½ Protein Exchange; 1 Bread Exchange; 1 Fat Exchange;
  ½ Fruit Exchange; ¼ Milk Exchange; 270 calories Optional Exchange
Per serving: 404 calories; 10 g protein; 20 g fat; 46 g carbohydrate; 281 mg calcium;
  572 mg sodium; 183 mg cholesterol

Almond Cookies ◐❷

CHEERS ∽ MAKES 4 SERVINGS, 3 COOKIES EACH

⅓ cup plus 2 teaspoons cake flour
¼ teaspoon double-acting baking
  powder
⅛ teaspoon baking soda
2 tablespoons each margarine,
  softened, and granulated sugar

1 egg
½ teaspoon almond extract
¼ teaspoon vanilla extract
12 blanched shelled almonds,
  lightly toasted

1. Preheat oven to 375°F. Onto sheet of wax paper or a paper plate sift together flour, baking powder, and baking soda; set aside.

2. In small mixing bowl, using electric mixer, cream margarine with sugar until light and fluffy; add sifted ingredients and beat until combined. Add egg and extracts and continue beating until batter is smooth.

3. Onto 2 nonstick baking sheets drop batter by heaping table-spoonsful, forming 6 cookies on each sheet and leaving a space of about 4 inches between each (batter will spread to form thin cookies, each about 3½ inches in diameter). Top each cookie with 1 almond and press lightly.

4. Bake until edges of cookies are dark brown, 8 to 10 minutes; using a spatula, remove cookies to wire rack to cool.

Each serving provides: ½ Bread Exchange; 1½ Fat Exchanges;
  70 calories Optional Exchange
Per serving: 160 calories; 3 g protein; 9 g fat; 16 g carbohydrate; 34 mg calcium;
  137 mg sodium; 69 mg cholesterol

Chocolate-Nut Squares ❷

SWEET DREAMS ∽ MAKES 16 SERVINGS, 1 SQUARE EACH

½ cup granulated sugar
1 egg
1 cup chunky-style peanut butter

1 teaspoon vanilla extract
2 ounces semisweet chocolate
  pieces

Preheat oven to 350°F. Spray an 8 x 8 x 2-inch baking pan with non-stick cooking spray; set aside.

In small mixing bowl combine sugar and egg and, using an electric mixer, beat until light and fluffy; add peanut butter and vanilla, beating until combined. Spread mixture evenly in sprayed pan and bake until top is lightly browned, about 20 minutes. Remove pan to wire rack and let cool for 5 minutes; invert pan onto rack to remove mixture. Let cool completely.

In small saucepan melt chocolate over low heat, stirring frequently. Spread melted chocolate over cooled mixture and let harden. Cut into sixteen 2-inch squares; wrap squares individually in plastic wrap and store in refrigerator.

Each serving provides: 1 Protein Exchange; 1 Fat Exchange;
  55 calories Optional Exchange
Per serving: 143 calories; 5 g protein; 10 g fat; 11 g carbohydrate; 8 mg calcium;
  80 mg sodium; 17 mg cholesterol

Variation: Week 4—Nut Squares—Prepare recipe as directed but omit chocolate. Decrease Optional Exchange to 35 calories.

Per serving: 123 calories; 5 g protein; 8 g fat; 9 g carbohydrate; 12 mg calcium;
  102 mg sodium; 17 mg cholesterol

Chocolate-Raisin Bars ❶

CHEERS ⌇ MAKES 12 SERVINGS, 1 BAR EACH

½ cup reduced-calorie margarine
1 packet reduced-calorie milk
  chocolate-flavored hot cocoa mix
¼ cup granulated sugar
2 eggs
1 teaspoon vanilla extract
⅔ cup all-purpose flour

½ teaspoon double-acting baking
  powder
¼ teaspoon salt
¾ cup raisins
2 ounces unsalted shelled roasted
  peanuts, chopped

Preheat oven to 350°F. Spray an 8 x 8 x 2-inch baking pan with non-stick cooking spray; set aside.

In medium bowl, using electric mixer, beat together margarine, cocoa mix, and sugar until combined; beat in eggs 1 at a time, beating after each addition until well blended. Beat in vanilla. Add flour, baking powder, and salt and beat until blended; fold in raisins and peanuts. Pour batter into sprayed pan and bake for 20 to 25 minutes (until a cake tester, inserted in center, comes out clean). Remove cake to wire rack and let cool. To serve, cut cake in half and cut each half into 6 equal bars.

Each serving provides: 1 Fat Exchange; ½ Fruit Exchange;
  95 calories Optional Exchange
Per serving: 148 calories; 4 g protein; 7 g fat; 19 g carbohydrate; 49 mg calcium;
  180 mg sodium; 46 mg cholesterol

Chocolate Figs with "Ice Cream" ◗

SWEET DREAMS ᔓ MAKES 2 SERVINGS

2 large fresh figs, stems removed
2 tablespoons water
2 strips orange peel
1 ounce semisweet chocolate
   pieces

6 ounces vanilla dietary frozen
   dessert

Place figs in small (about 1-cup) shallow baking dish that is just large enough to hold them; add water and orange peel and bake at 375°F. until figs are soft to the touch but still hold their shape, about 15 minutes.

In small saucepan melt chocolate over low heat, stirring frequently; set aside and keep warm. Cut each fig in half. For each portion serve 2 fig halves with 3 ounces frozen dessert; pour half of the melted chocolate and any liquid remaining from cooked figs over each serving.

Each serving provides: 2 Fruit Exchanges; ½ Milk Exchange;
   75 calories Optional Exchange
Per serving: 221 calories; 5 g protein; 6 g fat; 40 g carbohydrate; 177 mg calcium;
   71 mg sodium; 2 mg cholesterol

Frozen Strawberry Soufflé

CHEERS ᔓ MAKES 4 SERVINGS

2 cups strawberries,* divided
6 ounces vanilla dietary frozen
   dessert, softened
2 tablespoons each thawed frozen
   concentrated orange juice (no
   sugar added) and raspberry
   liqueur

2 egg whites (at room temperature)
2 teaspoons granulated sugar

In work bowl of food processor puree 1½ cups strawberries; add frozen dessert, orange juice, and liqueur and process until smooth. Transfer to freezer-safe bowl, cover with plastic wrap, and freeze until solid, about 45 minutes. Break into pieces and return to work bowl of food processor; process until smooth. Spoon into large bowl and set aside.

In medium bowl, using electric mixer on high speed, beat egg whites until soft peaks form; add sugar and continue beating until stiff peaks form. Using wire whisk, beat ⅓ of egg whites into strawberry mixture until combined; gently fold in remaining egg whites. Spoon mixture into 4 freezer-safe dessert dishes; cover with plastic wrap and freeze until firm. Remove from freezer 5 minutes before serving; to serve, slice remaining strawberries and top each soufflé with ¼ of berries.

Each serving provides: 1 Fruit Exchange; ¼ Milk Exchange;
  60 calories Optional Exchange
Per serving: 124 calories; 4 g protein; 1 g fat; 23 g carbohydrate; 90 mg calcium;
  61 mg sodium; 1 mg cholesterol

* If fresh strawberries are not available, frozen strawberries (no sugar added) may be used; thaw after measuring.

"Ice Cream" with Sugar-Coated Bananas ◐ ◑

CHEERS ∽ MAKES 2 SERVINGS

1 medium banana
1 tablespoon lemon juice
2 teaspoons margarine
2 tablespoons light rum

1 teaspoon granulated brown sugar
Dash ground cinnamon
2 scoops (3 ounces each) vanilla
  dietary frozen dessert

1. Peel banana and cut in half lengthwise, then cut each piece in half crosswise. Sprinkle banana quarters with lemon juice and set aside.

2. In small skillet heat margarine until bubbly and hot; add rum, brown sugar, and cinnamon and cook over low heat, stirring constantly, until sugar melts. Remove from heat.

3. Using a wooden spoon, roll banana pieces in rum-sugar mixture.

4. Into each of 2 champagne glasses or dessert dishes place 1 scoop frozen dessert; top each scoop with 2 banana quarters and half of any remaining rum-sugar mixture.

Each serving provides: 1 Fat Exchange; 2 Fruit Exchanges; ½ Milk Exchange;
  45 calories Optional Exchange
Per serving: 233 calories; 5 g protein; 5 g fat; 36 g carbohydrate; 157 mg calcium;
  117 mg sodium; 2 mg cholesterol

Spiced Fruit 'n' Honey Treat

CHEERS ⌁ MAKES 2 SERVINGS, 5 FRUIT BALLS EACH

¼ cup raisins, finely chopped
2 large dried figs, finely chopped
½ teaspoon apple pie spice
1 teaspoon honey

½ teaspoon lemon juice
½ ounce shelled almonds, toasted
    and finely ground

In small bowl combine raisins, figs, and apple pie spice; roll into 10 small balls, each about 1 inch in diameter. In metal measuring cup combine honey and lemon juice; place over low heat and stir constantly until honey melts. Remove from heat and immediately roll each fruit ball in honey-lemon mixture, then in ground almonds to coat. Arrange on plate, cover, and refrigerate until chilled.

Each serving provides: 2 Fruit Exchanges; 55 calories Optional Exchange
Per serving: 156 calories; 3 g protein; 4 g fat; 32 g carbohydrate; 63 mg calcium;
    5 mg sodium; 0 mg cholesterol

Variation: Substitute 2 dried apricot halves, finely chopped, for the figs; decrease Fruit Exchange to 1 Exchange and increase Optional Exchange to 65 calories.

Per serving: 117 calories; 2 g protein; 4 g fat; 21 g carbohydrate; 37 mg calcium;
    4 mg sodium; 0 mg cholesterol

Caramel Corn ◑

CHEERS ∿ MAKES 2 SERVINGS

1 tablespoon granulated sugar
1 tablespoon caramel topping,
  warmed
½ teaspoon vanilla extract
⅛ teaspoon white or cider vinegar

2 cups prepared plain popcorn
1 ounce unsalted shelled roasted
  peanuts

In small nonstick skillet heat sugar over *very* low heat, stirring constantly, until sugar melts and turns golden, about 2 minutes (*be careful not to burn*); add caramel topping, vanilla, and vinegar and cook, stirring vigorously, until all lumps disappear and mixture is bubbly.

Place popcorn and peanuts in flameproof bowl and set over *lowest* possible heat; add caramel mixture and toss until popcorn and peanuts are evenly coated. Moisten hands with cold water, then shape mixture into 4 equal balls; let cool before serving.

Each serving provides: ½ Bread Exchange; 145 calories Optional Exchange
Per serving: 168 calories; 5 g protein; 7 g fat; 22 g carbohydrate; 18 mg calcium;
  2 mg sodium; 0 mg cholesterol

Peanut-Popcorn Balls ◑❸

CHEERS ∾ MAKES 4 SERVINGS

2 tablespoons each granulated
   sugar and light corn syrup
¼ teaspoon white vinegar
2 tablespoons chunky-style peanut
   butter (at room temperature)

1 teaspoon vanilla extract
4 cups prepared plain popcorn
1 ounce unsalted shelled roasted
   peanuts

In small nonstick saucepan combine sugar, syrup, and vinegar; stirring constantly, bring to a boil. Reduce heat and let simmer for 2 minutes. Add peanut butter and vanilla and stir to combine.

Place popcorn and peanuts in flameproof bowl and set over *lowest* possible heat; add peanut butter mixture and toss until popcorn and peanuts are evenly coated. Moisten hands with cold water, then shape mixture into 4 equal balls; let cool before serving.

Each serving provides: ½ Protein Exchange; ½ Bread Exchange; ½ Fat Exchange;
   105 calories Optional Exchange
Per serving: 171 calories; 5 g protein; 8 g fat; 21 g carbohydrate; 8 mg calcium;
   46 mg sodium; 0 mg cholesterol

Banana-Pineapple Cocktail ◑

CHEERS ∾ MAKES 2 SERVINGS

1 medium banana, peeled
¼ cup light rum
1 tablespoon plus 1 teaspoon
   thawed frozen concentrated
   pineapple juice (no sugar added)

2 teaspoons lime juice (no sugar
   added)
1 teaspoon granulated sugar
¾ cup crushed ice

Chill two 8-ounce glasses. In blender container combine all ingredients except ice; process until smooth. With motor running gradually add ice, processing until all ice is dissolved and mixture is thick and frothy. Pour into chilled glasses and serve immediately.

Each serving provides: 1½ Fruit Exchanges; 80 calories Optional Exchange
Per serving: 154 calories; 1 g protein; 0.03 g fat; 21 g carbohydrate; 9 mg calcium;
   2 mg sodium; 0 mg cholesterol

Eggnog Crème ◑

CHEERS ∿ MAKES 2 SERVINGS

1 teaspoon unflavored gelatin
½ cup evaporated skimmed milk,
  divided
1 egg, separated
2 tablespoons light rum

2 teaspoons granulated sugar
1 teaspoon vanilla extract
2 tablespoons thawed frozen dairy
  whipped topping
Ground nutmeg

Chill 2 dessert dishes. In small saucepan sprinkle gelatin over ¼ cup milk and let stand to soften. In small bowl combine remaining ¼ cup milk with egg yolk, rum, sugar, and vanilla and, using a fork, beat until combined; pour into gelatin mixture and cook over low heat, stirring constantly, until gelatin is completely dissolved and mixture coats the back of a metal spoon. Remove from heat and let cool slightly; cover and refrigerate until mixture mounds slightly when dropped from a spoon, about 20 minutes.

In small bowl, using an electric mixer on high speed, beat egg white until stiff peaks form; fold into chilled milk mixture. Spoon mixture into chilled dessert dishes; cover with plastic wrap and refrigerate until firm. Serve each portion topped with 1 tablespoon whipped topping and dash nutmeg.

Each serving provides: ½ Protein Exchange; ½ Milk Exchange;
  70 calories Optional Exchange
Per serving: 165 calories; 9 g protein; 4 g fat; 13 g carbohydrate; 199 mg calcium;
  109 mg sodium; 140 mg cholesterol

Appendix

Dry and Liquid Measure Equivalents

Teaspoons	Tablespoons	Cups	Fluid Ounces
3 teaspoons	1 tablespoon		½ fluid ounce
6 teaspoons	2 tablespoons	⅛ cup	1 fluid ounce
8 teaspoons	2 tablespoons plus 2 teaspoons	⅙ cup	
12 teaspoons	4 tablespoons	¼ cup	2 fluid ounces
15 teaspoons	5 tablespoons	⅓ cup less 1 teaspoon	
16 teaspoons	5 tablespoons plus 1 teaspoon	⅓ cup	
18 teaspoons	6 tablespoons	⅓ cup plus 2 teaspoons	3 fluid ounces
24 teaspoons	8 tablespoons	½ cup	4 fluid ounces
30 teaspoons	10 tablespoons	½ cup plus 2 tablespoons	5 fluid ounces
32 teaspoons	10 tablespoons plus 2 teaspoons	⅔ cup	
36 teaspoons	12 tablespoons	¾ cup	6 fluid ounces
42 teaspoons	14 tablespoons	1 cup less 2 tablespoons	7 fluid ounces
45 teaspoons	15 tablespoons	1 cup less 1 tablespoon	
48 teaspoons	16 tablespoons	1 cup	8 fluid ounces

Note: Measurements of less than ⅛ teaspoon are considered a Dash or a Pinch.

Goal Weights
Women

Height Range Without Shoes	Age in Years				
	18	19-20	21-22	23-24	25 & Over
Ft. Inches	Weight in Pounds				
4 6 (54)	83- 99	84-101	85-103	86-104	88-106
4 7 (55)	84-100	85-102	86-104	88-105	90-107
4 8 (56)	86-101	87-103	88-105	90-106	92-108
4 9 (57)	89-102	90-104	91-106	92-108	94-110
4 10 (58)	91-105	92-106	93-109	94-111	96-113
4 11 (59)	93-109	94-111	95-113	96-114	99-116
5 0 (60)	96-112	97-113	98-115	100-117	102-119
5 1 (61)	100-116	101-117	102-119	103-121	105-122
5 2 (62)	104-119	105-121	106-123	107-125	108-126
5 3 (63)	106-125	107-126	108-127	109-129	111-130
5 4 (64)	109-130	110-131	111-132	112-134	114-135
5 5 (65)	112-133	113-134	114-136	116-138	118-139
5 6 (66)	116-137	117-138	118-140	120-142	122-143
5 7 (67)	121-140	122-142	123-144	124-146	126-147
5 8 (68)	123-144	124-146	126-148	128-150	130-151
5 9 (69)	130-148	131-150	132-152	133-154	134-155
5 10 (70)	134-151	135-154	136-156	137-158	138-159
5 11 (71)	138-155	139-158	140-160	141-162	142-163
6 0 (72)	142-160	143-162	144-164	145-166	146-167
6 1 (73)	146-164	147-166	148-168	149-170	150-171
6 2 (74)	150-168	151-170	152-172	153-174	154-175

Goal Weights
Men

Height Range Without Shoes	Age in Years				
	18	19-20	21-22	23-24	25 & Over
Ft. Inches	Weight in Pounds				
5 0 (60)	109-122	110-133	112-135	114-137	115-138
5 1 (61)	112-126	113-136	115-138	117-140	118-141
5 2 (62)	115-130	116-139	118-140	120-142	121-144
5 3 (63)	118-135	119-143	121-145	123-147	124-148
5 4 (64)	120-145	122-147	124-149	126-151	127-152
5 5 (65)	124-149	125-151	127-153	129-155	130-156
5 6 (66)	128-154	129-156	131-158	133-160	134-161
5 7 (67)	132-159	133-161	134-163	136-165	138-166
5 8 (68)	135-163	136-165	138-167	140-169	142-170
5 9 (69)	140-165	141-169	142-171	144-173	146-174
5 10 (70)	143-170	144-173	146-175	148-178	150-179
5 11 (71)	147-177	148-179	150-181	152-183	154-184
6 0 (72)	151-180	152-184	154-186	156-188	158-189
6 1 (73)	155-187	156-189	158-190	160-193	162-194
6 2 (74)	160-192	161-194	163-196	165-198	167-199
6 3 (75)	165-198	166-199	168-201	170-203	172-204
6 4 (76)	170-202	171-204	173-206	175-208	177-209

Goal Weights
Girls

Height Range Without Shoes	Age in Years							
	10	11	12	13	14	15	16	17
Ft. Inches	Weight in Pounds							
3 11 (47)	48- 55							
4 0 (48)	49- 58	51- 61						
4 1 (49)	50- 61	52- 65	53- 69					
4 2 (50)	51- 64	53- 67	55- 71	60- 73				
4 3 (51)	54- 67	55- 70	57- 73	62- 76	63- 84			
4 4 (52)	58- 70	59- 73	60- 76	64- 79	67- 88	77- 91		
4 5 (53)	59- 73	62- 76	63- 79	66- 82	71- 90	78- 93	79- 94	80- 96
4 6 (54)	62- 75	65- 77	66- 81	68- 85	74- 91	79- 94	80- 95	82- 98
4 7 (55)	64- 77	68- 78	69- 84	70- 88	76- 92	80- 95	81- 96	83- 99
4 8 (56)	66- 79	71- 80	72- 87	73- 91	78- 94	81- 96	82- 97	85-100
4 9 (57)	68- 83	74- 84	75- 90	76- 94	81- 97	84- 99	85-100	88-101
4 10 (58)	70- 86	76- 87	77- 93	79- 97	84-100	87-102	88-103	90-104
4 11 (59)	75- 89	78- 90	80- 96	82-100	87-103	90-105	91-106	92-108
5 0 (60)	80- 92	81- 93	82- 98	86-103	90-106	93-108	94-110	95-111
5 1 (61)	82- 95	84- 97	86-101	88-106	94-109	97-111	98-112	99-113
5 2 (62)	84- 98	86-102	89-104	92-109	98-112	101-115	102-117	103-118
5 3 (63)	87-101	89-104	92-106	96-112	101-115	103-122	104-123	105-124
5 4 (64)	90-103	93-106	97-109	100-115	104-118	106-124	107-126	108-128
5 5 (65)	94-105	98-108	102-111	104-118	107-121	109-126	110-129	111-131
5 6 (66)		103-111	106-116	108-121	111-124	113-131	114-132	115-134
5 7 (67)		107-114	110-120	112-124	116-127	118-134	119-135	120-137
5 8 (68)			114-124	117-127	119-130	120-135	121-138	122-140
5 9 (69)			118-127	122-130	124-133	126-141	128-142	129-144
5 10 (70)				127-134	128-137	130-143	132-146	133-148
5 11 (71)				132-138	133-141	135-146	136-150	137-152
6 0 (72)					136-145	138-148	140-151	141-156
6 1 (73)					140-150	142-155	144-158	145-160

Goal Weights
Boys

Height Range Without Shoes	Age in Years							
	10	11	12	13	14	15	16	17
Ft. Inches	Weight in Pounds							
3 11 (47)	48- 52							
4 0 (48)	50- 55	51- 57						
4 1 (49)	52- 57	53- 58						
4 2 (50)	54- 59	55- 60	56- 62					
4 3 (51)	58- 62	59- 63	60- 64					
4 4 (52)	60- 65	61- 66	62- 67					
4 5 (53)	63- 68	64- 69	65- 70	66- 71				
4 6 (54)	65- 71	66- 72	67- 73	68- 75				
4 7 (55)	70- 75	71- 76	72- 77	73- 79	74- 80			
4 8 (56)	75- 80	76- 81	77- 83	78- 85	79- 87			
4 9 (57)	79- 82	80- 84	81- 86	83- 89	84- 90	86- 95		
4 10 (58)	82- 86	83- 87	84- 88	88- 93	89- 94	92-100	95-108	
4 11 (59)	86- 90	87- 91	88- 92	93- 97	94- 98	96-104	98-110	101-114
5 0 (60)	90- 94	91- 95	92- 96	96-101	98-103	100-108	102-113	105-117
5 1 (61)	93- 97	95- 99	96-100	100-105	101-108	103-112	106-116	108-120
5 2 (62)	97-101	99-103	100-104	104-109	106-113	108-116	110-120	112-123
5 3 (63)	100-104	102-106	104-108	107-113	111-118	113-120	114-123	117-126
5 4 (64)	102-107	104-109	108-112	111-117	114-121	116-123	118-127	119-130
5 5 (65)	105-110	107-112	112-116	115-121	117-125	119-127	122-130	123-133
5 6 (66)		111-116	116-120	118-125	121-129	123-131	126-133	127-137
5 7 (67)		115-120	119-124	121-130	125-133	128-134	130-136	131-141
5 8 (68)			122-128	124-133	129-137	132-138	133-140	134-145
5 9 (69)			125-132	127-136	133-141	136-142	138-144	139-149
5 10 (70)				130-140	137-145	140-149	141-155	142-160
5 11 (71)				135-144	141-149	144-155	145-160	146-168
6 0 (72)					146-153	148-156	149-163	150-170
6 1 (73)					150-157	152-163	153-166	154-175
6 2 (74)						157-165	158-170	159-182
6 3 (75)						162-175	163-180	164-190
6 4 (76)						167-185	168-191	169-195

Index

Over 280 Winning Dishes from
Weight Watchers Members and Staff

❖❖❖❖❖❖❖❖❖❖❖❖❖❖❖❖❖❖❖❖❖❖❖❖❖❖❖❖❖❖❖❖❖❖

WEIGHT WATCHERS®
FAVORITE RECIPES

❖❖❖❖❖❖❖❖❖❖❖❖❖❖❖❖❖❖❖❖❖❖❖❖❖❖❖❖❖❖❖❖❖❖

BASED ON THE
QUICK START PLUS PROGRAM©

with 32 pages of full-color photos

Introducing Weight Watchers deliciously down-home cookbook featuring easy-to-make contest-winning recipes. From breakfasts and brunches to main dishes, snacks, and dazzling desserts, enjoy an enormous variety of culinary delights including:

- **Cheese Pancakes with Pineapple Topping**
- **Vegetable-Shrimp Quiche**
- **Spiced Apple-Carrot Bake**
- **Chocolate Soufflé**
- **and many more!**

With Food Plan Exchange Information and high-lighted quick recipes and budget stretchers.

☐ NAL Hardcover Edition: $17.50 U.S., $24.50 Can.
(0-453-01012-1)

To order, use the convenient coupon on the next page.

Savory, slimmed-down favorites from around the world.

Weight Watchers®
NEW INTERNATIONAL
COOKBOOK

With 32 pages of full-color photos

How in the world can you enjoy Arroz con Pollo, Shrimp with Lobster Sauce, and Deep-Dish Apple Pie—and still lose weight? With the help of this all-new collection of 300 worldly and wonderful recipes based on the 1986 Quick Start Plus Program®. Together, they represent the cuisines of over 40 countries and the world's most respected weight-loss organization.

To help you prepare these delightful dishes with maximum ease and authenticity, the cookbook includes:

- Typical menus for each region
- Substitutes for hard-to-find ingredients
- Symbols that highlight short preparation/cooking times
- Per-serving counts for calories, protein, fat, carbohydrate, sodium, and cholesterol

Plume Softcover Edition: $9.95 U.S., $13.95 Canada (0-452-25951-7)
NAL Hardcover Edition: $18.50 U.S., $24.50 Canada (0-453-01011-3)